Lecture Notes in Computer Science 1506

Edited by G. Goos, J. Hartmanis and J. van Leeuwen

T0217356

Springer

Berlin
Heidelberg
New York
Barcelona
Hong Kong
London
Milan
Paris
Singapore
Tokyo

Reinhard Koch   Luc Van Gool (Eds.)

3D Structure
from Multiple Images of
Large-Scale Environments

European Workshop, SMILE'98
Freiburg, Germany, June 6-7, 1998
Proceedings

Springer

Series Editors

Gerhard Goos, Karlsruhe University, Germany
Juris Hartmanis, Cornell University, NY, USA
Jan van Leeuwen, Utrecht University, The Netherlands

Volume Editors

Reinhard Koch
Luc Van Gool
ESAT-PSI, Katholieke Universiteit Leuven
Kardinaal Mercilaan 9, B-3001 Leuven, Belgium
E-mail: {Reinhard.Koch,Luc.Vangool}@esat.kuleuven.ac.be

Cataloging-in-Publication data applied for

Die Deutsche Bibliothek - CIP-Einheitsaufnahme

3D structure from multiple images of large scale environments : european
workshop, SMILE '98, Freiburg, Germany, June 6 - 7, 1998 ; proceedings / Koch ;
van Gool (ed.). - Berlin ; Heidelberg ; New York ; Barcelona ; Hong Kong ;
London ; Milan ; Paris ; Singapore ; Tokyo : Springer, 1998
  (Lecture notes in computer science ; Vol. 1506)
  ISBN 3-540-65310-4

CR Subject Classification (1998): I.4, I.2.10, I.5.4

ISSN 0302-9743
ISBN 3-540-65310-4 Springer-Verlag Berlin Heidelberg New York

Typesetting: Camera-ready by author
SPIN 10639005   06/3142 – 5 4 3 2 1 0   Printed on acid-free paper

Preface

The contributions in this volume give an overview of state-of-the-art results presented at the *Workshop on 3D Structure from Multiple Images of Large-scale Environments (SMILE)*. This workshop was held in conjunction with the Fifth European Conference on Computer Vision 1998 in Freiburg, Germany. SMILE was a joint effort of the European ACTS projects VANGUARD and PANORAMA and the Esprit project CUMULI, all of which are involved in the analysis and reconstruction of 3D scenes from image sequences.

The potential for 3D reconstructions of scenes and objects is tremendous. Much of the work reported here is to be seen especially against the background of a convergence between computer vision and computer graphics, and of a shift from signal-based to content-based image analysis in telecommunications. Accordingly, the requirements for 3D models and acquisition systems are also shifting. Visualization rather than mensuration is the primary issue. The perceptual quality of the models, the flexibility of the acquisition, and the cost of the system are three driving forces in the search for new methods.

The last few years have seen important steps toward genuine flexibility. A case in point is the use of multiple images to generate 3D models, without an explicit knowledge of the relative position of the cameras or the camera settings. The same developments also hold good promise to make 3D acquisition cheaper and more widely available.

The contributions in this volume focus on the latest developments in this and related areas. They demonstrate the feasibility of generating highly realistic 3D models from natural, uncalibrated video sequences, of using 3D models for telecommunications, and of integrating real and virtual objects into a single environment.

This volume is divided into five thematic sections and an appendix. First, an overview is given of the work performed in the three organizing projects with links to the related contributions. In his invited presentation, Richard Hartley then develops ideas to exploit the duality concept between points and cameras in scene reconstruction.

Section 2 discusses various approaches to formalize basic multiview relations and to reliably estimate image correspondences.

Section 3 exploits results given in the previous section. Different approaches for the estimation of 3D scene structure from image sequences are presented, with an emphasis on fully automatic algorithms.

Section 4 deals with the use of constraints to improve 3D modeling. Two basic approaches are discussed: introducing explicit geometrical constraints, and controlled user interaction.

Section 5 bridges the gap to real-world applications. The object models are integrated in real and virtual environments by using novel Augmented Reality techniques.

An appendix has been included to give the nonspecialist reader a comprehensive and intuitive introduction to multiview relations. It explains the geometry behind the image relationships and develops the underlying mathematical concepts.

We hope that you will enjoy this volume.

September 1998   Reinhard Koch and Luc Van Gool

Workshop Committee

Lutz Falkenhagen	University of Hannover
Olivier Faugeras	Inria Sophia Antipolis
Nick Holliman	Sharp Laboratories of Europe
Reinhard Koch	University of Leuven (Chair)
Roger Mohr	INPG Grenoble
Georgio Sakas	IGD Darmstadt
Amnon Shashua	Hebrew University of Jerusalem
Gunnar Sparr	Lund University
Bill Triggs	INRIA Grenoble
Andrew Zisserman	University of Oxford
Luc Van Gool	University of Leuven (Chair)

Table of Contents

Invited Presentations

Multiview Relations and Correspondence Search

3D Structure from Multiple Images

Calibration and Reconstruction Using Scene Constraints

Range Integration and Augmented Reality Applications

Appendix

Author Index

Cumuli[1], Panorama[2], and Vanguard[3] Project Overview

R. Mohr[1,1], R. Buschmann[2,2], L. Falkenhagen[2,3], L. Van Gool[3,4], and R. Koch[3,4]

[1] INRIA, ZIRST-655 avenue de l'Europe, 38330 Montbonnet, France
[2] Siemens AG, ZT IK 2, 81730 München, Germany
[3] University of Hannover, Germany
[4] K.U. Leuven, 3001 Leuven, Belgium

Abstract. This overview summarizes the goals of the European projects CUMULI, PANORAMA, and VANGUARD and references the various contributions in this volume. There are several overlaps between the projects which all evolve around the geometric analysis of scenes from multiple images. All projects attempt to reconstruct the geometry and visual appearance of complex 3D scenes that may be static or dynamic.

While CUMULI and VANGUARD deal with images from uncalibrated cameras and unrestricted camera position for general scenes, PANORAMA focusses on a highly calibrated setup used to capture 3D person models. CUMULI and VANGUARD developed techniques for handling multiview relations, object tracking and camera calibration, image and geometry based view synthesis, and 3D model generation. Interaction with the modeled scene and mixing of virtual and real objects leads to Virtual/Augmented Reality applications in VANGUARD and CUMULI, while the PANORAMA approach is tuned to fully automatic scene analysis for visual communication and 3D-telepresence. Visualisation aspects are handled by VANGUARD and PANORAMA with the development of auto-stereoscopic displays.

1 The CUMULI Project

CUMULI — "Computational Understanding of MULtiple Images" — is an ESPRIT Long term Research project focusing on multi-image geometry and its applications to 3D industrial metrology. It can be seen as a follow-up to the successful ESPRIT–BRA project VIVA, which involved three of CUMULI's academic partners: Lund University (G. Sparr), INRIA Sophia-Antipolis (O. Faugeras) and INRIA–IMAG in Grenoble (R. Mohr). On the industrial side, CUMULI's partners have expertise in image-based metrology: Innovativ Vision Image Systems in Linköping are specialists in motion measurement from high speed image sequences, *e.g.* car crash testing; and IMETRIC based in Courgenay (Switzerland) are world leaders in high precision industrial photogrammetry from still images. The final partner, Fraunhofer IGD in Darmstadt and Munich, specializes in visual modelling for augmented and virtual reality. D. Wang from the Leibniz

Reinhard Koch, Luc Van Gool (Eds.): SMILE '98, LNCS 1506, pp. 1–13, 1998.
© Springer-Verlag Berlin Heidelberg 1998

laboratory in Grenoble has also joined the academic team, bringing his expertise in algebraic proof for geometry.

VIVA provided deep insights into the geometry of 3D perception with uncalibrated cameras. CUMULI builds on this, considering on the one hand autocalibration, Euclidean structure and extensions to more general types of image features, and on the other the special problems introduced by image sequences. It also addresses a new basic research problem: how can we automate the geometric reasoning (consistency, integration of diverse types of information, ...) required to build large 3D models from image data.

1.1   Multi-camera Geometry, Discrete Images

The first part of CUMULI concentrates on the geometry of discrete sets of images of static scenes. The goal is to recover 3D scene structure under different assumptions:

- Unknown camera parameters and scenes: the basic structure of uncalibrated multi-camera geometry has been well studied in the past, so here we focus on a unification of the theory on one side, and practical numerical methods on the other;
- Partial camera or scene knowledge: in many applications some prior information is available (*e.g.* camera calibrations, the knowledge that points lie on a plane or curve, ...). Here we work on using this knowledge to extend the range or quality of the reconstruction, for example creating methods that allow reconstruction from the minimum amount of image data;
- Non-point-like image features: to date, much of the scientific and technical work has focused on point-like primitives. In many applications lines, curves, and surfaces are also important. The goal is to use the strong geometric constraints that such primitives induce to relax the conditions for reconstruction, and to improve its accuracy.

Some of our recent results improve our understanding of multi-camera geometry, for example [3,9]. Corresponding efficient reconstruction procedures have also been obtained, for instance [6,9].

Autocalibration is a potentially important means of moving towards Euclidean 3D structure. The basic autocalibration constraint has been reformulated in terms of the absolute dual quadric [8,2] and the direction frame formalisms [10], and this has lead to much stabler numerical algorithms. Autocalibration has also been considered under weaker conditions, for instance when the skew is the only constant camera parameter [3]. A complete characterization of the camera motions for which autocalibration is necessarily degenerate is given in [7]

Considering geometric features, one major extension is the fact that silhouettes of general surfaces can be used to compute both relative positioning (Euclidean case) and projective reconstruction [4]. Line features have been used in a fast linear algorithm for the affine camera case based on a '1D camera' (vanishing point to image line at infinity projection) [5].

The demonstrator for this part of the project will be integrated by IMETRIC. It will use the different types of features to initialize a photogrammetric bundle adjustment, for 3D metrology in scenes like the one illustrated in fig.1. The goal is to allow more flexible system initialization, minimizing the the amount of prior information and scene instrumentation required.

Fig. 1. A point scene of an industrial environment

1.2   3D Perception from Continuous Image Sequences

The second part of the project considers image sequences and non-rigid motion estimation. Although the same underlying theory applies to discrete and continuous images, the practical implementations tend to be rather different. For one thing, the geometry inherited from the discrete case becomes degenerate when the views are very close or the inter-image motions are aligned (see fig.2). The appropriate incremental geometry must be developed and integrated with the handling of uncertainty, compensating the degeneracy of close views with the redundancy of many images. A key problem is to specialize the multi-image matching constraints to the continuous case. An important result is that third order continuous constraints are needed to reconstruct the scene and motion [1]. Tracking tools and several efficient reconstruction methods are also being developed to deal with the large volume of image data.

Innovativ Vision will integrate a demonstrator of the tools coming out of this part of the project. The aim is to reconstruct the non-rigid 3D motion of points on a car or a test dummy during a car crash test, with as little prior calibration as possible. Fig. 2 shows some typical data provided by a high speed camera. Some camera vibration occurs, so static points in the scene will be tracked to provide a reference frame.

Fig. 2. Image of a car crash sequence

1.3   Algebraic Geometric Reasoning from Image Data

The final part of CUMULI addresses a new area: the use of automated algebraic and geometric reasoning tools in visual reconstruction. The geometric models in computer vision are more than just coordinates: they are complex networks of incidence relations, constraints, *etc.* To build such models from weak or uncertain data, we need methods that make efficient use of any known constraints on the environment, to reduce the uncertainty and improve the consistency and quality of the generated models. Often, many such constraints are available. They are often used informally when building models by hand, but it is currently difficult to automate this process. In particular, we are studying the integration of digital site maps with vision data, as these are an important source of constraints in urban modelling (see *The Use of Reality Models for Augmented Reality Applications*).

Another main focus is the use of automated geometric reasoning techniques for computer vision applications. However, although the need to manipulate abstract geometric knowledge (the constraints) strongly motivates their use, they must be adapted to the particular requirements of computer vision. One illustration of this approach is the automatic derivation of minimal parametrizations of constrained 3D geometric models (see *Imposing Euclidean Constraints during the Self-Calibration Process*). This is a crucial step towards enforcing the constraints, but given the intrinsic uncertainty and the potential complexity of the 3D models involved in computer vision (many primitives, complicated constraints), to actually impose the constraints the algebraic techniques need to be coupled to efficient numerical methods (see *Euclidean and Affine Structure/Motion for Uncalibrated Cameras from Affine Shape and Subsidary Information*).

2   The PANORAMA Project

This paper gives an overview over the ACTS PANORAMA project and additionally a more detailed look on the 3-D reconstruction approach developed in PANORAMA. The PANORAMA consortium consists of 14 European partners from Universities, Research Institutes and Industry. The objective of the PANORAMA project is to enhance the visual information exchange in telecommunications with 3-D telepresence. The main challenges of PANORAMA are:

- Multiview camera and autostereoscopic display which allows for movement of the observer (multiviewpoint capability)
- Realtime imaging system using special purpose hardware for analysis, vector coding and interpolation of intermediate views
- Imaging system based on offline image analysis using 3D model objects and state-of-the-art 3D graphic computers
- Application studies in field trials

2.1   Goals of PANORAMA

The ultimate goal for future telecommunication is highly effective interpersonal information exchange. The effectiveness of telecommunication is greatly enhanced by 3-D telepresence. In this concept it is crucial that visual information is presented in such a way that the viewer is under the impression of actually being physically close to the party with whom the communication takes place. Existing systems realise 3-D telepresence by stereoscopic imaging and display technologies. A natural 3-D impression is achieved if the camera positions correspond to the observers eye positions, and if the observer is stationary.

The objective of the PANORAMA project is to enhance the visual information exchange in telecommunication by alleviating two major drawbacks of existing 3-D telepresence systems. In the first place, an autostereoscopic display is realised that spatially separates the left and right view images according to the observers eye positions instead of the current techniques which require wearing polarised or active LCD glasses. Secondly, the communication system allows for movements of the observer while providing a 3-D view, which enables to look around objects.

In order to look around objects, intermediate images are synthesised at the receiver side appropriate to the observers head position. The synthesis of intermediate views uses the captured trinocular image sequences and 3-D scene information that is obtained my means of image analysis. Two different image synthesis approaches are considered in PANORAMA. A high-quality but complex off-line system based on 3-D reconstruction of dynamic scenes is realised that uses explicit 3-D models. With this approach, synthesis of intermediate images is carried out on-line using existing 3-D computer graphics hardware. On the other hand a real-time system is developed which is composed of disparity estimator, disparity field, video and audio codec for transmission over Dutch and German National Hosts and disparity compensated image synthesis of intermediate views.

The PANORAMA project demonstrates its achievements by application studies which are realised by demonstrator, prototype subsystems or services. Two demonstrators for video communication systems are currently developed, one for each of the investigated image synthesis approaches. Since also other 3-D imaging applications can greatly benefit from the developed technologies, three additional application studies are performed in PANORAMA in the fields of medicine, automation in 3-D modelling of industrial environments, and 3-D program production.

2.2   3-D Reconstruction Approach in PANORAMA

One of the two image synthesis approaches developed in PANORAMA for the generation of intermediate views is based on 3-D reconstruction and 3-D computer graphics. This approach uses a calibrated trinocular camera setup which is arranged around the autostereoscopic screen showing the other communication party(fig.3).

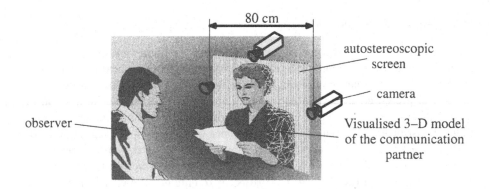

Fig. 3. Trinocular camera setup for video communication application

The camera triple is calibrated once after its installation by determining the relative extrinsic and intrinsic camera parameters. An accurate multi-camera calibration approach has been developed in PANORAMA [11] which is based on the Tsai calibration [12]. It exploits geometric constraints of the trinocular camera setup in order to manage calibration with a relatively simple planar calibration pattern.

The developed 3-D reconstruction approach for dynamic scenes represents the scene using explicit 3-D models, which are defined by 3-D shape, surface colour and 3-D motion parameters. This kind of representation is known from computer graphics [13,14]. In 3-D reconstruction, additional data like observation points and a data memory for information from preceding time instances is required. Thus, PANORAMA developed a new 3-D scene representation that supports 3-D reconstruction and is still compatible to computer graphics. This scene representation is currently implemented in more than 100 C++ classes.

The 3-D reconstruction can be subdivided into two phases: the initialisation phase, where new objects occurring in the scene are analysed, and an update phase, where temporal changes of already reconstructed objects are analysed and the quality of 3-D models is successively improved.

In the initialisation phase, a set of depth maps and 3-D edges are estimated from the input image triples [15]. The depth maps are back-projected into 3-D space, resulting in a cloud of 3-D points. These points are interpolated together with the 3-D edges into a coherent surface model. This model is further approximated using a triangular mesh that represents the shape of the objects [16]. The texture of the objects is represented by mapping parts of the image triple onto each triangle [17].

The update phase starts by analysing the motion of the objects, assuming that most of the changes result from motion of rigid objects [18,19]. In case of persons, the assumption of rigidity requires a subdivision of the 3-D models into articulated components. This subdivision is based on an evaluation of local 3-D motion information which is estimated in a robust manner for each triangle [20]. After compensating the motion of the object components, the shape of the 3-D models is updated. This update considers flexible deformations inside the models and evaluates the changes at object borders [21]. Finally the texture of the 3-D models is updated, compensating the changes of the objects surface colour. The resulting 3-D models are stored in order to analyse the next image triple and are transmitted to the receiver (see *Improving Block-based Disparity Estimation by Considering the non-uniform Distribution of the Estimation Error, Multi-Camera Acquisitions for High-Accuracy 3D Reconstruction*, and *Integration of Multiple Range Maps through Consistency Processing*).

2.3 Telepresence Visualization

At the receiver, two views of the scene are visualised on an autostereoscopic display according to the observers head position. Two techniques for a visualisation of the 3-D models were developed. On the one hand, interfaces to common computer graphics file formats like VRML1, VRML2 and OpenInventor were built which enable the visualisation with commercially available viewers. Since these file formats provide only limited representations of temporal changes, additionally a new viewer for direct visualisation of PANORAMA 3-D scene representation and a file format based on OpenGL was developed. With this viewer, also shape and texture updates can be easily visualised.

A distributed development of a common 3-D reconstruction software is performed in PANORAMA. The software is integrated and tested at one site to guarantee the interfacing and functionality. The overall approach is tested using image sequences of typical video communication scenes. The tests proved to provide realistically looking synthesised images of the other communication party for reasonable observer movements. An example of such a synthesised image is given in fig 4(left). Due to the fixed camera positions that show the other communication party from the front side, the 3-D models are not closed at their back. Therefore, the observer should not move his head outside the area that is covered by the real camera triple.

Fig. 4. (left) Image synthesised from automatically generated 3-D model, (right) Seamless integration of an automatically generated 3-D model into a virtual environment

Fig. 4(right) shows that the automatically generated 3-D models can be seamlessly integrated into virtual environments. This allows an integration of 3-D telecommunication into 3-D applications with communication requirements like e.g. 3-D teleshopping or cooperative CAD. Beyond that the seamless integration of automatically generated 3-D models and virtual environments will allow to design comfortable and intuitive teleconference systems where participants are brought together in a 3-D virtual conference room and to give the participants the impression of being physically close to each other.

The project itself and a number of recent results are also documented online at
http://www.tnt.uni-hannover.de/project/eu/panorama/

3   The VANGUARD Project

VANGUARD stands for *Visualisation Across Networks using Graphics and Uncalibrated Acquisition of Real Data*. The expertise of the consortium is in the fields of uncalibrated tracking and 3D reconstruction (University of Oxford, K.U.Leuven), image-based view synthesis and mosaicing (University of Jerusalem), augmented reality systems (IGD Darmstadt) and 3D displays (SHARP Laboratories Europe).

The primary goal of this project is automatic 3D model building from video sequences, and the use of these models for the rendering of scenes in telepresence applications. The scenes may contain both real and synthetic objects. This goal entails extracting both object geometry and surface descriptions (reflectance) at a level suitable for high quality graphical rendering.

3.1   Approach

Two key points underlie our approach:

- The camera motion is unknown and unconstrained,
- The camera internal parameters (e.g. focal length) are unknown.

Here, the goal is to arrive at 3D models from multiple images taken without any prior calibration of the internal or external camera parameters.

These points are essential for flexible and general purpose model acquisition because camera motion and calibration are usually not recorded (think of extracting 3D models of buildings from old newsreel footage, or from an unknown image sequence on the net).

The 3D geometrical models, together with appropriate surface information facilitate:

- Graphical rendering of novel views, and sequences of views, of the scenes.
- Integration of synthetic and real models and sequences.

The basic VANGUARD modules and the interaction between vision and graphics are sketched in fig.5. The main modules are:

Computer Vision This module handles all computer vision tasks such as tracking of features, self-calibration, and surface reconstruction [22,23]. It forms the backbone of the VANGUARD technology (see the contributions *Metric 3D Surface Reconstruction from Uncalibrated Image Sequences, Automatic 3D Model Construction for Turn-Table Sequences*, and *Matching and Reconstruction from Widely Separated Views*). Another important direction here is the development of image based view synthesis methods [25]and of panoramic image representations[24].

3D Geometry The geometrical models as produced by the vision tasks need post processing like mesh retriangulation and reduction [26], compact representation, model fusion and editing (see *Fitting Geometrical Deformable Models to Registered Range Images*).

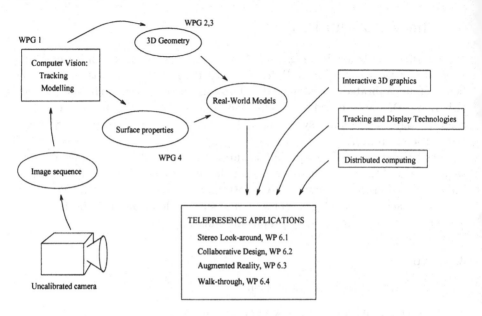

Fig. 5. Schematic overview of VANGUARD modules.

Surface properties In addition to the geometric properties VANGUARD aims at extracting surface albedo, reflectance and texture properties This information is used to control the rendering and to further increase the realism of the generated models.

3.2   Applications

All modules as mentioned above are tuned towards a set of applications that will use the extracted real-world models and enhance them with AR/VR techniques.
    The project has focussed on three major application areas:

3D surface modeling from an image sequence The goal of this very general application is to develop strategies for easy and efficient geometric modeling. Based on images of the scene alone highly realistic metric models of specific objects or scenes (e.g. buildings, landscapes) are generated that can be used for visualisation and demonstration purposes. As a test case for this approach, a reconstruction of parts of the archaeological excavation site in Sagalassos, Turkey, was performed. An example of 3D modeling shows the reconstruction of a corner of the Roman bath at the Sagalassos site, based on five uncalibrated views (fig. 6).

Stereo Visualisations of Objects and Scenes Given a monocular (single camera) sequence, the objective is to generate the image sequences that would have been seen had a *stereo-rig* moved along the same path. The stereo sequence will be used as an image source to drive 3D displays (e.g. shutter glasses on a workstation, and SHARP's autostereoscopic displays). By creating views that are "in-between"

Fig. 6. 2 Images of Roman bath sequence, reconstructed shape and textured model

the discrete set of images, an active "look-around" system can be built — a pseudo-holographic display.

Collaborative Scene Visualisation The objective of this application is to walk around objects with a video camera and then extract a 3D model. The objects will then be graphically rendered together with possible arrangements of previously modeled (e.g. CAD) objects and surroundings. Remote sites will be able to jointly change the configurations of real and virtual objects. The application will serve as a trial using ISDN or ATM (see *Applying Augmented Reality Techniques in the Field of Interactive Collaborative Design*).

These applications represent a significant integration of state-of-the-art computer vision and computer graphics techniques. Many other application areas could benefit from these capabilities: non-invasive surgery; heritage preservation; archeologists recording layouts and discovered artefacts at an excavation (a video sequence at each stage providing the basis for subsequent virtual reality walkthroughs), accident investigators recording a scene before it is cleared; architecture visualization; collaborative design; teleshopping, etc.

Walkthrough, look–around and model acquisition also have applications in the games industry, e.g. to create more realistic backgrounds than simple graphically rendered ones, to immerse the player more fully (by changing the scene when his/her viewing perspective changes), and to provide virtual objects. Finally, although not explored here, the work opens up the prospect of intelligent keying - the integration of two video sequences - based on the geometries of the viewed scenes; it also allows virtual "tele-porting" of objects, since a cloned model can be cut at a distant location using the geometry and surface description provided by a video of the original.

References

1. K. Åström and A. Heyden. Continous time matching constraints for image stream. *International Journal of Computer Vision*, page To appear, 1998.
2. A. Heyden and K. Åström. Euclidean reconstruction from constant intrinsic parameters. In *Proceedings of the 13th International Conference on Pattern Recognition, Vienna, Austria*, volume I, pages 339–343, August 1996.
3. A. Heyden and K. Åström. Euclidean reconstruction from image sequences with varying and unknown focal length and principal point. In *Proceedings of the Conference on Computer Vision and Pattern Recognition, Puerto Rico, USA*, pages 438–443. IEEE Computer Society Press, June 1997.
4. F. Kahl and K. Åström. Motion estimation in images sequences using the deformation of apparent contours. In *Proceedings of the 6th International Conference on Computer Vision, Bombay, India*, pages 939–944, 1998.
5. L. Quan and T. Kanade. Affine structure from line correspondences with uncalibrated affine cameras. IEEE *Transactions on Pattern Analysis and Machine Intelligence*, 19(8):834–845, August 1997.
6. G. Sparr. Simultaneous reconstruction of scene structure and camera locations from uncalibrated image sequences. In *Proceedings of the 13th International Conference on Pattern Recognition, Vienna, Austria*, volume I, pages 328–333. IEEE Computer Society Press, August 1996.
7. P. Sturm. *Vision 3D non calibrée : contributions à la reconstruction projective et étude des mouvements critiques pour l'auto-calibrage*. Thèse de doctorat, Institut National Polytechnique de Grenoble, December 1997.
8. B. Triggs. Autocalibration and the absolute quadric. In *Proceedings of the Conference on Computer Vision and Pattern Recognition, Puerto Rico, USA*, pages 609–614. IEEE Computer Society Press, June 1997.
9. B. Triggs. Linear projective reconstruction from matching tensors. *Image and Vision Computing*, 15(8):617–625, August 1997.
10. B. Triggs. Autocalibration from planar scenes. In *Proceedings of the 5th European Conference on Computer Vision, Freiburg, Germany*, 1998.
11. F. Pedersini, et. al, "Calibration and Self-Calibration of multi-Ocular Camera Systems", Int. Workshop on Synthetic-Natural Hybrid Coding and Three Dimensional Imaging - IWSNHC3DI'97, Rhodes, Greece, 1997.
12. R. Y. Tsai, "A Versatile Camera Calibration Technique for High-Accuracy 3D Machine Vision Metrology Using Off-the-Shelf TV Cameras and Lenses", Journal of Robotics and Automation, Vol. RA-3. No.4, August 1987, pp. 323-344.
13. "The Virtual Reality Modeling Language Specification", Version 2.0, Final Working Draft, ISO/IEC WD 14772, July 28, 1996, http://vrml.sgi.com/movingworlds/spec/

14. Foley, J. D., van Dam, A., Feiner, S. K., Hughes J. F., "Computer Graphics", Addison-Wesley Publi. Comp. 1990.
15. L. Falkenhagen, "Hierarchical Block-Based Disparity Estimation Considering Neighbourhood Constraints", Int. Workshop on Synthetic-Natural Hybrid Coding and Three Dimensional Imaging - IWSNHC3DI'97, Rhodes, Greece, 1997.
16. T. Riegel, et. al. "3-D Shape Approximation for Objects in Multiview Image Sequences", Int. Workshop on Synthetic-Natural Hybrid Coding and Three Dimensional Imaging - IWSNHC3DI'97, Rhodes, Greece, 1997.
17. W. Niem, H. Broszio, "Mapping Texture from Multiple Camera Views onto 3D Object models for Computer Animation", Int. Workshop on Stereoscopic and 3D Imaging - IWS3DI'95, Santorini, Greece, Sept. 1995.
18. R. Koch, "Dynamic 3-D Scene Analysis through Synthesis Feedback Control", IEEE Transactions on PAMI, Vol. 12, No. 6, June 1993
19. L. Falkenhagen, "3-D Motion Estimation of 3-D Model Objects", ACTS-PANORAMA Project Deliverable, AC092/UH/D006, 1996.
20. D. Tzovaras, et. al. "3D Motion Estimation of Small Surface Patches", ACTS-PANORAMA Project Deliverable, AC092/UT/D013, 1997.
21. A. Kopernik, et. al. "3D Shape Update and Subdivision of 3D Model Objects, First Results", ACTS-PANORAMA Project Deliverable, AC092/UT/D014, 1997.
22. Torr P., Fitzgibbon A. and Zisserman A., "Maintaining Multiple Motion Model Hypotheses Over Many Views to Recover Matching and Structure", To appear in *Intern. Journal on Computer Vision*, 1998.
23. M. Pollefeys, R. Koch and L. Van Gool: Self-Calibration and Metric Reconstruction in spite of Varying and Unknown Internal Camera Parameters.To appear in *Intern. Journal on Computer Vision*, 1998.
24. Avidan, S. and Shashua, A. Novel View Synthesis in Tensor Space. *IEEE Conference on Computer Vision and Pattern Recognition* (CVPR), June 1997.
25. Rousso, S. Peleg, I. Finci, and A. Rav-Acha. Universal Mosaicing using Pipe Projection. In *Sixth International Conference on Computer Vision*, Bombay, India, 1998.
26. P. J. Neugebauer and K. Klein: Adaptive Triangulation of Objects Reconstructed from Multiple Range Images. *Proc. IEEE Visualization '97, Phoenix, Arizona*

Dualizing Scene Reconstruction Algorithms

Richard Hartley and Gilles Debunne

GE–CRD, Schenectady, NY
iMAGIS-GRAVIR, Grenoble
hartley@crd.ge.com, Gilles.Debunne@imag.fr

Abstract. It has been known since the work of Carlsson [2] and Weinshall [17] that there is a dualization principle that allows one to interchange the role of points being viewed by several cameras and the camera centres themselves. In principle this implies the possibility of dualizing projective reconstruction algorithms to obtain new algorithms. In this paper, this theme is developed at a theoretical and algorithmic level. The nature of the duality mapping is explored and its application to reconstruction ambiguity is discussed. An explicit method for dualizing any projective reconstruction algorithm is given. At the practical implementation level, however, it is shown that there are difficulties which have so far defeated successful application of this dualization method to produce working algorithms.

1   Introduction

The theory and practice of projective and metric reconstruction from uncalibrated and semi calibrated views has reached a level of maturity in recent years that excellent results may now be achieved. Papers presented at this workshop and reported in this volume show the high quality of reconstruction that is now possible.

In particular, it would appear that many of the problems of reconstruction have now reached a level where one may claim that they are solved. Such problems include

1. Computation of the multifocal tensors, particularly the fundamental matrix and trifocal tensors (the quadrifocal tensor having not received so much attention) [19, 3].
2. Extraction of the camera matrices from these tensors, and subsequent projective reconstruction from two and three views.

Other significant successes have been achieved, though there may be more to learn about these problems.

1. Application of bundle adjustment to solve more general reconstruction problems.
2. Metric (Euclidean) reconstruction given minimal assumptions on the camera matrices ([7, 9, 16]).

Reinhard Koch, Luc Van Gool (Eds.): SMILE '98, LNCS 1506, pp. 14–31, 1998.
© Springer-Verlag Berlin Heidelberg 1998

3. Automatic detection of correspondences in image sequences, and elimination of outliers and false matches using the multifocal tensor relationships [14, 18].

In other areas the last word has clearly not been written. Notably, there is not any single satisfactory algorithm for projective reconstruction from several views. Many methods have been tried : iterative methods, methods based on tacking together reconstructions from small numbers of views [6], or factorization-based algorithms [15, 13], which need arbitrary guesses at depth.

This paper discusses a technique that, although known, seems not to have received as much attention as may be warranted. The method based on a dualization principle expounded by Carlsson and also Weinshall ([2, 17]) can in principle transform the problem of projective reconstruction from long image sequences into the problem of projective reconstruction from small numbers of views, for which (as claimed above) the reconstruction problem is essentially solved. It is shown that although this duality theoretically gives rise to the desired multiple-view algorithms, in reality there are practical difficulties. In this paper, the problem of how to obtain working algorithms from this method is not solved. The purpose is to highlight the fascinating properties of the duality method, here called Carlsson duality, with the hope of awaking enough interest to lead to a practical implementation of these methods.

Before we proceed to discuss duality, I claim the privilege of giving an opinion. At this point of maturity, the understanding of the underlying geometrical properties of multi-view vision and the implementation of high-quality geometrical algorithms have outstripped the less mathematically structured tasks of correspondence matching and 3D model building that are essential to building a good system (despite the excellent results achieved and reported at the workshop). In short, we seem to be able to obtain small robust sets of image correspondences and reconstruct these points in 3-space. But how does one find sufficiently many correspondences to build a complete model, and anyway, how does one build a complete 3D model, that is, fill in the gaps between the points ? We can still not do satisfactory automatic reconstruction from complex outdoor scenes (for instance a forest scene) or even indoor scenes such as a room with a jumble of furniture and equipment (such as my office). However, leaving for another day a consideration of these harder problem, we now turn to the main technical subject of this paper.

2   Carlsson Duality

Let $\mathbf{E}_1 = (1,0,0,0)^\top$, $\mathbf{E}_2 = (0,1,0,0)^\top$, $\mathbf{E}_3 = (0,0,1,0)^\top$ and $\mathbf{E}_4 = (0,0,0,1)^\top$ form part of a projective basis for $\mathcal{P}^3$. Similarly, let $\mathbf{e}_1 = (1,0,0)^\top$ $\mathbf{e}_2 = (0,1,0)^\top$ $\mathbf{e}_3 = (0,0,1)^\top$ $\mathbf{e}_4 = (1,1,1)^\top$ be a projective basis for the projective image plane $\mathcal{P}^2$.

Now, consider a camera with matrix P. We assume that the camera centre $\mathbf{C}$ does not sit on any of the axial planes, that is $\mathbf{C} = (\mathrm{X}, \mathrm{Y}, \mathrm{Z}, \mathrm{T})^\top$ and none of the four coordinates is zero. In this case, no three of the points $\mathrm{P}\mathbf{E}_i$ for $i = 1, \dots, 4$ are collinear in the image. Consequently, one may apply a projective transformation

H to the image so that $\mathbf{e}_i = \mathtt{HPE}_i$. We assume that this has been done, and henceforth denote HP simply by P. Since $\mathbf{PE}_i = \mathbf{e}_i$, one computes that the form of the matrix P is

$$P = \begin{bmatrix} \alpha^{-1} & & & -\delta^{-1} \\ & \beta^{-1} & & -\delta^{-1} \\ & & \gamma^{-1} & -\delta^{-1} \end{bmatrix} . \tag{1}$$

Further, the camera centre is $\mathbf{C} = (\alpha, \beta, \gamma, \delta)^\top$, as one verifies by solving $\mathbf{PC} = \mathbf{0}$. If $\mathbf{C} = (\alpha, \beta, \gamma, \delta)^\top$ is any point in $\mathcal{P}^3$, then the matrix in (1) will be denoted by $\mathbf{P_C}$.

Now, for any point $\mathbf{X} = (\mathtt{X}, \mathtt{Y}, \mathtt{Z}, \mathtt{T})^\top$ one verifies that

$$\mathbf{P_C X} = \begin{pmatrix} \alpha^{-1}\mathtt{X} - \delta^{-1}\mathtt{T} \\ \beta^{-1}\mathtt{Y} - \delta^{-1}\mathtt{T} \\ \gamma^{-1}\mathtt{Z} - \delta^{-1}\mathtt{T} \end{pmatrix} . \tag{2}$$

This observation leads to the following definition

Definition 1. *The mapping of $\mathcal{P}^3$ to itself given by*

$$(\mathtt{X}, \mathtt{Y}, \mathtt{Z}, \mathtt{T})^\top \mapsto (\mathtt{YZT}, \mathtt{ZTX}, \mathtt{TXY}, \mathtt{XYZ})^\top$$

will be called the Carlsson map, and will be denoted by Γ. We denote the image of a point $\mathbf{X}$ under Γ by $\overline{\mathbf{X}}$. The image of an object under Γ is sometimes referred to as the dual *object, for reasons that will be seen later.*

The Carlsson map is an example of a *Cremona* transformation. For more information on Cremona transformations, the reader is referred to Semple and Kneebone ([11]).

Note. If none of the coordinates of $\mathbf{X}$ is zero then we may divide $\overline{\mathbf{X}}$ by $\mathtt{XYZT}$. Then Γ is equivalent to $(\mathtt{X}, \mathtt{Y}, \mathtt{Z}, \mathtt{T})^\top \mapsto (\mathtt{X}^{-1}, \mathtt{Y}^{-1}, \mathtt{Z}^{-1}, \mathtt{T}^{-1})^\top$. This is the form of the mapping that we will usually use. In the case where one of the coordinates of $\mathbf{X}$ is zero, then the mapping will be interpreted as in the definition. Note that any point $(0, \mathtt{Y}, \mathtt{Z}, \mathtt{T})^\top$ is mapped to the point $(1, 0, 0, 0)^\top$ by Γ, provided none of the other coordinates is zero. Thus, the mapping is not one-to-one.

If two of the coordinates of $\mathbf{X}$ are zero, then $\overline{\mathbf{X}} = (0, 0, 0, 0)^\top$, which is an undefined point. Thus, Γ is not defined at all points. In fact, there is no way to extend Γ continuously to such points. Note that the points for which the mapping is undefined consists of the lines joining two of the points $\mathbf{E}_i$. We will call the four points $\mathbf{E}_i$ the vertices of the *reference tetrahedron*. The lines joining two vertices are the edges of the tetrahedron, and the planes defined by three vertices are the faces of the reference tetrahedron. As remarked, Γ is undefined on the edges of the reference tetrahedron. As for the faces of the reference tetrahedron, these are the points with a zero coordinate. Consequently (as shown above), each face is mapped by Γ to a single point, namely the opposite vertex of the reference tetrahedron.

The major importance of the Carlsson map derives from the following formula, which is easily derived from (2).

$$P_C X = P_{\overline{X}} \overline{C} \tag{3}$$

Thus, Γ interchanges the rôles of object points and camera centres. Thus, C acting on X gives the same result as $\overline{X}$ acting on $\overline{C}$. The consequences of this result will be investigated soon. However, first we will investigate the way in which Γ acts on other geometric objects.

Theorem (2.0.1). *The Carlsson map, Γ acts in the following manner :*

1. *It maps a line passing through two general points X_0 and X_1 to the twisted cubic ([11]) passing through $\overline{X}_0, \overline{X}_1$ and the the four reference vertices $E_1, \ldots, E_4$.*

2. *It maps a line passing through any of the points E_i to a line passing through the same E_i. We exclude the lines lying on the face of the reference tetrahedron, since such lines will be mapped to a single point.*

3. *It maps a quadric Q passing through the four points E_i, $i = 1, \ldots 4$ to a quadric surface (denoted $\overline{Q}$) passing through the same four points. If Q is a ruled quadric, then so is $\overline{Q}$. If Q is degenerate then so is $\overline{Q}$.*

Proof. **Part 1.** A line has parametric equation $(X_0 + a\theta, Y_0 + b\theta, Z_0 + c\theta, T_0 + d\theta)^\top$, and a point on this line is taken by the Carlsson map to the point

$$((Y_0 + b\theta)(Z_0 + c\theta)(T_0 + d\theta), \ldots, (X_0 + a\theta)(Y_0 + b\theta)(Z_0 + c\theta))^\top .$$

Thus, the entries of the vector are cubic functions of θ, and the curve is a twisted cubic. Now, setting $\theta = -X_0/a$, the term $(X_0 + a\theta)$ vanishes, and the corresponding dual point is $((Y_0 + b\theta)(Z_0 + c\theta)(T_0 + d\theta), 0, 0, 0)^\top \approx (1, 0, 0, 0)^\top$. The first entry is the only one that does not contain $(X_0 + a\theta)$, and hence the only one that does not vanish. This shows that the reference vertex $E_1 = (1, 0, 0, 0)^\top$ is on the twisted cubic. By similar arguments, the other points $E_2, \ldots, E_4$ lie on the twisted cubic also. Note that a twisted cubic is defined by 6 points, and this twisted cubic is defined by the given 6 points $E_i, \overline{X}_0, \overline{X}_1$ that lie on it, where X_0 and X_1 are any two points defining the line.

Part 2. We prove this for lines passing through the point $E_1 = (1, 0, 0, 0)^\top$. An analogous proof holds for the other points E_i. Choose another point $X = (X, Y, Z, T)^\top$ on the line, such that X does not lie on any face of the reference tetrahedron. Thus X has no zero coordinate. Points on a line passing through $(1, 0, 0, 0)^\top$ and $X = (X, Y, Z, T)^\top$ are all of the form $(X, Y, Z, T)^\top + k(1, 0, 0, 0)^\top = (\alpha, Y, Z, T)^\top$ for varying values of $\alpha = X + k$. These points are mapped by the transformation to $(\alpha^{-1}, Y^{-1}, Z^{-1}, T^{-1})^\top$. This represents a line passing through the two points $(1, 0, 0, 0)^\top$ and $\overline{X} = (X^{-1}, Y^{-1}, Z^{-1}, T^{-1})^\top$.

Part 3. Since the quadric Q passes through all the points E_i, the diagonal entries of Q must all be zero. This means that there are no terms involving a squared coordinate (such as X^2) in the equation for the quadric. Hence the equation for the quadric contains only mixed terms (such as XY, YZ or XT).

Therefore, a point $\mathbf{X} = (\text{X}, \text{Y}, \text{Z}, \text{T})^\top$ lies on the quadric Q if and only if $a\text{XY} + b\text{XZ} + c\text{XT} + d\text{YZ} + e\text{YT} + f\text{ZT} = 0$. Dividing this equation by XYZT, we obtain $a\text{Z}^{-1}\text{T}^{-1} + b\text{Y}^{-1}\text{T}^{-1} + c\text{Y}^{-1}\text{Z}^{-1} + d\text{X}^{-1}\text{T}^{-1} + e\text{X}^{-1}\text{Z}^{-1} + f\text{X}^{-1}\text{Y}^{-1} = 0$. Since $\overline{\mathbf{X}} = (\text{X}^{-1}, \text{Y}^{-1}, \text{Z}^{-1}, \text{T}^{-1})^\top$, this is a quadratic equation in the entries of $\overline{\mathbf{X}}$. Thus Γ maps quadric to quadric. Specifically, suppose Q is represented by the matrix

$$\mathsf{Q} = \begin{bmatrix} 0 & a & b & c \\ a & 0 & d & e \\ b & d & 0 & f \\ c & e & f & 0 \end{bmatrix} \quad \text{then} \quad \overline{\mathsf{Q}} = \begin{bmatrix} 0 & f & e & d \\ f & 0 & c & b \\ e & c & 0 & a \\ d & b & a & 0 \end{bmatrix}$$

and $\mathbf{X}^\top \mathsf{Q} \mathbf{X} = 0$ implies $\overline{\mathbf{X}}^\top \overline{\mathsf{Q}} \overline{\mathbf{X}} = 0$. The quadric $\overline{\mathsf{Q}}$ is a ruled quadric, since the generators of Q passing through the points $\mathbf{E}_i$ map to straight lines, lying on $\overline{\mathsf{Q}}$. One may further verify that $\det \mathsf{Q} = \det \overline{\mathsf{Q}}$, which implies that if Q is a non-degenerate quadric (that is $\det \mathsf{Q} \neq 0$), then so is $\overline{\mathsf{Q}}$. In this non-degenerate case, if Q is a hyperboloid of one sheet, then $\det \mathsf{Q} > 0$, from which it follows that $\det \overline{\mathsf{Q}} > 0$. Thus $\overline{\mathsf{Q}}$ is also a hyperboloid of one sheet.   □

We wish to interpret duality equation (3) in a coordinate-free manner. The matrix $\mathsf{P_C}$ has by definition the form given in (1), and maps $\mathbf{E}_i$ to $\mathbf{e}_i$ for $i = 1, \ldots, 4$. The image $\mathsf{P_C}\mathbf{X}$ is may be thought of as a representation of the projection of $\mathbf{X}$ relative to the projective basis $\mathbf{e}_i$ in the image. Alternatively, $\mathsf{P_C}\mathbf{X}$ represents the projective equivalence class of the set of the five rays $\overline{\mathbf{CE}_1}, \ldots, \overline{\mathbf{CE}_4}, \overline{\mathbf{CX}}$. Thus $\mathsf{P_C}\mathbf{X} = \mathsf{P_{C'}}\mathbf{X'}$ if and only if the set of rays from $\mathbf{C}$ to $\mathbf{X}$ and the four vertices of the reference tetrahedron is projectively equivalent to the set of rays from $\mathbf{C'}$ to $\mathbf{X'}$ and the four reference vertices.

The Duality Principle.

There is nothing special about the four points $\mathbf{E}_1, \ldots, \mathbf{E}_4$ used as vertices of the reference tetrahedron, other than the fact that they are non-coplanar. Given any four non-coplanar points, one may define a projective coordinate system in which these four points are the points $\mathbf{E}_i$ forming part of a projective basis. The Carlsson mapping may then be defined with respect to this coordinate frame. The resulting map is called the Carlsson map with respect to the given reference tetrahedron.

To be more precise, it should be observed that five points (not four) define a projective coordinate frame in $\mathcal{P}^3$. In fact, there is a 3-parameter family of projective frames for which four non-coplanar points have coordinates $\mathbf{E}_i$. Thus the Carlsson map with respect to a given reference tetrahedron is not unique. However, the mapping given by definition (1) with respect to any such coordinate frame may be used.

Given a statement or theorem concerning projections of sets of points with respect to one or more projection centres one may derive a dual statement. One requires that among the four points being projected, there are four non-coplanar points that may form a reference tetrahedron. Under a general duality mapping with respect to the reference tetrahedron

1. Points (other than those belonging to the reference tetrahedron) are mapped to centres of projection.
2. Centres of projection are mapped to points.
3. Straight lines are mapped to twisted cubics.
4. Ruled quadrics containing the reference tetrahedron are mapped to ruled quadrics containing the reference tetrahedron.

Points lying on an edge of the reference tetrahedron should be avoided, since the Carlsson mapping is undefined for such points. Using this as a sort of translation table, one may use existing theorems about point projection to be dualized, giving new theorems for which a separate proof is not needed.

Note : It is important to observe that only those points not belonging to the reference tetrahedron are mapped to camera centres by duality. The vertices of the reference tetrahedron remain points. In practice, in applying the duality principle, one may select any 4 points to form the reference tetrahedron, as long as they are non-coplanar. In general, in the results stated in the next section there will be an assumption (not always stated explicitly) that **point sets considered contain four non-coplanar points**, which may be taken as the reference tetrahedron.

2.1   Reconstruction Ambiguity

It will be shown in this section how various ambiguous reconstruction results may be derived simply from known, or obvious geometrical statements by applying duality.

We will be considering configurations of camera centres and 3D points, which will be denoted by $\{C_1, \ldots, C_m; X_1, \ldots, X_n\}$ or variations thereof. Implicit is that the symbols appearing before the semicolon are camera centres, and those that come after are 3D points. In order to make the statements of derived results simple, the concept of *image equivalence* is defined.

Definition 2. *Two configurations*

$$\{C_1, \ldots C_m; X_1, \ldots X_n\} \text{ and } \{C'_1, \ldots C'_m; X'_1, \ldots X'_n\}$$

are called image equivalent *if for all i the image of the set of points $X_1, \ldots, X_n$ observed from camera centre C_i is projectively equivalent to the image of points $X'_1, \ldots, X'_n$ observed from C'_i.*

This definition makes sense, only because an image is determined up to projective equivalence by the centre of projection. The image of the points $X_1, \ldots, X_n$ with respect to centre C_i may be thought of somewhat abstractly as the projective equivalence class of the set of rays $\{\overline{C_i X_j} : j = 1, \ldots, n\}$.

The concept of image equivalence is distinct from projective equivalence of the sets of points and camera centres involved. Indeed, the relevance of this to reconstruction ambiguity is that if a configuration $\{C_1, \ldots, C_m; X_1, \ldots, X_n\}$

allows another image-equivalent set which is not projective-equivalent, then this amounts to an ambiguity of the projective reconstruction problem, since the projective structure of the points and cameras is not uniquely defined by the set of images. In this case, we say that the configuration $\{C_1, \ldots, C_m, X_1, \ldots X_n\}$ *allows an alternative reconstruction.*

Single View Ambiguity

As a simple example of what can be deduced using Carlsson duality, consider the following simple question : when do two points project to the same point in an image. The answer is obviously, when the two points lie on the same ray (straight line) through the camera centre. From this simple observation, one may deduce the following result.

(2.1.2). *Consider a set of camera centres* $C_1, \ldots, C_m$ *and a point* X_0 *all lying on a single straight line. and let* $E_i : i = 1, \ldots, 4$ *be the vertices of a reference tetrahedron. Let* X *be another point. The the two configurations*

$$\{C_1, \ldots, C_m; E_1, \ldots, E_4, X\} \text{ and } \{C_1, \ldots, C_m; E_1, \ldots, E_4, X_0\}$$

are image-equivalent configurations if and only if X *lies on the same straight line.*

This is illustrated in Fig 1.

In passing to the dual statement, according to Theorem (2.0.1) the straight line becomes a twisted cubic through the four vertices of the reference tetrahedron. Thus the dual statement to ((2.1.2)) is :

(2.1.3). *Consider a set of points* X_i *and a camera centre* C_0 *all lying on a single twisted cubic also passing through four reference vertices* E_k. *Let* C *be any other camera centre. Then the configurations*

$$\{C; E_1, \ldots, E_4, X_1, \ldots, X_m\} \text{ and } \{C_0; E_1, \ldots, E_4, X_1, \ldots, X_m\}$$

are image equivalent if and only if C *lies on the same twisted cubic.*

Since the points E_i may be any four non-coplanar points, and a twisted cubic can not contain 4 coplanar points, one may state this last result in the following form :

Proposition 1. *Let* $X_1, \ldots, X_m$ *be a set of points and* C_0 *a camera centre all lying on a twisted cubic. Then for any other camera centre* C *the configurations*

$$\{C; X_1, \ldots, X_m\} \text{ and } \{C_0; X_1, \ldots, X_m\}$$

are image equivalent if and only if C *lies on the same twisted cubic.*

This is illustrated in Fig 2. It shows that camera pose can not be uniquely determined whenever all points and a camera centre lie on a twisted cubic.

Using similar methods one can show that this is one of only two possible ambiguous situations. The other case in which ambiguity occurs is when all points and the two camera centres lie in the union of a plane and a line. This arises as the dual of the case when the straight line through the camera centres meets one of the vertices of the reference tetrahedron. In this case, the dual of this line is also a straight line through the same reference vertex (see Theorem (2.0.1)), and all points must lie on this line or the opposite face of the reference tetrahedron. These results were brought to the attention of the computer-vision community by Buchanan ([1]).

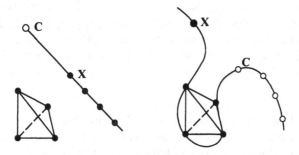

Fig. 1. **Left :** Any point on the line passing through **C** and **X** is projected to the same point from projection centre **C**. **Right :** The dual statement – from any centre of projection **C** lying on a twisted cubic passing through **X** and the vertices of the reference tetrahedron, the five points are projected in the same way (up to projective equivalence). Thus a camera is constrained to lie on a twisted cubic by its image of five known points.

The Horopter

Similar arguments can be used to derive the form of the horopter for two images. The horopter is the set of space points that map to the same point in two images. The following result is self-evident.

(2.1.4). *Given points* **X** *and* **X**$'$, *the set of camera centres* **C** *such that*

$$\{\mathbf{C}; \mathbf{E}_1, \ldots, \mathbf{E}_4, \mathbf{X}\} \text{ and } \{\mathbf{C}; \mathbf{E}_1, \ldots, \mathbf{E}_4, \mathbf{X}'\}$$

are image equivalent is the straight line passing through **X** *and* **X**$'$.

This is illustrated in Fig 2. The dual of this statement is

Proposition 2. *Given projection centres* **C** *and* **C**$'$, *non-collinear with the four points* **E**$_i$ *of a reference tetrahedron, the set of points* **X** *such that* $\{\mathbf{C}; \mathbf{E}_1, \ldots, \mathbf{E}_4, \mathbf{X}\}$ *and* $\{\mathbf{C}'; \mathbf{E}_1, \ldots, \mathbf{E}_4, \mathbf{X}\}$ *are image-equivalent is a twisted cubic passing through* **E**$_1, \ldots,$ **E**$_4$ *and the two projection centres* **C** *and* **C**$'$.

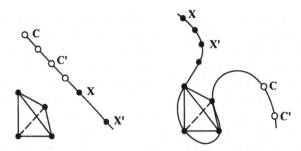

Fig. 2. Left : From any centre of projection $\mathbf{C}, \mathbf{C}', \ldots$ lying on the line passing through $\mathbf{X}$ and $\mathbf{X}'$, the points $\mathbf{X}$ and $\mathbf{X}'$ are projected to the same ray. That is, $\{\mathbf{C}; \mathbf{E}_i, \mathbf{X}\}$ is image-equivalent to $\{\mathbf{C}; \mathbf{E}_i, \mathbf{X}'\}$ for all $\mathbf{C}$ on the line. **Right :** The dual statement – all points on the twisted cubic passing through $\mathbf{C}$ and $\mathbf{C}'$ and the vertices of the reference tetrahedron are projected in the same way relative to the two projection centres. That is, $\{\mathbf{C}; \mathbf{E}_i, \mathbf{X}\}$ is image-equivalent to $\{\mathbf{C}'; \mathbf{E}_i, \mathbf{X}\}$ for all $\mathbf{X}$ on the twisted cubic. This curve is called the *horopter* for the two centres of projection.

Note in both these examples how the use of duality has taken intuitively obvious statements concerning projections of collinear points and derived a result somewhat less obvious about points lying on a twisted cubic.

Two-View Ambiguity

The basic ([8]) result about critical surfaces from two views may be stated as follows.

Theorem (2.1.5). *A configuration $\{\mathbf{C}_1, \mathbf{C}_2; \mathbf{X}_1, \ldots, \mathbf{X}_n\}$ of two camera centres and n points allows an alternative reconstruction if and only if both camera centres $\mathbf{C}_1, \mathbf{C}_2$ and all the points $\mathbf{X}_j$ lie on a ruled quadric surface. Furthermore, when an alternative reconstruction exists, then there will always exist a third distinct reconstruction.*

One may write down the dual statement straight away as follows.

Theorem (2.1.6). *A configuration $\{\mathbf{C}_1, \ldots, \mathbf{C}_n; \mathbf{X}_1, \ldots, \mathbf{X}_6\}$ of any number of cameras and six points allows an alternative reconstruction if and only if all camera centres $\mathbf{C}_1, \ldots, \mathbf{C}_n$ and all the points $\mathbf{X}_1, \mathbf{X}_6$ lie on a ruled quadric surface. Furthermore, when an alternative reconstruction exists, then there will always exist a third distinct reconstruction.*

This result was proven in [12]. Observe that in this dual statement, the value of n is not the same as the value of n in Theorem (2.1.5). Indeed, in the transition to the dual result, four of the original n points $\mathbf{X}_j$ are selected as the reference tetrahedron, and remain points. The remaining $n-4$ points become camera centres. The two original camera centres become points, making six points in total. The ruled quadric becomes a ruled quadric according to Theorem (2.0.1).

The minimum interesting case of Theorem (2.1.6) is when $n = 3$, as studied in [10]. In this case one has nine points in total (three cameras and six points). One can construct a quadric surface passing through these nine points (a quadric is defined by nine points). If the quadric is a ruled quadric (a hyperboloid of one sheet in the non-degenerate case), then there are three possible distinct reconstructions. Otherwise the reconstruction is unique.

3   Dual Algorithms

The method of duality will now be given for deriving a dual algorithm from a given algorithm. Specifically, it will be shown that if one has an algorithm for doing projective reconstruction from n views of $m + 4$ points, then there is an algorithm for doing projective reconstruction from m views of $n + 4$ points. This result, observed by Carlsson [2], will be made specific by explicitly describing the steps of the dual algorithm.

We consider a projective reconstruction problem, which will be referred to as $\mathcal{P}(m, n)$. It is the problem of doing reconstruction from m views of n points. We denote image points by $\mathbf{x}_j^i$, which represents the image of the j-th object space point in the i-th view. Thus, the upper index indicates the view number, and the lower index represents the point number. Such a set of points $\{\mathbf{x}_j^i\}$ is called **realizable** if there are a set of camera matrices P^i and a set of 3D points $\mathbf{X}_j$ such that $\mathbf{x}_j^i = \mathrm{P}^i \mathbf{X}_j$. The projective reconstruction problem $\mathcal{P}(m, n)$ is that of finding such camera matrices P^i and points $\mathbf{X}_j$ given a realizable set $\{\mathbf{x}_j^i\}$ for m views of n points.

Let $\mathcal{A}(n, m + 4)$ represent an algorithm for solving the projective reconstruction problem $\mathcal{P}(n, m+4)$. An algorithm will now be exhibited for solving the projective reconstruction $\mathcal{P}(m, n + 4)$. This algorithm will be denoted $\mathcal{A}^*(m, n+4)$, the dual of the algorithm $\mathcal{A}(n, m + 4)$.

Initially, the steps of the algorithm will be given without proof. In addition, difficulties will be glossed over so as to give the general idea without getting bogged down in details. In the description of this algorithm it is important to keep track of the range of the indices, and whether they index the cameras or the points. Thus, the following may help to keep track.

- Upper indices represent the view number.
- Lower indices represent the point number.
- i ranges from 1 to m.
- j ranges from 1 to n.
- k ranges from 1 to 4.

The Dual Algorithm

Given an algorithm $\mathcal{A}(n, m+4)$ the goal is to exhibit a dual algorithm $\mathcal{A}^*(m, n+4)$.

Input:

The input to the algorithm $\mathcal{A}^*(m, n+4)$ consists of a realizable set of $n+4$ points seen in m views. This set of points can be arranged in a table as in Fig 3(left).

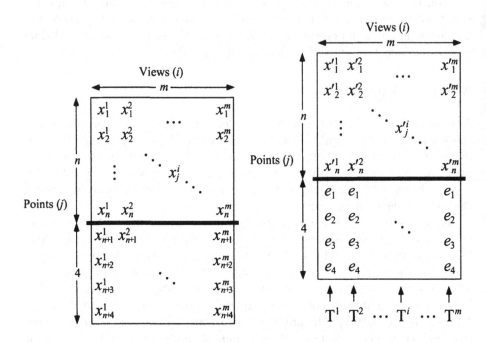

Fig. 3. Left : Input to algorithm $\mathcal{A}^*(m, n+4)$ **Right :** Input data after transformation.

In this table, the points $\mathbf{x}^i_{n+k}$ are separated from the other points $\mathbf{x}^i_j$, since they will receive special treatment.

Step 1 : Transform.

The first step is to compute for each i, a transformation $\mathbf{T}^i$ that maps the points $\mathbf{x}^i_{n+k}$, $k = 1, \ldots, 4$ in the i-th view to the points $\mathbf{e}_k$ of a canonical basis for projective 2-space $\mathcal{P}^2$. The transformation $\mathbf{T}^i$ is applied also to each of the points $\mathbf{x}^i_j$ to produce transformed points $\mathbf{x}'^i_j = \mathbf{T}^i \mathbf{x}^i_j$. The result is the transformed point array shown in Fig 3(right). A different transformation $\mathbf{T}^i$ is computed and applied to each column of the array, as indicated.

Step 2 : Transpose.

The last four rows of the array are dropped, and the remaining block of the array is transposed. One defines $\hat{\mathbf{x}}^j_i = \mathbf{x}'^i_j$. At the same time, one does a mental switch of points and views. Thus the point $\hat{x}_i^j$ is now conceived as being the image of the j-th point in the i-th view, whereas the point $x_j'^i$ was the image of the i-th point in the j-th view. What is happening here effectively is that one is swapping the roles of points and cameras – the basic concept behind Carlsson duality expressed by (3). The resulting transposed array is shown in Fig 4(left).

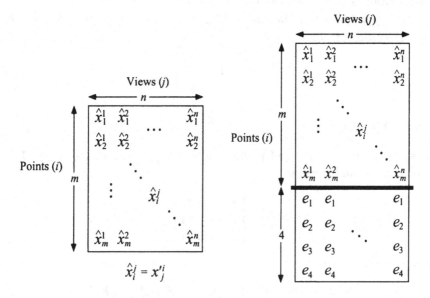

Fig. 4. Left : Transposed data. **Right :** Transposed data extended by addition of extra points.

Step 3 : Extend.

The array of points is now extended by the addition of four extra rows containing points e_k in all positions of the $(m + k)$-th row of the array, as shown in Fig 4(right).

Step 4 : Solve.

The array of points resulting from the last step has $m + 4$ rows and n columns, and may be regarded as the positions of $m + 4$ points seen in n views. As such, it is a candidate for solution by the algorithm $\mathcal{A}(n, m+4)$, which we have assumed is given. Essential here is that the points in the array form a realizable set of point correspondences. Justification of this is deferred for now. The result of the algorithm $\mathcal{A}(n, m+4)$ is a set of cameras $\widehat{\mathsf{P}}^j$ and points $\widehat{\mathbf{X}}_i$ such that $\hat{x}_i^j = \widehat{\mathsf{P}}^j \widehat{\mathbf{X}}_i$. In addition, corresponding to the last four rows of the array, there are points $\widehat{\mathbf{X}}_{m+k}$ such that $e_k = \widehat{\mathsf{P}}^j \widehat{\mathbf{X}}_{m+k}$ for all j.

Step 5 : 3D Transform.

Since the reconstruction obtained in the last step is a projective reconstruction, one may transform it (equivalently, choose a projective coordinate frame) such that the points $\widehat{\mathbf{X}}_{m+k}$ are the four points $\mathbf{E}_k$ of a partial canonical basis for $\mathcal{P}^3$. The only requirement is that the points $\widehat{\mathbf{X}}_{m+k}$ obtained in the projective reconstruction not be coplanar. This assumption is validated later.

At this point, one sees that $\mathbf{e}_k = \widehat{\mathsf{P}}^j \widehat{\mathbf{X}}_{m+k} = \widehat{\mathsf{P}}^j \mathbf{E}_k$. From this it follows that $\widehat{\mathsf{P}}^j$ has the special form

$$\widehat{\mathsf{P}}^j = \begin{bmatrix} a^j & & d^j \\ & b^j & d^j \\ & & c^j & d^j \end{bmatrix} . \tag{4}$$

Step 6 : Dualize.

Let $\widehat{\mathbf{X}}_i = (\mathsf{X}_i, \mathsf{Y}_i, \mathsf{Z}_i, \mathsf{T}_i)^\top$, and $\widehat{\mathsf{P}}^j$ be as given in (4). Now define points $\mathbf{X}_j = (a^j, b^j, c^j, d^j)^\top$ and cameras

$$\mathsf{P}'^i = \begin{bmatrix} \mathsf{X}_i & & \mathsf{T}_i \\ & \mathsf{Y}_i & \mathsf{T}_i \\ & & \mathsf{Z}_i & \mathsf{T}_i \end{bmatrix} .$$

Then one verifies that

$$\begin{aligned} \mathsf{P}'^i \mathbf{X}_j &= (\mathsf{X}_i a^j + \mathsf{T}_i d^j, \mathsf{Y}_i b^j + \mathsf{T}_i d^j, \mathsf{Z}_i c^j + \mathsf{T}_i d^j)^\top \\ &= \widehat{\mathsf{P}}^j \widehat{\mathbf{X}}_i \\ &= \widehat{\mathbf{x}}_i^j \\ &= \mathbf{x}_j'^i . \end{aligned}$$

If in addition, one defines $\mathbf{X}_{n+k} = \mathbf{E}_k$ for $k = 1, \ldots, 4$, then $\mathsf{P}'^i \mathbf{X}_{n+k} = \mathbf{e}_k$. It is then evident that the cameras P'^i and points $\mathbf{X}_j$ and $\mathbf{X}_{n+k}$ form a projective reconstruction of the transformed data array obtained in Step 1 of this algorithm.

Step 7 : Reverse Transform.

Finally, defining $\mathsf{P}^i = (\mathsf{T}^i)^{-1}\mathsf{P}'^i$, and with the points $\mathbf{X}_j$ and $\mathbf{X}_{n+k}$ obtained in the previous step, one has a projective reconstruction of the original data. Indeed, one verifies

$$\mathsf{P}^i \mathbf{X}_j = (\mathsf{T}^i)^{-1} \mathsf{P}'^i \mathbf{X}_j = (\mathsf{T}^i)^{-1} \mathbf{x}_j'^i = \mathbf{x}_j^i .$$

This completes the description of the algorithm. One can see that it takes place in various stages.

1. In Step 1, the data is transformed into canonical image reference frames based on the selection of 4 distinguished points.

2. In Steps 2 and 3 the problem is mapped into the dual domain, resulting in a dual problem $\mathcal{P}(n, m + 4)$.
3. The dual problem is solved in step 4 and 5.
4. Step 6 maps the solution back into the original domain.
5. Step 7 undoes the effects of the initial transformation.

3.1 Justification of the Algorithm.

To justify this algorithm, one needs to be sure that at Step 4 there indeed exists a solution to the transformed problem. Before considering this, it is necessary to explain the purpose of Step 3, which extends the data by the addition of rows of image points $\mathbf{e}_k$, and Step 5, which transforms the arbitrary projective solution to one in which four points are equal to the 3D basis points $\mathbf{E}_k$.

The purpose of these steps is to ensure that one obtains a solution to the dual reconstruction problem in which $\widehat{\mathbf{P}}^j$ has the special form given by (4) in which the camera matrix is parametrized by only 4 values. The dual algorithm is described in this manner so that it will work with any algorithm $\mathcal{A}(n, m + 4)$ whatever. However, both Steps 3 and 5 may be eliminated if the known algorithm $\mathcal{A}(n, m+4)$ has the capability of enforcing this constraint on the camera matrices directly. Algorithms based on the fundamental matrix, trifocal or quadrifocal tensors may easily be modified in this way, as will be seen.

In the mean time, since $\widehat{\mathbf{P}}^j$ of the form (4) is called a *reduced camera matrix*, we call any reconstruction in which each camera matrix is of this form a *reduced reconstruction*. Not all sets of realizable point correspondences allow a reduced reconstruction, however, the following result characterizes sets of point correspondences that do have this property.

(3.1.7). *A set of image points* $\{\mathbf{x}_j^i \; : \; i = 1, \ldots, m \; ; \; j = 1, \ldots, n\}$ *permits a reduced reconstruction if and only if it may be augmented with supplementary correspondences* $\mathbf{x}_{n+k}^i = \mathbf{e}_k$ *for* $k = 1, \ldots, 4$ *such that*

1. *The total set of image correspondences is realizable, and*
2. *The reconstructed points* $\mathbf{X}_{n+k}$ *corresponding to the supplementary image correspondences are non-coplanar.*

Proof. The proof is straight-forward enough. Suppose the set permits a reduced reconstruction, and let $\mathbf{P}^i$ be the set of reduced camera matrices. Let points $\mathbf{X}_{n+k} = \mathbf{E}_k$ for $k = 1, \ldots, 4$ be projected into the m images. The projections are $\mathbf{x}_{n+k}^i = \mathbf{P}^i \mathbf{X}_{n+k} = \mathbf{P}^i \mathbf{E}_k = \mathbf{e}_k$ for all i.

Conversely, suppose the augmented set of points are realizable and the points $\mathbf{X}_{n+k}$ are non-coplanar. In this case, a projective basis may be chosen such that $\mathbf{X}_{n+k} = \mathbf{E}_k$. Then for each view, one has $\mathbf{e}_k = \mathbf{P}^i \mathbf{E}_k$ for all k. From this it follows that each $\mathbf{P}^i$ has the desired form (4). $\qquad\square$

One other remark must be made before proving the correctness of the algorithm.

(3.1.8). *If a set of image points $\{\mathbf{x}_j^i \ : \ i = 1,\ldots,m \ ; \ j = 1,\ldots,n\}$ permits a reduced reconstruction then so does the transposed set $\{\hat{\mathbf{x}}_i^j \ : \ j = 1,\ldots,n \ ; \ i = 1,\ldots,m\}$ where $\hat{\mathbf{x}}_i^j = \mathbf{x}_j^i$ for all i and j.*

This is the basic duality property, effectively proven by the construction given in Step 6 of the algorithm above. Now it is possible to prove the correctness of the algorithm.

Proposition 3. *Let $\mathbf{x}_j^i$ and $\mathbf{x}_{n+k}^i$ as in Fig 3(left) be a set of realizable image point correspondences, and suppose*

1. *for each i, the four points $\mathbf{x}_{n+k}^i$ are non-collinear, and*
2. *the four points $\mathbf{X}_{n+k}$ in a projective reconstruction are non-coplanar.*

Then the algorithm of section 3 will succeed.

Proof. Because of the first condition of the theorem, transformations $\mathbf{T}^i$ exist for each i, transforming the input data to the form shown in Fig 3(right). This transformed data is also realizable, since the transformed data differ only by a projective transformation of the image.

Now, according to ((3.1.7)) applied to Fig 3(right), the correspondences $\mathbf{x}_j'^i$ admit a reduced realization. By ((3.1.8)) the transposed data Fig 4(left) also admits a reduced realization. Applying ((3.1.7)) once more shows that the extended data Fig 4(right) is realizable, Furthermore, the points $\widehat{\mathbf{X}}_{m+k}$ are non-coplanar, and so Step 5 is valid. The subsequent steps 6 and 7 go forward without problems. □

The first condition may be checked from the image correspondences $\mathbf{x}_j^i$. It may be thought that to check the second condition requires reconstruction to be carried out. It is, however possible to check whether the reconstructed points will be coplanar without carrying out the reconstruction. This is left as an exercise for the reader.

4   Refinements to the Dual Algorithm

The dual algorithm as presented above gives a way of dualizing any given projective reconstruction algorithm. The main weakness of this approach is that it ignores possible noise in the measurements. Noise ought to be considered at several points.

Direct Enforcement of Reduced Reconstruction.

Steps 3 and 5 of the algorithm are used to make sure that the camera matrices in the computed reconstruction are of the form (4). The trouble with this is that the points $\hat{\mathbf{x}}_{m+k}^j = \mathbf{e}_k$ are treated as any other point in the reconstruction. In the presence of noise, most algorithms, such as those based on multifocal tensors find reconstructions for which the input point correspondences are only approximately satisfied, to the extent that is possible given the level of noise. However, in order that the camera matrices should be of the correct form, it is necessary that the correspondences $\hat{\mathbf{x}}_{m+k}^j = \mathbf{e}_k$ be satisfied exactly. Thus, these correspondences must be treated differently from the others.

Preferable would be to enforce the constraint that the camera matrices are of the form (4) directly. In the case where $n = 2$ the algorithm $\mathcal{A}(n, m+4)$ used to obtain the reconstruction in the dual domain may be the 8-point algorithm. Apart from assuming that each of the camera matrices is reduced, one may assume further that the first one has the special canonical form $\widehat{\mathbf{P}}^1 = [\mathbf{I} \mid \mathbf{0}]$. In this case with $\widehat{\mathbf{P}}^2$ given as in (4) one computes that the fundamental matrix has the form (up to a scale factor)

$$\widehat{\mathbf{F}} = \begin{bmatrix} 0 & -b & c \\ a & 0 & -c \\ -a & b & 0 \end{bmatrix} \tag{5}$$

The 8-point algorithm may easily be modified so that the computed fundamental matrix has this form. The retrieval of the reduced camera matrix $\widehat{\mathbf{P}}^2$ from (5) is then trivial.

In the case where $n = 3$, one may use an algorithm based on the trifocal tensor. For three general camera matrices $[\mathbf{I} \mid \mathbf{0}]$, $\mathbf{A} = [a_i^j]$ and $\mathbf{B} = [b_i^k]$ the general formula for the trifocal tensor was given in [4] to be

$$T_i^{jk} = a_i^j b_4^k - a_4^j b_i^k \tag{6}$$

for $1 \leq i, j, k \leq 3$. Translated into the notation of the present paper and applied to reduced camera matrices $\widehat{\mathbf{P}}^1 = [\mathbf{I} \mid \mathbf{0}]$, $\widehat{\mathbf{P}}^2$ and $\widehat{\mathbf{P}}^3$ of the form (4) (and assuming that $d^1 = d^2 = 1$) one sees that there are only 15 non-zero entries of T_i^{jk} and these entries of T_i^{jk} are linear in terms of the values a^i, b^i and c^i for $i = 2, 3$. Thus, one may solve linearly for the T_i^{jk} corresponding to reduced camera matrices, and in fact find the entries of the reduced camera matrices linearly.

The Transformations $\mathbf{T}^i$

The most serious difficulty is finding a well-performing algorithm using this dualization scheme to reduce to a known algorithm is how to handle the transformations $\mathbf{T}^i$. Application of projective transformations to the image data has the effect of distorting any noise distribution that may apply to the data. The problem also exists of choosing four points that are non-collinear in any of the images. If the points are close to collinear in any of the images, then the projective transformation applied to the image in Step 1 of the algorithm may entail extreme distortion of the image. In the algorithm discussed in [5] for computing the quadrifocal tensor, this sort of distortion was shown to degrade performance of the algorithm severely.

5   Experimental Performance

Algorithms based on the fundamental matrix (the 8-point algorithm) for two views and the trifocal tensor (three views) were dualized, resulting in algorithms for 6 or 7 points in any number of views. The results of these tests were reported as a student report in August 1996 by Gilles Debunne. Since this report is effectively unavailable, the results are summarized here.

Performance of the algorithms was generally unsatisfactory, mainly due to the distortion of the noise by the application of the transformations T^i. It was observed that errors due to noise may be minimized in Step 4 of the algorithm. Reversing the dualization in Step 6 of the algorithm results in the same small errors. However, when the inverse projective transformations are applied in Step 7, the average error became very large. Some points retained quite small error, whereas in those images where distortion was significant, quite large errors resulted.

Normalization in the sense of [3] is also a problem. It has been shown to be essential for performance of the linear reconstruction algorithms to apply data normalization. However what sort of normalization should be applied to the transformed data of Fig 3(right) which is geometrically unrelated to actual image measurements is a mystery.

To get good results, it would seem that one would need to propagate assumed error distributions forward in Step 1 of the algorithm to get assumed error distributions for the transformed data Fig 3(right), and then during reconstruction to minimize residual error relative to this propagated error distribution. However, the fundamental matrix and trifocal tensor algorithms do not provide ways of dealing with arbitrary error distributions.

6   Conclusion

Duality as introduced by Carlsson is a very interesting theoretical tool for understanding camera projection. It seems also to have potential to provide algorithms for reconstruction from image sequences containing a large number of images. To this point, however, problems with dealing with noise distributions are an impediment to good performance.

There seems to be good hope, however for eventually using methods like this for finding linear algorithms for carrying out reconstruction from extended image sequences. Finding such a method would represent a significant advance, since at present linear methods for reconstruction have been limited to reconstruction from small numbers of views.

References

[1] T. Buchanan. The twisted cubic and camera calibration. *Computer Vision, Graphics, and Image Processing*, 42:130–132, 1988.

[2] Stefan Carlsson. Duality of reconstruction and positioning from projective views. In *Workshop on Representations of Visual Scenes*, 1995.

[3] R. I. Hartley. In defense of the eight-point algorithm. *IEEE Trans. on Pattern Analysis and Machine Intelligence*, 19(6):580 – 593, October 1997.

[4] Richard I. Hartley. Lines and points in three views and the trifocal tensor. *International Journal of Computer Vision*, 22(2):125–140, March 1997.

[5] Richard I. Hartley. Computation of the quadrifocal tensor. In *Computer Vision - ECCV '98, Volume I, LNCS-Series Vol. 1406, Springer-Verlag*, pages 20 – 35, 1998.

[6] Anders Heyden. Reconstruction from image sequences by means of relative depth. In *Proc. International Conference on Computer Vision*, pages 1058 – 1063, 1995.

[7] Anders Heyden and Kalle Å ström. Euclidean reconstruction from image sequences with varying and unknown focal length and principal point. In *Proc. IEEE Conf. on Computer Vision and Pattern Recognition*, pages 438–443, 1997.

[8] S. J. Maybank. The projective geometry of ambiguous surfaces. *Phil. Trans. R. Soc. Lond.*, A 332:1 – 47, 1990.

[9] Marc Pollefeys, Reinhard Koch, and Luc Van Gool. Self-calibration and metric reconstruction in spite of varying and unknown internal camera parameters. In *Proc. International Conference on Computer Vision*, pages 90 – 95, 1998.

[10] Long Quan. Invariants of 6 points from 3 uncalibrated images. In *Computer Vision - ECCV '94, Volume II, LNCS-Series Vol. 801, Springer-Verlag*, pages 459–470, 1994.

[11] J.G. Semple and G. T. Kneebone. *Algebraic Projective Geometry*. Oxford University Press, Oxford, 1952.

[12] S.J.Maybank and A. Shashua. Ambiguity in reconstruction from images of six points. In *Proc. International Conference on Computer Vision*, pages 703–708, 1998.

[13] Peter Sturm and Bill Triggs. A factorization based algorithm for multi-image projective structure and motion. In *Computer Vision - ECCV '96, Volume II, LNCS-Series Vol. 1065, Springer-Verlag*, pages 709–720, 1996.

[14] P.H.S. Torr and D.W.Murray. A review of robust methods to estimate the fundamental matrix. IJCV – to appear.

[15] B. Triggs. Factorization methods for projective structure and motion. In *Proc. IEEE Conf. on Computer Vision and Pattern Recognition*, pages 845–851, 1996.

[16] Bill Triggs. Autocalibration and the absolute quadric. In *Proc. IEEE Conf. on Computer Vision and Pattern Recognition*, pages 609–614, 1997.

[17] D. Weinshall, M. Werman, and A. Shashua. Shape descriptors : Bilinear, trilinear and quadrilinear relations for multi-point geometry and linear projective reconstruction algorithms. In *Workshop on Representations of Visual Scenes*, 1995.

[18] Z. Zhang, R. Deriche, O. Faugeras, and Q.-T. Luong. A robust technique for matching two uncalibrated images through the recovery of the unknown epipolar geometry. *Artificial Intelligence Journal*, 78:87–119, October 1995.

[19] Zhengyou Zhang. Determining the epipolar geometry and its uncertainty : A review. *International Journal of Computer Vision*, 27(2):161 – 195, 1998.

Geometry of Multiple Affine Views

Long Quan[1], Yuichi Ohta[2], and Roger Mohr[1]

[1] CNRS-GRAVIR-INRIA
ZIRST – 655 avenue de l'Europe
38330 Montbonnot, France
`Long.Quan, Roger.Mohr@inrialpes.fr`
`http://www.inrialpes.fr/movi/people/Quan,Mohr/index.html`
[2] University of Tsukuba
Institute of Information Sciences
Tsukuba, Ibaraki, 305-8573, JAPAN
`ohta@image.is.tsukuba.ac.jp`

Abstract. We introduce a unified framework for developing matching constraints of multiple affine views and rederive 2-view (affine epipolar geometry) and 3-view (affine image transfer) constraints within this framwork. With the insight into the particular structure of these multiple-view constraints, we first describe a new linear method for Euclidean motion and structure from 3 calibrated affine images. Compared with the existing linear method of Huang and Lee [6], the new method uses different and more appropriate constraints. It has no failure mode of the Euclidean factorisation method of Tomasi and Kanade [20]. We then describe how to integrate points and lines and establish some minimal point/line configurations for structure recovery. The method is demonstrated on real image sequences.

1 Introduction

Motion/structure from orthographic or weak perspective views is a very old and popular topic. It is well known that at least 4 non-planar points over 3 orthographic or weak perspective views are sufficient to uniquely determine motion/structure up to a reflection about the image plane [22,6,7]. Many algorithms have been published for this problem: the linear methods of Huang and Lee [6,8], non-linear algebric methods of Koenderink and Van Doorn [7,2] and non-linear numerical method of Shapiro *et al.* [18]. A good review of the different methods can be found in [18].

In this paper, we introduce a unified framework for developing matching constraints of multiple affine views. In particular, 2-view and 3-view constraints will be derived, and all existing methods could be recast into this framework. Our key observation is that classical linear methods for metric motion/structure from 3 orthographic or weak perspective views were heavily based on affine epipolar geometry and did not use the full set of 3 image constraints, thus leading to over-parameterisation and inconsitent motion recovery. Based on insight into the particular structure of these constraints, we will propose a linear algorithm

Reinhard Koch, Luc Van Gool (Eds.): SMILE '98, LNCS 1506, pp. 32–46, 1998.
© Springer-Verlag Berlin Heidelberg 1998

that uses 9 linear parameters to encode the 8 Euclidean motion parameters of 3 weak perspective views. After that, we investigate how points and lines can be integrated into the same framework thanks to the common matching constraints.

This work was also partly motivated by the application of novel image synthesis from example images, as Euclidean reconstruction from a minimal number of images is required here [9,25] Part of this work was also presented in [17].

The paper is organised as follows. In Section 2, we review the affine camera model. Then, we introduce a unified framwork for studying the geometric constraints among multiple affine images in Section 3. The linear method for Euclidean motion/structure from 3 calibrated affine images is developed in Section 4. The integration of points and lines will be described in Section 5. Experimental results are presented in Section 6 and a short conclusion is given in Section 7

Throughout the paper, matrices are denoted in upper case boldface, vectors in lower case boldface and scalars are either in lower case or lower case Greek.

2   Review of the Affine Camera Model

For a restricted class of camera models, by setting the third row of the perspective camera $\mathbf{P}_{3\times4}$ to $(0,0,0,\lambda)$, we obtain the affine camera initially introduced by Mundy and Zisserman in [10,1]

$$\mathbf{A}_{3\times4} = \begin{pmatrix} p_{11} & p_{12} & p_{13} & p_{14} \\ p_{21} & p_{22} & p_{23} & p_{24} \\ 0 & 0 & 0 & p_{34} \end{pmatrix} = \begin{pmatrix} \mathbf{M}_{2\times3} & \mathbf{t}_{3\times1} \\ \mathbf{0}_{1\times3} & \end{pmatrix}. \tag{1}$$

The affine camera $\mathbf{A}_{3\times4}$ subsumes the orthographic, weak perspective and para-perspective. For more detailed relations and applications, one can refer to [18,13].

Finite points in affine spaces $\mathcal{R}^n$, are naturally embedded into $\mathcal{P}^n$ by the mapping $\mathbf{u}_a \mapsto \mathbf{u} = (\mathbf{u}_a, 1)^T$ and $\mathbf{x}_a \mapsto \mathbf{x} = (\mathbf{x}_a, 1)^T$. We have therefore $\mathbf{u}_a = \mathbf{M}_{2\times3}\mathbf{x}_a + \mathbf{t}_0$, where $\mathbf{t}_0 = (t_1/t_3, t_2/t_3)^T = (p_{14}/p_{34}, p_{24}/p_{34})^T$. If we further use relative coordinates of the points with respect to a given reference point (for instance, the centroid of a set of points), the vector $\mathbf{t}_0$ is cancelled, and we obtain the following linear mapping between relative space points and relative image points:

$$\Delta\mathbf{u} = \mathbf{M}_{2\times3}\Delta\mathbf{x}. \tag{2}$$

Equation (2) is the basic projection equation for points in an affine camera when relative coordinates are used. The reference point to determine the relative coordinates determines uniquely the translational component of the affine projection matrix. Throughout this paper, the reference point is always taken to be the centroid in each image.

3   Unifying 2-View and 3-View Geometry of Points

For projective cameras, the geometric constraints among multiple projective views have been thoroughly studied in [21,19,5,4,15]. There has been no similar effort for affine camera case, although the geometric constraints among affine views are well known.

For notational simplicity, rewrite Equation (2) as $\mathbf{u} = \mathbf{M}_{2 \times 3} \mathbf{x}$.

We can now examine the matching constraints between multiple views of the same point. Let the three views of the same point $\mathbf{x}$ be given as follows:

$$\begin{cases} \mathbf{u} = \mathbf{M}\mathbf{x}, \\ \mathbf{u}' = \mathbf{M}'\mathbf{x}, \\ \mathbf{u}'' = \mathbf{M}''\mathbf{x}. \end{cases} \tag{3}$$

These can be rewritten together in matrix form as

$$\begin{pmatrix} \mathbf{M} & \mathbf{u} \\ \mathbf{M}' & \mathbf{u}' \\ \mathbf{M}'' & \mathbf{u}'' \end{pmatrix} \begin{pmatrix} \mathbf{x} \\ \lambda \end{pmatrix} = 0, \tag{4}$$

where $\lambda \neq 0$ encodes the (unrecoverable) global scale factor of the reconstruction.

As the vector $(\mathbf{x}, \lambda)^T$ can not be zero, the rank of the coefficient matrix is at most 3, so all of its 4×4 minors vanish. There are $C_6^4 = 15 = 3 + 4 + 4 + 4$ such minors, which can be divided into two types:

- 2-view constraints involving only two views with two rows from each view,
- 3-view constraints involving all three views with two rows from one view and one from each of the others.

There are three 2-view and three sets of four 3-view constraints. Among the 3 sets of 3-view constraints, only one of them is independent due to the symmetry.

Each expansion of these 4×4 minors is linear in the image coordinates $\mathbf{u}$, $\mathbf{u}'$ and $\mathbf{u}''$ with the coefficients t_i coming from the 3×3 minors of the following 6×3 joint projection matrix: $\begin{pmatrix} \mathbf{M} \\ \mathbf{M}' \\ \mathbf{M}'' \end{pmatrix} = (1\ 2\ 1'\ 2'\ 1''\ 2'')^T$.

There are in total $C_6^3 = 20 = 8 + 4 + 8$ such minors, as we will see later that 4 of the 20 minors are common to the 2-view and 3-view constraints. All these minors provide a linear coordinate system to span the joint projection matrix. The constraints for more than 3 views will be briefly discussed in Section 7.

3.1   Two-View Constraints

There are three 2-view constraints corresponding to the 3 pairs of the 3 views, namely the vanishing of the determinants $[121'2']$, $[121''2'']$ and $[1'2'1''2'']$:

$$t_{13}u + t_{14}v + t_{10}u' + t_9 v' = 0,$$
$$t_{15}u' + t_{16}v' + t_{17}u'' + t_{18}v'' = 0,$$
$$t_{19}u + t_{20}v + t_{12}u'' + t_{11}v'' = 0.$$

These are the affine epipolar geometry. The set of $3 \times 4 = 12$ coefficients t_i for $i = 9, \ldots, 20$ are 12 of the 20 minors of the joint projection matrix.

Each point correspondence from two images gives one homogeneous linear equation, taking into account of the reference point for relative coordinates, 4 points are sufficient for uniquely determining the affine epipolar geometry.

The affine epipolar geometry equation was introduced in [6] for orthography, and later in [8] for weak perspective and also in [18]. Shapiro *et al.* nicely related the affine epipolar geometry with Koenderink and Van Doorn's rotation parameterisation [7]. But Koenderink's method is equivalent to Lee and Huang's [8].

3.2   Three-View Constraints

There are four 3-view constraints from the vanishing of the determinants $[121'1'']$, $[122'1'']$, $[121'2'']$ and $[122'2'']$. By careful inspection of the minors (for example, using the computer algebra tool Maple), we have:

$$
\begin{aligned}
t_4\, u &+ t_8\, v &+ t_{11}u' &+ t_9\, u'' &= 0, \\
t_2\, u &+ t_6\, v &+ t_{11}v' &+ t_{10}u'' &= 0, \\
t_3\, u &+ t_7\, v &+ t_{12}u' &+ t_9\, v'' &= 0, \\
t_1\, u &+ t_5\, v &+ t_{12}v' &+ t_{10}v'' &= 0.
\end{aligned}
$$

Among 12 minors, 8 of them are new (t_1 to t_8) and 4 of them are common with 2-view constraints (t_9 to t_{12}).

These are the transfer equations over three views [23]. Any orthographic view of a point set can be expressed as a linear combination of two other views if this point set undergoes a linear transformation in space. This has been extensively used in object recognition.

Since each point correspondence gives 4 linearly independent 3-view constraints, 4 points give $(4 - 1) \times 4 = 12$ linear equations for solving these minors.

The appearance of common minors between 2-view and 3-view constraints is not accidental, as we have 3+4=7 constraints, each of them has 4 coefficients, that amounts to $4 \times 7 = 28$. As there are only 20 minors, so 8 of them should appear at least more than once.

4   Euclidean Motion/Structure from 3 Calibrated Affine Views

So far, the linear estimates of the 2-view and 3-view constraints yield, directly but implicitly, the affine motion/structure. To get Euclidean or more exactly similarity motion/structure, we need at least 3 calibrated affine images. Here we use the unified formulation introduced in [13] for calibrated affine cameras, thus the method developed will be valid for all calibrated orthographic, weak-perspective and para-perspective models.

Each projection matrix $\mathbf{M}_{2\times3}$ can be decomposed [13] into $\mathbf{M} = s\mathbf{KR}$, where s is a scaling factor of the whole image, $\mathbf{K}$ is the intrinsic parameter matrix (for instance, $\mathbf{K} = \begin{pmatrix} \xi & 0 \\ 0 & 1 \end{pmatrix}$, where ξ is the aspect ratio for the weak-perspective case), and $\mathbf{R}_{2\times3}$ represents 2 rows of a 3D rotation matrix. As we are assuming calibrated cameras, the intrinsic parameter matrix $\mathbf{K}$ is known and its inverse can be directly applied to the image points so that its effect is removed completely. So the projection matrix $\mathbf{M}$ for normalised image coordinates becomes $\mathbf{M} = s\mathbf{R}$, i.e. a scaled 2×3 rotation matrix. There are in total $8 = 2 \times 3 + 2$ Euclidean parameters for a set of 3 views: two relative 3D rotations $\mathbf{R}$ and $\mathbf{G}$ each having 3 d.o.f. and 2 relative scale factors s and s' between (say) the first view and the remaining ones.

Any linear algorithm will consist of first estimating linearly the minors using multiple view constraints, then extract the 8 Euclidean parameters from these minors by identifying the projection matrices $\mathbf{M}$ and $\mathbf{M}'$ with the scaled rotation matrices $s\mathbf{R}$ and $s'\mathbf{G}$.

Combining 2-view and 3-view constraints We should keep in mind that although all 7 constraints are linearly independent, only $3 = (6-3) \times (4-3)$ of them are algebraically independent due to Grassmanian relations. There are in total 20 homogeneous coefficients—minors of the joint projection matrix. How to choose the most appropriate constraints is of primary importance. The selected constraints should be algebraically independent and contain as few coefficients as possible.

Taking only the three 2-view constraints is a poor choice since the third one is partially dependent on the first two by the composition rule on the rigid motions and each one is completely separate from the others. Taking only the 3-view constraints leads to a complicated algebraic manipulation for the extraction of Euclidean parameters. Hence we combine 2-view and 3-view constraints.

The key observation is that there are common coefficients between 2-view and 3-view constraints: two of the three 2-view constraints share 4 minors t_9, t_{10}, t_{11} and t_{12} with the 3-view constraints. This allows us to use the following combination: two 2-view constraints plus one of the 3-view constraints.

$$\begin{cases} t_4\,u & +\,t_8\,v & +\,t_{11}u' & +\,t_9\,u'' = 0, \\ t_{13}u & +\,t_{14}v & +\,t_{10}u' & +\,t_9\,v' = 0, \\ t_{15}u & +\,t_{16}v & +\,t_{12}u'' & +\,t_{11}v'' = 0. \end{cases}$$

These 10 unknown minors can be solved as a single homogeneous vector under the constraint $\|\mathbf{t}_{10}\| = 1$:

$$\begin{pmatrix} u & v & u'' & 0 & u' & 0 & 0 & 0 & 0 & 0 \\ 0 & 0 & v' & u' & 0 & 0 & u & v & 0 & 0 \\ 0 & 0 & 0 & 0 & v'' & u'' & 0 & 0 & u & v \end{pmatrix} \mathbf{t} = 0.$$

Any ratio t_i/t_j of the minors is therefore obtained.

Obtaining partial solutions from 2-view constraints First, from the estimated minors of the 2-view constraint, we can easily obtain the partial Euclidean solution based on Shapiro et al.'s reformulation of Koenderink and Van Doorn's rotation representation. Koenderink and Van Doorn's representation is probably the most appropriate parameterisation, since it distinguishes clearly between the entities which can be obtained from two views and those that can not.

Assume that the affine epipolar geometry of two views is estimated as

$$(a, b, c, d)(u, v, u', v')^T = 0.$$

From 3 ratios $a : b : c : d$, exactly 3 Euclidean parameters can be extracted. Using a scaled rotation matrix instead of $\mathbf{M}$, the following relation holds: $a : b : c : d = sr_{32} : -sr_{31} : r_{23} : -r_{13}$.

Therefore, the relative scale factor between the two views is immediately given as $s = \frac{a^2 + b^2}{c^2 + d^2}$.

According to Koenderink and Van Doorn, the entire rotation can be decomposed into a rotation in the image plane (assume this rotation angle to be θ) and a rotation through an angle ρ about an axis (angled at ϕ to the positive x axis) in a frontoparallel plane. The rotation matrix in terms of Koenderink and Van Doorn's $\theta - \phi - \rho$ representation [18] can be recomposed as $\mathbf{R}_{3 \times 3}$:

$$\begin{pmatrix} (1 - c(\rho))c(\phi)c(\phi - \theta) + c(\rho)c(\theta) & (1 - c(\rho))c(\phi)s(\phi - \theta) - c(\rho)s(\theta) & s(\phi)s(\rho) \\ (1 - c(\rho))s(\phi)c(\phi - \theta) + c(\rho)s(\theta) & (1 - c(\rho))s(\phi)s(\phi - \theta) + c(\rho)c(\theta) & -c(\phi)s(\rho) \\ -s(\rho)s(\phi - \theta) & s(\rho)c(\phi - \theta) & c(\rho) \end{pmatrix}.$$

Therefore,

$$a : b : c : d = s \sin \rho \cos(\phi - \theta) : s \sin \rho \sin(\phi - \theta) : -\cos \phi \sin \rho : -\sin \phi \sin \rho$$

hence, the rotation angle in the image plane is easily determined by $\tan \phi = \frac{d}{c}$, and the rotation axis modulo π out of the image plane by $\tan(\phi - \theta) = \frac{b}{a}$.

Obtaining the full solution with the 3-view constraint Up to this point, the only unknown is the rotation angle out of the image plane ρ, which is the only component that generates depth information. The one-parameter family of solutions for the rotation matrix between the two views is

$$\mathbf{R}_{3 \times 3}(\rho) = \begin{pmatrix} \mathbf{D}_{2 \times 2} + \cos \rho \mathbf{E}_{2 \times 2} & \sin \rho \mathbf{F}_{2 \times 1} \\ \sin \rho \mathbf{G}_{1 \times 2} & \cos \rho \end{pmatrix},$$

where $\mathbf{D}_{2 \times 2}, \mathbf{E}_{2 \times 2}, \mathbf{F}_{2 \times 1}$ and $\mathbf{G}_{1 \times 2}$ are the known quantities.

Similarly, with the second 2-view constraint, we get another one-parameter family of solutions for the rotation matrix $\mathbf{G}_{3 \times 3}(\rho')$ of the other 2 views in terms of the unknown rotation angle out of the image plane ρ'.

Now, it is time to use the 3-view constraint to fully determine the motion/structure. It can be easily verified that

$$t_4 : t_8 : t_{11} : t_9 = ss'(r_{11}g_{13} - g_{11}r_{13}) : ss'(r_{12}g_{13} - g_{12}r_{13}) : -s'g_{13} : sr_{13}.$$

Substituting the ratio t_9/t_{11} into t_4/t_{11} and t_8/t_{11}, we get exactly 2 linear equations in $\cos\rho$ and $\cos\rho'$,

$$\frac{t_4}{t_{11}} = a \ \cos\rho + b \ \cos\rho' + c \ ,$$
$$\frac{t_8}{t_{11}} = a' \cos\rho + b' \cos\rho' + c' ,$$

i.e.

$$\mathbf{A}_{2\times 2} \begin{pmatrix} \cos\rho \\ \cos\rho' \end{pmatrix} = \mathbf{B}_{2\times 1}.$$

Remarks

– This new formulation contains only $9 = 10 - 1$ independent parameters, compared with the 8 Euclidean motion parameters of the set of 3 views, it is a minimal linear parameterisation.
– The advantage of solving **t** as a whole is that it provides more information, for instance the knowledge of the ratio $t_9 : t_{11}$ which could not be recovered from 2-view constraints is the key for a linear solution in $\cos\rho$ and $\cos\rho'$. Huang and Lee had to re-compute this ratio at the very begining of the second step with the rotation composition constraint.
– Solving directly and linearly for $\cos\rho$ and $\cos\rho'$ is of great significance. On the one hand, the intrinsic two-way ambiguity is nicely expressed by the fact that

$$\cos(-\rho) = \cos\rho.$$

This parameterisation indeed makes a linear solution possible since the two equations are solved together. On the other hand, the only failure mode of the entire linear algorithm is the possibility that $\cos\rho > 1$ which may happen due to numerical error when $\cos\rho$ is close to 1. Since

$$\cos\rho \approx 1 \Rightarrow \rho \approx 0,$$

this means that actually there is almost no rotation out of the image plane. As rotation out of the image plane is the only component which contains depth information, this means that the 2D images we used do not contain the desired 3D structure, or equivalently we can report that $\rho = 0$ for the motion. Essentially, this algorithm does not have the failure mode that the factorisation method suffers in its linear version.

4.1   Comparison with Related Work

We first make a comparison with the existing linear algorithms of Huang and Lee and the factorisation method of Tomasi and Kanade.

Basically, there are two steps in Huang and Lee's method [6], the first step computes the coefficients of the three 2-view constraints. Any 3-view constraint was totally absent during the batch solution step and was introduced in the second step by the composition rule of rotation matrices $\mathbf{R}_{13} = \mathbf{R}_{23}\mathbf{R}_{12}$. In our new linear algorithm, the 3-view constraint has been already integrated in the first numerical step. No any other constraint was used afterwards. Since Euclidean depth information is only contained in 3-view constraints, therefore, it is dangerous to not use any 3-view constraint during the numerical step. Although 3 2-view constraints have also $9 = 3 \times 3$ independent parameters if each one is estimated individually, but they are essentially a set of 12 homogeneous parameters which breaks up into 3 sets of 4 homogeneous parameters. If we examine carefully the second step of Huang and Lee's method, it has to recompute this set of 12 homogeneous parameters (via the ratios between these 3 sets of 4 homogeneous parameters) using the 3-view constraint. In conclusion, Huang and Lee's method does not use the appropriate constraints. It will inevitably lead to the inconsistencies of the rotation matrix.

Compared with the factorization method of Tomasi and Kanade [20,11,24]— most suitable for redundant views, the major problem is to impose the 'metric constraint'. The linearly estimated matrix which is the product of an affine transformation and its transpose may not be positive definite, the whole Euclidean reconstruction process fails. The exact Cholesky parameterisation of the matrix introduced in [13] needs to solve simultaneous quadratic equations.

Other important work include Koenderink and Van Doorn [7]. The method consists of three steps. The first step shows that the scale change between 2 views, the rotation in the image plane around the viewing direction and the projection of the rotation axis out of the image plane can be obtained with 2 views of 4 points. The second step is to parameterise the remaining Euclidean structure with the angle of the rotation out of the image plane and the 2 depths of the reference triangle, then eliminate the unknown angle to get a quadratic equation on the 2 Euclidean depths. Finally, with the third view, a second quadratic equation is obtained. Intersecting these two quadratics gives 4 possible solutions for the two depths. These intersections represent either one or two pairs of solutions that are related through a reflection in the fronto-parallel plane.

We can see that the first step of Koenderink and Van Doorn's method is similar to that of Huang and Lee [6] and Lee and Huang [8], it uses 2-view constraint to get partial solutions although Koenderink and Van Doorn's is more geometrically oriented. One major difference is that Koenderink and Van Doorn do not use the third 2-view constraint as Huang and Lee did. Unfortunately, Koenderink's method needs to intersect two quadratics for each pair of points, and can not handle all available points.

Shapiro et al. [18] extended Koenderink and Van Doorn's first step by nicely relating the Koenderink and Van Doorn's rotation representation to the affine epipolar geometry. Unfortunately they failed to get a closed form solution and adopted a non linear numerical optimisation approach for the 3-view case.

Ullman and Basri [23] and Poggio [12] considered the 3-view constraint for linear combination for recognition. Although they essentially show the equivalence with motion/structure, they do not concentrate on motion/structure recovery, in fact there is no closed form solution which allows Euclidean structure extracted directly from linear combination coefficients.

5 Unifying 3-View Geometry of Points and Lines

Using only line segments for motion/structure within the affine camera framework has been adressed in [16,14]. We can now examine the possibility of combining points and line segments into the same framework.

5.1 Trifocal Tensor of Lines

Recall that there exists a linear mapping between directions of 3D lines $\mathbf{x}$ and those of 2D lines $\mathbf{u}$ [16,14]. It can be derived even more directly using projective geometry, by considering that the line with direction $\mathbf{d}_x$ is the point at infinity $\mathbf{x}_\infty = (\mathbf{d}_x^T, 0)^T$ in $\mathcal{P}^3$ and the line with direction $\mathbf{d}_u$ is the point at infinity $\mathbf{u}_\infty$ in $\mathcal{P}^2$.

These can be rewritten in matrix form as

$$\begin{pmatrix} \mathbf{M} & \mathbf{u} & 0 & 0 \\ \mathbf{M}' & 0 & \mathbf{u}' & 0 \\ \mathbf{M}'' & 0 & 0 & \mathbf{u}'' \end{pmatrix} \begin{pmatrix} \mathbf{x} \\ -\lambda \\ -\lambda' \\ -\lambda'' \end{pmatrix} = 0,$$

which is the basic reconstruction equation for a one-dimensional camera. The vector $(\mathbf{x}, -\lambda, -\lambda', -\lambda'')^T$ cannot be zero, and so

$$\begin{vmatrix} \mathbf{M} & \mathbf{u} & 0 & 0 \\ \mathbf{M}' & 0 & \mathbf{u}' & 0 \\ \mathbf{M}'' & 0 & 0 & \mathbf{u}'' \end{vmatrix} = 0. \tag{5}$$

The expansion of this determinant produces a trilinear constraint of three views

$$T_{ijk} u^i u'^j u''^k = 0, \tag{6}$$

where T_{ijk} is a $2 \times 2 \times 2$ homogeneous tensor whose components T_{ijk} are 3×3 minors of the following 6×3 joint projection matrix:

$$\begin{pmatrix} \mathbf{M} \\ \mathbf{M}' \\ \mathbf{M}'' \end{pmatrix} = \begin{pmatrix} 1 \\ 2 \\ 1' \\ 2' \\ 1'' \\ 2'' \end{pmatrix}. \tag{7}$$

The components of the tensor can be made explicit as

$$T_{ijk} = [\bar{i}\bar{j}'\bar{k}''], \text{ for } i, j', k'' = 1, 2.$$

where the bracket $[ij'k'']$ denotes the 3×3 minor of i-th,j'-th and k''-th row vector of the above joint projection matrix and bar " $^-$ " in $\bar{i}$, $\bar{j}$ and $\bar{k}$ denotes the mapping

$$(1, 2) \mapsto (2, -1).$$

5.2   Trifocal Tensor of Points

Let re-take the 3-view constraints for points,

$$t_4 u + t_8 v + t_{11} u' + t_9 u'' = 0,$$
$$t_2 u + t_6 v + t_{11} v' + t_{10} u'' = 0,$$
$$t_3 u + t_7 v + t_{12} u' + t_9 v'' = 0,$$
$$t_1 u + t_5 v + t_{12} v' + t_{10} v'' = 0$$

By eliminating t_9 and t_{10}, we get two bilinear forms and furhter elimination between the bilinear forms gives the following trilinear form:

$$T_{ijk} u^i u'^j u''^k = 0,$$

with the tensor-vector mapping defined by $4(i-1) + 2(j-1) + k$.

5.3   Method 1—Using the Trifocal Tensor

As both points and lines share exactly the same trifocal tensor T_{ijk}, an immediate integration method consists of estimating this common tensor with both points and lines.

$$T_{ijk} u^i u'^j u''^k = 0.$$

As a matter of fact, it's not surprising at all, since each point in relative coordinates may be considered as a line segment. Even more, a set of n points is equivalent to C_n^2 lines. I.e. points are just normal points and line directions are properly "scaled" points.

One major drawback of this method is that we are not using the information on the known scales of the "points".

5.4   Method 2—Using 3-View Constraints and Trifocal Tensor

Another method of integrating points and lines is to look for the common minors among multiple view constraints and the trifocal tensor.

As we have seen that the trifocal tensor shares all its 8 minors with the 3-view constraints (it's reasonable that the tensor has nothing common with the 2-view constraints) via

$$T_{ijk} \Leftrightarrow t_{4(i-1)+2(j-1)+k}.$$

We can therefore solve the following homogeneous linear system of equations:

$$\begin{cases} t_4 u + t_8 v + t_{11} u' + t_9 u'' = 0, \\ t_2 u + t_6 v + t_{11} v' + t_{10} u'' = 0, \\ t_3 u + t_7 v + t_{12} u' + t_9 v'' = 0, \\ t_1 u + t_5 v + t_{12} v' + t_{10} v'' = 0, \\ T_{ijk} u^i u'^j u''^k = 0, \end{cases}$$

i.e.

$$\mathbf{A}(t_1, t_2, \ldots, t_{12})^T = 0.$$

5.5   Some Minimal Configurations

By suitable switching between two methods, we can establish the following minimal geometric configurations for points and lines:

- 4 points + 0 line
- 3 points + 3 lines ($2 \times 4 + 3$)
- 2 points + 6 lines (1+6)
- 1 point + 7 lines (0+7)
- 0 point + 7 lines

Generally we may proceed as follows:

- when lines outnumbers points, estimate the trifocal tensor both for points and lines—method 1;
- when points outnumbers lines, estimate 12 components—method 2.

6   Experimental Results

The linear method for motion/structure from 3 calibrated affine images developed in this paper has been implemented and applied to real image sequences.

We first acquired a sequence of images of a calibration pattern with a standard camera mounted on a robot. It is important to stress that the imaging conditions were not chosen to be close to affine. The triplet of images we used is shown in Figure 1. The 69 points have been automatially identified and tracked for the triplet.

Fig. 1. The triplet of images of the calibration pattern.

The 8 Euclidean motion parameters are estimated by the linear method as $s = 1.06$, $\phi = -1.51$, $\theta = -0.33$, $\rho = 0.33$ and $s' = 1.11$, $\phi' = -1.53$, $\theta' = -0.47$, $\rho' = 0.43$. The resulting shape reconstruction from these motion parameters is shown in Figure 2.

To evaluate the reconstruction quality, we did the same 3D reconstruction using a full perspective camera model, for instance the method described in [3] is used. The two reconstructions differ by a 3D similarity transformation which can be easily estimated. The normalised relative error of the Euclidean reconstruction with affine camera with respect to perspective camera one is 3.6 percent.

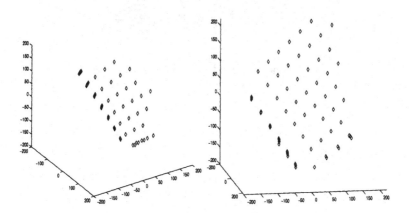

Fig. 2. Two views of the resulting 3D reconstruction.

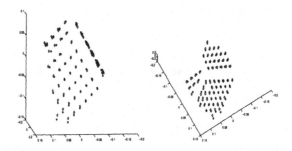

Fig. 3. Two different views of the two superimposed 3D reconstructions, one uses weak-perspective camera model (marked by a square) and the other full perspective (marked by a circle).

We also tried our method on the popular hotel sequence kindly provided by Poelman and Kanade at CMU. In this sequence, the camera motion included substantial translation away from the camera and across the field of view. 197 points throughout the sequence of 181 images are automatically identified and traced. For a more detailed description of this set-up, consult [11]. The triplet of images we used are displayed in Figure 4. The resulting 3D reconstruction is shown in Figure 5.

Fig. 4. The triplet of hotel image sequence.

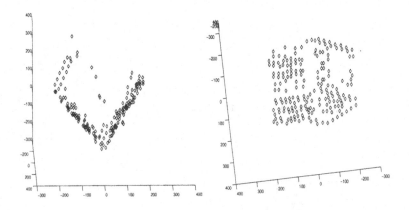

Fig. 5. Two views of the 3D reconstruction of the hotel.

7   Conclusion

We have introduced a unified approach to 2-view and 3-view geometric constraints of affine images, and a new linear method for Euclidean motion/structure from 3 calibrated affine images. What is also important for the framework of multiple affine views developed in this paper is that line segment features could also be incorporated. The method has been validated on real image sequences.

Acknowledgements

This work is in part supported by CUMULI.

References

1. J.Y. Aloimonos. Perspective approximations. *Image and Vision Computing*, 8(3):179–192, August 1990.
2. B.M. Bennet, D.D. Hoffman, J.E. Nicola, and C. Prakash. Structure from two orthographic views of rigid motion. *Journal of the Optical Society of America*, 6(7):1052–1069, 1989.
3. S. Christy and R. Horaud. Euclidean shape and motion from multiple perspective views by affine iterations. IEEE *Transactions on Pattern Analysis and Machine Intelligence*, 18(11):1098–1104, November 1996.
4. O. Faugeras and B. Mourrain. On the geometry and algebra of the point and line correspondences between n images. In *Proceedings of the 5th International Conference on Computer Vision, Cambridge, Massachusetts, USA*, pages 951–956, June 1995.
5. R.I. Hartley. Lines and points in three views and the trifocal tensor. *International Journal of Computer Vision*, 22(2):125–140, 1997.
6. T.S. Huang and C.H. Lee. Motion and structure from orthographic projections. IEEE *Transactions on Pattern Analysis and Machine Intelligence*, 11(5):536–540, 1989.
7. J. Koenderink and A. van Doorn. Affine structure from motion. *Journal of the Optical Society of America A*, 8(2):377–385, 1991.
8. C.H. Lee and T. Huang. Finding point correspondences and determining motion of a rigid object from two weak perspective views. *Computer Vision, Graphics and Image Processing*, 52:309–327, 1990.
9. Y. Mukaigawa, Y. Nakamura, and Y. Ohta. Synthesis of arbitrarily oriented face views from two images. In *Proceedings of the Second Asian Conference on Computer Vision*, pages 718–722, 1995.
10. J.L. Mundy and A. Zisserman, editors. *Geometric Invariance in Computer Vision*. The MIT Press, Cambridge, MA, USA, 1992.
11. C.J. Poelman and T. Kanade. A paraperspective factorization method for shape and motion recovery. In J.O. Eklundh, editor, *Proceedings of the 3rd European Conference on Computer Vision, Stockholm, Sweden*, pages 97–108. Springer-Verlag, May 1994.
12. T. Poggio and S. Edelman. A network that learns to recognize three-dimensional objects. *Nature*, 343(6255):263–266, January 1990.
13. L. Quan. Self-calibration of an affine camera from multiple views. *International Journal of Computer Vision*, 19(1):93–105, May 1996.
14. L. Quan. Uncalibrated 1D projective camera and 3D affine reconstruction of lines. In *Proceedings of the Conference on Computer Vision and Pattern Recognition, Puerto Rico, USA*, pages 60–65, June 1997.
15. L. Quan. Algebraic relations among matching constraints of multiple images. Technical report, INRIA, January 1998. Also TR Lifia-Imag 1995.
16. L. Quan and T. Kanade. Affine structure from line correspondences with uncalibrated affine cameras. IEEE *Transactions on Pattern Analysis and Machine Intelligence*, 19(8):834–845, August 1997.
17. L. Quan and Y. Ohta. A new linear method for euclidean motion/structure from three calibrated affine views. In *Proceedings of the Conference on Computer Vision and Pattern Recognition, Santa Barbara, California, USA*, June 1998.
18. L.S. Shapiro, A. Zisserman, and M. Brady. 3D motion recovery via affine epipolar geometry. *International Journal of Computer Vision*, 16(2):147–182, 1995.

19. A. Shashua. Algebraic functions for recognition. IEEE *Transactions on Pattern Analysis and Machine Intelligence*, 17(8):779–789, August 1995.
20. C. Tomasi and T. Kanade. Shape and motion from image streams under orthography: A factorization method. *International Journal of Computer Vision*, 9(2):137–154, November 1992.
21. B. Triggs. Matching constraints and the joint image. In E. Grimson, editor, *Proceedings of the 5th International Conference on Computer Vision, Cambridge, Massachusetts, USA*, pages 338–343. IEEE, IEEE Computer Society Press, June 1995.
22. S. Ullman. *The Interpretation of Visual Motion.* The MIT Press, Cambridge, MA, USA, 1979.
23. S. Ullman and R. Basri. Recognition by linear combinations of models. IEEE *Transactions on Pattern Analysis and Machine Intelligence*, 13(10):992–1006, 1991.
24. D. Weinshall and C. Tomasi. Linear and incremental acquisition of invariant shape models from image sequences. In *Proceedings of the 4th International Conference on Computer Vision, Berlin, Germany*, pages 675–682. IEEE, May 1993.
25. Z. Zhang, K. Isono, and S. Akamatsu. Euclidean structure from uncalibrated images using fuzzy domain knowledge: Application to facial images synthesis. In *Proceedings of the 6th International Conference on Computer Vision, Bombay, India*, 1998. to appear.

Tensor Embedding of the Fundamental Matrix

Shai Avidan and Amnon Shashua

Institute of Computer Science, The Hebrew University,
91904 Jerusalem, Israel.
{avidan,shashua}@cs.huji.ac.il

Abstract. We revisit the bilinear matching constraint between two perspective views of a 3D scene. Our objective is to represent the constraint in the same manner and form as the trilinear constraint among three views. The motivation is to establish a common terminology that bridges between the fundamental matrix F (associated with the bilinear constraint) and the trifocal tensor T_i^{jk} (associated with the trilinearities). By achieving this goal we can unify both the properties and the techniques introduced in the past for working with multiple views for geometric applications.

Doing that we introduce a $3 \times 3 \times 3$ tensor $\mathcal{F}_i^{jk}$, we call the bifocal tensor, that represents the bilinear constraint. The bifocal and trifocal tensors share the same form and share the same contraction properties. By close inspection of the contractions of the bifocal tensor into matrices we show that one can represent the family of rank-2 homography matrices by $[\delta]_\times F$ where δ is a free vector. We then discuss four applications of the new representation: (i) Quasi-metric viewing of projective data, (ii) triangulation, (iii) view synthesis, and (iv) recovery of camera ego-motion from a stream of views.

1 Introduction

The geometry of multiple views is governed by certain multi-linear constraints, bilinear for pairs of views and trilinear for triplets of views — all other multi-linear constraints (four views and beyond) are spanned by the bilinear and trilinear constraints.

The traditional representation of the coefficients of the bilinear constraint is by a 3×3 matrix, F, that satisfies $p'^\top F p = 0$ for all matching image points p, p' (represented in the 2D projective space) across two views. On the other hand, the three-view relations are represented by a set of 4 trilinear constraints, each of the form $p^i s_j r_k T_i^{jk} = 0$ where s and r are lines coincident with the matching points p' and p'', respectively. In other words, the bilinear constraint represents a "point+point" relation, whereas each of the trilinear constraints represents a "point+line+line" relation.

Because of the difference in form between the fundamental matrix and the trifocal tensor, the analysis tools are different and the properties discovered for one do not easily carry over to the other. For example, the trifocal tensor contracts (reduces) to matrix forms that carry geometric information: one type

Reinhard Koch, Luc Van Gool (Eds.): SMILE '98, LNCS 1506, pp. 47–62, 1998.
© Springer-Verlag Berlin Heidelberg 1998

of contraction produces subgroups of 2D homography matrices and another type of contraction produces a subgroup of 2D correlation matrices. There is no such equivalence known for the fundamental matrix, for instance.

In this paper we revisit the bilinear constraint and represent it using a $3 \times 3 \times 3$ tensor $p^i s_j r_k \mathcal{F}_i^{jk} = 0$ where s, r are two coincident lines with the matching point p'. We call the tensor $\mathcal{F}_i^{jk}$ the "bifocal" tensor and show that not only it shares the same form as the trifocal tensor but it also shares the same properties. We can therefore consider contractions of the bifocal tensor just was is done with the trifocal counterpart.

Through the inspection of tensor contractions we derive the representation of the subgroup of rank-2 homography matrices in the simple form of $[\delta]_\times F$ where δ is a free vector. We introduce the group of "primitive homographies" and discuss 4 applications of the new representation: (i) Quasi-metric viewing of projective data, (ii) triangulation, (iii) view synthesis, and (iv) recovery of camera ego-motion from a stream of views. This work in its initial form was presented at the meeting found in [1].

2   Notations

A point x in the 3D projective space $\mathcal{P}^3$ is projected onto the point p in the 2D projective space $\mathcal{P}^2$ by a 3×4 camera projection matrix $\mathbf{A} = [A, v']$ that satisfies $p \cong \mathbf{A}x$, where $\cong$ represents equality up to scale. The left 3×3 minor of $\mathbf{A}$, denoted by A, stands for a 2D projective transformation of some arbitrary plane (the reference plane) and the fourth column of $\mathbf{A}$, denoted by v', stands for the epipole (the projection of the center of camera 1 on the image plane of camera 2). In a calibrated setting the 2D projective transformation is the rotational component of camera motion (the reference plane is at infinity) and the epipole is the translational component of camera motion. Since only relative camera positioning can be recovered from image measurements, the camera matrix of the first camera position in a sequence of positions can be represented by $[I; 0]$.

We will occasionally use tensorial notations, which are briefly described next. We use the covariant-contravariant summation convention: a point is an object whose coordinates are specified with superscripts, i.e., $p^i = (p^1, p^2, ...)$. These are called contravariant vectors. An element in the dual space (representing hyper-planes — e.g., lines in $\mathcal{P}^2$), is called a covariant vector and is represented by subscripts, i.e., $s_j = (s_1, s_2, ...)$. Indices repeated in covariant and contravariant forms are summed over, i.e., $p^i s_i = p^1 s_1 + p^2 s_2 + ... + p^n s_n$. This is known as a contraction. For example, if p is a point incident to a line s in $\mathcal{P}^2$, then $p^i s_i = 0$. Vectors are also called 1-valence tensors. 2-valence tensors (matrices) have two indices and the transformation they represent depends on the covariant-contravariant positioning of the indices. For example, a_i^j is a mapping from points to points, and hyper-planes to hyper-planes, because $a_i^j p^i = q^j$ and $a_i^j s_j = r_i$ (in matrix form: $Ap = q$ and $A^\top s = r$); a_{ij} maps points to hyper-planes; and a^{ij} maps hyper-planes to points. When viewed as a matrix the row and column positions are determined accordingly: in a_i^j and a_{ji} the index i runs over the columns and j runs over the rows, thus $b_j^k a_i^j = c_i^k$ is $BA = C$ in matrix form. An outer-product of two 1-valence tensors (vectors), $a_i b^j$, is a 2-valence tensor c_i^j whose i, j entries are $a_i b^j$ — note that in matrix form $C = ba^\top$. An n-valence tensor described as an outer-product of n vectors is a rank-1 tensor. Any n-valence tensor can be described as a sum of rank-1 n-valence tensors. The rank of an n-valence tensor is the *smallest* number of rank-1 n-valence tensors with sum equal to the tensor. For example, a rank-1 trivalent tensor is $a_i b_j c_k$ where a_i, b_j and c_k are three vectors. The rank of a trivalent tensor α_{ijk} is the smallest r such that,

$$\alpha_{ijk} = \sum_{s=1}^{r} a_{is} b_{js} c_{ks}. \tag{1}$$

We will make extensive use of the "cross-product tensor" ϵ defined next. The cross product (vector product) operation $c = a \times b$ is defined for vectors in $\mathcal{P}^2$. The vector c is the line joining the points a, b, or the point of intersection of the lines a, b. The product operation can also be represented as the product $c = [a]_\times b$ where $[a]_x$ is called the "skew-symmetric matrix of a" and has the form:

$$[a]_\times = \begin{pmatrix} 0 & -a_3 & a_2 \\ a_3 & 0 & -a_1 \\ -a_2 & a_1 & 0 \end{pmatrix}$$

In tensor form we have $\epsilon_{ijk} a^i b^j = c_k$ representing the cross products of two points (contravariant vectors) resulting in the line (covariant vector) c_k. Similarly, $\epsilon^{ijk} a_i b_j = c^k$ represents the point intersection of the to lines a_i and b_j. The tensor ϵ is defined such that $\epsilon_{ijk} a^i$ produces the matrix $[a]_\times$ (i.e., ϵ contains $0, -1, 1$ in its entries such that its operation on a single vector produces the skew-symmetric matrix of that vector).

3   Tensor Embedding of the Fundamental Matrix

Our goal is to derive a trivalent tensor representation (i.e., a $3 \times 3 \times 3$ tensor) of the 3×3 fundamental matrix and to illuminate the advantages of doing so. In particular, once we have the trivalent tensor representation in our hand we wish to investigate its contraction properties (as was done for the trifocal tensor in [22]) and recast them back in matrix form.

We start with deriving the fundamental matrix from basic principles. Let A be a 2D homography (collineation) from image 1 to image 2 due to some plane π, i.e., if p is a point in image 1, then Ap is a point coincident with the epipolar line $p' \times v'$ in image 2, where the exact location of Ap on the epipolar line is determined by the position of the plane π. Thus, $(v' \times p')^\top Ap = 0$, or in tensor notation,

$$0 = \epsilon_{lj\rho} p'^j v'^\rho p^i a_i^l$$
$$= p'^j \underbrace{\left(\epsilon_{lj\rho} v'^\rho a_i^l \right)}_{F_{ji}} p^i$$

where $\epsilon_{lj\rho}p'^{j}v'^{\rho}$ is the cross-product $p' \times v'$. The matrix $F_{ji} = \epsilon_{lj\rho}v'^{\rho}a_{i}^{l}$ is the fundamental matrix that satisfies the bilinear constraint $p^{i}p'^{j}F_{ji} = 0$ (cf. [14,6]). In matrix form, since $\epsilon_{lj\rho}v'^{\rho}$ is the skew-symmetric matrix $[v']_{\times}$, then $F = [v']_{\times}A$.

Next, we begin with the bilinear constraint $p^{i}p'^{j}F_{ji} = 0$ and consider replacing the point p' with a cross product of any two incident lines s, r, i.e., $p'^{l} = \epsilon^{ljk}s_{j}r_{k}$. The reason for doing so will be apparent later on. We have therefore a "point+line+line" relationship $p^{i}s_{j}r_{k}\mathcal{F}_{i}^{jk} = 0$ as follows:

$$p^{i}p'^{l}F_{li} = p^{i}\underbrace{\left(\epsilon^{ljk}s_{j}r_{k}\right)}_{p'^{l}}F_{li}$$

$$= p^{i}s_{j}r_{k}\underbrace{\left(\epsilon^{ljk}F_{li}\right)}_{\mathcal{F}_{i}^{jk}}$$

$$= 0$$

and the tensor $\mathcal{F}_{i}^{jk} = \epsilon^{ljk}F_{li}$ is a trivalent form of the fundamental matrix. This form is equivalent to considering the trifocal tensor of views 1,2,3 where views 2,3 are identical. Thus we obtain a relationship between three views, but only two of the views are distinct. We can represent the "bifocal" tensor $\mathcal{F}_{i}^{jk}$ directly as a function of v' and A as follows:

$$\mathcal{F}_{i}^{jk} = v'^{j}a_{i}^{k} - v'^{k}a_{i}^{j}.$$

The importance of the trivalent tensor embedding of the fundamental matrix (which we will denote by bifocal tensor from now on) is that we have arrived to an equivalent representation with 3-view geometry: both the trifocal and bifocal tensors are $3 \times 3 \times 3$ and operate on a configuration of a point+line+line. In the case of three views, the lines are in two distinct views (the line s coincides with p' and the line r coincides with p'') and there are 4 such relationships (due to the fact that there are two choices for each line). In the case of two views the two lines are in the same view and therefore there is only one configuration of point+line+line.

The advantage of this equivalence in form between the trifocal and bifocal tensors appears when one considers contractions into bivalent forms (matrices). The properties of contractions of the trifocal tensor are well understood (see [22,18] and in the appendix here) and provide the building blocks for making use of the trifocal tensor in applications. We can apply now an identical analysis on the bifocal tensor which we will do next.

3.1   Bifocal Tensor Contractions

Given an arbitrary vector δ, the trifocal tensor reduces to a matrix of three types: $\delta^{i}\mathcal{T}_{i}^{jk}, \delta_{j}\mathcal{T}_{i}^{jk}$ and $\delta_{k}\mathcal{T}_{i}^{jk}$. Note that when $\delta = (1,0,0),(0,1,0)$ or $(0,0,1)$ we obtain "slices" of the tensor. The first type produces a rank-2 correlation matrix, i.e., a mapping from all 2D lines to collinear points (where the orientation of collinearity is determined by δ) — by slicing the tensor in that way

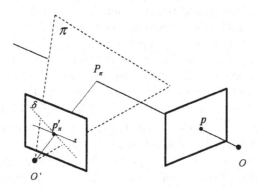

Fig. 1. The matrix $[\delta]_{\times} F$ is a homography matrix due to a plane π coincident with the center of projection O' and the line δ in view 2. The line s is the epipolar line and the point P_{π} is at the intersection of the optic ray from the first view and the plane π. The point p'_{π} is the projection of P_{π} onto view 2. Therefore the point+line+line configuration of p, δ, s satisfies the bifocal tensor relation $p^{i} s_{j} \delta_{k} \mathcal{F}_{i}^{jk} = 0$, where $\delta_{k} \mathcal{F}_{i}^{jk}$ is the matrix $[\delta]_{\times} F$.

we obtain the three matrices of "line geometry" introduced in the calibrated context by [23,24,28]. The second and third types produce homography matrices (collineations). The second type is a homography matrix from view 1 to 3 due to a plane determined by the line δ_{j} in view 2 and the center of projection of camera 2. Likewise, the third type is a homography from view 1 to 2 via a plane determined by the line δ_{k} in view 3 and the center of projection of camera 3. These homography matrices were introduced in [22] and are described in more detail in the appendix here.

We wish to consider the same types of contractions on the bifocal tensor $\mathcal{F}_{i}^{jk}$ — by equivalence of form, we should obtain collineations and correlations as well. Consider the contraction

$$\delta_{k} \mathcal{F}_{i}^{jk}$$

for some arbitrary vector δ. By substitution in the definition of $\mathcal{F}_{i}^{jk}$ we obtain

$$\delta_{k} \mathcal{F}_{i}^{jk} = \underbrace{\left(\epsilon^{ljk} \delta_{k} \right)}_{[\delta]_{\times}} F_{li}$$

which in matrix form becomes $[\delta]_{\times} F$. Our question therefore is about the geometric interpretation of this matrix (for an arbitrary δ). Given the form-equivalence of the two tensors the answer is immediate: $[\delta]_{\times} F$ is a homography matrix from view 1 to view 2 via a plane coincident with the center of projection O' of camera 2 and the line δ in view 2. The family of such matrices over all choices of δ

corresponds to the family of homography matrices whose planes are coincident with O'. The family is spanned by three matrices (since δ is spanned by three vectors), and for example, the three slices using $\delta = (1,0,0), (0,1,0)$ or $(0,0,1)$ will provide the basis for this subgroup of homography matrices.

More formally, consider the plane π defined by the point O' and the line δ in view 2. Consider a point p in view 1 and the ray from the center of projection O of the first camera and the point p. The ray intersects π at P_π which projects to a point p'_π in view 2 which is coincident with the line δ (by construction). Let s_j be the epipolar line of p in view 2, thus $p^i s_j \delta_k \mathcal{F}_i^{jk} = 0$ because they provide a point+line+line configuration, and this holds for all points p (see Fig. 1). Thus, the matrix $\delta_k \mathcal{F}_i^{jk}$ maps view 1 onto points along the corresponding epipolar lines and is therefore a homography matrix, and since the projected points are collinear the rank of the matrix is 2. We have the following result:

Theorem 1. *The matrix $[\delta]_\times F$ is a homography matrix of rank 2 from view 1 to view 2 due to the plane coincident with the center of projection of camera 2 and the line δ in view 2.*

Note that the theorem generalizes the observation due to [16] that $[v']_x F$ is a homography matrix. We see that this is true for any choice of skew-symmetric matrix $[\delta]_\times$.

The same result applies for the contraction $\delta_j \mathcal{F}_i^{jk}$ (with a change of sign). Note that with the trifocal tensor there is a difference between the contractions $\delta_j T_i^{jk}$ and $\delta_k T_i^{jk}$ in which the former produces a homography matrix from view 1 to 3 and the latter produces a homography matrix from view 1 to 2. In the case of the bifocal tensor views 2 and 3 coincide thus the two types of contractions are equivalent.

The remaining contraction type is $\delta^i \mathcal{F}_i^{jk}$. In the case of the trifocal tensor the contraction $\delta^i T_i^{jk}$ produces a *correlation* matrix which maps the space of lines from view 2 to a set of collinear points (on the epipolar line of the point δ in view 1) in view 3. The transpose of that matrix is the same type of mapping, but from view 3 to view 2 (see Appendix). We should obtain something similar for the bifocal tensor and since view 2 and 3 coincide the matrix $\delta^i \mathcal{F}_i^{jk}$ should map the space of lines in view 2 onto collinear points in view 2 that define the epipolar line, $F\delta$, of the point δ. Indeed, by substitution we obtain:

$$\delta^i \mathcal{F}_i^{jk} = \epsilon^{ljk} \delta^i F_{li}$$
$$= [F\delta]_\times \tag{2}$$

Thus, $[F\delta]_\times s$ for all lines s in view 2 is the point of intersection of the epipolar line $F\delta$ and the line s. In other words, the matrix $[F\delta]_\times$ is the correlation matrix we described above. Note that the reason we have obtained a trivial mapping is due to fact that this type of contraction is associated with reconstruction for lines. The three matrices $\delta^i T_i^{jk}$ for $\delta = (1,0,0), (0,1,0)$ and $(0,0,1)$ are known to arise from considerations of matching lines across three views (cf. [23,28,10]). However, the relative camera positions cannot be recovered from matching lines across two views only (only from matching points), which is why the corresponding correlation matrices $\delta^i \mathcal{F}_i^{jk}$ of the bifocal tensor become trivial.

To summarize, the embedding of the fundamental matrix in trivalent tensor format (the bifocal tensor) provides a unified terminology of a "point+line+line" that applies for both the bifocal and trifocal relationships across multiple views. In particular, as is the case with the trifocal tensor, contractions of the bifocal tensor into reduced forms (matrices) have a geometric significance. The contractions properties of the bifocal tensor are listed in Table 1. We see a clear analogy to the type of resulting matrices (homography and correlations) one obtains from the same contractions applied to the trifocal tensor. Furthermore, the homography contraction provides the basis for all rank-2 homography matrices whose planes are coincident with the center of projection of camera 2. All linear combinations of the rank-2 homography matrices are of the form $[\delta]_\times F$ for some vector δ.

Table 1. *The three types of contractions of the bifocal tensor (embedding of the fundamental matrix F as a trivalent tensor $\mathcal{F}_i^{jk}$), their matrix form, and the property they produce. Note that the first two contractions produce a homography matrix of a plane whose orientation is determined by the vector of contraction δ.*

Contraction	Matrix Form	Result
$\delta_k \mathcal{F}_i^{jk}$	$[\delta]_\times F$	Homography Matrix.
$\delta_j \mathcal{F}_i^{jk}$	$[\delta]_\times F$	Same as above.
$\delta^i \mathcal{F}_i^{jk}$	$[F\delta]_\times$	Trivial Correlation Mapping.

4   The Primitive Homography Matrices

We have seen that the family of matrices $[\delta]_\times F$ parameterized by the choice of the vector δ spans the family of homography matrices from view 1 to view 2 due to the planes coincident with the center of projection O' of camera 2. The vector δ determines the orientation of the plane and is the line of intersection of the plane and view 2. Since δ is spanned by three vectors, say $(1, 0, 0), (0, 1, 0)$ and $(0, 0, 1)$, the bifocal tensor contractions provide three distinct homography matrices that span the subgroup of homography matrices (those whose planes are coincident with O'). Since the entire group of all homography matrices lies in a 4 dimensional subspace [20], i.e., spanned by 4 homography matrices whose planes do not all coincide with a single point, we must produce an additional homography matrix in order to complete the basis of the subgroup defined by $[\delta]_\times F$ to a full basis for the entire group. The elements (matrices) of the full basis will be called "primitive homographies". The additional homography matrix we seek must therefore be associated with a plane coincident with the center of projection O of camera 1 (and is therefore of rank 1). We have the following Lemma which is adapted from [17]:

Lemma 1. *Given the fundamental matrix F and the epipole v' defined by $F^\top v' = 0$, then the family of matrices $v'\delta^\top$ are homography matrices from view 1 to view 2 due to planes coincident with the center of projection O of camera 1 and the vector δ is the intersection line of the plane and view 1.*

Proof: Let A_1, A_2 be any two homography matrices. Thus, A_1p, A_2p and v' are collinear for all points p in view 1. Let $q \neq v$, where v is the epipole in view 1 ($Fv = 0$), be some point in view 1 and let λ be a scalar defined such that $A_1q - \lambda A_2q \cong v'$. Let $H = A_1 - \lambda A_2$ be a homography matrix (because all homography matrices are closed under linear combinations). Clearly, since $Hq \cong v'$, then $Hp \cong v'$ for all p (because $Hv \cong v'$ as well). Thus $H = v'\delta^\top$ for some vector δ. □

Therefore, as long as $\delta^\top v \neq 0$, where v is the epipole in view 1 (i.e., $Fv = 0$), then the homography matrix $v'\delta^\top$ does not coincide with O' (only with O) and thus can be used to complete the full basis for the group of homography matrices. Without loss of generality assume that $(1, 0, 0)$ is not coincident with v, thus we have a basis of 4 homography matrices $H_1, ..., H_4$, denoted as "primitive homographies", defined below:

$$H_i = [e_i]_\times F, \quad i = 1, 2, 3 \tag{3}$$
$$H_4 = v'e_1^\top \tag{4}$$

where e_i are the identity vectors: $e_1 = (1, 0, 0), e_2 = (0, 1, 0)$ and $e_3 = (0, 0, 1)$.

5   Applications Using Primitive Homography Matrices

The primitive homography matrices are a useful tool for representing geometric data. We will consider two examples here, the first on obtaining a "quasi-metric" representation of 3D space from a pair of uncalibrated cameras, and the second on "triangulation" from 3 views.

5.1   Quasi-Metric Reference Plane

Let $p_i, p'_i, i = 1, ..., N$, be matching points in view 1 and 2 respectively. Given the fundamental matrix F and the epipole v' in view 2, then the 3D projective representation of the object space points P_i can be described relative to a reference plane π:

$$p'_i \cong A_\pi p_i + \rho_i v' = [A_\pi, v']P_i$$

where A_π is the homography matrix mapping view 1 onto view 2 due to the plane π. The scalar ρ_i represents the relative deviation of the point P_i from the plane π and is called the "relative affine structure"[21]. The choice of the plane π determines the projective representation of object space. For purposes of visualization, it is useful to choose π such that it is situated "in-between" the space points making it possible to treat ρ_i as simple depth variable. In other words, let $A_\pi = \sum_j \alpha_j H_j$, we seek to solve for the scalar α_j, $j = 1, ..., 4$, that minimize:

$$\sum_{j=1}^{4}(\alpha_j H_j)p_i \cong p'_i \quad i = 1, ..., N$$

which provides an over-determined linear set of equations. We will refer to π as the "quasi-metric" plane. The choice of the quasi-metric plane provides a better chance that the projective viewing of the object (treating the coordinates x_i, y_i, ρ_i as Euclidean coordinates by the viewing program) will have less projective distortions than other choices.

5.2 Triangulation from 3 Views

Hartley and Sturm [11] considered the problem, they called "triangulation", of modifying the locations of input matching points $\hat{p}, \hat{p}'$ that are given with noise to new locations p, p' that satisfy $p'^{\top} F p = 0$ such that $(p - \hat{p})^2 + (p' - \hat{p}')^2$ is minimized. The triangulation problem in 3 views can be stated in a similar manner: given p in view 1, the matching process produces an error in the matches in view 2 and 3. The input matches are $\hat{p}'$ and $\hat{p}''$ and we wish to find new matches p', p'' with p such that the triplet p, p', p'' satisfy the trilinear equations while $(p' - \hat{p}')^2 + (p'' - \hat{p}'')^2$ is minimized. Note that we do not add an error term to p and rather take p as a reference. The reason for that is twofold: first due to the asymmetry of the trifocal tensor with respect to view ordering as it is defined with respect to a reference view (unlike the fundamental matrix which remains fixed under view ordering). Secondly, in most matching approaches that use a correlation principle, like the popular Lucas-Kanade [15] method with the coarse-to-fine implementation by Sarnoff Corp. [4], there is also an intrinsic asymmetry that assumes one of the views as a reference. Taken together, we can without loss of generality assume that the effect of error in the matching process is represented in the displacement of $\hat{p}'$ and $\hat{p}''$ from their true locations p', p''.

The triangulation process using the trifocal tensor can proceed as follows. We first note that the following relationship exists:

$$p' \cong Ap + \rho v' \tag{5}$$
$$p'' \cong Bp + \rho v'' \tag{6}$$

where A, B are two homography matrices from view 1 to 2 and from view 1 to 3 via some reference plane π (any plane). Given the trifocal tensor T_i^{jk} one can recover the epipoles v', v'' (and fundamental matrices) [10,22] and proceed to recover a pair of homography matrices A, B as described below.

One can solve for A be either choosing some linear combination of the primitive homographies or solving for the quasi-metric plane as described in the previous section. Thus we can assume that A is known. The corresponding homography B cannot be chosen arbitrarily because it must be associated with the same plane π that was associated with the homography A.

Let $\bar{H}_l$, $l = 1, ..., 4$, be the primitive homographies from view 1 to 3. Let the sought after matrix B be represented by $B = \sum_l \beta_l \bar{H}_l$. We seek a solution of the scalars β_l. We have the following relationship:

$$T_i^{jk} = v'^j b_i^k - v''^k a_i^j$$
$$= v'^j (\Sigma_{l=1}^4 \beta_l \bar{H}_l)_i^k - \lambda v''^k a_i^j \tag{7}$$

where the left-hand side is known (the trifocal tensor) and the right-hand side contains 5 unknowns which together form an over-determined linear system. The scalar λ fixes the scale because v', v'', A are all determined up to scale. Taken together, from the trifocal tensor and with the use of the primitive homographies we can extract a set of compatible homographies (associated with the same plane) and the epipoles v', v''.

We are now left with minimizing the following expression:

$$\min_\rho \{ (\hat{x}' - \frac{a_1^\top p + \rho v_1'}{a_3^\top p + \rho v_3'})^2 + (\hat{y}' - \frac{a_2^\top p + \rho v_2'}{a_3^\top p + \rho v_3'})^2 + (\hat{x}'' - \frac{b_1^\top p + \rho v_1''}{b_3^\top p + \rho v_3''})^2 + (\hat{y}'' - \frac{b_2^\top p + \rho v_2''}{b_3^\top p + \rho v_3''})^2 \}$$

which is minimized with respect to ρ. This yields a 4th order polynomial in ρ which thus has a closed-form solution. The geometric interpretation of this minimization process is that the solution ρ determines the points p', p'' on their corresponding epipolar lines such that the distance $(p' - \hat{p}')^2 + (p'' - \hat{p}'')^2$ is minimized. Note that unlike the case of two views, one cannot place p' and p'' anywhere on their epipolar lines because they are coupled together by a 1-parameter degree of freedom. In particular, the projections of $\hat{p}'$ and $\hat{p}''$ on their epipolar lines may not be an admissible solution.

6 Other Applications of the Bifocal Tensor Representation

In the previous sections we presented applications of the primitive homographies which in turn are due to the discovery of $[\delta]_\times F$ representing the family of rank-2 homographies which in turn are due to the bifocal tensor representation. However, one could possibly re-derive the result $[\delta]_\times F$ from purely matrix considerations without relying on the bifocal tensor. Nevertheless, there are applications that critically rely on the tensor embedding of the fundamental matrix in the form of the bifocal tensor — and in this section we briefly discuss two of them.

6.1 View-Synthesis

The notion of image-based rendering is gaining momentum both in the computer graphics and computer vision communities. Using the trifocal tensor for image-based rendering was proposed by [2]. In a nutshell, the method links together two real views of a 3D scene with a third virtual view of the scene. The tensor is

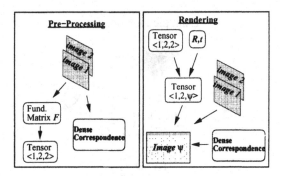

Fig. 2. View synthesis is divided into two parts. In the pre-processing stage, done only once, we compute the dense correspondence and the bifocal tensor. The rendering stage, done for every novel image, transforms the "seed" bifocal tensor to a general three-view trifocal tensor, using user-specified parameters R, t and renders the novel view using the transformed tensor, the model images and the dense correspondence.

then used to reproject a point appearing in the first two views directly onto the virtual view, without ever recovering 3D structure. Moving the virtual camera in space is done by modifying the tensor to reflect the change in the relative position of the virtual view. To bootstrap the seed tensor one would need three real views of the object, but only two of them will be later used for the generation of the virtual view. However, using the tensor-embedded fundamental matrix, one can use only two real images to generate the bifocal "seed tensor".

One starts with the bifocal tensor which is then transformed using the user specified motion of the virtual camera to the appropriate trifocal tensor (of the original two model views and the virtual view to be synthesized). From there on the trifocal tensors transform as the virtual camera changes positions (see Fig. 2). Thus, for this application to work it is necessary to have a uniform terminology for handling 2 and 3 views.

6.2 Ego-motion Recovery

When considering the problem of recovering the camera ego-motion (projection matrices) from a stream of views, one faces the problem of maintaining a consistency of pairwise fundamental matrices. The consistency requirement arises from the simple fact that from an algebraic standpoint a camera trajectory must be *concatenated* from pairs or triplets of images. Therefore, a sequence of independently computed fundamental matrices or trifocal tensors, maybe optimally consistent with the image data, but not necessarily consistent with a unique camera trajectory (see Figure 3).

The consistency problem can be approached by introducing the following equation which relates the trifocal tensor between views 1,2,3 and the bifocal

Example in 4 Images

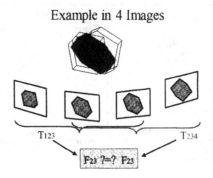

Fig. 3. One can compute two tensors T_{123}, T_{234} from the four images of the 3D scene. However, each tensor can give rise to a different reconstruction of the 3D structure due to noise or errors in measurements, and therefor the camera trajectory between images 2 and 3, as captured by the fundamental matrix F_{23}, is inconsistent between the two tensors. Figure taken from [3]

tensor between views 1,2 and the elements of the fundamental matrix between views 2,3:

$$T_i^{jk} = c_l^k \mathcal{F}_i^{jl} - v'''^k a_i^j \tag{8}$$

where T_i^{jk} is the tensor of views 1,2,3, the matrix A, whose elements are a_i^j, is a homography from views 1 to 2 via some arbitrary plane π, $\mathcal{F}_i^{jl}$ is the bifocal tensor of views 1,2, and $\mathbf{C} = [C; v''']$ is the camera motion from view 2 to 3 where c_l^k is a homography matrix from view 2 to 3 via the (same) plane π.

As a result, given the fundamental matrix between views 1,2 and (at least) 6 matching points between views 1,2,3 one can solve for the fundamental matrix between views 2 and 3 (i.e., $[v''']_\times C$) which is consistent with the trifocal relationship among views 1,2,3. Also, as a byproduct, the projection matrix $[C, v''']$ is consistent with the same projective representation due to the fact that the homographies A, C are of the same reference plane. The details and demonstration of this idea can be found in [3].

7   Summary

We have introduced a new representation of the bilinear matching constraint between a pair of views in terms of a $3 \times 3 \times 3$ tensor which we termed the "bifocal" tensor. The motivation for the new representation is to establish a unified terminology between the elements of 2-view and 3-view constraints. The unified terminology is achieved by representing the 2-view constraint in a way analogously (and identical in form) to the trifocal tensor relationship. As a result, we were able to transfer the properties known today about the trifocal tensor (especially the contraction into homography matrices) to the realm of the 2-view case.

The byproduct of the new representation is twofold. First, we have derived the family of rank-2 homography matrices represented by $[\delta]_\times F$ and introduced the "primitive homographies" and their applications. Second, we mentioned two other applications for which the unified terminology is necessary.

Taken together, it is useful to have a common language for analyzing the geometric constraints arising from multiple-view geometry — both at the theoretical level for purposes of obtaining a clean representation and for applications where the common language is sometimes necessary (as was shown in Section 6).

Acknowledgments

We thank Richard Hartley for comments on the previous version of this work (in [1]) which led to a simpler representation of $\mathcal{F}_i^{jk}$. A.S. also thanks Nir Avrahami for noticing the need for the scale factor λ in eqn. 7 and Jacob Goldberg for suggesting the use of the relative-affine invariant for "triangulation" in Section 5.2.

References

1. S. Avidan and A. Shashua. Unifying two-view and three-view geometry. In *ARPA, Image Understanding Workshop*, 1997.
2. S. Avidan and A. Shashua. Novel view synthesis by cascading trilinear tensors. *IEEE Transactions on Visualization and Computer Graphics*, 4(3), 1998. Short version can be found in CVPR'97.
3. S. Avidan and A. Shashua. Threading fundamental matrices. In *Proceedings of the European Conference on Computer Vision*, Frieburg, Germany, June 1998. Springer, LNCS 1406.
4. J.R. Bergen, P. Anandan, K.J. Hanna, and R. Hingorani. Hierarchical model-based motion estimation. In *Proceedings of the European Conference on Computer Vision*, Santa Margherita Ligure, Italy, June 1992.
5. A. Criminisi, I. Reid, and A. Zisserman. Duality, rigidity and planar parallax. In *Proceedings of the European Conference on Computer Vision*, Frieburg, Germany, 1998. Springer, LNCS 1407.
6. O.D. Faugeras. Stratification of three-dimensional vision: projective, affine and metric representations. *Journal of the Optical Society of America*, 12(3):465–484, 1995.
7. O.D. Faugeras and B. Mourrain. On the geometry and algebra of the point and line correspondences between N images. In *Proceedings of the International Conference on Computer Vision*, Cambridge, MA, June 1995.
8. O.D. Faugeras and T. Papadopoulo. A nonlinear method for estimating the projective geometry of three views. In *Proceedings of the International Conference on Computer Vision*, Bombay, India, January 1998.
9. R. Hartley. Lines and points in three views — a unified approach. In *Proceedings of the DARPA Image Understanding Workshop*, Monterey, CA, November 1994.
10. R.I. Hartley. Lines and points in three views and the trifocal tensor. *International Journal of Computer Vision*, 22(2):125–140, 1997.

11. R.I. Hartley and P. Sturm. Triangulation. In *Proceedings of the DARPA Image Understanding Workshop*, pages 972–966, Monterey, CA, Nov. 1994.
12. A. Heyden. Reconstruction from image sequences by means of relative depths. In *Proceedings of the International Conference on Computer Vision*, pages 1058–1063, Cambridge, MA, June 1995.
13. M. Irani, P. Anandan, and D. Weinshall. From reference frames to reference planes: Multiview parallax geometry and applications. In *Proceedings of the European Conference on Computer Vision*, Frieburg, Germany, 1998. Springer, LNCS 1407.
14. H.C. Longuet-Higgins. A computer algorithm for reconstructing a scene from two projections. *Nature*, 293:133–135, 1981.
15. B.D. Lucas and T. Kanade. An iterative image registration technique with an application to stereo vision. In *Proceedings IJCAI*, pages 674–679, Vancouver, Canada, 1981.
16. Q.T. Luong and T. Vieville. Canonic representations for the geometries of multiple projective views. In *Proceedings of the European Conference on Computer Vision*, pages 589–599, Stockholm, Sweden, May 1994. Springer Verlag, LNCS 800.
17. A. Shashua. Algebraic functions for recognition. *IEEE Transactions on Pattern Analysis and Machine Intelligence*, 17(8):779–789, 1995.
18. A. Shashua. Trilinear tensor: The fundamental construct of multiple-view geometry and its applications. In G. Sommer and J.J. Koenderink, editors, *Algebraic Frames For The Perception Action Cycle*, number 1315 in Lecture Notes in Computer Science. Springer, 1997. Proceedings of the workshop held in Kiel, Germany, Sep. 1997.
19. A. Shashua and P. Anandan. The generalized trilinear constraints and the uncertainty tensor. In *Proceedings of the DARPA Image Understanding Workshop*, Palm Springs, CA, February 1996.
20. A. Shashua and S. Avidan. The rank4 constraint in multiple view geometry. In *Proceedings of the European Conference on Computer Vision*, Cambridge, UK, April 1996.
21. A. Shashua and N. Navab. Relative affine structure: Canonical model for 3D from 2D geometry and applications. *IEEE Transactions on Pattern Analysis and Machine Intelligence*, 18(9):873–883, 1996.
22. A. Shashua and M. Werman. Trilinearity of three perspective views and its associated tensor. In *Proceedings of the International Conference on Computer Vision*, June 1995.
23. M.E. Spetsakis and J. Aloimonos. Structure from motion using line correspondences. *International Journal of Computer Vision*, 4(3):171–183, 1990.
24. M.E. Spetsakis and J. Aloimonos. A unified theory of structure from motion. In *Proceedings of the DARPA Image Understanding Workshop*, 1990.
25. G. Stein and A. Shashua. Model based brightness constraints: On direct estimation of structure and motion. In *Proceedings of the IEEE Conference on Computer Vision and Pattern Recognition*, Puerto Rico, June 1997.
26. G. Stein and A. Shashua. On degeneracy of linear reconstruction from three views: Linear line complex and applications. In *Proceedings of the European Conference on Computer Vision*, Frieburg, Germany, 1998. Springer, LNCS 1407.
27. B. Triggs. Matching constraints and the joint image. In *Proceedings of the International Conference on Computer Vision*, pages 338–343, Cambridge, MA, June 1995.
28. J. Weng, T.S. Huang, and N. Ahuja. Motion and structure from line correspondences: Closed form solution, uniqueness and optimization. *IEEE Transactions on Pattern Analysis and Machine Intelligence*, 14(3), 1992.

A   Appendix

A.1   Trilinearities and the Trifocal Tensor

Three views, $p = [I; 0]x, p' \cong Ax$ and $p'' \cong Bx$, are known to produce four trilinear forms whose coefficients are arranged in a tensor representing a bilinear function of the camera matrices A, B:

$$T_i^{jk} = v'^j b_i^k - v''^k a_i^j \tag{1}$$

where $A = [a_i^j, v'^j]$ (a_i^j is the 3×3 left minor and v' is the fourth column of A) and $B = [b_i^k, v''^k]$. The tensor acts on a triplet of matching points in the following way:

$$p^i s_j^\mu r_k^\rho T_i^{jk} = 0 \tag{2}$$

where s_j^μ are any two lines (s_j^1 and s_j^2) intersecting at p', and r_k^ρ are any two lines intersecting p''. Since the free indices are μ, ρ each in the range 1,2, we have 4 trilinear equations (unique up to linear combinations). If we choose the *standard* form where s^μ (and r^ρ) represent vertical and horizontal scan lines, i.e.,

$$s_j^\mu = \begin{bmatrix} -1 & 0 & x' \\ 0 & -1 & y' \end{bmatrix}$$

then the four trilinear forms, referred to as *trilinearities* [17], have the following explicit form:

$$x'' T_i^{13} p^i - x'' x' T_i^{33} p^i + x' T_i^{31} p^i - T_i^{11} p^i = 0,$$
$$y'' T_i^{13} p^i - y'' x' T_i^{33} p^i + x' T_i^{32} p^i - T_i^{12} p^i = 0,$$
$$x'' T_i^{23} p^i - x'' y' T_i^{33} p^i + y' T_i^{31} p^i - T_i^{21} p^i = 0,$$
$$y'' T_i^{23} p^i - y'' y' T_i^{33} p^i + y' T_i^{32} p^i - T_i^{22} p^i = 0.$$

These constraints were first derived in [17]; the tensorial derivation leading to eqns. 1 and 2 was first derived in [19]. The tensor is often referred to as "trilinear" or "trifocal", and we adopt here the term trifocal tensor. The trifocal tensor has been well known in disguise in the context of Euclidean line correspondences and was not identified at the time as a tensor but as a collection of three matrices (a particular contraction of the tensor, correlation contractions, as explained next) [23,24,28]. The link between the trilinearities and the matrices of line geometry was identified later by Hartley [9,10]. Additional work in this area can be found in [22,7,27,12,20,3,2,25,8,13,5,26].

The tensor has certain contraction properties and can be sliced in three principled ways into matrices with distinct geometric properties. These properties is what makes the tensor distinct from simply being a collection of three matrices and will be briefly discussed next — further details can be found in [22,18].

A.2   Contraction Properties and Tensor Slices

Consider the matrix arising from the contraction,

$$\delta_k T_i^{jk} \tag{3}$$

which is a 3×3 matrix, we denote by E, obtained by the linear combination $E = \delta_1 T_i^{j1} + \delta_2 T_i^{j2} + \delta_3 T_i^{j3}$ (which is what is meant by a contraction), and δ_k is an *arbitrary* covariant vector. The matrix E has a general meaning introduced in [22]:

Proposition 1 (Homography Contractions).   *The contraction $\delta_k T_i^{jk}$ for some arbitrary δ_k is a homography matrix from image one onto image two determined by the plane containing the third camera center C'' and the line δ_k in the third image plane. Generally, the rank of E is 3. Likewise, the contraction $\delta_j T_i^{jk}$ is a homography matrix from image one onto image three.*

For proof see [22]. Clearly, since δ is spanned by three vectors, we can generate up to at most three distinct homography matrices by contractions of the tensor. We define the *Standard Homography Slicing* as the homography contractions associated by selecting δ be $(1, 0, 0)$ or $(0, 1, 0)$ or $(0, 0, 1)$, thus the three standard homography slices between image one and two are T_i^{j1}, T_i^{j2} and T_i^{j3}, and we denote them by E_1, E_2, E_3 respectively, and likewise the three standard homography slices between image one and three are T_i^{1k}, T_i^{2k} and T_i^{3k}, and we denote them by W_1, W_2, W_3 respectively.

Similarly, consider the contraction

$$\delta^i T_i^{jk} \tag{4}$$

which is a 3×3 matrix, we denote by T, and where δ^i is an *arbitrary* contravariant vector. The matrix T has a general meaning is well, as detailed below [18]:

Proposition 2. *The contraction $\delta^i T_i^{jk}$ for some arbitrary δ^i is a rank 2 correlation matrix from image two onto image three, that maps the dual image plane (the space of lines in image two) onto a set of collinear points in image three that form the epipolar line corresponding to the point δ^i in image one. The null space of the correlation matrix is the epipolar line of δ^i in image two. Similarly, the transpose of T is a correlation from image three onto image two with the null space being the epipolar line in image three corresponding to the point δ^i in image one.*

For proof see [18]. We define the *Standard Correlation Slicing* as the correlation contractions associated with selecting δ be $(1, 0, 0)$ or $(0, 1, 0)$ or $(0, 0, 1)$, thus the three standard correlation slices are T_1^{jk}, T_2^{jk} and T_3^{jk}, and we denote them by T_1, T_2, T_3, respectively. The three standard correlations date back to the work on structure from motion of lines across three views [23,28] where these matrices were first introduced.

Optimal Estimation of Matching Constraints

Bill Triggs

INRIA Rhône-Alpes, 655 avenue de l'Europe, 38330 Montbonnot St. Martin, France
Bill.Triggs@inrialpes.fr — http://www.inrialpes.fr/movi/people/Triggs

Abstract. We describe work in progress on a numerical library for estimating multi-image matching constraints, or more precisely the multi-camera geometry underlying them. The library will cover several variants of homographic, epipolar, and trifocal constraints, using various different feature types. It is designed to be modular and open-ended, so that (*i*) new feature types or error models, (*ii*) new constraint types or parametrizations, and (*iii*) new numerical resolution methods, are relatively easy to add. The ultimate goal is to provide practical code for stable, reliable, statistically optimal estimation of matching geometry under a choice of robust error models, taking full account of any nonlinear constraints involved. More immediately, the library will be used to study the relative performance of the various competing problem parametrizations, error models and numerical methods. The paper focuses on the overall design, parametrization and numerical optimization issues. The methods described extend to many other geometric estimation problems in vision, *e.g.* curve and surface fitting.
Keywords: Matching constraints, multi-camera geometry, geometric fitting, statistical estimation, constrained optimization.

1 Introduction and Motivation

This paper describes work in progress on a numerical library for the estimation of multi-image matching constraints. The library will cover several variants of homographic, epipolar, and trifocal constraints, using various common feature types. It is designed to be modular and open-ended, so that new feature types or error models, new constraint types or parametrizations, and new numerical resolution methods are relatively easy to add. The ultimate goal is to provide practical code for stable, reliable, statistically optimal estimation of matching geometry under a choice of robust error models, taking full account of any nonlinear constraints involved. More immediately, the library is being used to study the relative performance of the various competing problem parametrizations, error models and numerical methods. Key questions include: (*i*) how much difference does an *accurate statistical error model* make; (*ii*) which *constraint parametrizations, initialization methods* and *numerical optimization schemes* offer the best reliability/speed/simplicity. The answers are most interesting for *near-degenerate* problems, as these are the most difficult to handle reliably. This paper focuses on architectural, parametrization and numerical optimization issues. I have tried to give an overview of the relevant choices and technology, rather than going into

Reinhard Koch, Luc Van Gool (Eds.): SMILE '98, LNCS 1506, pp. 63–77, 1998.
© Springer-Verlag Berlin Heidelberg 1998

too much detail on any one subject. The methods described extend to many other geometric estimation problems, such as curve and surface fitting.

After motivating the library and giving notation in this section, we develop a general statistical framework for geometric fitting in §2 and discuss parametrization issues in §3. §4 summarizes the library architecture and numerical techniques, §5 discusses experimental testing, and §6 concludes.

Why study matching constraint estimation? — Practically, matching constraints are central to both feature grouping and 3D reconstruction, so better algorithms should immediately benefit many geometric vision applications. But there are many variations to implement, depending on the feature type, number of images, image projection model, camera calibration, and camera and scene geometry. So a systematic approach seems more appropriate than an *ad hoc* case-by-case one. Matching constraints also have a rather delicate algebraic structure which makes them difficult to estimate accurately. Many common camera and scene geometries correspond to degenerate cases whose special properties need to be detected and exploited for stability. Even in stable cases it is not yet clear how best to parametrize the constraints — usually, they belong to fairly complicated algebraic varieties and redundant or constrained parametrizations are required. Some numerical sophistication is needed to implement these efficiently, and the advantages of different models and parametrizations need to be studied experimentally: the library is a vehicle for this.

It is also becoming clear that in many cases no single model suffices. One should rather think in terms of a continuum of nested models linked by specialization/generalization relations. For example, rather than simply assuming a generic fundamental matrix, one should use inter-image homographies for small camera motions or large flat scenes, affine fundamental matrices for small, distant objects, essential matrices for constant intrinsic parameters, fundamental matrices for wide views of large close objects, lens distortion corrections for real images, *etc.* Ideally, the model should be chosen to maximize the statistically expected end-to-end system performance, given the observed input data. Although there are many specific decision criteria (ML, AIC, BIC, ...), the key issue is always the *bias* of over-restrictive models versus the *variability* of over-general ones with superfluous parameters poorly controlled by the data. Any model selection approach requires several models to be fitted so that the best can be chosen. Some of the models must always be inappropriate — either biased or highly variable — so fast, reliable, accurate fitting in difficult cases is indispensable for practical model selection.

Terminology and notation: We use homogeneous coordinates throughout, with upright bold for 3D quantities and italic bold for image ones. Image projections are described by 3×4 perspective **projection matrices P**, with specialized forms for calibrated or very distant cameras. Given m images of a static scene, our goal is to recover as much information as possible about the camera calibrations and poses, using only image measurements. We will call the recoverable information the **inter-image geometry** to emphasize that no explicit 3D structure is involved. The ensemble of projection matrices is defined only up to a 3D coordinate transformation (projectivity or similarity) $\mathbf{T}$: $(\boldsymbol{P}_1, \dots, \boldsymbol{P}_m) \rightarrow (\boldsymbol{P}_1\mathbf{T}, \dots, \boldsymbol{P}_m\mathbf{T})$. We call such coordinate freedoms **gauge freedoms**. So our first representation of the inter-image geometry is as **projection matrices modulo a transformation group**. In the uncalibrated case this gives an $11m$ parameter representation with 15 gauge freedoms, leaving $11m - 15$ essential d.o.f. ($= 7, 18, 29$ for $m = 2, 3, 4$). In the calibrated case there are $6m - 7$ essential degrees of freedom.

Any set of four (perhaps not distinct) projection matrices can be combined to form a **matching tensor** [14, 5] — a multi-image object independent of the 3D coordinates. The possible types are: **epipoles** e_i^j; 3×3 **fundamental matrices** $\boldsymbol{F}_{ij}$; $3 \times 3 \times 3$ **trifocal tensors** $\boldsymbol{G}_i^{jk}$; and $3 \times 3 \times 3 \times 3$ **quadrifocal tensors** $\boldsymbol{H}^{ijkl}$. Their key property is that they are the coefficients of inter-image **matching constraints** — the consistency relations linking corresponding features in different images. *E.g.*, for images $\boldsymbol{x}, \boldsymbol{x}', \boldsymbol{x}''$ of a 3D point we have the 2-image **epipolar constraint** $\boldsymbol{x}^\mathsf{T}\boldsymbol{F}\,\boldsymbol{x}' = 0$; the 3-image **trinocular constraint** which can be written symbolically as $[\,\boldsymbol{x}'\,]_\times(\boldsymbol{G}\cdot\boldsymbol{x})[\,\boldsymbol{x}''\,]_\times = \boldsymbol{0}$ where $[\,\boldsymbol{x}\,]_\times$ is the matrix generating the cross product $[\,\boldsymbol{x}\,]_\times\boldsymbol{y} \equiv \boldsymbol{x}\wedge\boldsymbol{y}$; and a 4-image **quadrinocular constraint**. The matching tensors also characterize the inter-image geometry. This is attractive because they are intimately connected to the image measurements — it is much easier to get linearized initial estimates of matching tensors than of projection matrices. Unfortunately, this linearity is deceptive. Matching tensors are not really linear objects: they only represent a valid, realizable inter-image geometry if they satisfy a set of nonlinear algebraic **consistency constraints**. These rapidly become intractable beyond 2–3 images, and are still only partially understood [4, 14, 5, 9, 6]. Our second parametrization of the inter-image geometry is as *matching tensors subject to consistency constraints*.

We emphasize that camera matrices or matching tensors are only a means to an end: it is the underlying inter-image geometry that we are really trying to estimate. Unfortunately, this is abstract and somewhat difficult to pin down because it is a **nontrivial algebraic variety** — there *are* no simple, minimal, global parametrizations.

2   Optimal Geometric Fitting

2.1   Direct Approach

Matching constraint estimation is an instance of an **abstract geometric fitting problem** which also includes curve and surface fitting and many other geometric estimation problems: estimate the parameters of a model $\mathbf{u}$ defining implicit constraints $\mathbf{c}_i(\mathbf{x}_i, \mathbf{u}) = \mathbf{0}$ on underlying features $\mathbf{x}_i$, from noisy measurements of the features. More specifically we assume:

1. There are unknown **true underlying features** $\overline{\mathbf{x}}_i$ and an unknown **true underlying model** $\overline{\mathbf{u}}$ which exactly satisfy implicit **model-feature consistency constraints** $\mathbf{c}_i(\overline{\mathbf{x}}_i, \overline{\mathbf{u}}) = \mathbf{0}$. (For matching constraint estimation, these 'features' are actually ensembles of several corresponding image ones).

2. Each underlying feature $\bar{\mathbf{x}}_i$ is linked to observations $\underline{\mathbf{x}}_i$ or other prior information by an additive **posterior statistical error measure** $\rho_i(\mathbf{x}_i) \equiv \rho_i(\mathbf{x}_i | \underline{\mathbf{x}}_i)$. For example, ρ_i might be (robustified, bias corrected) **posterior log likelihood**. There may also be a **model prior** $\rho_{\text{prior}}(\mathbf{u})$. These distributions are independent.

3. The model parametrization $\mathbf{u}$ may itself be complex, *e.g.* with internal constraints $\mathbf{k}(\mathbf{u}) = \mathbf{0}$, gauge freedoms, *etc.*

4. We want to find **optimal consistent point estimates** $(\hat{\mathbf{x}}_i, \hat{\mathbf{u}})$ of the true underlying model $\bar{\mathbf{u}}$ and features $\bar{\mathbf{x}}_i$

$$(\hat{\mathbf{x}}_i, \ldots, \hat{\mathbf{u}}) \equiv \arg \min \left(\rho_{\text{prior}}(\mathbf{u}) + \sum_i \rho_i(\mathbf{x}_i | \underline{\mathbf{x}}_i) \,\middle|\, \mathbf{c}_i(\mathbf{x}_i, \mathbf{u}) = \mathbf{0}, \ \mathbf{k}(\mathbf{u}) = \mathbf{0} \right)$$

Consistent means that $(\hat{\mathbf{x}}_i, \hat{\mathbf{u}})$ exactly satisfy all the constraints. **Optimal** means that they minimize the total error over all such estimates. **Point estimate** means that we are attempting to "summarize" the joint posterior distribution $\rho(\mathbf{x}_i, \ldots, \mathbf{u} | \underline{\mathbf{x}}_i, \ldots)$ with just the few numbers $(\hat{\mathbf{x}}_i, \ldots, \hat{\mathbf{u}})$.

We call this the **direct approach** to geometric fitting because it involves direct numerical optimization over the "natural" variables $(\mathbf{x}_i, \mathbf{u})$. Its most important characteristics are: (i) It gives exact, optimal results — no approximations are involved. (ii) It produces optimal consistent estimates $\hat{\mathbf{x}}_i$ of the underlying features $\bar{\mathbf{x}}_i$. These are useful whenever the measurements need to be made coherent with the model. For matching constraint estimation such feature estimates are "pre-triangulated" or "implicitly reconstructed" in that they have already been made exactly consistent with exactly one reconstructed 3D feature. (iii) Natural variables are used and the error function is relatively simple, typically just a sum of (robustified, covariance weighted) squared deviations $\|\mathbf{x}_i - \underline{\mathbf{x}}_i\|^2$. ($iv$) However, a sparse constrained nonlinear optimization routine is required: the problem is large, constrained and usually nonlinear, but the features couple only to the model, not to each other.

As an example, for the uncalibrated epipolar geometry: the "features" are pairs of corresponding underlying image points $(\boldsymbol{x}_i, \boldsymbol{x}_i')$; the "model" $\mathbf{u}$ is the fundamental matrix $\boldsymbol{F}$ subject to the consistency constraint $\det(\boldsymbol{F}) = 0$; the "model-feature constraints" are the epipolar constraints $\boldsymbol{x}_i^{\mathsf{T}} \boldsymbol{F} \boldsymbol{x}_i' = 0$; and the "feature error model" $\rho_i(\mathbf{x}_i)$ might be (a robustified, covariance-weighted variant of) the squared feature-observation distance $\|\boldsymbol{x} - \underline{\boldsymbol{x}}\|^2 + \|\boldsymbol{x}' - \underline{\boldsymbol{x}}'\|^2$.

2.2   Reduced Approach

If explicit estimates of the underlying features are not required, one can attempt to replace step 4 above with an optimization over $\mathbf{u}$ alone:

4′. Find an **optimal consistent point estimate** $\hat{\mathbf{u}}$ of the true underlying model $\bar{\mathbf{u}}$

$$\hat{\mathbf{u}} \equiv \arg \min \left(\rho_{\text{prior}}(\mathbf{u}) + \sum_i \rho_i(\mathbf{u} | \underline{\mathbf{x}}_i) \,\middle|\, \mathbf{k}(\mathbf{u}) = \mathbf{0} \right)$$

Here, the **reduced error functions** $\rho_i(\mathbf{u}|\underline{\mathbf{x}}_i)$ are obtained by freezing $\mathbf{u}$ and eliminating the unknown features from the problem using either: (i) **point estimates** $\mathbf{x}_i(\underline{\mathbf{x}}_i, \mathbf{u}) \equiv \arg\min\left(\rho_i(\mathbf{x}_i|\underline{\mathbf{x}}_i) \mid \mathbf{c}_i(\mathbf{x}_i, \mathbf{u}) = 0\right)$ of $\mathbf{x}_i$ given $\underline{\mathbf{x}}_i$ and $\mathbf{u}$, with $\rho_i(\mathbf{u}|\underline{\mathbf{x}}_i) \equiv \rho_i(\mathbf{x}_i(\underline{\mathbf{x}}_i, \mathbf{u})|\underline{\mathbf{x}}_i)$; or ($ii$) **marginalization** with respect to $\mathbf{x}_i$: $\rho_i(\mathbf{u}|\underline{\mathbf{x}}_i) \equiv \int_{\mathbf{c}_i(\mathbf{x}_i, \mathbf{u})=0} \rho_i(\mathbf{x}_i|\underline{\mathbf{x}}_i)\, d\mathbf{x}_i$. These two methods are not equivalent in general, although their answers happen to agree in the linear/Gaussian limit. But both represent reasonable estimation techniques.

We call this the **reduced approach** to geometric fitting, because the problem is **reduced** to one involving only the model parameters $\mathbf{u}$. The main advantage is that the optimization is over relatively few variables $\mathbf{u}$. The constraints $\mathbf{c}_i$ do not appear, so a non-sparse and (perhaps) unconstrained optimization routine can be used. The disadvantage is that the reduced cost $\rho(\mathbf{u})$ is seldom available in closed form. Usually, it can only be evaluated to first order in a linearized + central distribution approximation. In fact, the direct method (with $\mathbf{u}$ frozen, and perhaps limited to a single iteration) is often the easiest way to evaluate the point-estimate-based reduced cost. The only real difference is that the direct method explicitly calculates and applies feature updates $d\mathbf{x}_i$, while the reduced method restarts each time from $\mathbf{x}_i \equiv \underline{\mathbf{x}}_i$. But the feature updates are relatively easy to calculate given the factorizations needed for cost evaluation, so it seems a pity not to use them.

The first order reduced cost can be estimated in two ways, either (i) directly from the definition by projecting $\underline{\mathbf{x}}_i$ Mahalanobis-orthogonally onto the local first-order constraint surface $\mathbf{c}_i + \frac{d\mathbf{c}_i}{d\mathbf{x}_i}\cdot d\mathbf{x}_i = 0$; or ($ii$) by treating $\mathbf{c}_i \equiv \mathbf{c}_i(\underline{\mathbf{x}}_i, \mathbf{u})$ as a random variable, using covariance propagation w.r.t. $\underline{\mathbf{x}}_i$ to find its covariance, and calculating the χ^2-like variable $\mathbf{c}_i^T \mathrm{Cov}(\mathbf{c}_i)^{-1}\mathbf{c}_i$. In either case we obtain the **gradient weighted least squares** cost function[1] [13]

$$\rho(\mathbf{u}) = \sum_i \mathbf{c}_i^T \left(\frac{d\mathbf{c}_i}{d\mathbf{x}_i}\left(\frac{d^2\rho_i}{d\mathbf{x}_i^2}\right)^{-1}\frac{d\mathbf{c}_i}{d\mathbf{x}_i}^T\right)^{-1}\mathbf{c}_i \Bigg|_{(\underline{\mathbf{x}}_i, \mathbf{u})}$$

This is simplest for problems with scalar constraints. *E.g.* for the uncalibrated epipolar constraint we get the well-known form [10]

$$\rho(\mathbf{u}) = \sum_i \frac{(\underline{\mathbf{x}}_i^T \mathbf{F}\, \underline{\mathbf{x}}_i')^2}{\underline{\mathbf{x}}_i^T \mathbf{F}\, \mathrm{Cov}(\underline{\mathbf{x}}_i')\, \mathbf{F}^T\, \underline{\mathbf{x}}_i + \underline{\mathbf{x}}_i'^T \mathbf{F}^T\, \mathrm{Cov}(\underline{\mathbf{x}}_i)\, \mathbf{F}\, \underline{\mathbf{x}}_i'}$$

2.3   Robustification — Total Distribution Approach

Outliers are omnipresent in vision data and it is essential to protect against them. In general, they are distinguished only by their failure to agree with the consensus established by the inliers, so one should really think in terms of *inlier* or *coherence* detection. The hardest part is establishing a reliable initial estimate, *i.e.* the combinatorial problem of finding enough inliers to estimate the

---

[1] If any of the covariance matrices is singular (which happens for redundant constraints or homogeneous data $\mathbf{x}_i$), the matrix inverses can be replaced with pseudo-inverses.

model, without being able to tell in advance that they *are* inliers. Exhaustive enumeration is usually impracticable, so one falls back on either RANSAC-like random sampling or (in low dimensions) Hough-like voting. Initialization from an outlier-polluted linear estimate is seldom completely reliable.

Among the many approaches to robustness, I prefer M-like estimators and particularly the **total distribution** approach: hypothesize a parametric form for the **total observation distribution** — *i.e.* including *both* inliers *and* outliers — and fit this to the data using some standard criterion, *e.g.* maximum likelihood. No explicit inlier/outlier decision is needed: the correct model is located simply because it provides an explanation more probable than randomness for the coherence of the inliers[2]. The total approach is really just classical parametric statistics with a more realistic or "robust" choice of parametric family. Any required distribution parameters can in principle be estimated during fitting (*e.g.* covariances, outlier densities). For centrally peaked mixtures one can view the total distribution as a kind of M-estimator, although it long predates these and gives a much clearer meaning to the rather arbitrary functional forms usually adopted for them. As with other M-like-estimators, the estimation problem is nonlinear and numerical optimization is required. With this approach, both of the above geometric fitting methods are 'naturally' robust — we just need to use an appropriate total likelihood.

Reasons for preferring M-like estimators over trimmed ones like RANSAC's consensus and rank-based ones like least median squares include: (*i*) to the extent that the total distribution is realistic, the total approach is actually the statistically optimal one; (*ii*) only M-like cost functions are smooth and hence easy to optimize; (*iii*) the 'soft' transitions of M-like estimators allow better use of weak 'near outlier' data, *e.g.* points which are relatively uncertain owing to feature extraction problems, or "false outliers" caused by misestimated covariances or a skewed, biased, or badly initialized model; (*iv*) including an explicit covariance scale makes the results more reliable and increases the *expected* breakdown point — 'scale free' rank based estimators can not tell whether the measurements they are including are "plausible" or not; (*v*) all of these estimators assume an underlying ranking of errors 'by relative size', and none are robust against mismodelling of this — rank based estimators only add a little extra robustness against the likelihood *vs.* error size assignment.

3 Parametrizing the Inter-image Geometry

As discussed above, what we are really trying to estimate is the **inter-image geometry** — the part of the multi-camera calibration and pose that is recoverable from image measurements alone. However, this is described by a nontrivial algebraic variety — it has *no* simple, minimal, concrete, global parametrization.

---

[2] If the total distribution happens to be an inlier/outlier *mixture* — *e.g.* Gaussian peak + uniform background — posterior inlier/outlier probabilities are easily extracted as a side effect.

For example, the uncalibrated epipolar geometry is "the variety of all homographic mappings between line pencils in the plane", but it is unclear how best to parametrize this. We will consider three general parametrization strategies for algebraic varieties: (i) redundant parametrizations with internal gauge freedoms; (ii) redundant parametrizations with internal constraints; (iii) overlapping local coordinate patches. *Mathematically* these are all equivalent — they only differ in relative convenience and numerical properties. Different methods are convenient for different uses, so it is important to be able to convert between them. Even the numerical differences are slight for strong geometries and careful implementations, but for weak geometries there can be significant differences.

3.1 Redundant Parametrizations with Gauge Freedom

In many geometric problems, **arbitrary choices of coordinates** are required to reduce the problem to a concrete algebraic form. Such choices are called **gauge freedoms** — 'gauge' just means coordinate system. They are associated with an internal **symmetry** or **coordinate transformation** group and its representations. Formulae expressed in gauged coordinates reflect the symmetry by obeying well-defined transformation rules under changes of coordinates, *i.e.* by belonging to well-defined group representations. 3D Cartesian coordinates are a familiar example: the gauge group is the group of rigid motions, and the representations are (roughly speaking) Cartesian tensors.

Common gauge freedoms include: (i) 3D projective or Euclidean coordinate freedoms in reconstruction and projection-matrix-based camera parametrizations; (ii) arbitrary homogeneous-projective scale factors; and (iii) choice-of-plane freedoms in **homographic parametrizations** of the inter-image geometry. These latter represent matching tensors as products of epipoles and inter-image homographies induced by an arbitrary 3D plane. The gauge freedom is the 3 d.o.f. choice of plane. The fundamental matrix can be written as $F \simeq [\,e\,]_{\times} H$ where e is the epipole and H is any inter-image homography [11, 3]. Redefining the 3D plane changes H to $H + e\,a^{\mathrm{T}}$ for some image line 3-vector a. This leaves F unchanged, as do rescalings $e \to \lambda e$, $H \to \mu H$. So there are $3 + 1 + 1$ gauge freedoms in the $3 + 3 \times 3 = 12$ variable parametrization $F \simeq F(e, H)$, leaving the correct $12 - 5 = 7$ degrees of freedom of the uncalibrated epipolar geometry. Similarly [8], the image $(1, 2, 3)$ trifocal tensor G can be written in terms of the epipoles (e', e'') and inter-image homographies (H', H'') of image 1 in images 2 and 3

$$G \simeq e' \otimes H'' - H' \otimes e'' \quad \text{with freedom} \quad \begin{pmatrix} H' \\ H'' \end{pmatrix} \to \begin{pmatrix} H' \\ H'' \end{pmatrix} + \begin{pmatrix} e' \\ e'' \end{pmatrix} a^{\mathrm{T}}$$

The gauge freedom corresponds to the choice of 3D plane and 3 scale d.o.f. — the relative scaling of (e', H') *vs.* (e'', H'') being significant — so the 18 d.o.f. of the uncalibrated trifocal geometry are parametrized by $3 + 3 + 9 + 9 = 24$ parameters modulo $3 + 1 + 1 + 1 = 6$ gauge freedoms. For calibrated cameras it is useful to place the 3D plane at infinity so that the resulting absolute homographies are represented by 3×3 rotation matrices. This gives well-known 6 and 12 parameter representations of the calibrated epipolar and trifocal geometries, each with just one redundant scale d.o.f.: $E \simeq [e]_\times R$, $G \simeq e' \otimes R'' - R' \otimes e''$. All of these homography + epipole parametrizations can also be viewed as projection matrix based ones, in a 3D frame where the first projection takes the form $(I_{3\times3}|0)$. The plane position freedom a corresponds to the 3 remaining d.o.f. of the 3D projective frame [8]. These methods seem to be a good compromise: compared to 'free' projections, they reduce the number of extraneous d.o.f. from 15 to 3. However their numerical stability does depend on that of the key image.

Gauged parametrizations have the following advantages: (*i*) they are very natural when the inter-image geometry is derived from the 3D one; (*ii*) they are close to the underlying geometry, so it is relatively easy to derive further properties from them (projection matrices, reconstruction methods, matching tensors); (*iii*) a single homogeneous coordinate system covers the whole variety; (*iv*) they are numerically fairly stable. Their main disadvantage is that they include extraneous, strictly irrelevant degrees of freedom which have no effect at all on the residual error. Hence, gauged Jacobians are exactly rank deficient: specially stabilized numerical methods are needed to handle them. The additional variables and stabilization also tend to make gauged parametrizations slow.

3.2   Constrained Parametrizations

Another way to define a variety is in terms of **consistency constraints** that "cut the variety out of" a larger, usually linear space. Any coordinate system in the larger space then parametrizes the variety, but this is an over-parametrization subject to nonlinear constraints. Points which fail to satisfy the constraints have no meaning in terms of the variety. **Matching tensors** are the most familiar example. In the 2- and 3-image cases a single fundamental matrix or trifocal tensor suffices to characterize the inter-image geometry. But this is a linear over-parametrization, subject to the tensor's nonlinear consistency constraints — only so is a coherent, realizable inter-image geometry represented. Such parametrizations are valuable because they are close to the image data, and (inconsistent!) linear initial estimates of the tensors are easy to obtain. Their main disadvantages are: (*i*) the consistency conditions rapidly become complicated and non-obvious; (*ii*) the representation is only implicit — it is not immediately obvious how to go from the tensor to other properties of the geometry such as projection matrices. The first problem is serious and puts severe limitations on the use of (ensembles of) matching tensors to represent camera geometries, even in transfer-type applications where explicit projection matrices are not required. Three images seems to be about the practical limit if a guaranteed-consistent geometry is required, although — at the peril of a build-up of rounding error — one can chain together a series of such three image solutions [12, 15, 1].

For the fundamental matrix the codimension is 1 and the consistency constraint is $\det(F) = 0$ — this is perhaps the simplest of all representations of the uncalibrated epipolar geometry. For the essential matrix E the codimension is 3, spanned either by the requirement that E should have two equal (which counts for 2) and one zero singular values, or by a local choice of 3 of the 9 Demazure constraints $(\boldsymbol{E}\boldsymbol{E}^{\mathrm{T}} - \frac{1}{2}\mathrm{trace}(\boldsymbol{E}\boldsymbol{E}^{\mathrm{T}}))\,\boldsymbol{E} = \boldsymbol{0}$ [4]. For the uncalibrated trifocal tensor $\boldsymbol{G}$ we locally need $26 - 18 = 8$ linearly independent constraints. Locally (only!) these can be spanned by the 10 determinantal constraints $\frac{\mathrm{d}^3}{\mathrm{dx}^3}\det(\boldsymbol{G}\cdot\mathbf{x}) = \boldsymbol{0}$ — see [6] for several global sets. For the quadrifocal tensor $\boldsymbol{H}$ the codimension is $80 - 29 = 51$ which is locally (but almost certainly not globally) spanned by the $3! \cdot 3 \cdot 3 = 54$ determinantal constraints $\det_{ij}(\boldsymbol{H}^{ijkl}) = \boldsymbol{0}$ + permutations.

Note that the redundancy and complexity of the matching tensor representation rises rapidly as more images or calibration constraints are added. Also, **constraint redundancy** is common. Many algebraic varieties require a number of generators greater than their codimension. Intersections of the minimal number of polynomials *locally* give the correct variety, but typically have other, unwanted components elsewhere in the space. Extra polynomials must be included to suppress these, and it rapidly becomes difficult to say which sets of polynomials are globally sufficient.

3.3   Local Coordinate Patches / Minimal Parametrizations

Both gauged and constrained parametrizations are redundant and require specialized numerical methods. Why not simplify life by using a **minimal set of independent parameters**? — The basic problem is that no such parametrization can cover the whole of a topologically nontrivial variety without singularities. Minimal parametrizations are intrinsically *local*: to cover the whole variety we need several such partially overlapping 'local coordinate patches', and also code to select the appropriate patch and manage any inter-patch transitions that occur. This can greatly complicate the optimization loop.

Also, although infinitely many local parametrizations exist, they are not usually very 'natural' and finding one with good properties may not be easy. Basically, starting from some 'natural' redundant representation, we must either come up with some inspired nonlinear change of variables which locally removes the redundancy, or algebraically eliminate variables by brute force using consistency or gauge fixing constraints. For example, Luong *et al* [10] guarantee $\det(\boldsymbol{F}) = 0$ by writing each row of the fundamental matrix as a linear combination of the other two. Each parametrization fails when its two rows are linearly dependent, but the three of them suffice to cover the whole variety. In more complicated situations, intuition fails and we have to fall back on algebraic elimination, which rapidly leads to intractable results. Elimination-based parametrizations are usually highly anisotropic: they do not respect the symmetries of the underlying geometry. This tends to mean that they are messy to implement, and numerically ill-behaved, particularly near the patch boundaries.

The above comments apply only to *algebraically* derived parametrizations. Many of the numerical techniques for gauged or constrained problems eliminate redundant variables *numerically* to first order, using the constraint Jacobians. Such local parametrizations are much better behaved because they are always used at the centre of their valid region, and because stabilizing techniques like pivoting can be used. *It is usually preferable to eliminate variables locally and numerically rather than algebraically.*

4   Library Architecture and Numerical Methods

The library is designed to be modular so that different problems and approaches are easy to implement and compare. We separate: (i) the matching geometry type and parametrization; (ii) each contributing feature-group type, parametrization and error model; (iii) the numerical optimization method, and its associated linear algebra; (iv) the search controller (step acceptance and damping, convergence tests). This decomposition puts some constraints on the types of algorithms that can be implemented, but these do not seem to be too severe in practice. Modularization also greatly simplifies the implementation.

Perhaps the most important assumption is the adoption throughout of a "square root" or normalized residual vector based framework, and the associated use of Gauss-Newton techniques. **Normalized residual vectors** are quantities $\mathbf{e}_i$ for which the squared norm $\|\mathbf{e}_i\|^2$ — or more generally a robust, nonlinear function $\rho_i(\|\mathbf{e}_i\|^2)$ — is a meaningful statistical error measure. *E.g.* $\mathbf{e}_i(\mathbf{x}_i) \equiv \text{Cov}(\underline{\mathbf{x}}_i)^{-\frac{1}{2}}(\mathbf{x}_i - \underline{\mathbf{x}}_i)$. This allows a nonlinear-least-squares-like approach. Whenever possible, we work directly with the residual $\mathbf{e}$ and its Jacobian $\frac{d\mathbf{e}}{d\mathbf{x}}$ rather than with $\|\mathbf{e}\|^2$, its gradient $\frac{d(\|\mathbf{e}\|^2)}{d\mathbf{x}} = \mathbf{e}^{\mathsf{T}}\frac{d\mathbf{e}}{d\mathbf{x}}$ and its Hessian $\frac{d^2(\|\mathbf{e}\|^2)}{d\mathbf{x}^2} = \mathbf{e}^{\mathsf{T}}\frac{d^2\mathbf{e}}{d\mathbf{x}^2} + \frac{d\mathbf{e}}{d\mathbf{x}}^{\mathsf{T}}\frac{d\mathbf{e}}{d\mathbf{x}}$. We use the **Gauss-Newton approximation**, *i.e.* we discard the second derivative term $\mathbf{e}^{\mathsf{T}}\frac{d^2\mathbf{e}}{d\mathbf{x}^2}$ in the Hessian. This buys us simplicity (no second derivatives are needed) and also numerical stability because we can use stable **linear least squares** methods for step prediction: by default we use **QR decomposition with column pivoting** of $\frac{d\mathbf{e}}{d\mathbf{x}}$, rather than Cholesky decomposition of the normal matrix $\frac{d\mathbf{e}}{d\mathbf{x}}^{\mathsf{T}}\frac{d\mathbf{e}}{d\mathbf{x}}$. This is potentially slightly slower, but for ill-conditioned Jacobians it has much better resistance to rounding error. (The default implementation is intended for use as a reference, so it is deliberately rather conservative). The main disadvantage of Gauss-Newton is that convergence may be slow if the problem has both *large residual* and *strong nonlinearity* — *i.e.* if the ignored Hessian term $\mathbf{e}^{\mathsf{T}}\frac{d^2\mathbf{e}}{d\mathbf{x}^2}$ is large. However, *geometric vision problems usually have small residuals* — the noise is usually much smaller than the scale of the geometric nonlinearities.

4.1   Numerical Methods for Gauge Freedom

The basic numerical difficulty with gauge freedom is that because gauge motions represent exact redundancies that have no effect at all on the residual error, in a classical optimization framework there is nothing to say what they should be: the error gradient and Hessian in a gauge direction both vanish, so the Newton step is undefined. If left undamped, this leads to **large gauge fluctuations** which can destabilize the rest of the system, prevent convergence tests from operating, *etc.* There are two ways around this problem:

1. **Gauge fixing conditions** break the degeneracy by adding **artificial constraints**. Unless we are clever enough to choose constraints that eliminate variables in closed form, this reduces the problem to constrained optimization. The constraints are necessarily non-gauge-invariant, *i.e.* non-tensorial under the

gauge group. For example, to fix the 3D projective coordinate freedom, Hartley [8] sets $P_1 \equiv (I_{3\times3}|0)$ and $\sum_i e^i H_j^i = 0$ where $P_2 = (H|e)$. Neither of these constraints is tensorial — the results depend on the chosen image coordinates.

2. Free gauge methods — like photogrammetric **free bundle** ones — leave the gauge free to drift, but ensure that it does not move too far at each step. Typically, it is also monitored and reset "by hand" when necessary to ensure good conditioning. The basic tools are **rank deficient least squares** methods (*e.g.* [2]). These embody some form of damping to preclude large fluctuations in near-deficient directions. The popular **regularization** method minimizes $\|\text{residual}\|^2 + \lambda^2 \|\text{step size}\|^2$ for some small $\lambda > 0$ — an approach that fits very well with Levenberg-Marquardt-like search control schemes. Alternatively, a **basic solution** — a solution where certain uncontrolled components are set to zero — can be calculated from a standard pivoted QR or Cholesky decomposition, simply by ignoring the last few (degenerate) columns. One can also find vectors spanning the local gauge directions and treat them as 'virtual constraints' with zero residual, so that the gauge motion is locally zeroed. **Householder reduction**, which orthogonalizes the rows of $\frac{de}{dx}$ w.r.t. the gauge matrix by partial QR decomposition, is a nice example of this.

4.2 Numerical Methods for Constrained Optimization

There are at least three ways to handle linear constraints numerically: (*i*) **eliminate variables** using the constraint Jacobian; (*ii*) introduce **Lagrange multipliers** and solve for these too; (*iii*) **weighting methods** treat the constraints as heavily weighted residual errors. Each method has many variants, depending on the matrix factorization used, the ordering of operations, *etc.* As a rough rule of thumb, for dense problems variable elimination is the fastest and stablest method, but also the most complex. Lagrange multipliers are slower because there are more variables. Weighting is simple, but slow and inexact — stable orthogonal decompositions are needed as weighted problems are ill-conditioned.

For efficiency, direct geometric fitting requires a sparse implementation — the features couple to the model, but not to each other. The above methods all extend to sparse problems, but the implementation complexity increases by about one order of magnitude in each case. My initial implementation [16] used Lagrange multipliers and Cholesky decomposition, but I currently prefer a stabler, faster 'multifrontal QR' elimination method. There is no space for full details here, but it works roughly as follows (NB: the implementation orders the steps differently for efficiency): For each constrained system, the constraint Jacobian $\frac{dc}{dx}$ is factorized and the results are propagated to the error Jacobian $\frac{de}{dx}$. This eliminates the dim(c) variables best controlled by the constraints from $\frac{de}{dx}$, leaving a 'reduced' dim(e) $\times$ (dim(x) $-$ dim(c)) least squares problem. Many factorization methods can be used for the elimination and the reduced problem. I currently use column pivoted QR decomposition for both, which means that the elimination step is essentially Gaussian elimination. All this is done for each feature system. The elimination also carries the $\frac{dc}{du}$ columns into the reduced system. The residual error of the reduced system can not be reduced by changing $\mathbf{x}$, but it is affected by changes in $\mathbf{u}$ acting via these reduced $\frac{d\mathbf{c}}{d\mathbf{u}}$ columns, which thus give contributions to an effective reduced error Jacobian $\frac{d\mathbf{e(u)}}{d\mathbf{u}}$ for the model $\mathbf{u}$. (This is the reduced geometric fitting method's error function). The resulting model system is reduced against any model constraints and factorized by pivoted QR. Back-substitution through the various stages then gives the required model update and finally the feature updates.

4.3   Search Control

All of the above techniques are linear. For nonlinear problems they must be used in a loop with appropriate step damping and search control strategies. This has been an unexpectedly troublesome part of the implementation — there seems to be a lack of efficient, reliable search control heuristics for constrained optimization. The basic problem is that the dual goals of reducing the constraint violation and reducing the residual error often conflict, and it is difficult to find a compromise that is good in all circumstances. Traditionally, a **penalty function** [7] is used, but all such methods have a 'stiffness' parameter which is difficult to set — too weak and the constraints are violated, too strong and the motion along the constraints towards the cost minimum is slowed. Currently, rather than a strict penalty function, I use a heuristic designed to allow a reasonable amount of 'slop' during motions along the constraints. The residual/constraint conflict also affects **step damping** — the control of step length to ensure acceptable progress. The principle of a **trust region** — a dynamic local region of the search space where the local function approximations are thought to hold good — applies, but interacts badly with **quadratic programming** based step prediction routines which try to satisfy the constraints exactly no matter how far away they are. Existing heuristics for this seemed to be poor, so I have developed a new 'dual control' strategy which damps the towards-constraint and along-constraint parts of the step separately using two Levenberg-Marquardt parameters linked to the same trust region.

Another difficulty is **constraint redundancy**. Many algebraic varieties require a number of generators greater than their codimension to eliminate spurious components elsewhere in the space. The corresponding constraint Jacobians theoretically have rank = codimension on the variety, but usually rank > codimension away from it. Numerically, a reasonably complete and well-conditioned set of generators is advisable to reduce the possibility of convergence to spurious solutions, but the high degree of rank degeneracy on the variety, and the rank transition as we approach it, are numerically troublesome. Currently, my only effective way to handle this is to assume known codimension r and numerically project out and enforce only the r strongest constraints at each iteration. This is straightforward to do during the constraint factorization step, once r is known. As examples: the trifocal point constraints $[\mathbf{x}']_\times (\mathbf{G} \cdot \mathbf{x})[\mathbf{x}'']_\times = \mathbf{0}$ have rank 4 in $(\mathbf{x}, \mathbf{x}', \mathbf{x}'')$ for most invalid tensors, but only rank 3 for valid ones; and the trifocal consistency constraints $\frac{d^3}{d\mathbf{x}^3} \det(\mathbf{G} \cdot \mathbf{x}) = \mathbf{0}$ have rank 10 for most invalid tensors, but only rank 8 for valid ones. In both cases, overestimating the rank causes severe ill-conditioning.

4.4 Robustification

We assume that each feature has a **central** robust cost function $\rho_i(\mathbf{x}_i) \equiv \rho_i(\|\mathbf{e}_i(\mathbf{x}_i)\|^2)$ defined in terms of a covariance-weighted **normalized residual error** $\mathbf{e}_i(\mathbf{x}_i) \equiv \mathbf{e}_i(\mathbf{x}_i|\underline{\mathbf{x}}_i)$. This defines the 'granularity' — entire 'features' (for matching constraints, ensembles of corresponding image features) are robustified, not their individual components. The robust cost ρ_i is usually some M-estimator, often a total log likelihood. For a uniform-outlier-polluted Gaussian it has the form $\rho(z) \equiv -2\log\left(e^{-z/2} + \beta\right)$, where β is related to outlier density. Typically, $\rho(z)$ is linear near 0, monotonic but sublinear for $z > 0$ and tends to a constant at $z \to \infty$ if distant outliers have vanishing influence. Hence, $\rho' \equiv \frac{d\rho}{dz}$ decreases monotonically to 0 and $\rho'' \equiv \frac{d^2\rho}{dz^2}$ is negative.

Robustification can lead to numerical problems, so care is needed. Firstly, since the cost is often nonconvex for outlying points, strong regularization may be required to guarantee a positive Hessian and hence a cost reducing step. This can slow convergence. To partially compensate for this curvature, and to allow us to use a 'naïve' Gauss-Newton step calculation while still accounting for robustness, we define a weighted, rank-one-corrected **effective residual** $\tilde{\mathbf{e}} \equiv \frac{\sqrt{\rho'}}{1-\alpha}\mathbf{e}$ and **effective Jacobian** $\frac{\widetilde{d\mathbf{e}}}{d\mathbf{x}} \equiv \sqrt{\rho'}\left(\mathbf{I} - \frac{\alpha}{\|\mathbf{e}\|^2}\,\mathbf{e}\,\mathbf{e}^{\mathsf{T}}\right)\frac{d\mathbf{e}}{d\mathbf{x}}$ where $\alpha \equiv \mathrm{RootOf}(\frac{1}{2}\alpha^2 - \alpha - \frac{\rho''}{\rho'}\|\mathbf{e}\|^2)$. These definitions ensure that to second order in ρ and $d\mathbf{x}$ and up to an irrelevant constant, the true robust cost $\rho(\|\mathbf{e} + \frac{d\mathbf{e}}{d\mathbf{x}}d\mathbf{x}\|^2)$ is the same as the naïve effective squared error $\|\tilde{\mathbf{e}} + \frac{\widetilde{d\mathbf{e}}}{d\mathbf{x}}d\mathbf{x}\|^2$. *I.e.* the same step $d\mathbf{x}$ is generated, so if we use effective quantities, we need think no further about robustness[3]. Here the $\sqrt{\rho'}$ weighting is the first order correction, and the α terms are the second order one. Usually $\rho' \to 0$ for distant outliers. Since the whole feature system is scaled by $\sqrt{\rho'}$, this might cause numerical conditioning or scaling problems in the direct method. To avoid this, we actually apply the $\sqrt{\rho'}$-weighting at the last possible moment — the contribution of the feature to the model error — and leave the feature systems themselves unweighted.

5   Measuring Performance

We currently test mainly on synthetic data, to allow systematic comparisons over a wide range of problems. We are particularly concerned with verifying theoretical statistical performance bounds, as these are the best guarantee that we are doing as well as could reasonably be expected. Any tendency to return occasional outliers is suspect and needs to be investigated. Histograms of

---

[3] If $\frac{\rho''}{\rho'}\|\mathbf{e}\|^2 < -\frac{1}{2}$ the robust Hessian has negative curvature and there is no real solution for α. In practice we limit $\alpha < 1 - \epsilon$ to prevent too much ill-conditioning. We would have had to regularize this case away anyway, so nothing is lost.

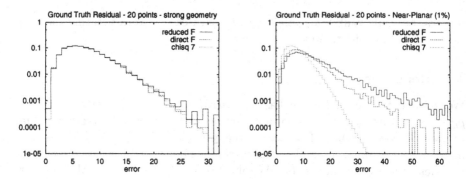

Fig. 1. Ground feature residuals for strong and near-coplanar epipolar geometries.

the **ground-truth-feature residual** (GFR) have proven particularly useful for this. These plot frequency *vs.* size of the total squared deviation of the *ground truth* values of the noisy features used in the estimate, from the estimated matching relations. This measures how *consistent* the estimated geometry is with the underlying noise-free features. For weak feature sets the geometry might still be far from the true one, but consistency is the most we can expect given the data. In the linear approximation the GFR is χ_ν^2 distributed for any sufficient model and number of features, where ν is the number of d.o.f. of the underlying inter-image geometry. This makes GFR easy to test and very sensitive to residual biases and oversized errors, as these are typically proportional to the number of features n and hence easily seen against the fixed χ_ν^2 background for $n \gg \nu$. For example, fig.1 shows GFR histograms for the 7 d.o.f. uncalibrated epipolar geometry for direct and reduced F-matrix estimators and strong and weak (1% non-coplanar) feature sets. For the strong geometry both methods agree perfectly with the theoretical χ_7^2 distribution without any sign of outliers, so both methods do as well as could be hoped. This holds for any number of points from 9 to 1000 — the estimated geometry (error per point) becomes more accurate, but the total GFR error stays constant. For the weak geometry both methods do significantly worse than the theoretical limit — in fact they turn out to have a small but roughly constant residual error *per point* rather than in total — with the direct method being somewhat better than the reduced one. We are currently investigating this: in theory it should be possible to get near the limit, even for exactly singular geometries.

6   Summary

We have described work in progress on a generic, modular library for the optimal nonlinear estimation of matching constraints, discussing especially the overall approach, parametrization and numerical optimization issues. The library will cover many different constraint types & parametrizations and feature types & error models in a uniform framework. It aims to be efficient and stable even in near-degenerate cases, *e.g.* so that it can be used reliably for model selection. Several fairly sophisticated numerical methods are included, including a sparse constrained optimization method designed for **direct geometric fitting**. Future work will concentrate mainly on (*i*) implementing and comparing different constraint types and parametrizations, feature types, and numerical resolution methods; and (*ii*) improving the reliability of the initialization and optimization stages, especially in near-degenerate cases.

References

[1] S. Avidan and A. Shashua. Threading fundamental matrices. In *European Conf. Computer Vision*, pages 124–140, Freiburg, 1998.

[2] Åke Björk. *Numerical Methods for Least Squares Problems*. SIAM Press, Philadelphia, PA, 1996.

[3] B. Boufama and R. Mohr. Epipole and fundamental matrix estimation using the virtual parallax property. In E. Grimson, editor, *IEEE Int. Conf. Computer Vision*, pages 1030–1036, Cambridge, MA, June 1995.

[4] O. Faugeras. *Three-dimensional computer vision: a geometric viewpoint*. MIT Press, 1993.

[5] O. Faugeras and B. Mourrain. On the geometry and algebra of the point and line correspondences between *n* images. In *IEEE Int. Conf. Computer Vision*, pages 951–6, Cambridge, MA, June 1995.

[6] O. Faugeras and T. Papadopoulo. Grassmann-Cayley algebra for modeling systems of cameras and the algebraic equations of the manifold of trifocal tensors. *Transactions of the Royal society A*, 1998.

[7] R. Fletcher. *Practical Methods of Optimization*. John Wiley, 1987.

[8] R.I. Hartley. Lines and points in three views and the trifocal tensor. *Int. J. Computer Vision*, 22(2):125–140, 1997.

[9] Anders Heyden. *Geometry and Algebra of Multiple Projective Transformations*. Ph.D. Thesis, University of Lund, 1995.

[10] Q.-T. Luong, R. Deriche, O. Faugeras, and T. Papadopoulo. On determining the fundamental matrix: Analysis of different methods and experimental results. Technical Report RR-1894, INRIA, Sophia Antipolis, France, 1993.

[11] Q.-T. Luong and T. Viéville. Canonic representations for the geometries of multiple projective views. In *European Conf. Computer Vision*, pages 589–599, 1994.

[12] P. Sturm and B. Triggs. A factorization based algorithm for multi-image projective structure and motion. In *European Conf. Computer Vision*, pages 709–20, Cambridge, U.K., 1996. Springer-Verlag.

[13] G. Taubin. Estimation of planar curves, surfaces and nonplanar space curves defined by implicit equations with applications to edge and range image segmentation. *IEEE Trans. Pattern Analysis & Machine Intelligence*, 13(11):1115–38, 1991.

[14] B. Triggs. Matching constraints and the joint image. In E. Grimson, editor, *IEEE Int. Conf. Computer Vision*, pages 338–43, Cambridge, MA, June 1995.

[15] B. Triggs. Linear projective reconstruction from matching tensors. In *British Machine Vision Conference*, pages 665–74, Edinburgh, September 1996.

[16] B. Triggs. A new approach to geometric fitting. Available from http://www.inrialpes.fr/movi/people/Triggs, 1997.

Matching and Reconstruction from Widely Separated Views

Philip Pritchett and Andrew Zisserman

Department of Engineering Science
University of Oxford, Oxford OX1 3PJ, UK.
{pcp, az}@robots.ox.ac.uk
http://www.robots.ox.ac.uk/~vgg

Abstract. The objective of this work is to automatically estimate the trifocal tensor and feature correspondences over images triplets, under unrestricted camera motions and changes in internal parameters between views. To this end we extend a previous wide baseline 2-view algorithm to 3-views. The algorithm is based on establishing feature correspondences between views together with a homography which enables a viewpoint invariant affinity score. The input is the three images, and the output the trifocal tensor and image correspondences, which in turn facilitate a projective reconstruction of the cameras and scene.

We also investigate the direct computation of the fundamental matrix for view pairs, and the trifocal tensor for view triplets, from the homographies alone. This method is successful, but not as yet as accurate as computation from point correspondences.

Finally, it is shown that the 3-view algorithm allows reconstruction of 3D points, lines and cameras from a disparate set of 11 views. All the algorithms have been implemented and assessed on real images, and processing is automatic throughout.

1 Introduction

Over the past decade algorithms have been developed which simultaneously compute feature correspondences and the epipolar geometry between pairs of images [23, 28]; and feature correspondences and the trifocal geometry between triplets of images [25]. These algorithms are robust and reliable and require only information derived from the images. In particular no information on the camera internal parameters or camera motion need be supplied. However, the algorithms require a restricted camera motion and limited change in internal parameters between views. If these restrictions are not satisfied then the algorithms will fail. In previous work we have extended 2-view algorithms to enable feature matching and geometry estimation between two quite disparate views — "Wide baseline stereo matching" [13]. We review this approach in section 2.

In this paper we extend this work in two ways: first, a matching and geometry estimation algorithm is developed for three views. The input is three images of a scene acquired from unrestricted viewpoints, and with unrestricted camera

Reinhard Koch, Luc Van Gool (Eds.): SMILE '98, LNCS 1506, pp. 78–92, 1998.

internal parameters. The output is a set of corresponding point features and the estimated trifocal tensor [11, 18, 20] for the view triplet. This is described in section 3.

The second extension is an algorithm for 2-view and 3-view geometry estimation which does not require point (corner) correspondences. In this case the fundamental matrix and trifocal tensor are computed directly from planar homographies. The algorithm is applicable to images where corner correspondences are not available, but planar homographies can be computed by other means, e.g. from line correspondences. This is ideally suited to piecewise planar scenes [5]. The algorithm is described in section 4.

Once the trifocal tensor is available for three views it supports the automatic matching of lines and curves [16], and enables correspondences to be established over a large set of views by concatenating triplet matches [2, 7, 12]. It is then possible to reconstruct scenes, of buildings for example, acquired from many disparate views — such as a set of photographs — and also determine the viewpoint of each image. There have been a number of recent photogrammetry applications where such wide baseline matching is required [8, 22, 27]. These applications are generally aimed at reconstruction from multiple views, where the baseline is large to improve the accuracy of reconstruction or a small number of views is used to cover all aspects of the object. Currently these applications are only partly automated, and require some or all correspondences to be supplied by hand. In contrast, the algorithms of this paper enable automatic computation of cameras and 3D point and line structure over a set of wide baseline views. This is demonstrated in section 5.

2   Recapitulation of the Two View Case

2.1   Failure of Small Baseline Algorithm

The first step of algorithms such as [23, 25, 28] is to establish a set of interest point correspondences across views. It is not necessary that all of these correspondences are correct, since robust estimation is used, but a significant proportion must be. Establishing these correspondences rests on two assumptions: first, that the intensity of *fixed-size and orientation* image neighbourhoods around images of a 3D point are similar. Cross-correlation on these intensity neighbourhoods then provides an affinity measure to disambiguate image point correspondences between views; second, that the image point motion is limited between views. This latter assumption enables a restricted search region to be defined, which in turn limits the number of potential matches, and thus lessens the reliance on the disambiguating power of the affinity measure.

Both of these assumptions are violated when there is significant change in either the internal camera parameters or a significant motion between views. Consider a camera motion consisting of a translation parallel to the image x-axis, followed by a 90° rotation clockwise about the camera principal axis (i.e. a rotation with axis perpendicular to the image plane). Cross-correlation of an intensity neighbourhood will fail (because of the rotation) and the position of an imaged point can move entirely across the image, e.g. A point on the left side of the image will move to the top.

2.2   Viewpoint Invariant Affinity Measure

Both of these problems are corrected by using a homography (a plane projective transformation) to map between the images. Continuing with the above example, a homography which provides a $90°$ rotation will return the situation to the small baseline conditions. A correction of this type is based only on the camera motion and is similar to classical rectification where images are projectively warped to align the epipolar lines with corresponding scan-lines. This will be referred to as employing a *global* homography.

However, global homographies will not always be sufficient since if there is a significant change in perspective effects between images, the correct mapping is a homography induced by the tangent plane of the surface at the 3D point of interest. This is a scene dependent homography, and several *local* homographies may well be required for a particular pair of images.

Thus, the small baseline algorithm is augmented with a homography which is used for two functions

1. The homography provides the map between interest point neighbourhoods for the cross-correlation affinity measure.
2. The homography is also used to transfer the point from one image to another in order to define the centre of the search region. A similar idea is used in [4] for the case of dense stereo matching.

For both functions the homography need only approximate the point-to-point map between the images — we are only seeking to improve the disambiguation power of cross-correlation and restrict the search region.

The problem of wide baseline stereo matching is thus reduced to homography estimation followed by small baseline matching. A single (global) homography may suffice, or a set of local homographies may be required.

2.3   Wide Baseline Stereo Matching Algorithm

The algorithm consists of 3 main steps:

1. **Automatically generate a (set of local) planar homographies.**
   A global homography may be computed by standard pyramid search techniques [1, 9]. Often a similarity transformation suffices.
   Local (scene-dependent) homographies may be computed using matching techniques similiar to those used in model-based recognition [14]. For example, using feature-focus [3] to identify and match distinctive image features. In [13] four-line groupings are matched between images. Homographies are then computed from the corresponding lines.

2. **For each homography generate a set of interest point matches.**
   Interest point matches are consistent with the homography if both their position and intensity neighbourhood are similar after mapping by the homography.
3. **Estimate the fundamental matrix and consistent correspondences.**
   Sets of matches are generated from each local homography and then combined. The fundamental matrix, F, and consistent matches are estimated using the RANSAC [6] robust estimator in the manner of the small baseline algorithms [24] (the RANSAC sample consists of 7 correspondences in this case). A maximum likelihood estimate of F and the correspondences is then obtained via a robust non-linear minimization.

Further details are given in [13].

3   Extension to Three Views: Trifocal Tensor Estimation

The small baseline trifocal estimation algorithm [7, 25] is extended to a wide baseline in a similar manner to the previous section. Point correspondences are here required over three views, and again homographies enable the small baseline algorithms to be used.

The algorithm for simultaneously estimating the trifocal tensor, T, and consistent 3-view point correspondences has the following steps:

1. **Generate homographies:** Compute a (set of) homographies between views 1 & 2, and 2 & 3 using the methods of section 2.3.
2. **2 view correspondences:** Compute interest point correspondences (and the fundamental matrix) between views 1 & 2, and 2 & 3 using the wide baseline stereo algorithm. Each correspondence has an association with a homography.
3. **Putative three view correspondences:** Compute a set of interest point correspondences over three views by joining the 2-view match sets: 3-view matches are formed from those 2-view matched points that share a common point in one of the images.
4. **RANSAC robust estimation:** of T based on samples of 6 point correspondences.
5. **Maximum Likelihood Estimation (MLE):** by minimizing reprojection error, re-estimate T, and perfectly consistent correspondences, from all the measured correspondences classified as inliers.
6. **Guided matching:** Further interest point correspondences are determined using the estimated T. Putative two view matches are obtained for views 1 & 2, and then verified using view 3. Verification involves two tests: first, there is a threshold on the image distance between the measured point in the third view, and the point transferred by T from its two view match; second, there is a threshold on the affinity measure computed using the homography associated with the two-view match.

The last three steps can be iterated until the number of correspondences is stable.

Fig. 1. *Valbonne images.*

3.1   Results

Table 1 shows the number of corner correspondences for various triplets of the Valbonne image set (shown in figure 1). Typical examples of Valbonne triplets are given in figure 2. Further examples of automatically estimating the trifocal tensor and correspondences are shown for different scenes in figures 3 – 4.

Triplet	Joined Pair Matches	Inliers to $\mathcal{T}$	$\mathcal{T}$ Guided Matches	Inliers to $\mathcal{T}$	Matches after Iteration
3 4 5	71	60	71	64	102
4 5 6	94	90	85	72	109
5 6 7	98	92	102	81	134
6 7 8	46	42	48	39	84
7 8 9	70	56	62	48	57
8 9 10	109	75	72	43	72
9 10 11	120	106	110	86	137
10 11 12	189	172	169	144	185
11 12 13	207	187	185	150	219
12 13 14	191	164	165	135	209

Table 1. *Three view matching for triplets from the Valbonne set (see figures 1 - 2). The Joined Pair Matches are the matches formed by taking points in the second image which have been paired with matches in both the first and third images. An estimate of $\mathcal{T}$ is then computed using RANSAC, the number of inliers to this solution are given. The $\mathcal{T}$ Guided Matches are found using the method described in section 3. The Matches after Iteration are found by iterating the guided matching and re-estimation of $\mathcal{T}$. See discussion in section 3.1.*

We first describe matching a triplet from the Valbonne set (figure 1) in greated depth and then discuss the results for the entire set of triplets.

Triplet V11–V13 In order to clarify the results of Table 1, we examine each stage of the matching process for the triplet V11 V12 and V13 (the first triplet of figure 2).

- The Harris corner detector [10] is used to find 970, 970, and 976 corners respectively in the three images.
- Global similarity transformations that approximately register the images are computed between pairs V11 & V12, and V12 & V13.
- The widebaseline stereo matching algorithm with global homographies gives 372 corner matches between V11 & V12, and 362 matches between V12 & V13.
- The join of the pair matches gives 207 triplet matches.
- An initial estimate of $\mathcal{T}$, generated from the initial triplet matches using RANSAC, has 187 matches as inliers.

- Using this estimate of $\mathcal{T}$, guided matching finds 185 matches, of which 150 are inliers to a second estimate of $\mathcal{T}$ using RANSAC.
- After further iterations of guided matching, and re-estimation of $\mathcal{T}$, a final 219 are found.

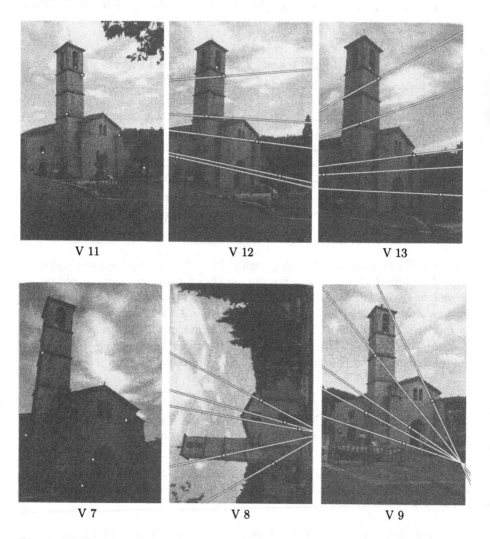

Fig. 2. Valbonne Triplets. *The trifocal tensor is estimated using corner matches and a global homography affinity score. Five of the matched points are shown together with their corresponding epipolar lines in the second and third images. The epipolar geometry is determined from the estimated trifocal tensor. The trifocal geometry is illustrated in this manner in all of the following triplet figures. The number of matched points for these examples is given in table 1.*

D 0   D 6   D 12

Fig. 3. Model house triplet. *The trifocal tensor is computed from point matches supported by three local homographies for the affinity score. 140 points are matched over the 3 images. The local homographies are computed from matched line groupings. In the first, second and third views there are 25, 21 and 30 respectively four-line groupings. Three groupings are matched between views D0 & D6, and views D6 & D12, and provide the local homographies. The angle between views D0 and D12 is approximately 60°.*

Discussion In examining table 1 horizontally, it can be seen that for all but two of the triplets (V7–V9 and V8–V10) the number of matches produced after repeated iteration of the guided matching is greater than the number of matches produced by joining the pair match sets. However, these two triplets are the ones with the smallest proportion of correct joined pair matches (as indicated by inliers to T). Guided matching is productive because putative matches that have previously been eliminated as "love-triangles" [17] are no longer erroneously excluded.

Examining the table vertically, it is evident that the number of matches produced between triplets is primarily related to the stability of corners between images. As the camera motion is increased, more corners become occluded and new corners are introduced which increases the likelihood of mismatches. Also, the matching algorithm is dependent upon the stability of the Harris corners. The stability of the corners is determined by the resolution at which patches in the world are imaged [15], corners found in one image are more likely to be lost as the camera is zoomed more significantly, or the surface viewed at an increasingly oblique angle.

4   Direct Estimation of View Relations from Homographies

This section describes how homographies alone can be used to compute the fundamental matrix and trifocal tensor. This is useful in situations where point correspondences are not available, but where homographies arising from world planes can be computed.

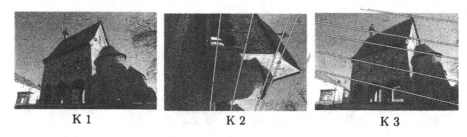

K 1   K 2   K 3

Fig. 4. Kapel (chapel) triplet. *The trifocal tensor is computed using point matches and a global homography affinity score. 62 points are matched over the triplet.*

4.1   Using Planes to Compute the Fundamental Matrix

Suppose there are two planes, π_A and π_B, in the scene, and these planes induce homographies, H_A and H_B respectively, between two views. Then the homography $H = H_B^{-1}H_A$ is a mapping from the first image onto itself with the following properties:

- H is a planar homology (see [21, 26]). It has a line of fixed points, which is the image of the intersection of the two planes, and a distinct fixed point which is the epipole e in the first image.
- A planar homology H has two equal eigenvalues. The corresponding eigenvectors define the line of fixed points. The eigenvector corresponding to the non-degenerate eigenvalue is the epipole in this case.

The action of the homology is shown in figure 5. The fundamental matrix is computed as (see [19])

$$F = [H_i e]_\times H_i \qquad \text{for } i = A \text{ or } B \tag{1}$$

4.2   Using Planes to Compute the Trifocal Tensor

Similarly, the trifocal tensor can be estimated from two planes which induce homographies over three views. Denote these homographies by H_{12}^A, H_{12}^B, between the first and second views, and H_{13}^A, H_{13}^B, between the first and third.

The trifocal tensor is determined indirectly from the camera matrices. The 3×4 camera matrices for the three views may be written using the homography induced by the first plane as

$$P = [I \mid 0], \quad P' = [H_{12}^A \mid e'], \quad P'' = [H_{13}^A \mid \lambda e''] \tag{2}$$

Since the epipoles, e' and e'', can be obtained from the two view homographies, as described above, only the scale factor λ is unknown. This scale factor can be

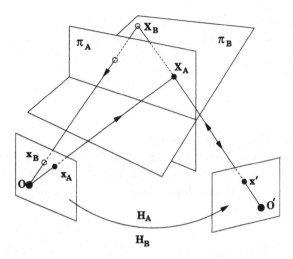

Fig. 5. *The action of the map* $H = H_B^{-1} H_A$ *on a point* $\mathbf{x}_A$ *in the first image, is to first transfer it to* $\mathbf{x}'$ *as though it was the image of the 3D point* $\mathbf{X}_A$, *and then map it back to the first image as though it was the image of the 3D point* $\mathbf{X}_B$. *Points in the first image on the image of the intersection of the two planes will be mapped to themselves, so are fixed points under this action. The epipole* $\mathbf{e}$ *is also a fixed point under this map.*

computed from the homography induced by the second plane. For this homography to be consistent with the first, the following relations must be satisfied:

$$H_{12}^B = H_{12}^A + \mathbf{e}'\mathbf{v}^\top \quad (3) \qquad\qquad H_{13}^B = H_{13}^A + \lambda \mathbf{e}''\mathbf{v}^\top \quad (4)$$

The 3-vector $\mathbf{v}$ here represents the plane π_B in the projective frame defined by cameras P and P'. Once $\mathbf{v}$ has been found we can then compute λ. The computational procedure is the following

1. Solve for $\mathbf{v}$ using (3).
   - To solve for $\mathbf{v}$ a scale factor α must be explicitly included

   $$H_{12}^B = \alpha(H_{12}^A + \mathbf{e}'\mathbf{v}^\top)$$

   - Solve for α by pre-multiplying both sides by $[\mathbf{e}']_\times$ giving

   $$[\mathbf{e}']_\times H_{12}^B = \alpha[\mathbf{e}']_\times H_{12}^A$$

   - Solve for $\mathbf{v}$ by taking the scalar product on the left with $\mathbf{e}'$ giving

   $$\mathbf{v} = (H_{12}^B/\alpha - H_{12}^A)^\top \mathbf{e}'/\|\mathbf{e}'\|^2$$

2. Given $\mathbf{v}$ determine λ from (4).
   - This proceeds in the same manner as above with a scale factor β, giving

   $$\lambda\mathbf{v} = (H_{13}^B/\beta - H_{13}^A)^\top \mathbf{e}''/\|\mathbf{e}''\|^2$$

3. Compute the camera matrices P, P', P''.

4. The trifocal tensor is then computed from the three camera matrices as described in [11].

4.3   Results

Estimation of F The homographies used to compute F are generated by using RANSAC on the 153 widebaseline point matches to pick out the two largest sets of points consistent with homographies from the pair D0 & D6 - shown in figure 6. The homographies, H_A, H_B, correspond to the planes of the house wall and ground.

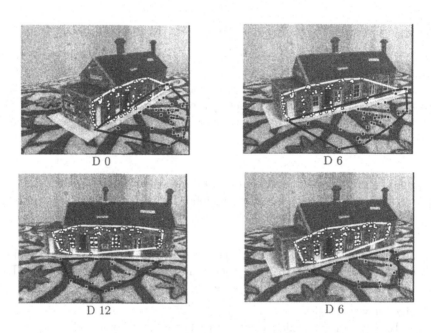

Fig. 6. *For each image pair, D0 & D6, and D6 & D12, the two homographies with most support are searched for amongst the matches resulting from the wide baseline stereo matching. For each pair the points contributing to the first homography are represented by circles and their convex hull is drawn in white, and the points consistent with the second homography are represented by squares and their convex hull is drawn in black.*

Using these homographies estimated independently, the matrix $H = H_B^{-1} H_A$ has eigenvalues -1.47, -0.93, -0.99. This indicates that the matrix is close to a homology (for which the last two eigenvalues would be exactly equal), but that the two homographies are not exactly consistent with the epipolar geometry. The next step is to estimate the homographies such that they are consistent, we return to this in section 6.

Estimation of T The homographies used to estimate T are determined, in a similar manner to above, by using RANSAC to pick out the two largest sets of points consistent with homographies from pairs D0 & D6, and D6 & D12. These points are shown in figure 6.

Figure 7 shows the accuracy of T by displaying the epipolar lines (derived from the trifocal tensor) for points lying both on and off the planes.

| D 0 | D 6 | D12 |

Fig. 7. *Model house triplet. The trifocal tensor is computed from the homographies relating the planes shown in figure 6.*

5 Matching and Reconstruction over Multiple Views

When more than three views are available, the three view matches and tensors can be integrated into a consistent reconstruction over all views [7]. This enables the cameras for all views to be determined in the same coordinate system, and

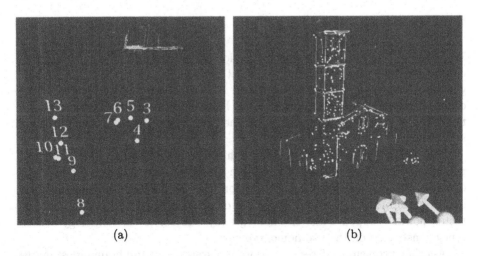

| (a) | (b) |

Fig. 8. *Views of recovered 3D point and line structure and cameras. There are 316 points and 92 lines. (a) a plan view of the church and the centers of cameras computed from 11 views of the scene. (b) a close up, including the directions of the camera's principal axes.*

for accurate 3D structure estimation by minimizing reprojection error over all views in which a feature appears.

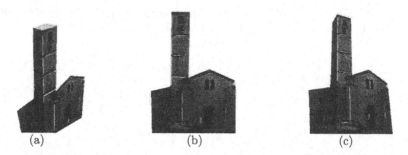

(a)   (b)   (c)

Fig. 9. *Views of the piecewise planar model generated from the 3D point and line structure shown in figure 9. The model has been texture-mapped using the original images from the Valbonne set - figure 1.*

The tensors and correspondences are determined for triplets from 11 images of the Valbonne set (figure 1) using the algorithm of section 3. The structure contains 316 points. Using the line matching algorithm of Schmid [16], together with the computed camera matrices, 92 lines are recovered. Views of the 3D points, lines and cameras are shown in figure 8. The lines are used to create the polygonal model shown in figure 9, which is texture mapped from the original images.

6   Discussion

We have demonstrated that a reconstruction of cameras and 3D scene structure can be generated automatically from a set of disparate views. Two types of algorithms have been engineered, one based on interest point correspondences the other on direct computation from planar homographies. The point based algorithm is the more mature, and achieves the sub-pixel accuracy of small baseline algorithms.

The direct estimation from homographies is more preliminary and standard problems arising in multiple view relation estimation are still to be solved. For example, a maximum likelihood estimation of F (or $\mathcal{T}$) from two planes would involve minimizing the "reprojection" error between measured points and corrected points mapped under the homography, subject to the homology consistency constraints on the two homographies.

Another problem that requires more investigation is in obtaining estimates of F or $\mathcal{T}$ when homographies arising from more than two world planes are available. In the case of estimating these 2-view and 3-view relations from point correspondences - it is well understood how best to use more than the minimum number of correspondences to improve the estimate of the view relation, but this has yet to be formulated for the estimation from homographies case.

A final extension of this work is that of estimating homographies for scene types where obtaining point or line correspondences may not be possible e.g. for a room with untextured walls.

Acknowledgements We are grateful for images provided by RobotVis INRIA Sophia Antipolis, and Fraunhofer IGD, and for financial support from EU ACTS Project Vanguard amd Sharp Labs of Europe. We are also indebted to Jesper Göransson for the software used in the post-processing of the 3D model.

References

[1] E.H. Adelson and P.J. Burt. Image data compression with the laplacian pyramid. In *PRIP81*, pages 218–223, 1981.

[2] P. Beardsley, P. Torr, and A. Zisserman. 3D model acquisition from extended image sequences. In *Proc. ECCV*, LNCS 1064/1065, pages 683–695. Springer-Verlag, 1996.

[3] R. C. Bolles and R. Horaud. 3DPO: A three-dimensional part orientation system. In T. Kanade, editor, *Three Dimensional Vision*, pages 399–450. Kluwer Academic Publishers, 1987.

[4] P. E. Debevec, C. J. Taylor, and J. Malik. Modeling and rendering architecture from photographs: A hybrid geometry- and image- based approach. In *Proceedings, ACM SIGGRAPH*, pages 11–20, 1996.

[5] O.D. Faugeras and F. Lustman. Motion and structure from motion in a piecewise planar environment. *International Journal of Pattern Recognition and Artificial Intelligence*, 2:485–508, 1988.

[6] M. A. Fischler and R. C. Bolles. Random sample consensus: A paradigm for model fitting with applications to image analysis and automated cartography. *Comm. ACM*, 24(6):381–395, 1981.

[7] A. W. Fitzgibbon and A. Zisserman. Automatic camera recovery for closed or open image sequences. In *Proc. ECCV*, pages 311–326, 1998.

[8] N. Georgis, M. Petrou, and J. Kittler. Error guided design of a 3d vision system. *IEEE T-PAMI*, 20:366–379, 4 1998.

[9] F. Glazer, G. Reynolds, and P. Anandan. Scene matching by hierarchical correlation. In *Proc. CVPR*, pages 432–441, 1983.

[10] C. J. Harris and M. Stephens. A combined corner and edge detector. In *Alvey Vision Conf.*, pages 147–151, 1988.

[11] R. I. Hartley. A linear method for reconstruction from lines and points. In *Proc. ICCV*, pages 882–887, 1995.

[12] S. Laveau. *Geometry of a system of N cameras. Theory, estimation, and applications.* PhD thesis, INRIA, 1996.

[13] P. Pritchett and A. Zisserman. Wide baseline stereo matching. In *Proc. ICCV*, pages 754–760, January 1998.

[14] C. Rothwell, A. Zisserman, D. Forsyth, and J. Mundy. Planar object recognition using projective shape representation. *IJCV*, 16(2), 1995.

[15] C. Schmid, R. Mohr, and C. Bauckhage. Comparing and evaluating interest points. In *Proc. ICCV*, pages 230–235, 1998.

[16] C. Schmid and A. Zisserman. Automatic line matching across views. In *Proc. CVPR*, pages 666–671, 1997.

[17] L. S. Shapiro. *Affine Analysis of Image Sequences*. PhD thesis, University of Oxford, England, 1993.

[18] A. Shashua. Trilinearity in visual recognition by alignment. In *Proc. ECCV*, volume 1, pages 479–484, May 1994.

[19] D. Sinclair, H. Christensen, and C. Rothwell. Using the relation between a plane projectivity and the fundamental matrix. SCIA, 1995.

[20] M. E. Spetsakis and J. Aloimonos. Structure from motion using line correspondences. *IJCV*, 4(3):171–183, 1990.

[21] C. E. Springer. *Geometry and Analysis of Projective Spaces*. Freeman, 1964.

[22] C. Taylor, P. Debevec, and J. Malik. Reconstructing polyhedral models of architectural scenes from photographs. In *Proc. ECCV*. Springer-Verlag, 1996.

[23] P. H. S. Torr and D. W. Murray. Outlier detection and motion segmentation. In *Proc SPIE Sensor Fusion VI*, pages 432–443, Boston, Sep 1993.

[24] P. H. S. Torr and A. Zisserman. Performance characterizaton of fundamental matrix estimation under image degradation. *Machine Vision and Applications*, 9:321–333, 1997.

[25] P. H. S. Torr and A. Zisserman. Robust parameterization and computation of the trifocal tensor. *Image and Vision Computing*, 15:591–605, 1997.

[26] L. Van Gool, M. Proesmans, and A. Zisserman. Grouping and invariants using planar homologies. In *Workshop on Geometrical Modeling and Invariants for Computer Vision*. Xidian University Press, 1995.

[27] C. Zeller. *Projective, Affine and Euclidean Calibration in Compute Vision and the Application of Three Dimensional Perception*. PhD thesis, RobotVis Group, INRIA Sophia-Antipolis, 1996.

[28] Z. Zhang, R. Deriche, O. Faugeras, and Q. Luong. A robust technique for matching two uncalibrated images through the recovery of the unknown epipolar geometry. *Artificial Intelligence*, 78:87–119, 1995.

Improving Block-Based Disparity Estimation by Considering the Non-uniform Distribution of the Estimation Error

Lutz Falkenhagen and Thomas Wedi

Institut für Theoretische Nachrichtentechnik und Informationsverarbeitung,
Universität Hannover, Appelstr. 9A, 30167 Hannover, Germany
falken,wedi@tnt.uni-hannover.de

Abstract. A block-based disparity estimator is proposed that considers the non-uniform spatial distribution of the estimation error inside an image block that is mapped into another image plane using projective 2-D transformations. For this purpose, first the error variance distribution inside the image block is analytically derived. The derived error variance distribution shows four eccentric minima. As a consequence, the proposed disparity estimator arranges the image block eccentrically around the picture element (pel) to be evaluated. Thus, a reduction of the estimation error variance by a factor between 1.5 and 2 can be achieved compared to known block-based disparity estimation techniques. Since the error distribution shows four minima, four possible arrangements of the image blocks and hence four independent estimates can be made. A further reduction of the estimation error variance by a factor up to 2.6 can be achieved, when the four estimates are averaged. Additionally, an outlier detection and removal in the set of four estimates enables an increased robustness. The proposed estimator is tested using both, synthetic image pairs of known disparity and real images. The expected error reduction performance of the estimator and its increased robustness are verified.

1   Introduction

A key problem in motion and depth estimation of real objects is to find corresponding image content in a pair of images which result from a projection of the same object into both image planes [1]. Object motion leads to a *displacement* between corresponding image content in a consecutive pair of images of a monoscopic image sequence [2]. On the other hand, object depth causes a *disparity* between corresponding image content in a stereoscopic pair of images [3]. Since the estimation of disparity and displacement can be put down to the problem of finding corresponding image content, similar estimation techniques are applied.

In order to estimate displacement for a particular picture element (pel), block-based estimation approaches arrange a reference block of $N \cdot N$ pel around the pel to be evaluated. This reference block is mapped into the other image plane using a 2-D transformation and its luminance signal is compared to the

Reinhard Koch, Luc Van Gool (Eds.): SMILE '98, LNCS 1506, pp. 93–108, 1998.
© Springer-Verlag Berlin Heidelberg 1998

luminance signal in the other image. The 2-D transformation parameters specify the displacement of the evaluated pel. They are estimated by minimising the differences between the luminance signals.

Essentially, three different 2-D transformations for displacement estimation are known from literature which differ in their number of transformation parameters:

- *translational transformation* using 2 transformation parameter [4] [5] [6]
- *affine transformation* using 6 transformation parameters [7] [8] [9] [10] [11]
- *bilinear transformation* using 8 transformation parameters [12] [13]

In general, the relation between two projections of the same physical object into two different image planes can not be modelled perfectly by a 2-D transformation of an image block. This leads to so-called model failures and thus to inaccurate estimation results. In order to determine the accuracy of displacement estimates, Buschmann recently derived a method for determining the *displacement estimation error variance* [14]. Since the real displacement vector field is unknown, the real displacement vector field is modeled as a zero-mean stochastic AR(1) process with given power spectral density. By relating the estimation results of the transformation parameters to the spatial displacement distribution inside the reference image block, an estimation error measure is derived that depends on the parameters of the stochastic process.

In [13], Buschmann extended the analysis of the displacement estimation error variance. He determined the displacement estimation error not only for the evaluated pel but also for all pels inside the reference image block depending on their position inside the block. With this extension, the *spatial distribution* of the displacement estimation error variance inside the reference image blocks is obtained. For an numerical evaluation of the spatial distribution, Buschmann empirically determined the parameters of the stochastic process by evaluating the displacement vector field of a set of videophone sequences. It turned out that the minimum of the displacement error is only in the center of the block in case of translational transformation. In case of affine and bilinear transformation, four eccentric minima were found. So far, the eccentric position of the minima is not analytically determined and not experimentally verified. All known displacement estimation approaches arrange the reference image block concentrically around the evaluated pel, where the estimation error variance is not minimal. Thus, the knowledge about the eccentric position of the minima is not yet used for an improvement of the displacement estimator.

In this paper, Buschmann's approach for calculating the displacement estimation error variance [13] is applied to disparity estimation and extended in order to improve the estimator. In case of disparity estimation, the transformation is constrained by the epipolar geometry of the stereo camera setup. Thus, the number of required transformation parameters is reduced by a factor of two. Furthermore, the stochastic properties of disparity fields are different from those of displacement vector fields. This difference is caused by the specific setup of a stereoscopic camera that introduces a disparity offset and scales the disparity variance depending on the distance between the cameras. Thus, the stochastic process has to be adapted.

In order to improve the block-based disparity estimator, the distribution of the estimation error variance is analytically derived depending on the parameters of the stochastic process. In particular, the positions of minimal estimation error variance inside the reference image block are determined. Depending on their positions, the reference image blocks are arranged eccentrically around the evaluated pel, such that an estimator with minimum estimation error variance is obtained. The decrease of the estimation error variance of the new estimator is analytically determined and verified using synthetic noisy images and real images.

In Section 2, the applied transformations are introduced. The estimation error variance distribution is specified in Section 3 for bilinear, affine and translational transformations. The proposed estimator is introduced in Section 4. Section 5 presents experimental results, followed by conclusions in Section 6.

2   Block-Based Disparity Estimation

The task of binocular disparity estimation in a 3-D reconstruction approch is to find corresponding image points in a stereoscopic pair of images and compute the according 3-D point position by a triangulation of the lines of sight of both image points. For correspondence analysing block-based disparity estimation approaches arrange a reference block around the pel to be evaluated. This reference block is mapped into the other image plane using a projective 2-D transformation. The transformation specifies the disparity between the evaluated pel and the corresponding pel in the other image plane.

In this section, at first the applied block-based 2-D transformations with their transformation parameters are defined. Then, the estimation of transformation parameters with an Maximum-Likelihood estimator is introduced.

2.1   Definition of Image Block Transformation

In Figure 1, a reference block and the homologous block are shown. The vector $\boldsymbol{p}_i = (x_i, y_i)^T$ denotes the position of an image point in the local coordinate system of the reference block. The vector $\boldsymbol{p}_i^h = (x_i^h, y_i^h)^T$ denotes the position of the transformed, homologous point.

A review in recent publications shows that currently mainly three different 2-D transformations are used to approximate the real mapping of image content from one image into another: translational, affine and bilinear transformation. Assuming standard stereo geometry with horizontal epipolar lines, the y-coordinate is not effected by the transformation, i.e. $y_i^h = y_i$. The mapping function of the x-coordinate is expressed by $x_i^h = \boldsymbol{B}^T \cdot \boldsymbol{A}$. In this function the vector $\boldsymbol{A}$ contains the transformation parameters and $\boldsymbol{B}$ describes the relation between the local coordinates inside the block and the transformation parameters. For the three applied 2-D transformations, the mapping functions and the vectors $\boldsymbol{A}$ and $\boldsymbol{B}$ are given in Tab. 1

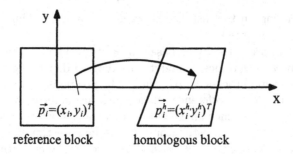

Fig. 1. Transformation of a reference block into a homologous block in case of horizontal epipolar lines.

Table 1. Definition of 2-D transformations

transformation	mapping function	B^T	A
translational	$x_i^h = a_1 + x_i$	$(1, x_i)$	$(a_1, 1)^T$
affine	$x_i^h = a_1 + a_2 x_i + a_3 y_i$	$(1, x_i, y_i)$	$(a_1, a_2, a_3)^T$
bilinear	$x_i^h = a_1 + a_2 x_i + a_3 y_i + a_4 x_i y_i$	$(1, x_i, y_i, x_i y_i)$	$(a_1, a_2, a_3, a_4)^T$

In the following only bilinear transformation is considered, since affine and translational transformation are subsets of it and can be easily extracted by omitting the higher order transformation parameters.

The disparity $d(\boldsymbol{p}_i)$ at position $\boldsymbol{p}_i$ inside the reference block is given by the difference between the x-coordinates of $\boldsymbol{p}_i$ and $\boldsymbol{p}_i^h$. With the parameter vector of the identical transformation

$$E = (\,0, 1, 0, 0\,)^T, \tag{1}$$

which maps a point onto itself, the disparity can be written as a function of the used transformation and their transformation parameters

$$d(\boldsymbol{p}_i) = x_i - x_i^h = B^T \cdot E - B^T \cdot A = -B^T \cdot \Delta a \tag{2}$$

The differential transformation parameter vector Δa is given by

$$\Delta a = A - E \tag{3}$$

2.2   Maximum-Likelihood (ML) Disparity Estimator

In order to estimate the disparity $d(\boldsymbol{p}_i)$, the differential transformation parameters Δa have to be estimated (2). This is done by evaluating the luminance difference between the left and right image-block [13], [15], [16]

$$fd(\boldsymbol{p}_i) = s_l(\boldsymbol{p}_i) - s_r(\boldsymbol{p}_i) = s_r(\boldsymbol{p}_i^h) - s_r(\boldsymbol{p}_i). \tag{4}$$

With the mapping functions of table 1 and a linearisation concerning the transformation parameters, equation (4) can be calculated to

$$fd(\boldsymbol{p}_i) = \sum_{k=1}^{m} \left(\frac{\partial s_r(\boldsymbol{p}_i)}{\partial a_k} \right)_E \Delta a_k = \boldsymbol{H}^T(\boldsymbol{p}_i)\boldsymbol{\Delta a} \tag{5}$$

In (5) the index k denotes one of the m transformation parameters. Assuming that the observation of the luminance signal is only disturbed by Gaussian noise, the ML-estimation of the differential transformation parameters leads to the method of leads squares [15], [16]. Therefore, the estimation result is given by

$$\boldsymbol{\hat{\Delta a}} = \left(\underline{H}^T \underline{H} \right)^{-1} \underline{H}^T \cdot \boldsymbol{fd} \tag{6}$$

In $\underline{H}$ and $\boldsymbol{fd}$ the N_B observations inside the transformation block are collected:

$$\begin{aligned}
\underline{H} &= \left(\boldsymbol{H}^T(\boldsymbol{p}_1),\ \boldsymbol{H}^T(\boldsymbol{p}_2),\ \cdots,\ \boldsymbol{H}^T(\boldsymbol{p}_{N_B}) \right)^T \\
\boldsymbol{fd} &= \left(fd(\boldsymbol{p}_1),\ \ fd(\boldsymbol{p}_2),\ \cdots,\ \ fd(\boldsymbol{p}_{N_B}) \right)
\end{aligned} \tag{7}$$

With (6) and (2) the estimated disparity is given by

$$\hat{d}(\boldsymbol{p}_i) = -\boldsymbol{B}^T \left(\underline{H}^T \underline{H} \right)^{-1} \underline{H}^T \cdot \boldsymbol{fd}. \tag{8}$$

In order to compensate for the linearisation errors, the estimation is carried out iteratively. The estimated differential transformation parameters are accumulated over all iterations. In case of large disparities, where a differential estimation technique fails because of the assumption of a monotonic image signal, a robust disparity search technique [17] is applied for an initialisation of the disparities.

3   Local Disparity Estimation Error Variance Distribution

For a derivation of the spatial distribution of the disparity estimation error inside the blocks, the disparity estimation error is defined by

$$de(\boldsymbol{p}_i) = d(\boldsymbol{p}_i) - \hat{d}(\boldsymbol{p}_i). \tag{9}$$

The stochastic properties of the disparity estimation error are described by the error variance

$$\sigma_{de}^2(\boldsymbol{p}_i) = E\left[(de(\boldsymbol{p}_i) - m_{de}(\boldsymbol{p}_i))^2 \right]. \tag{10}$$

In order to compute the error variance of the estimator without knowing the real displacement vector field, Buschmann described the real displacement vector field using a stationary stochastic process. In particular an AR(1)-process is used which is described by its variance σ_{de}^2 and its autocorrelation coefficient ρ_{dd}. In contrast to displacement estimation, where a zero mean vector field is expected, an additional mean value m_d is considered in case of disparity fields since the shift between the two cameras introduces an offset. Assuming an isotropic ACF-model, the ACF of the process is defined by

$$R_{dd}(\Delta x, \Delta y) = \sigma_d^2 \rho_{dd}^{\sqrt{\Delta x^2 + \Delta y^2}} + m_d^2 \tag{11}$$

With this model, Buschmann analytically derived the spatial error distribution for translational, affine and bilinear transformation. By restricting the image block transformations to horizontal epipolar geometry, the horizontal component of the displacements is turning into disparity and the vertical displacement is equal to zero. Since Buschmann assumed statistically independent displacement components, also the estimation error variance distribution of the horizontal displacement component corresponds to the one of the disparity estimate. For translational transformation the error variance is

$$\sigma_{de,d}^2(x_i, y_i) = \sigma_d^2 + m_d^2 - \frac{2}{MN} \int_{-\frac{M}{2}}^{\frac{M}{2}} \int_{-\frac{N}{2}}^{\frac{N}{2}} R_{dd}(x_i - \tau_x, y_i - \tau_x) d\tau_y d\tau_x \tag{12}$$

$$+ \frac{1}{M^2 N^2} \int_{-M}^{M} \int_{-N}^{N} (M - |\tau_x|)(N - |\tau_y|) R_{dd}(\tau_x, \tau_y) d\tau_y d\tau_x$$

In case the affine transformation the error variance is

$$\sigma_{de,d}^2(x_i, y_i) = \sigma_d^2 + m_d^2 \tag{13}$$

$$- \frac{2}{MN} \int_{-\frac{M}{2}}^{\frac{M}{2}} \int_{-\frac{N}{2}}^{\frac{N}{2}} \left(1 + \frac{x_i \tau_x}{M^2/12} + \frac{y_i \tau_y}{N^2/12}\right) R_{dd}(x_i - \tau_x, y_i - \tau_x) d\tau_y d\tau_x$$

$$+ \frac{1}{M^2 N^2} \int_{-M}^{M} \int_{-N}^{N} \left((M - |\tau_x|)(N - |\tau_y|) \right.$$

$$+ \frac{x_i^2 [(M - |\tau_x|)^3 - 3(M - |\tau_x|)\tau_x^2]}{M^4/12}(N - |\tau_y|)$$

$$\left. + \frac{y_i^2 [(N - |\tau_y|)^3 - 3(N - |\tau_y|)\tau_y^2]}{N^4/12}(M - |\tau_x|) \right) \cdot$$

$$R_{dd}(\tau_x, \tau_y) d\tau_y d\tau_x$$

and for bilinear tranformation it is defined by

$$\sigma_{de,d}^2(x_i, y_i) = \sigma_d^2 + m_d^2 \tag{14}$$

$$- \frac{2}{MN} \int_{-\frac{M}{2}}^{\frac{M}{2}} \int_{-\frac{N}{2}}^{\frac{N}{2}} \left(1 + \frac{x_i \tau_x}{M^2/12}\right)\left(1 + \frac{y_i \tau_y}{N^2/12}\right) R_{dd}(x_i - \tau_x, y_i - \tau_x) d\tau_y d\tau_x$$

$$+ \frac{1}{M^2 N^2} \int_{-M}^{M} \int_{-N}^{N} \left((M - |\tau_x|) + \frac{x_i^2[(M - |\tau_x|)^3 - 3(M - |\tau_x|)\tau_x^2]}{M^4/12}\right) \cdot$$

$$\left((N - |\tau_y|) + \frac{y_i^2[(N - |\tau_y|)^3 - 3(N - |\tau_y|)\tau_y^2]}{N^4/12}\right) \cdot$$

$$R_{dd}(\tau_x, \tau_y) d\tau_y d\tau_x$$

These integrals give the error variance distribution inside the reference image blocks in relation to the ACF of the AR(1)-process. An evaluation of equation (14) with (11) shows, that the variance σ_d^2 of the real disparity scales the error variance σ_{de}^2 linearly. Therefore, the normalized error variance σ_{de}^2/σ_d^2 is shown in Fig. 2 in dependence on the local coordinate $\boldsymbol{p}_i = (x_i, y_i)^T$ inside the image block. A typical autocorrelation coefficient of $\rho_{dd} = 0.95$ is chosen. In addition to

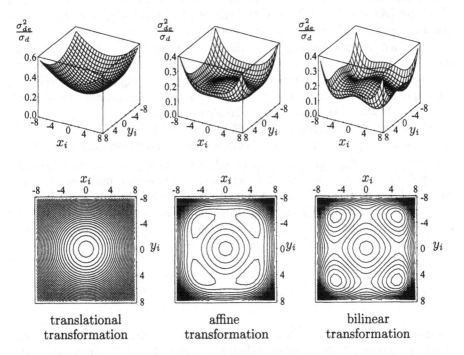

Fig. 2. Spatial disparity error variance distribution inside blocks of the size 17x17 pel. Visualised as 3-D diagram and height contours for three different transformations (other scale for translational transformation).

the 3-D diagrams of the spatial error variance distribution, the height contours are shown. There, the position of the minimum can be recognised more easily.

The first remarkable result is that the error variance in the central postition is exactly the same for all three transformations. This means that the estimation error variance can not be decreased by using more sophisticated transformations, if the transformed image block is concentrically arranged arround the evaluated pel. This seems to contradict to previous investigations which showed that affine transformation is superior to translational even in case of concentrically arranged blocks [7]. Of course, this derivation is only valid, when the real desparity field can be modeled using an AR(1)-process. This applies to natural objects with curved surfaces. In case of large planar surfaces which are arbitrarilly oriented in 3-D space, the model of an AR(1) process is not appropriate. Thus, affine or bilinear estimation can provide more accurate estimates than translational transformation even if the reference block is concentrically arranged around the evaluated pel.

The second result is that there are four eccentric minima in case of affine and bilinear transformation, which are eccentrically arranged arround the center of the block. An investigation with varying autocorrelation coefficients shows that their position (x_{min}, y_{min}) is proportional to the chosen block size N and varies slightly with ρ_{dd}. It varies less than $0.03N$ for $0.75 < \rho_{dd} < 1$, the typical range of autocorrelation coefficients of real disparity fields. In case of a block size of 17x17 pel (N=17) the position of the minimum is $x_{min} = y_{min} = 4$ for affine and $x_{min} = y_{min} = 5$ for bilinear transformation.

The third result is that ρ_{dd} effects the error variance itself. The error variance rises with decreasing autocorrelation ρ_{dd} between neighbouring disparities. The reason is that with small statistcal bindings between neighbouring disparities the implicit assumption about deterministic course of the disparity that results from the 2-D transformation involves larger model failures.

The fourth result is that ρ_{dd} also effects the ratio between the error variance in the center $\sigma^2_{de,cen}$ and the error variance in the eccentric minimum $\sigma^2_{de,ecc}$. The ratio $g_{ecc} = \sigma^2_{de,cen}/\sigma^2_{de,ecc}$ is denoted as the gain, since an according gain is expected from an estimator that arranges the reference block eccentrically instead of concentrically. In case of affine transformation the gain varies between 1.2 and 1.35. In case of bilinear transformation a gain between 1.45 and 1.95 can be archieved. Since the gain is higher in case of bilinear transformation it is applied to the new estimator.

4   Disparity Estimation with Eccentric Image Blocks

As shown in Fig. 2, the error distribution inside the image blocks shows four eccentric minima. This knowledge shall now be exploited for an improvement of the estimator. In all known approaches [4] [7] [10] [12], the image blocks are arranged concentrically arround the evaluated pel, where the estimation error variance is not minimal according to the analytically derived error distribution.

A new estimator is therefore proposed that arranges the image blocks eccentrically arround the evaluated pel. Since four minima exist, there are four possible arrangements of the image block such that the evaluated pel lies in one of the minima (Fig. 3).

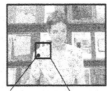

pel to be evaluated   reference window

Fig. 3. Four possible eccentric arrangements of the reference block around the pel to be evaluated

With the eccentric arrangement of the image blocks, a gain in terms of reducing the estimation error variance is obtained. This gain depends on the ratio between the error variance in the center $\sigma^2_{de,cen}$ and the error in the minima $\sigma^2_{de,ecc}$ and is expressed by $g_{ecc} = \sigma^2_{de,cen}/\sigma^2_{de,ecc}$.

A further improvement is expected by estimating with all four possible arrangements of the image block. Thus, the proposed estimator averages the four possible estimates arithmetically (15).

$$d_{res} = \frac{1}{4}(d_1 + d_2 + d_3 + d_4) \tag{15}$$

Assuming that the error involved by each observed pel in the image block is uncorrelated and has the same statistical properties, the estimation error variance decreases reciprocally with the number of observed pels when using an Maximum-Likelihood (ML) estimator. Since the four eccentric image blocks partly overlap, the number of observed pels is not increased by a factor of 4. The computation of the number of observed pels is derived in Fig. 4 results in 2.64 times more observed pels. Thus a maximum gain due to averaging of $g_{av} < 2.64$ is expected from the new estimator.

The same gain can not be expected from a single estimation with a block size b_4, because a single estimation with larger blocks leads to additional model failures that decrease the accuracy of the estimator. In case of the new estimator the block size of each individual estimation is not changed and thus no additional model failures are caused.

Beside the possibility of arithmetically averaging the four estimates, also a more appropriate averaging might be used that leads to more robust estimates. Such improvements are envisaged as a next step, but have not been investigated so far.

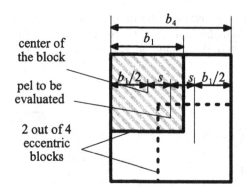

Shift s between center of the block and position of minimal estimation error

$$s = \frac{5}{16} \cdot b_1$$

Resulting areas A of evaluated pels

$A_1 = b_1^2$

$A_4 = b_4^2 = (b_1+2{\cdot}s)^2 = 2.64 \cdot b_1^2$

Fig. 4. Relation between the number of observation points in a single block of size b_1 and four partly overlapping blocks of size b1 which cover the same area as a single block of size b_4

5   Experimental Results

In this section the theoretically derived error variance distribution and the gain obtained by the proposed estimator are experimentally verified. For a numerical verification of the error variance distribution and the derived gain of the new estimator, the real disparity of the evaluated image pair has to be known. Therefore, two synthetic image pairs were created by rendering two virtual 3-D objects. In order to consider the camera noise, an additional Gaussian noise was added to the synthetic images. Since the real disparity is known, the disparity estimation error can be measured.

In Fig. 5 the left luminance image and the real disparity field of a synthetic image pair called SynAR is shown.

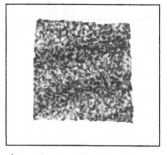

a) synthesised luminance image   b) real disparity field

Fig. 5. Synthetic image SynAR

A lowpass filtered random noise is chosen for the texture of the SynAR object. The surface of the object approximates a depth map which results from a stationary AR(1) process. Thus the disparity estimation results should confirm the analytically derived disparity estimation error variance distribution. The real disparity field has an autocorrelation coefficient of $\rho_{dd} = 0.995$.

The second image pair was created from a virtual 3-D object that is reconstructed from a real video communication scene. It is called SynLudo and is shown in Fig. 6. The real disparity field of SynLudo shows discontinuities and is not stationary. Therefore the AR(1)-process can not approximate it as accurately as in case of SynAR. The real disparity field has an autocorrelation coefficient of $\rho_{dd} = 0.98$.

a) synthesised luminance image   b) real disparity field

Fig. 6. Synthetic image SynLudo

A block size of 17x17 pel was chosen for the experimental verification. In table 2 the estimation errors variances of the different estimators are shown.

Table 2. Measured estimation error variances of the different estimators

Estimation		SynAR	SynLudo
One concentrically arranged block:	$\sigma^2_{de,cen}$	0.4803 pel^2	0.1214 pel^2
One eccentrically arranged block:	$\sigma^2_{de,ecc}$	0.3096 pel^2	0.0901 pel^2
Four averaged, eccentrically arranged blocks:	$\sigma^2_{de,av}$	0.2070 pel^2	0.0698 pel^2

The gain of the proposed estimator is computed from the measured error variances. In case of SynAR the following gain is optained:

$$g_{ecc} = \frac{\sigma^2_{de,cen}}{\sigma^2_{de,ecc}} = \frac{0.4803}{0.3096} = 1.5514 \quad , \quad g_{av} = \frac{\sigma^2_{de,ecc}}{\sigma^2_{de,av}} = \frac{0.3096}{0.2070} = 1.4967$$

In case of SynLudo the gain is

$$g_{ecc} = \frac{\sigma^2_{de,cen}}{\sigma^2_{de,ecc}} = \frac{0.1214}{0.0901} = 1.3474 \quad , \quad g_{av} = \frac{\sigma^2_{de,ecc}}{\sigma^2_{de,av}} = \frac{0.0901}{0.0698} = 1.2908$$

Fig. 7 shows the comparison between the theoretically derived and experimentally found disparity estimation error variance distribution.

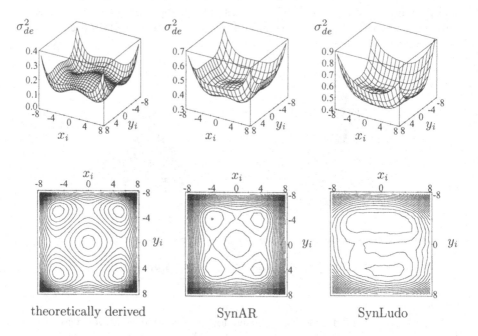

theoretically derived   SynAR   SynLudo

Fig. 7. Comparison between the theoretically derived disparity estimation error variance distribution inside the image blocks and the experimentally found one. Visualised as 3-D diagram and height contours.

The theoretically derived and the measured error distributions are quite similar. The measured position of the minima almost fits to the analytically derived one. But there is a difference between the expected error variance ratio of $g_{ecc} = 1.93$ and the measured one of $g_{ecc} = 1.55$ in case of SynAR. This difference is caused by restricted accuracy of the virtuel 3-D object and error during the image synthesis. On the one hand, the object surface is represented by a triangular mesh causing piecewise linear surfaces that differ from an ideal AR(1) process. On the other hand the applied image synthesis approach just uses bilinear texture interpolation and does no anti-aliasing filtering. In case of SynLudo a gain of $g_{ecc} = 1.35$ is achieved.

From averaging, a maximum gain of $g_{av} = 2.64$ can be expected. It turns out that only a gain of $g_{av} < 1.5$ is achieved during the experimental investigations.

This indicates that the error between neighbouring pels is correlated. The total gain of the presented estimator is therefore $g = g_{ecc} \cdot g_{av} = 1.55 \cdot 1.5 = 2.33$.

With real images, a subjective assessment of the estimates is carried out by visualising the 3-D cloud of points which results from a triangulation of corresponding image points. It turns out that the robustness is obviously improved due to averaging the four estimates using a simple outlier detection and removal that evaluates the empirical variance of the four estimates.

6   Conclusions

A block-based disparity estimator is proposed in this paper that considers the non-uniform spatial distribution of the disparity estimation error inside an image block.

The presented approach is based on Buschmann's analytical derivation of the spatial distribution of the displacement estimation error inside image blocks which are mapped into another image plane using a 2-D transformation [13]. By restricting the image block transformations to horizontal epipolar geometry, the horizontal component of the displacements is turning into disparity and the vertical displacement is equal to zero. Since Buschmann assumed statistically independent displacement components, also the estimation error variance distribution of the horizontal displacement component corresponds to the one of the disparity estimate.

For the derivation of the estimation error variance, the stochastic process for modelling displacement vector fields [13] is adapted to model disparity fields. The zero-mean AR(1) process is extended by an additional mean value which models the offset in disparity fields that origins from the stereoscopic camera setup. The real disparity field is thus described by its autocorrelation coefficient ρ_{dd}, its variance σ_d^2 and its mean value m_d.

The dependency of the spatial distribution of the disparity estimation error variance inside the reference block on the parameters of the AR(1) process is derived in a next step. It turns out that m_d does not influence the distribution and that σ_d^2 scales the error variance linearly. The error distribution non-linearly depends on ρ_{dd}. Comparing the three different investigated transformations, it is shown that the estimation error variance in the center of the blocks is identical for translational, affine and bilinear transformations. This observation seems to contradict to previous investigations which showed that affine transformation is superior to translational transformation in case of almost planar surfaces and an estimation technique that uses concentrically arranged image blocks [7]. The reason for this contradiction is that the disparity field of planar surfaces, having a deterministic linear course, can not be modeled by an AR(1) process. An AR(1) process rather models disparity fields caused by more complex surfaces.

The position of the four minima is analytically determined for affine and bilinear transformation. It is proportional to the chosen block size N and varies slightly with ρ_{dd}. It varies less than $0,03N$ for $0.75 < \rho_{dd} < 1$. In case of bilinear transformation the position is around $(\pm 5, \pm 5)$ and in case of affine transformation around $(\pm 4, \pm 4)$ with respect to a local coordinate system in the center of the block and a block size of 17x17 pel.

Based on the evaluation of the estimation error distribution, a new estimator is proposed. It arranges the image block eccentrically around the evaluated pel such that it lies in one of the minima of the estimation error variance distribution. Since the position of the minima is almost constant the arrangement does not depend on the statistic properties of the disparity field.

The gain of the proposed estimator compared to conventional estimation with a concentrically arranged block is expressed by a gain factor g. The gain obtained by eccentrically arranging the blocks is expressed by the ratio between the error variance in the minimum $\sigma^2_{de,ecc}$ and the error variance in the center of the block $\sigma^2_{de,cen}$, leading to $g_{ecc} = \sigma^2_{de,cen}/\sigma^2_{de,ecc}$. This gain non-linearly depends on ρ_{dd}. For common autocorrelation values around $\rho_{dd} = 0.995$, a gain around $g_{ecc} = 1.93$ is obtained in case of bilinear transformation and a gain around $g_{ecc} = 1.83$ is achieved in case of affine transformation. Since the error variance is smaller in case of bilinear transformation, bilinear transformation is applied in the proposed estimator.

The estimation error variance is further decreased by arithmetically averaging the four possible estimates. Assuming that the error of each observed pel is uncorrelated, the error variance decreases reciprocally with the total number of pels in the reference blocks when using a Maximum-Likelihood estimator. Because the eccentric blocks partly overlap, the number of pels increases by a factor of 2,64. Accordingly, a maximum additional gain of $g = 2.64$ can be obtained by averaging the four estimates. The same gain can not be obtained by using a single block with the same number of pels, since this would cause additional model failures.

The proposed estimator is tested in order to verify the analytically derived gain using synthetic and real images and a constant block size of $N = 17$ pel. Synthetic images are created by rendering two virtual 3-D objects: one with a surface whose depth is created using a AR(1) process, called SynAR, and another object that was reconstructed from a videocommunication scene, called SynLudo. The disparity fields of both objects can not be modelled correctly by the investigated transformations.

The analytically determined and measured error distribution are quite similarity. The measured position of the minima almost fits to the analytically derived one. But there is a difference between the expected error variance ratio of $g_{ecc} = 1.93$ and the measured one of $g_{ecc} = 1.55$ in case of SynAR. This difference is caused by restricted accuracy of the virtuel 3-D object and error during the image synthesis. On the one hand, the object surface is represented by a triangular mesh causing piecewise linear surfaces that differ from an ideal AR(1) process. On the other hand the applied image synthesis approach just uses bilinear texture interpolation and does no anti-aliasing filtering. In case of SynLudo a gain of $g_{ecc} = 1.35$ is achieved.

For a further reduction of the estimation error due to averaging, a maximum value of $g_{av} = 2.64$ can be expected. It turns out that only a gain of $g_{av} = 1.5$ is achieved. This indicates that the error between neighbouring pels is correlated. The total gain of the presented estimator is therefore $g = g_{ecc} \cdot g_{av} = 2.33$.

With real images a subjective assessment of the estimates is carried out. It turns out that the robustness is obviously improved due to averaging the four estimates using a simple outlier detection and removal that evaluates the empirical variance of the four estimates. Further improvements are expected but not yet verified by a more appropriate averaging of the estimates, considering disparity discontinuities and individual disparity estimation errors.

References

1. M. J. P. M. Lemmens, "A survey on stereo matching techniques", International Archives of Photogrammetry and Remote Sensing, Vol. 27, Comm. V., pp. 11-23, 1988.
2. J. K. Aggarwal, N. Nandhakumar, "On the computation of Motion from Sequences of Images - A Review", Proceedings of the IEEE, Vol. 76, No. 8, August 1988.
3. U. R. Dhond, J. K. Aggarwal, "Structure from Stereo - A Review", IEEE Trans. on Systems, Man, and Cybernetics, Vol.19, No. 6, Nov./Dec. 1989.
4. H.G. Musmann, P. Pirsch, H.J. Grallert, "Advances in picture coding", Proceedings of the IEEE, Vol. 73, No. 4, S. 523-548, April 1985
5. M. Bierling, "Displacement estimation by hierarchical block matching", Proc. 3rd SPIE Symposium on Visual Communications and Image Processing, Cambridge, USA, pp. 942-951, November 1988
6. J.W. Kim, S.U. Lee,"On the hierarchical variable block size motion estimation technique for motion sequence coding", Proc. SPIE Visual Communications and Image Processing '93, Vol. 2094-I, pp. 372-383, Cambridge, MA, USA, November 1993
7. W. Foerstner, "Quality assessment of object location and point transfer using digital image correlation techniques", Int. Arch. of Photogrammetry and Remote Sensing, Vol. 25, Part A3a, C3, 1984.
8. C. Fuh and P. Maragos, "Motion displacement estimation using an affine model image matching", Optical Engineering, Vol. 30, No. 7, pp. 881-887, July 1991
9. H. Li and R. Forchheimer, "A new motion compensation technique for video compression", Proc. IEEE Int. Conf. Acoust., Speech. Signal Processing, Minneapolis, MN, USA, pp. 441-444, May 1993
10. A. W. Gruen, E. Baltsavias, "Geometrically Constrained Multiphoto Matching", Photogrammetric Engineering and Remot Sensing, Vol. 54, No. 5, May 1988, pp 633-641.
11. Y. Xiong, S. Shafer, " Hypergeometric Filters for Optical Flow and Affine Matching", Int. Journal of Computer Vision, Vol. 24, No. 2 1997, pp 163-177.
12. V. Seferidis, M. Ghanbari, "Generalized block matching motion estimation", SPIE Symposium on Visual Communications and Image Processing, Boston, USA, Vol. 1818, S. 110-118, November 1992.
13. R. Buschmann, "Analytische Bestimmung der Schätzfehlervarianzen von Displacementschätzverfahren der Bewegtbildcodierung", Ph. D Thesis, Hannover, Germany, 1997.
14. R. Buschmann, "Efficiency of displacement estimation techniques", Image Communication, 10/1997, pp. 43-61.

15. R. Koch, "Automatische Oberflächenmodellierung starrer dreidimensionaler Objekte aus stereoskopischen Rundum-Ansichten", Dissertation, Universität Hannover, 1996

16. D. E. Wells, E. J. Krakiwsky,"Method of least squares", Dept. of Surveying Eng. Reports, University of New Brunswick, Frederikton, Canada, 1971.

17. L. Falkenhagen, "Hierarchical Block-Based Disparity Estimation Considering Neighbourhood Constraints", International workshop on SNHC and 3D Imaging, September 5-9, 1997, Rhodes, Greece.

Beyond the Epipolar Constraint: Integrating 3D Motion and Structure Estimation*

Tomáš Brodský, Cornelia Fermüller, and Yiannis Aloimonos

Computer Vision Laboratory, Center for Automation Research,
University of Maryland, College Park, MD 20742

Abstract. This paper develops a novel solution to the problem of recovering the structure of a scene given an uncalibrated video sequence depicting the scene. The essence of the technique lies in a method for recovering the rigid transformation between the different views in the image sequence. Knowledge of this 3D motion allows for self-calibration and for subsequent recovery of 3D structure. The introduced method breaks away from applying only the traditionally used epipolar constraint and introduces a new constraint based on the interaction between 3D motion and shape.

Up to now, structure from motion algorithms proceeded in two well defined steps, where the first and most important step is recovering the rigid transformation between two views, and the subsequent step is using this transformation to compute the structure of the scene in view. Here both aforementioned steps are accomplished in a synergistic manner. Existing approaches to 3D motion estimation are mostly based on the use of optic flow which however poses a problem at the locations of depth discontinuities. If we knew where depth discontinuities were, we could (using a multitude of approaches based on smoothness constraints) estimate accurately flow values for image patches corresponding to smooth scene patches; but to know the discontinuities requires solving the structure from motion problem first. In the past this dilemma has been addressed by improving the estimation of flow through sophisticated optimization techniques, whose performance often depends on the scene in view. In this paper the main idea is based on the interaction between 3D motion and shape which allows us to estimate the 3D motion while at the same time segmenting the scene. If we use a wrong 3D motion estimate to compute depth, then we obtain a distorted version of the depth function. The distortion, however, is such that the worse the motion estimate, the more likely we are to obtain depth estimates that are locally unsmooth, i.e., they vary more than the correct ones. Since local variability of depth is due either to the existence of a discontinuity or to a wrong 3D motion estimate, being able to differentiate between these two cases provides the correct motion, which yields the "smoothest" estimated depth as well as the image locations of scene discontinuities. Although no optic flow values are computed, we show that our algorithm is very much related to minimizing the epipolar constraint when the scene in view is smooth.

* The support of the Office of Naval Research under Contract N00014-96-1-0587, and IBM under Grant 50000293, is gratefully acknowledged.

Reinhard Koch, Luc Van Gool (Eds.): SMILE '98, LNCS 1506, pp. 109–123, 1998.
© Springer-Verlag Berlin Heidelberg 1998

When however the imaged scene is not smooth, the introduced constraint has in general different properties from the epipolar constraint and we present experimental results with real sequences where it performs better.

Keywords: Structure from motion, 3D motion estimation, shape segmentation, epipolar constraint, self-calibration

1   Introduction and Motivation

One of the biggest challenges of contemporary computer vision is to create robust and automatic procedures for recovering the structure of a scene given multiple views. This is the well known problem of structure from motion (SFM) [6,10]. Here the problem is treated in the differential sense, that is, assuming that a camera moving in an unrestricted rigid manner in a static environment continuously takes images. Regardless of particular approaches, the solution always proceeds in two steps: first, the rigid motion between the views is recovered and, second, the motion estimate is used to recover the scene structure.

Traditionally, the problem has been treated by first finding the correspondence or optic flow and then optimizing an error criterion based on the epipolar constraint. Although considerable progress has been made in minimizing deviation from the epipolar constraint [12,14,15], the approach is based on the values of flow whose estimation is an ill-posed problem.

The values of flow are obtained by applying some sort of smoothing to the locally computed image derivatives. When smoothing is done in an image patch corresponding to a smooth scene patch, accurate flow values are obtained. When, however, the patch corresponds to a scene patch containing a depth discontinuity, the smoothing leads to erroneous flow estimates there. This can only be avoided if a priori knowledge about the locations of depth discontinuities is available. Thus, flow values close to discontinuities often contain errors (and these affect the flow values elsewhere) and when the estimated 3D motion (containing errors) is used to recover depth, it is unavoidable that an erroneous scene structure will be computed. The situation presents itself as a chicken-and-egg problem. If we had information about the location of the discontinuities, then we would be able to compute accurate flow and subsequently accurate 3D motion. Accurate 3D motion implies, in turn, accurate location of the discontinuities and estimation of scene structure. Thus 3D motion and scene discontinuities are inherently related through the values of image flow and the one needs the other to be better estimated. Researchers avoid this problem by attempting to first estimate flow using sophisticated optimization procedures that could account for discontinuities, and although such techniques provide better estimates, their performance often depends on the scene in view, they are in general very slow and require a large number of resources [8,13,16].

In this paper, instead of attempting to estimate flow at all costs before proceeding with structure from motion, we ask a different question: Would it be possible to utilize any available local image motion information, such as normal flow for example, in order to obtain knowledge about scene discontinuities which would allow better estimation of 3D motion? Or, equivalently, would it be possible to devise a procedure that estimates scene discontinuities while at the same time estimating 3D motion? We show here that this is the case and we present a novel algorithm for 3D motion estimation. The idea behind our approach is based on the interaction between 3D motion and scene structure that only recently has been formalized [4]. If we have a 3D motion estimate which is wrong and we use it to estimate depth, then we obtain a distorted version of the depth function. Not only do incorrect estimates of motion parameters lead to incorrect depth estimates, but the distortion is such that the worse the motion estimate, the more likely we are to obtain depth estimates that locally vary much more than the correct ones. The correct motion then yields the "smoothest" estimated depth and we can define a measure whose minimization yields the correct egomotion parameters. The measure can be computed from normal flow only, so the computation of optical flow is not needed by the algorithm. Intuitively, the proposed algorithm proceeds as follows: first, the image is divided into small patches and a search — for the 3D motion — which as explained in Section 3 takes place in the two-dimensional space of translation directions — is performed. For each candidate 3D motion, using the local normal flow measurements in each patch, the depth of the scene corresponding to the patch is computed. If the variation of depth for all patches is small, then the candidate 3D motion is close to the correct one. If, however, there is a significant variation of depth in a patch, this is either because the candidate 3D motion is inaccurate or because there is a discontinuity in the patch. The second situation is differentiated from the first if the distribution of the depth values inside the patch is bimodal with the two classes of values spatially separated. In such a case the patch is subdivided into two new ones and the process is repeated. When the depth values computed in each patch are smooth functions, the corresponding motion is the correct one and the procedure has at the same time given rise to the location of a number of discontinuities. The rest of the paper formalizes these ideas and presents a number of experimental results.

1.1 Organization of the Paper

Section 2 defines the imaging model and describes the equations of the motion field induced by rigid motion; it also makes explicit the relationship between distortion of depth and errors in 3D motion. Section 3 is devoted to the description of the algorithm and it also analyzes the introduced constraints and formalizes the relationship of the approach to algorithms utilizing the epipolar constraint. Section 4 reviews the self-calibration method used in the paper and Section 5 describes a number of experimental results with real image sequences.

2   Preliminaries

We consider an observer moving rigidly in a static environment. The camera is a standard uncalibrated pinhole with internal calibration parameters described by matrix $\mathbf{K}$,

$$\mathbf{K} = \begin{pmatrix} f_x & s & \Delta_x \\ 0 & f_y & \Delta_y \\ 0 & 0 & f \end{pmatrix}$$

The coordinate system $OXYZ$ is attached to the camera, with Z being the optical axis.

Image points are represented as vectors $\mathbf{r} = [x, y, f]^T$, where x and y are the image coordinates of the point and f is a chosen constant of the same magnitude as x, y. A scene point $\mathbf{R}$ is projected onto the image point

$$\mathbf{r} = \frac{\mathbf{KR}}{\mathbf{R} \cdot \hat{\mathbf{z}}} \tag{1}$$

where $\hat{\mathbf{z}}$ is the unit vector in the direction of the Z axis.

Let the camera move in a static environment with instantaneous translation $\mathbf{t}$ and instantaneous rotation $\boldsymbol{\omega}$ (measured in the coordinate system $OXYZ$). Then a scene point $\mathbf{R}$ moves with velocity (relative to the camera)

$$\dot{\mathbf{R}} = -\mathbf{t} - \boldsymbol{\omega} \times \mathbf{R} \tag{2}$$

The image motion field is then [3]

$$\dot{\mathbf{r}} = -\frac{(\hat{\mathbf{z}} \times (\mathbf{Kt} \times \mathbf{r}))}{f(\mathbf{R} \cdot \hat{\mathbf{z}})} + \frac{1}{f}(\hat{\mathbf{z}} \times (\mathbf{r} \times (\mathbf{K}[\boldsymbol{\omega}]_\times \mathbf{K}^{-1}\mathbf{r}))) = \frac{1}{Z}\mathbf{u}_{tr}(\mathbf{Kt}) + \mathbf{u}_{rot}(\mathbf{K}[\boldsymbol{\omega}]_\times \mathbf{K}^{-1}) \tag{3}$$

where Z is used to denote the scene depth $(\mathbf{R} \cdot \hat{\mathbf{z}})$, and $\mathbf{u}_{tr}, \mathbf{u}_{rot}$ the direction of the translational and the rotational flow respectively.

The rotational component $\mathbf{u}_{rot}$ is determined by the matrix $\mathbf{A} = \mathbf{K}[\boldsymbol{\omega}]_\times \mathbf{K}^{-1}$ with seven degrees of freedom. As shown in [3], for a given translation $\mathbf{t}'$, matrix $\mathbf{A}$ can be decomposed into

$$\mathbf{A} = \mathbf{A}_c + \mathbf{A}_t = \mathbf{A}_c + f\,\mathbf{t}'\mathbf{w}^T + w_0\mathbf{I} \tag{4}$$

Matrix $\mathbf{A}_c$ (also called copoint matrix) depends on five independent parameters and is the component of $\mathbf{A}$ that can be estimated (together with the direction of $\mathbf{Kt}$) from a single flow field. The vector $\mathbf{w}$ determines the plane at infinity and it cannot be obtained from a single flow field. Finally, w_0 can be computed from the condition trace $\mathbf{A} = 0$.

For a hypothesized epipole $\mathbf{t}'$, the copoint matrix $\mathbf{A}_c$ is a suitable parameterization of the remaining parameters of the instantaneous fundamental matrix; $\mathbf{t}'$ and $\mathbf{A}_c$ define the epipolar geometry of the instantaneous motion [17].

Also, due to linearity, we have:

$$\mathbf{u}_{rot}(\mathbf{A}) = \mathbf{u}_{rot}(\mathbf{A}_c) + \mathbf{u}_{rot}(f\,\mathbf{tw}^T) + \mathbf{u}_{rot}(w_0\mathbf{I}) = \mathbf{u}_{rot}(\mathbf{A}_c) + (\mathbf{w} \cdot \mathbf{r})\mathbf{u}_{tr}(\mathbf{t})$$

i.e., the rotational flow due to $\mathbf{A}_t$ is equal to the translational flow of a certain scene plane.

In the sequel, $\hat{\mathbf{t}}$ is used to denote an estimate of the apparent translation $\mathbf{Kt}$ and $\hat{\mathbf{A}}_c$ denotes an estimate of the copoint matrix $\mathbf{A}_c$.

2.1 Depth Estimation from Motion Fields

This section introduces the novel criterion of "smoothness of depth" which is used to evaluate the consistency of the normal flow field with the estimated 3D motion and also to segment the scene at its depth boundaries. The idea is based on the interrelationship of estimated 3D motion $(\hat{\mathbf{t}}, \hat{\mathbf{A}}_c)$ and estimated depth of the scene $\hat{Z}$.

The structure of the scene, i.e., computed depth, can be expressed as a function of the motion parameters. Suppose we have estimated the apparent translation $\hat{\mathbf{t}}$ and the copoint matrix $\hat{\mathbf{A}}_c$ (for that particular $\hat{\mathbf{t}}$).

At an image point $\mathbf{r}$ where the normal flow direction is $\mathbf{n}$, we can compute inverse depth (up to an projective ambiguity [17])

$$\frac{1}{\hat{Z}'} = \frac{\dot{\mathbf{r}} \cdot \mathbf{n} - \mathbf{u}_{\mathrm{rot}}(\hat{\mathbf{A}}_c) \cdot \mathbf{n}}{\mathbf{u}_{\mathrm{tr}}(\hat{\mathbf{t}}) \cdot \mathbf{n}} \tag{5}$$

Substituting into (5) from (3) and (4), we obtain:

$$\frac{1}{\hat{Z}'} = \frac{\frac{1}{Z}\mathbf{u}_{\mathrm{tr}}(\mathbf{t}) \cdot \mathbf{n} - \mathbf{u}_{\mathrm{rot}}(\delta\mathbf{A}_c) \cdot \mathbf{n}}{\mathbf{u}_{\mathrm{tr}}(\hat{\mathbf{t}}) \cdot \mathbf{n}} + \mathbf{w} \cdot \mathbf{r} \tag{6}$$

where $\mathbf{u}_{\mathrm{rot}}(\delta\mathbf{A}_c)$ is the rotational flow due to the rotational error $\delta\mathbf{A}_c = (\hat{\mathbf{A}}_c - \mathbf{A}_c)$. Notice that when $\hat{\mathbf{t}}$ and $\hat{\mathbf{A}}_c$ are correct estimates of $\mathbf{t}$ and $\mathbf{A}_c$ respectively, we have

$$\frac{1}{\hat{Z}'} = \frac{1}{Z} + \mathbf{w} \cdot \mathbf{r}$$

Obviously, it is not enough to recover $\mathbf{w}$ to obtain Euclidean scene reconstruction, we still need the calibration matrix $\mathbf{K}$.

For incorrect motion estimates, we obtain distorted estimates of the scene depth and the amount of distortion depends on the normal flow direction $\mathbf{n}$. The larger the angle between vectors $\mathbf{u}_{\mathrm{tr}}(\hat{\mathbf{t}})$ and $\frac{1}{Z}\mathbf{u}_{\mathrm{tr}}(\mathbf{t}) - \mathbf{u}_{\mathrm{rot}}(\delta\mathbf{A}_c)$, the more the distortion will be spread out over the different directions. Thus, considering a patch of a smooth surface in space and assuming that normal flow measurements are taken along many directions, a rugged (i.e., unsmooth) surface will be computed on the basis of wrong 3D motion estimates.

The above observation constitutes the main idea behind our algorithm. For a candidate 3D motion estimate we evaluate the smoothness of estimated depth within image patches, compensating for the unknown linear function $\mathbf{w} \cdot \mathbf{r}$. If the chosen image patches correspond to smooth 3D scene patches the correct 3D motion will certainly give rise to the overall smoothest image patches. To obtain such a situation we attempt a segmentation of the scene on the basis of estimated depth while at the same time testing the candidate 3D motions. As all computations are based on normal flow and we thus have available the full statistics of the raw data, a good segmentation generally is possible.

3   Estimation of Viewing Geometry and Segmentation

To measure estimated depth smoothness, it is certainly possible to utilize the inverse depth directly and evaluate its variation over small image regions. However, we may run into instability problems, as division by small $\mathbf{u}_{tr} \cdot \mathbf{n}$ can greatly amplify measurement errors.

To address such potential problems, we improve the method of [3] and formulate a criterion in terms of image measurements. Instead of computing variation of estimated depth, we assume that the depth is smooth, i.e., in a small image region, we choose the smooth depth that best corresponds to the image measurements. The goodness of the fit is the error measure for that image region.

Consider a small image region $\mathcal{R}$. We define a measure that is small if there exists a smooth estimated inverse depth that, combined with the estimated motion parameters, matches the image measurements well.

It is not sufficient to assume a constant inverse depth because of the unknown parameters. We approximate the inverse depth $1/Z'$ in the region by a linear function, $1/\hat{Z}' = \mathbf{z} \cdot \mathbf{r}$ (note that the third component of $\mathbf{r}$ is a constant f, so $\mathbf{z} \cdot \mathbf{r}$ is a general linear function in the image coordinates). As the unknown component of inverse depth is a linear function $\mathbf{w} \cdot \mathbf{r}$, it can be incorporated into $\mathbf{z} \cdot \mathbf{r}$ and the smoothness criterion thus does not depend on the unknown parameters.

In the region $\mathcal{R}$ that contains a set of measurements $\dot{\mathbf{r}}_i$ with directions $\mathbf{n}_i$ we can define

$$\Theta_0(\hat{\mathbf{t}}, \hat{\mathbf{A}}_c, \mathbf{z}, \mathcal{R}) = \sum_i \left(\dot{\mathbf{r}}_i \cdot \mathbf{n}_i - (\mathbf{z} \cdot \mathbf{r}_i)(\mathbf{u}_{tr}(\hat{\mathbf{t}}) \cdot \mathbf{n}_i) - \mathbf{u}_{rot}(\hat{\mathbf{A}}_c) \cdot \mathbf{n}_i \right)^2 \quad (7)$$

Minimization of Θ_0 with respect to $\mathbf{z}$ provides the best smooth depth. We have

$$\frac{\partial \Theta_0}{\partial \mathbf{z}} = \sum_i (\mathbf{z} \cdot \mathbf{r}_i)(\mathbf{u}_{tr}(\hat{\mathbf{t}}) \cdot \mathbf{n}_i)^2 \mathbf{r}_i - \sum_i (\dot{\mathbf{r}}_i \cdot \mathbf{n} - \mathbf{u}_{rot}(\hat{\mathbf{A}}_c) \cdot \mathbf{n}_i)(\mathbf{u}_{tr}(\hat{\mathbf{t}}) \cdot \mathbf{n}_i) \mathbf{r}_i = 0 \quad (8)$$

a set of three linear equations for the three elements of $\mathbf{z}$. Substituting the solution of (8) into (7), we obtain $\Theta_1(\hat{\mathbf{t}}, \hat{\mathbf{A}}_c, \mathcal{R})$, a second order function of $\hat{\mathbf{A}}_c$. Notice that the computation can be performed even when $\hat{\mathbf{A}}_c$ is not known.

To estimate $\hat{\mathbf{A}}_c$, we sum up all the local functions and obtain a global function:

$$\Theta_2(\hat{\mathbf{t}}, \hat{\mathbf{A}}_c) = \sum_{\mathcal{R}} \Theta_1(\hat{\mathbf{t}}, \hat{\mathbf{A}}_c, \mathcal{R}) \quad (9)$$

Finally, global minimization yields the best copoint matrix $\hat{\mathbf{A}}_c$ and also a measure of depth smoothness for the apparent translation $\hat{\mathbf{t}}$:

$$\Phi(\hat{\mathbf{t}}) = \min \Theta_2(\hat{\mathbf{t}}, \hat{\mathbf{A}}_c) \quad (10)$$

3.1   Algorithm Description

The epipole is found by localizing the minimum of function $\Phi(\hat{\mathbf{t}})$ described above. We first summarize the computation of $\Phi(\hat{\mathbf{t}})$ and then explain the algorithm. To obtain $\Phi(\hat{\mathbf{t}})$:

1. Partition the image into small regions, in each region compute $\Theta_0(\hat{\mathbf{t}}, \hat{\mathbf{A}}_c, \mathbf{z}, \mathcal{R})$ and perform local minimization of $\mathbf{z}$ (the computation is symbolic in the unknown elements of $\hat{\mathbf{A}}_c$). The minimum is denoted by $\Theta_1(\hat{\mathbf{t}}, \hat{\mathbf{A}}_c, \mathcal{R})$.
2. Add all the local functions $\Theta_1(\hat{\mathbf{t}}, \hat{\mathbf{A}}_c, \mathcal{R})$ and minimize the resulting $\Theta_2(\hat{\mathbf{t}}, \hat{\mathbf{A}}_c)$ to obtain $\hat{\mathbf{A}}_c$.
3. $\Phi(\hat{\mathbf{t}})$ is the minimum of $\Theta_2(\hat{\mathbf{t}}, \hat{\mathbf{A}}_c)$.

Smoothness must only be enforced in image patches corresponding to smooth parts of the scene. Thus, once we have obtained preliminary estimates of $\Phi(\hat{\mathbf{t}})$ and $\hat{\mathbf{A}}_c$, we compute the inverse depth and try to perform depth segmentation. A detailed description of the segmentation algorithm is given in the next section.

After the segmentation, we recompute $\Phi(\hat{\mathbf{t}})$ by enforcing smoothness only within image regions that do not contain depth discontinuity. Notice that it is not necessary to recompute Θ_1 for all the image regions as we can locally compute the change of Θ_1 for the regions that are segmented. The improved $\Theta_2(\hat{\mathbf{t}}, \hat{\mathbf{A}}_c)$ then provides new $\hat{\mathbf{A}}_c$ and a new value of $\Phi(\hat{\mathbf{t}})$.

The edge detection and re-computation process could be iteratively repeated, but in practice a single iteration seems to be sufficient, as we explain in the next section.

One may ask whether depth segmentation using an incorrect copoint matrix (due to incorrect information from regions with depth discontinuities) can actually improve the estimation of the viewing geometry. The answer is yes, almost always. For most scenes, a majority of the image regions correspond to smooth scene patches and should yield the correct copoint matrix. Regions with depth discontinuities often provide the correct solution or at least relatively small errors for the correct motion. Such regions may give better results for some incorrect motion, but usually different motions would be the best for different patches.

Computation of $\hat{\mathbf{A}}_c$ uses information from the whole image and when we ignore depth discontinuities in the first stage of the algorithm, we may bias the solution, but in most cases not by much. If the estimated copoint matrix is relatively close to the true $\mathbf{A}_c$, the major depth discontinuities (and those are the ones we are most interested in) should certainly appear in the segmentation.

To find the minimum of Φ and thus the apparent translation, we perform a hierarchical search over the two-dimensional space of epipole positions. In practice, the function Φ is quite smooth, that is small changes in $\hat{\mathbf{t}}$ give rise to only small changes in Φ. One of the reasons for this is that for any $\hat{\mathbf{t}}$, the value of $\Phi(\hat{\mathbf{t}})$ is influenced by all the normal flow measurements and not only by a small subset.

For most sequences, the motion of the camera does not change abruptly and we can use the computed epipole as a starting point of the search in the next frame.

3.2   Patch Segmentation

Given an inverse depth map computed using $(\hat{\mathbf{t}}, \hat{\mathbf{A}}_c)$, we apply a Canny edge detector with special precautions taken to handle sparse input data. However, we also need to take into account the unknown linear term $\mathbf{w} \cdot \mathbf{r}$. The term cannot be estimated, but to improve the edge detection process, we add a linear function to the inverse estimated depth so that the average depth in different parts of the image is approximately the same.

By segmenting a patch, we decrease its contribution to $\Phi(\hat{\mathbf{t}})$. Ideally, an image patch should be segmented if it contains two smooth scene surfaces separated by a depth discontinuity and the depth is estimated using the correct 3D motion. It would be the best to not segment any patches when the 3D motion is incorrect and no depth discontinuities are present, but this of course cannot be guaranteed.

We use a simple segmentation criterion. If the edge detection algorithm finds an edge that divides an image region into two coherent subregions, we split that region. On the other hand, we do not split regions containing more complicated edge structure (that may be expected for a distorted depth estimates, since distortion depends on the normal flow direction).

It is simple to show that this strategy can be expected to yield good patch segmentation. When the motion estimate is correct, also the depth estimates are correct and patches with large amount of depth variation contain depth discontinuities.

For incorrect motions, the distortion factor depends on the direction of normal flow. While for any patch we can split the depth estimates into two groups and decrease the error measure, it is highly unlikely that the two groups of measurements define two spatially coherent separate subregions. Consequently, several edges can be expected in such a patch and it will not be split by the algorithm.

However, as the segmentation is based on local information only, we cannot expect it to perfectly distinguish the depth discontinuities from depth variation due to incorrect 3D motion. Sometimes, if a patch contains two subregions with different distributions of normal flow directions, we may split the patch even for incorrect 3D motion. An improvement, however, could be achieved by taking into account also the distribution of normal flow directions in relation to the estimated depth.

The local results are used in a global measure and occasional segmentation errors are unlikely to change the overall results. For the segmentation to cause an incorrect motion to yield the smallest $\Phi(\hat{\mathbf{t}})$, special normal flow configurations would have to occur in many patches in the image.

3.3   Algorithm Analysis

A single image region $\mathcal{R}$ contributes the value $\Theta_1(\hat{\mathbf{t}}, \hat{\mathbf{A}}_c, \mathcal{R})$ to the global criterion. It is shown below that the function can be decomposed into two parts; the first part is a multiple of the epipolar error and thus measures the error of the motion estimate. The second part is equal to the residual of the least squares fitting of optical flow to the measurements in the region.

The vectors $\mathbf{u}_{tr}(\hat{\mathbf{t}})$ and $\mathbf{u}_{rot}(\mathbf{A}_c)$ are polynomial functions of image position $\mathbf{r}$ and can usually be approximated by constants within a small image region. To simplify the analysis we use a rotated local coordinate system so that

$$\begin{aligned} \mathbf{u}_{tr}(\hat{\mathbf{t}}) &= [1,0,0]^T, & \mathbf{u}_{rot}(\mathbf{A}_c) &= [u_{rx}, u_{ry}, 0]^T \\ u_{n_i} &= \dot{\mathbf{r}}_i \cdot \mathbf{n}_i, & \mathbf{n}_i &= [\cos\psi_i, \sin\psi_i, 0]^T \end{aligned} \tag{11}$$

We can then rewrite (7) as

$$\Theta_0 = \sum_i W_i \left(u_{n_i} - (\mathbf{z}\cdot\mathbf{r}_i)\cos\psi_i - u_{rx}\cos\psi_i - u_{ry}\sin\psi_i\right)^2 \tag{12}$$

Note that u_{rx} can be incorporated into $\mathbf{z}$ (writing $\mathbf{z}' = \mathbf{z} + [0,0,u_{rx}/f]^T$) and we thus obtain the same minimum for the simplified:

$$\Theta_0 = \sum_i W_i \left(u_{n_i} - (\mathbf{z}\cdot\mathbf{r}_i)\cos\psi_i - u_{ry}\sin\psi_i\right)^2 \tag{13}$$

Now consider the least squares estimation of optical flow in the region using weights W_i. Allowing linear depth changes, in the local coordinate system we fit flow $(\mathbf{u}_x\cdot\mathbf{r}, u_y)$, i.e., a linear function along the direction of $\mathbf{u}_{tr}(\hat{\mathbf{t}})$ and a constant in the perpendicular direction. We would minimize

$$\sum_i W_i \left(u_{n_i} - (\mathbf{u}_x\cdot\mathbf{r}_i)\cos\psi_i - u_y\sin\psi_i\right)^2 \tag{14}$$

Expressions (13) and (14) are almost identical, but there is one important difference. The optical flow minimization (14) is strictly local, using only measurements from the region. On the other hand, in (13), the rotational flow (u_{rx}, u_{ry}) is determined by the global motion parameters.

Let us denote the least squares solution of (14) as $(\hat{u}_x, \hat{u}_y)$ and the residual as E_F. After some vector and matrix manipulation we can obtain

$$\Theta_1 = (m_{ss} - \mathbf{m}_{cs}^T \mathbf{M}_{cc}^{-1} \mathbf{m}_{cs})\,\delta u_{ry}^2 + E_F = K\,\delta u_{ry}^2 + E_F \tag{15}$$

where

$$m_{ss} = \sum_i W_i \sin^2\psi_i, \quad \mathbf{m}_{cs} = \sum_i W_i \cos\psi_i \sin\psi_i \mathbf{r}_i, \quad \mathbf{M}_{cc} = \sum_i W_i \cos^2\psi_i \mathbf{r}_i \mathbf{r}_i^T$$

and $\delta u_{ry} = u_{ry} - \hat{u}_y$ is the difference of the globally determined rotational component u_{ry} and the best local optical flow component $\hat{u}_y$. Both of the components are in the direction perpendicular to the translational flow and δu_{ry} is therefore the epipolar distance as shown in detail in the following section.

Equation (15) provides an interpretation of the criterion used in this paper. The component E_F, evaluates whether the depth in the region is smooth. The first term $K\,\delta u_{ry}^2$, is a product of the squared epipolar distance and a factor K

that only depends on the geometric configuration of measurements within the region. The complete analysis is complicated by the fact that K also depends on the point positions. One simple observation is the boundedness of K: matrix $\mathbf{M}_{cc}$ is positive definite, so $0 \leq K \leq m_{ss} \leq \sum_i W_i$.

Since the image regions are small, some intuition can be obtained by assuming that all the measurements are taken at a single point. Then both matrix $\mathbf{M}_{cc}$ and vector $\mathbf{m}_{cs}$ simplify into scalars and K becomes

$$K = \frac{(\sum_i W_i \cos^2 \psi_i)(\sum_i W_i \sin^2 \psi_i) - (\sum_i W_i \cos \psi_i \sin \psi_i)^2}{\sum_i W_i \cos^2 \psi_i} \tag{16}$$

Applying the Cauchy-Schwartz inequality to the numerator, we see that expression (16) can only be zero if sequences $\sqrt{W_1} \sin \psi_1, \ldots, \sqrt{W_n} \sin \psi_n$ and $\sqrt{W_1} \cos \psi_1, \ldots, \sqrt{W_n} \cos \psi_n$ are proportional. If we use weights W_i that only depend on the angle ψ_i, the sequences are proportional if all the normal flow directions are the same. Thus a small range of normal flow directions yields a small K. There is only one special case. K reaches the maximum $\sum_i W_i$ when all the normal flow measurements are perpendicular to the estimated translational flow, so that $\sin \psi_i = 1$. This is a desirable property. The epipolar error depends on the projection of the flow onto the direction perpendicular to the translational flow. If all the measurements are in that direction, they provide a maximum amount of information about the needed flow projection.

In general, K measures the range of normal flow directions within the region while preferring measurements that provide more information about the epipolar error. Compared to the epipolar constraint, the depth smoothness measure for smooth patches emphasizes regions with larger variation of normal flow directions and can thus be expected to yield better results for noisy data.

Finally, let us examine the behavior of Θ_1 for a smooth scene patch. Ignoring noise, we obtain $E_F = 0$ and the estimated $(\hat{u}_x, \hat{u}_y)$ is equal to the true motion field vector. For any translation, we can make Θ_1 zero by choosing a rotation that yields $\delta u_{ry} = 0$. But the rotation is not determined locally!

For the correct translation, the global rotation estimate should be correct and we should obtain zero Θ_1 for all the smooth patches. Now consider an incorrect translation candidate. It is easy to find a rotation to make Θ_1 zero for one or several smooth patches. But if we are able to find a rotation that yields zero Θ_1 for many different patches, we can obtain exactly the same motion field for two different 3D motions and the scene (or large parts of it) has to be close to an ambiguous surface [9,2].

Thus except for ambiguous surfaces we should obtain the correct 3D motion if most of the regions used correspond to smooth patches.

3.4   The Epipolar Constraint

The depth smoothness measure is closely related to the traditional epipolar constraint and we examine the relationship here. In the instantaneous form the epipolar constraint can be written as

$$(\hat{\mathbf{z}} \times \mathbf{u}_{tr}(\hat{\mathbf{t}})) \cdot (\dot{\mathbf{r}} - \mathbf{u}_{rot}(\hat{\mathbf{A}}_c)) = 0 \tag{17}$$

Note that we can use $\hat{\mathbf{A}}_c$ instead of $\hat{\mathbf{A}}$, since the flow $\mathbf{u}_{\text{rot}}(\hat{\mathbf{A}} - \hat{\mathbf{A}}_c)$ is parallel to the translational flow $\mathbf{u}_{\text{tr}}(\hat{\mathbf{t}})$ and therefore $(\hat{\mathbf{z}} \times \mathbf{u}_{\text{tr}}(\hat{\mathbf{t}})) \cdot \mathbf{u}_{\text{rot}}(\hat{\mathbf{A}} - \hat{\mathbf{A}}_c) = 0$.

Usually, the distance of the flow vector $\dot{\mathbf{r}}$ from the epipolar line (determined by $\mathbf{u}_{\text{tr}}(\hat{\mathbf{t}})$ and $\mathbf{u}_{\text{rot}}(\hat{\mathbf{A}}_c)$) is computed, and the sum of the squared distances, i.e.,

$$\sum \left((\hat{\mathbf{z}} \times \mathbf{u}_{\text{tr}}(\hat{\mathbf{t}})) \cdot (\dot{\mathbf{r}} - \mathbf{u}_{\text{rot}}(\hat{\mathbf{A}}_c)) \right)^2 \tag{18}$$

is minimized.

Methods based upon (18) suffer from bias [5], however, and a scaled epipolar constraint has been used to give an unbiased solution:

$$\sum \frac{\left((\hat{\mathbf{z}} \times \mathbf{u}_{\text{tr}}(\hat{\mathbf{t}})) \cdot (\dot{\mathbf{r}} - \mathbf{u}_{\text{rot}}(\hat{\mathbf{A}}_c)) \right)^2}{\|\mathbf{u}_{\text{tr}}(\hat{\mathbf{t}})\|^2} \tag{19}$$

Again we use the coordinate system and notation of (11). Suppose that the flow vector $\dot{\mathbf{r}}$ has been obtained by minimization of (14) and write it as (u_x, u_y). Substituting into (19) we obtain

$$\frac{\left((\hat{\mathbf{z}} \times \mathbf{u}_{\text{tr}}(\hat{\mathbf{t}})) \cdot (\dot{\mathbf{r}} - \mathbf{u}_{\text{rot}}(\hat{\mathbf{A}}_c)) \right)^2}{\|\mathbf{u}_{\text{tr}}(\hat{\mathbf{t}})\|^2} = (u_y - u_{\text{ry}})^2 = \delta u_{\text{ry}}^2 \tag{20}$$

Equations (20) and (15) illustrate the relationship of the epipolar constraint (albeit possibly using non-standard weights to estimate flow) and the smoothness measure Θ_1.

4   Self-Calibration

So far we have shown how to estimate the apparent translation $\hat{\mathbf{t}}$ and the copoint matrix $\hat{\mathbf{A}}_c$. To perform camera self-calibration, and thus subsequently derive structure, we can use the method developed in [3], combining the partial information assuming that the internal camera parameters are constant throughout the image sequence.

According to (3), the rotational component of the motion field is determined by matrix $\mathbf{A} = \mathbf{K}[\boldsymbol{\omega}]_\times \mathbf{K}^{-1}$. Matrix $[\boldsymbol{\omega}]_\times$ is skew-symmetric, i.e., $[\boldsymbol{\omega}]_\times + [\boldsymbol{\omega}]_\times^{\text{T}} = 0$. This is the constraint we use, expressed in terms of $\mathbf{K}$ and $\mathbf{A}$ as:

$$\mathbf{K}^{-1}\mathbf{A}\mathbf{K} + (\mathbf{K}^{-1}\mathbf{A}\mathbf{K})^{\text{T}} = 0 \tag{21}$$

Suppose we have a set of copoint matrices $\hat{\mathbf{A}}_{ci}$ and based on (4) we solve for w_0 using trace $\mathbf{A} = 0$. We may write

$$\hat{\mathbf{A}}_i = \hat{\mathbf{A}}_{ci} + f\hat{\mathbf{t}}_i\mathbf{w}_i^{\text{T}} - \frac{1}{3}\text{trace}\,(\hat{\mathbf{A}}_{ci} + f\hat{\mathbf{t}}_i\mathbf{w}_i^{\text{T}})\mathbf{I}$$

The error measure is based on (21):

$$\mathcal{E}(\mathbf{K}) = \sum_i \|\mathbf{K}^{-1}(\hat{\mathbf{A}}_i)\mathbf{K} + (\mathbf{K}^{-1}(\hat{\mathbf{A}}_i)\mathbf{K})^{\text{T}}\|^2 \tag{22}$$

Function $\mathcal{E}(\mathbf{K})$ can be minimized with respect to all the unknown vectors $\mathbf{w}_i$ (it is a second order function of the unknown vectors), yielding an error measure in terms of the calibration parameters alone. Levenberg-Marquardt minimization is then used to obtain the calibration parameters. For details, the reader is referred to [3].

5   Experimental Results

We present various experiments testing the different aspects of the introduced method, namely the competence of the technique to extract depth edges and a comparison between the smoothness measure and the epipolar constraint. The optical flow used in the epipolar error minimization was computed by the method of Lucas and Kanade [11], as implemented in [1].

One sequence used was the Yosemite fly-through sequence (one frame is shown in Figure 1(a)). The images also show independently moving clouds and each image frame was thus clipped to contain only the mountain range. One frame from an indoor lab sequence is shown in Figure 1(b).

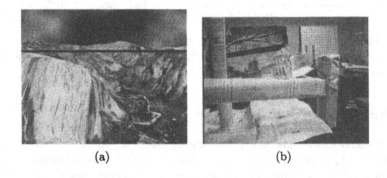

(a)   (b)

Fig. 1. (a) One frame of the Yosemite sequence. Only the bottom part of the image was used. (b) One frame of the lab sequence.

Experiment 1. We show examples of the depth estimation and segmentation process for the lab sequence, specifically for the frame in Figure 1(b). In Figure 2 the inverse estimated depth is displayed for the correct translation (as estimated by the algorithm) and for one incorrect translation. The corresponding depth segmentation results are shown in Figure 3.

Experiment 2. For the Yosemite sequence, both our method and the epipolar minimization perform quite well. The known epipole location in the image plane was $(0, -100)$. The estimated epipole locations for different methods are summarized in Table 1.

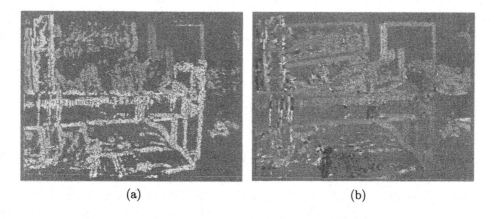

(a)   (b)

Fig. 2. (a) Inverse depth estimated for the correct epipole $((397, -115)$ pixels from the image center). (b) Inverse depth for an incorrect FOE $((-80, 115)$ pixels from image center). The grey-level value represents inverse estimated depth with mid-level grey shown in places where no information was available, white representing positive $1/Z$ and black representing negative $1/Z$.

method	epipole
ground truth	$(0.0, -100.0)$
epipolar minimization	$(0.5, -98.8)$
$\Phi(\hat{t})$ (no segmentation)	$(2.4, -96.7)$
$\Phi(\hat{t})$ (incl. segmentation)	$(0.0, -103.6)$

Table 1. Estimated epipole locations for the Yosemite sequence

Experiment 3. The lab sequence contained several significant depth discontinuities and for the majority of frames our method performed better than the epipolar minimization. No ground truth was available, but we visually inspected the instantaneous scene depth recovered. Out of a 90 frame subsequence tested with both methods, the epipolar minimization yielded 25 frames with clearly incorrect depth (i.e., many negative depth estimates or reversed depth order for large parts of the scene). The performance of our method was significantly better, as only 7 frames yielded clearly incorrect depth.

Experiment 4. The lab sequence was taken by a hand-held Panasonic D5000 camera with a zoom setting of approximately 12mm. Unfortunately, the effective focal length of the pinhole camera model was also influenced by the focus setting and we thus knew the intrinsic parameters only approximately. The internal parameters were fixed and approximately: $f_x = f_y = 450$, $\Delta_x = \Delta_y = s = 0$. The focal lengths were slightly overestimated, but consistent for different parts of the sequence. Calibration results are summarized in Table 2.

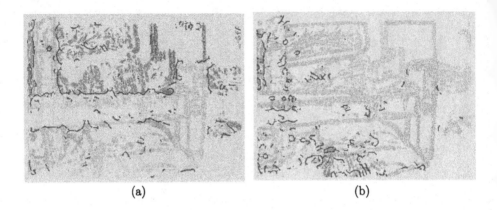

(a)   (b)

Fig. 3. Depth edges (drawn in black) found for the correct translation, overlaid on the computed depth. (a) Correct translation $(397, -115)$. (b) Incorrect translation $(-80, 115)$.

frames	f_x	f_y	Δ_x	Δ_y	s
001–300	536	522	16	26	3
001–100	541	543	-33	6	-25
101–200	544	475	26	-38	14
201–300	548	513	-11	8	6

Table 2. Self-calibration results for the lab sequence.

6   Conclusions

There exists a lot of structure in the world. With regard to shape, this structure manifests itself in surface patches that are smooth, separated by abrupt discontinuities. This paper exploited this fact in order to provide an algorithm that estimates 3D motion while at the same time it recovers scene discontinuities.

The basis of the technique lies in the understanding of the interaction between 3D shape and motion. Wrong 3D motion estimates give rise to depth values that are locally unsmooth, i.e., they vary more than the correct ones. This was exploited in order to obtain the 3D motion that locally provides the "smoothest" depth while recovering scene discontinuities. Finally, it was shown that the technique is very much related to epipolar minimization since the function to be minimized in image areas corresponding to smooth scene patches takes the same values as deviation from the epipolar constraint.

Although the properties of the new constraint are not fully developed, it appears to have a different behavior from the epipolar constraint for image areas corresponding to non-smooth patches apparently causing [7] less confusion between translation and rotation and thus producing more accurate results. It was generally believed in the computer vision community that a good algorithm for structure from motion is one that doesn't involve the scene in view. This is probably the reason behind the prominence of the epipolar constraint where one recovers the viewing geometry from image flow or correspondences without any reference to the scene. The present paper demonstrates that this may not be the case. The recovery of epipolar geometry is inherently connected to the scene in view and the best ways to achieve structure from motion may be the algorithms that recover motion and structure in a synergistic manner. Further study of the introduced constraint opens new avenues for research on the problem of recovering structure from image sequences, and its associated applications.

References

1. J. L. Barron, D. J. Fleet, and S. S. Beauchemin. Performance of optical flow techniques. *Int. Journal of Computer Vision*, 12(1):43–77, 1994.
2. T. Brodský, C. Fermüller, and Y. Aloimonos. Directions of motion fields are hardly ever ambiguous. *Int. Journal of Computer Vision*, 26:5–24, 1998.
3. T. Brodský, C. Fermüller, and Y. Aloimonos. Self-calibration from image derivatives. In *Proc. Int. Conf. Computer Vision*, pages 83–89, 1998.
4. L.-F. Cheong, C. Fermüller, and Y. Aloimonos. Effects of errors in viewing geometry on shape estimation. *Computer Vision and Image Understanding*, 1996. In press. Earlier version available as technical report CS-TR-3480, June 1996.
5. K. Daniilidis and M. Spetsakis. Understanding noise sensitivity in structure from motion. In Y. Aloimonos, editor, *Visual Navigation: From Biological Systems to Unmaned Ground Vehicles*, chapter 4. Lawrence Erlbaum, 1996.
6. O. D. Faugeras. *Three-Dimensional Computer Vision*. MIT Press, Cambridge, MA, 1992.
7. C. Fermüller and Y. Aloimonos. What is computed by structure from motion algorithms? Technical Report CS-TR-3809, Center for Automation Research, University of Maryland, College Park, 1997.
8. S. Geman and D. Geman. Stochastic relaxation, Gibbs distribution and Bayesian restoration of images. *IEEE Trans. PAMI*, 6:721–741, 1984.
9. B. K. P. Horn. Motion fields are hardly ever ambiguous. *Int. Journal of Computer Vision*, 1(3):259–274, 1987.
10. J. J. Koenderink and A. J. van Doorn. Affine structure from motion. *Journal of the Optical Society of America*, 8:377–385, 1991.
11. B. D. Lucas. *Generalized Image Matching by the Method of Differences*. PhD thesis, Dept. of Computer Science, Carnegie-Mellon University, 1984.
12. Q.-T. Luong and O. D. Faugeras. The fundamental matrix: Theory, algorithms, and stability analysis. *Int. Journal of Computer Vision*, 17:43–75, 1996.
13. J. Marroquin. *Probabilistic Solution of Inverse Problems*. PhD thesis, Massachusetts Institute of Technology, 1985.
14. S. J. Maybank. Algorithm for analysing optical flow based on the least-squares method. *Image and Vision Computing*, 4:38–42, 1986.
15. S. J. Maybank. *A Theoretical Study of Optical Flow*. PhD thesis, University of London, England, 1987.
16. D. Mumford and J. Shah. Boundary detection by minimizing functionals. In *Proc. IEEE Conf. Computer Vision and Pattern Recognition*, pages 22–25, 1985.
17. T. Viéville and O. Faugeras. The first-order expansion of motion equations in the uncalibrated case. *Computer Vision and Image Understanding*, 64(1):128–146, 1996.

Multi-Camera Acquisitions for High-Accuracy 3D Reconstruction

Federico Pedersini, Augusto Sarti, Stefano Tubaro

Dip. di Elettronica e Informazione (DEI), Politecnico di Milano
Piazza L. Da Vinci 32, 20133 Milano, Italy
E-mail: pedersin/sarti/tubaro@elet.polimi.it

Abstract. In this paper we present our global approach to accurate 3D reconstruction with a calibrated multi-camera system. In particular, we illustrate a simple and effective adaptive technique for the self-calibration of CCD-based multi-camera acquisition systems. We also propose a general and robust approach to the problem of close-range partial 3D reconstruction of objects from stereo-correspondences. Finally, we introduce a method for performing an accurate patchworking of the partial reconstructions, based on 3D feature matching.

1. Introduction

In the past few years, there has been a fast proliferation of methods for the 3D reconstruction of objects from the analysis of camera images. A large number of these applications are aimed at the problem of *content creation* for the market of multi-media applications. There is a considerable number of applications, however, in which the accuracy of the 3D reconstruction plays a crucial role. For example, applications of close-range digital photogrammetry aimed at the preservation and restoration of 3D works of art require effective methods for accurate, quantitative, reproducible and repeatable 3D reconstruction. In this case, in fact, suitable 3D modeling methods should be sufficiently accurate as to match the performance of the methods that are commonly adopted for the 3D relief of works of art; and to guarantee that such measurements will be reproducible and can be repeated along time for monitoring purposes.

The most popular non-invasive approaches to 3D reconstruction of mid-sized objects are based on stereo-correspondences. Such methods are based on the detection of features (e.g. points, edges, luminance profiles) on the available images of the object. When the camera parameters (position, orientation and other intrinsic physical parameters) are known (*calibrated* case), the process of determining the correspondences is helped by some rigidity constraints such as the coplanarity of corresponding visual rays (epipolar constraint), and the 3D coordinates of the features can be determined through geometric triangulation [1,2]. When, on the contrary, the camera parameters are not known (*uncalibrated* analysis), the determination of the feature correspondences becomes more complex as it can only rely on projective constraints and invariants. Several robust matching techniques have been developed for uncalibrated acquisitions [19]; such methods are usually based on the progressive application of a variety of projective constraints on sets of uncalibrated views, in order to narrow-down a list of candidate matches (generated through a correlation-based approach) to a final set of confidence matches.

Reinhard Koch, Luc Van Gool (Eds.): SMILE '98, LNCS 1506, pp. 124-138, 1998.

In general, the 3D reconstruction methods based on feature matching can be classified into two categories:

- *monocular approach*: a number of uncalibrated views are acquired and processed all together (*global* approach) or in subgroups (*local* approach) in order to jointly estimate camera motion and object structure. In the global approach, one or more cameras are employed for acquiring a number of images of the object from a variety of viewpoints [6]. The pose of the cameras and the 3D coordinates of the features are found through a joint analysis of the image features extracted from all the available views. In the local approach a video sequence of the object is acquired in such a way to "cover" all portions of the object. Then the views are partitioned into subgroups to be processed separately using uncalibrated methods based on projective invariants and constraints.
- *multi-ocular approach*: a set of cameras is mounted on a rigid support and calibrated, so that all camera parameters are known beforehand. Several multi-ocular views of the object are acquired from a variety of viewpoints. From the analysis of each multi-view a "local" surface is generated. All local surfaces are then fused together into a single one, by using some global constraints [6,7,8].

In general, the global monocular approach estimates the 3D coordinates of some object features with best accuracy. Due to its global treatment of the data, however, it tends to produce a sparse set of 3D features that cannot be easily interpolated into a global surface unless some *a-priori* information on the object is available. Partitioning the views into smaller groups for a more "local" approach makes it easier to deal with the complexity of the surface topology but generally causes a reduction of the accuracy and is quite difficult to perform on an automatic basis. This partitioning becomes necessary when dealing with video sequences, but the subgroups of views tend to be "aligned" with each other, which is not the optimal positioning for feature matching purposes. On the other hand, acquiring a monocular sequence is certainly the simplest way to perform an acquisition campaign.

The local multi-camera approach, exhibits some interesting characteristics:

- a multi-camera acquisition system induces a "natural" partition of the views, which becomes optimal when the cameras are well-positioned on the rigid frame;
- the acquisition system can be quite easily calibrated, and the estimated parameters can be used for validating all feature matches; the calibration can be made adaptive in order to compensate for the drift of the parameters throughout the acquisition process;
- the accuracy of a well-calibrated system is at photogrammetric level;
- each calibrated triplet generates a "local" surface *patch* of modest topological complexity; all patches can be merged into a more complex global surface through "patchworking".

In this article we illustrate our calibrated reconstruction approach based on adaptive self-calibration, local stereo-matching approach and global patchworking, with the goal of obtaining a high-accuracy reconstruction of unstructured 3D objects.

2. Calibration

All calibrated 3D reconstruction methods are critically dependent on the accuracy with which the camera parameters, i.e. the geometrical, optical and electric characteristics of the camera system (camera position and orientation, focal length, pixel size, location of the optical center, nonlinear distortion coefficients, etc.) are known. In the past few years several approaches to the calibration problem have been proposed. Such methods apply to electronic cameras the same techniques that were traditionally used for the calibration of photogrammetric cameras [9,10,11]. The camera characteristics are, in fact, computed through a proper processing of the image of a test object (calibration target-frame) placed in the scene. The accuracy of the camera model can be arbitrarily improved by employing an adequate number of parameters therefore, when the goal is that of improving the calibration accuracy as much as possible, the pattern accuracy becomes the major bottleneck. For this reason, we developed an advanced photogrammetric method that jointly estimate the camera parameters and the geometry of the calibration target-set in a more accurate fashion (*self-calibration*). This method is based on a *multi-camera, multi-view* calibration approach, and performs an accurate self-calibration on the multi-camera system from the analysis of several views of a simpler calibration target-frame, such as a marked planar surface (a printed sheet of paper glued on a glass surface) or some other even simpler structure. In fact, not only is this technique able to estimate the camera parameters, but it can also determine the 3D position of the targets on the calibration frame, which can be just roughly known or not known at all. Finally, we developed method for making the calibration robust against the inevitable parameter drift that takes place during the acquisition process. Such method detects and tracks some "safe" features that are naturally present in the scene, and use their image coordinates for making the calibration process adaptive.

2.1 Calibration Strategy

The camera model allows us to compute the image coordinates of the projection of an object point P, given its coordinates. This model can also be seen as a function g that maps a point m in the model space into a point d in the observation space. This set of equations is called *direct model*. For each fiducial point P_i and for each camera C_j, the direct model provides us image coordinates in the form

$$d_{i,j} = g(P_i, C_j) = g(m_{i,j}); \qquad d_{i,j} = \begin{bmatrix} x_i & y_i \end{bmatrix}; \qquad m_{i,j} = \begin{bmatrix} P_i & C_j \end{bmatrix};$$

where C_j is the set of the 11 parameters which define the model of the j-th camera

$$C_j = \begin{bmatrix} \phi, \theta, \psi, \ t_X, t_Y, t_Z, f, \ k_3, k_5, \ c_X, c_Y \end{bmatrix},$$

ϕ, θ and ψ are the 3 angles that characterize the rotation matrix R, $T = \{t_X, t_Y, t_Z\}$ is the translation vector, f is the focal length of the lens, k_3 and k_5 are the radial lens distortion coefficients, $OC = \{c_X, c_Y\}$ is the optical center on the image plane. R and T are usually referred to as *extrinsic parameters*, while the other five are called *intrinsic parameters*, as they characterize the camera. Rewriting the above equations in matrix form and extending them to all the considered fiducial points and all the cameras, the direct model becomes

$$g(\cdot): \quad \Re^{3N+11\cdot V} \quad \rightarrow \quad \Re^{2N\cdot V}$$

$$\mathbf{m} \qquad \mapsto \quad \overline{\mathbf{d}} = g(\mathbf{m})$$

$g(\cdot)$ being the nonlinear function that maps the 3D world coordinates of N fiducial points, given the camera parameters of V cameras, into the V sets of N two-dimensional image coordinates of the perspective projection in each camera.

With this formalization of the camera model, the problem of camera calibration becomes that of computing the model vector $\mathbf{m}$ by exploiting the knowledge about the observed data $\mathbf{d}$ and the direct model $g(\cdot)$. In other words, the solution of the problem is given by the inverse of the model function $\mathbf{m}=g^{-1}(\mathbf{d})$, where $\mathbf{d}$ and $g()$ are known. This corresponds to the classical formulation of an inverse problem. In this sense, the camera calibration problem is a typical inverse problem.

Multi-view, multi-camera calibration - It is well-known that, in order to obtain satisfactory and reliable calibration results, it is necessary for the fiducial points to "fill up" the entire scene space. This fact usually forces to construct 3D calibration patterns that are as large as the object to be reconstructed. In this case, calibration is possible only for scenes of limited spatial extension. When scenes of larger size are considered, 3D pattern cannot be employed anymore. In fact, an accurate 3D pattern is very expensive to build and quite cumbersome to handle. For this reason a *multi-view* calibration set-up has been developed, that allows us to generate the desired 3D set of fiducial points through multiple acquisition of a smaller and simpler calibration pattern, such as a planar target. In fact, the pattern can be placed in several different positions, so that the entire 3D volume of interest will be "scanned". The relative motion between different positions of the pattern is not measured, therefore the position of the fiducial points in the scene is only partially known. This, of course, complicates the calibration problem, as the relative motion of the pattern must be estimated. In fact, we have six extra unknowns per additional target position. However, as the motion of the pattern from view to view, is the same for all the cameras, each camera will give its contribution to the estimation of the pattern motion. In fact, with respect to the case of calibrating one camera with V pattern views, each new camera to calibrate adds 11 more unknowns, while providing approx. $2NV$ equations (the image coordinates of NV fiducial points).

Self-calibration - Thanks to the large number of constraints and to the fact that, through multiple pattern positioning, the fiducial points end up covering the whole scene space, the self-calibrating approach can lead to the best results that can be obtained with such low-cost calibration setups, in terms of global accuracy throughout the scene space. In fact, experimental results have shown that, under proper conditions, the achieved calibration accuracy, with this approach, reaches the limit imposed by the accuracy with which the position of the fiducial points is known, with respect to the pattern frame. In order to further improve the accuracy of the calibration, it is either necessary to use calibration patterns of higher precision, for which the fiducial point coordinates have been determined with high accuracy (e.g. with photogrammetric techniques) or to adopt a self-calibrating approach, which, besides estimating the camera parameters, refines the estimates of the a-priori given coordinates of the fiducial points. The complexity of the former solution is the same as in the previous case, but it requires expensive calibration patterns. As the aim of this work to obtain high performance at low cost, we focused on the latter solution.

The self-calibration problem is much more undetermined than the previously considered one, because the calibration points coordinates *WP* are considered only approximately known. In other words, also the data points become, to some extent, unknowns to be estimated. The a-priori knowledge about the data generally consists of a rough estimate of the world-coordinates. The proposed technique is able not only to further improve the accuracy of the estimated camera parameters, but to refine the a-priori given estimate of the world coordinates as well.

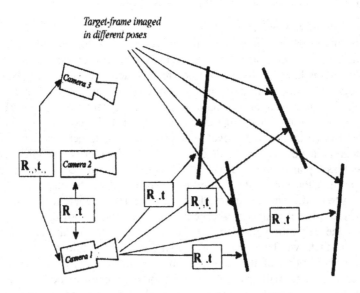

Fig. 1. General scheme for the multi-view multi-camera approach to self-calibration

The calibration target-set that we adopted is planar as the pixel size is assumed known [9]. A planar target-set is much simpler to build compared to a 3D target-frame as it can be easily constructed, for example, by gluing a laser-printed sheet of paper on a rigid planar surface. This procedure also gives us some *a-priori* information on the coordinates of the targets (and their uncertainty), relative to a frame attached to the surface. A 3D calibration target-frame, on the other hand, would require an accurate 3D measurement of the coordinates of the targets (generally through some photogrammetric technique [11]). An example of application of our self-calibration approach is reported in Fig. 2.

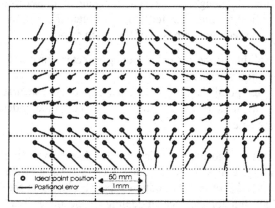

Fig. 2. *A-priori* coordinates of the fiducial points of the target-set (laser-printed circles on a sheet of A4 paper, glued to a flat surface) and corresponding *a-posteriori* corrections estimated through self-calibration. The orientation of the (magnified) correction vectors denotes the deformation of the sheet of paper due to the action of the dragging mechanism of the laser printer.

2.2 Adaptive Calibration

In order to extract 3D information from the scene views the *camera parameters* must be known with good accuracy throughout the whole acquisition campaign. As *camera calibration* is performed before the beginning of an acquisition session, problems of parameter drift may occur. In fact, when long video sequences are acquired, the stability of the camera parameters measured at the beginning becomes a crucial problem as mechanical shocks, vibrations or thermal effects on cameras and supports, can cause small variations of the initial camera set-up. This drift of the camera parameters leads to significant 3D reconstruction errors, as the 3D back-projection is rather ill-conditioned with respect to the camera parameters. In order to overcome this problem, we detect and track any changes in the acquisition system and, whenever possible, we apply an on-the-fly correction of the camera parameters. By doing so, the calibration holds accurate throughout the acquisition campaign.

Our approach does not require us to place targets in the scene or to use any *a-priori* knowledge, but exploits luminance features that are already present in the scene (e.g. corners and spots) which can be located in the image with high precision. After the localization process, which is performed with sub-pixel accuracy, a matching operation is performed among the n sets (n being the number of cameras) of feature points, which returns a set of n-tuples of homologous points. The matched n-tuples will be then back-projected into the 3D scene space. If the camera parameters change, then the back-projection will be affected by larger errors, with respect to the predicted pre-calibration accuracy. A proper analysis of the magnitude and the temporal changes of the back-projection error allows us to reveal and characterize any incidental modifications of the camera parameters. Furthermore, if the set of matched *n*-tuples is informative enough, the proposed technique allows to accurately measure the occurred modification and, therefore, to re-calibrate the system.

Our approach can be seen as composed of two main steps

- check on the validity of the current camera parameters through the estimation of the back-projection's accuracy
- analysis of the temporal changes of the back-projection's accuracy, in order to reveal increments in the reconstruction error that could likely denote a change in the system parameter

The first step of the algorithm consists in the detection of the significant image features that will be used as control points. Our method is based on the techniques presented in [13,14,15]. In order to obtain super-resolution in the image localization accuracy, an algorithm for the local modeling of the image Laplacian function has been developed and employed in the localization procedure. The obtained results show that the introduced improvements has allowed to reach a localization accuracy better than 0.2 pixel [18].

Over the obtained sets of image points, an *n*-partite matching algorithm is applied, in order to find the stereo-corresponding *n*-tuples. The matching criterion is based not only on the epipolar geometry defined by the current calibration, as the calibration is not considered as reliable in this application, but also on the similarity of the local luminance profiles. All the matched *n*-tuples are then back-projected in the 3D scene space, and an "*accuracy index*" is computed for each match, based on the back-projection error. The statistical distribution of this index over the matched points and its temporal behavior are then analyzed, in order to reveal any increment of the accuracy index that could very likely denote a change in the system parameters. Moreover, at the beginning of the sequence, the back-projected points that are most accurate and are fixed in the scene are selected as *control points*. These are the points that could then be used as 3D fiducial points for the re-calibration of the system. In fact, if the number of matched points is sufficient, it is possible to perform a reliable re-calibration of the system. When a change in the camera system has been detected, the current set of matched *n*-tuples of image features is exploited, in order to recover the new camera parameters.

Assuming that the camera system is not subjected to a rigid motion with respect to the scene throughout the acquisition session, at the beginning of the sequence the most accurate and stable (fixed) back-projected points are detected and used as *control points*. These are the candidate points to be used as 3D targets for parameter correction, provided that their number is sufficient. When a parameter change is detected, the current set of matched *n*-tuples of image features is used for recovering the new camera parameters.

Depending on the previous knowledge of the 3D position of the matched points, the algorithm adopts either a calibration or a self-calibration approach. More precisely, if the 3D position of some points had been measured at the beginning of the sequence when the system was still calibrated, then re-calibration is performed through a standard procedure that uses the available 3D points as markers. If, on the contrary, no reliable information is available about the actual 3D position of the matched points, the calibration can only be corrected through a self-calibration procedure. Self-calibration allows to simultaneously determine the camera parameters and the 3D position of the fiducial points.

This method, however, requires a larger number of matched points for accurate results, as the self-calibration problem is much more ill-conditioned than the calibration problem. We are currently working on a modified version of the method that is able to determine a *rigid* (rather than *fixed*) set of points and perform calibration with respect to a relative (rather than absolute) frame.

The proposed technique has been tested on real sequences acquired with different trinocular camera systems, with both simulated and real variations of the camera parameters. In all experimental situations, the algorithm has been able to detect the modification of the camera parameters. Moreover, after artificial modifications of the camera system, of the same characteristics and entity of accidental ones (artificial shocks, change of focal length, etc.), the algorithm has been able to measure the drift of the parameters, thus allowing the re-calibration of the system. The results have shown that the accuracy of the re-calibration, in all cases, has reached the same accuracy of the original calibration.

3. Partial Reconstruction

Our approach to local reconstruction is based on feature correspondence. Image features that are most often used for 3D reconstruction are points, luminance edges and luminance profiles. Such features tend to provide information of different nature. Point and edge matching is generally a very precise and reliable process, but it usually results in a sparse set of 3D data. Conversely, matching the luminance profiles of small areas tends to generate a much denser set of 3D data but it is rather sensitive to the unavoidable viewer-dependent perspective/radiometric distortions, therefore this approach tends to be less stable and reliable. For this reason we developed a general and robust solution to the problem of 3D reconstruction from stereo correspondence of luminance patches. The method is largely independent on the camera geometry, and employs a calibrated set of three or more standard TV-resolution CCD cameras, which provides enough redundancy for removing possible matching ambiguities. The robustness of the approach can also be attributed to the *physicality* of the matching process, which is actually performed in the 3D space rather than on the image plane. In order to do so, besides the 3D location of the surface patches, it estimates their local orientation in 3D space as well, so that the geometric distortion of the luminance patch can be included in the model. Finally, the method takes into account the viewer-dependent radiometric distortion.

3.1 Edge-Based Approach

As a preliminary operation, we perform partial reconstruction from edge matching, in order to obtain reliable and accurate 3D data to begin with. The same type of features will later be used for egomotion estimation as well (which is based on 3D contour matching in object space). In order to be able to use edges for accurate egomotion estimation, however, we need to detect them with great accuracy. We do this by first using a traditional edge detector, we then retrieve the subpixel location of the edge points through an interpolation process which takes the luminance gradient into account. Finally, a rule-based contour tracking method is employed for determining the correct connection between edge points.

The search for homologous edges on different views is performed along *epipolar lines*. Notice that using more than two cameras allows us to avoid problems of matching ambiguity. With three cameras, in fact, not only can we always select the best pair of views for a specific stereo-correspondence (sharp intersection between edge and epipolar lines), but we can validate the match through a check on the third view. In fact, the edge point must lie on the intersection of the two epipolar lines associated to the homologous edge points on the other views. Once the matches are found, each set of corresponding contours is back-projected onto the 3D scene space by looking for the point at minimum distance from the three homologous visual rays.

3.2 Area-Based Approach

The luminance patches used by most area-matching techniques are normally assumed to have the same shape in all views. It is quite clear, however, that this hypothesis is acceptable only when the angles between the viewing directions of the three cameras are not too wide, which is not our case. As a consequence, we need to take into account the perspective distortion of the shape of the patch, when back-projected onto the object surface and then re-projected onto the other image plane. In order to do so, we assume the 3D surface to be locally flat, which means that it can be approximated by a plane within the back-projected surface patch.

In the other view we search, along the distorted (due to radial distortion) epipolar line, for the patch that best matches the first one. The projective distortion of the patch is accounted for by estimating, both position and orientation of the patch. In practice, the minimum of a *similarity function* between a patch of the actual image and a re-projected patch after perspective warping is searched for as a function of position and local orientation of the tangent plane of the object surface.

Area matching requires a comparison between the actual luminance profile of a patch with the one that we obtain by *transferring* luminance profiles of other views through a specific 3D surface model. Let S be a surface patch in object space, obtained by back-projecting a reference image patch of any of the views onto the plane $\mathbf{s}^T\mathbf{x}=0$, and let $S^{(i)}$ be its i-th view. The transfer of projective coordinates from the j-th view to the i-th view through the plane $\mathbf{s}^T\mathbf{x}=0$, can be expressed as a homography (an invertible linear projective transformation) of the form

$$\mathbf{u}^{(i)} = \mathbf{M}_{ij}(\mathbf{s})\mathbf{u}^{(j)} = 0 \ ,$$

where $\mathbf{M}_{ij}(\mathbf{s})$ is a 3 by 3 matrix which depends on the parameters of the plane over which the patch lies. This homography allows us to express the luminance transfer from the j-th view to the i-th view as

$$I_j^{(i)}(\mathbf{u}^{(i)}) = g_j^{(i)} I^{(i)}(\mathbf{M}_{ji}(\mathbf{s})\mathbf{u}^{(i)}) + \Delta_j^{(i)}$$

where $g^{(i)}_j$ is a correction factor (*gain*) that accounts for electrical differences in the camera sensors, while $\Delta^{(i)}_j$ is an additive radiometric correction (*offset*) which accounts for non-Lambertian effects of the surface reflectivity (reflection's migration with the viewpoint). Notice that the Lambertian component of the surface reflectivity does not appear in the above expression as it is the same for all views.

If a reference patch produces reliable 3D information, then it can be used for 3D surface reconstruction. Once all reference regions have been considered, surface interpolation is carried out and the area matching process can start over with a smaller patch size. In this case the previously estimated surface can be used for initializing the search in the next step and speeding up the process.

As a general rule, we need to make sure that the maximum size of the patch is small enough to guarantee a limited matching error. On the other hand, we know that the area matching process is based on the minimization of a highly nonlinear similarity function, therefore we can expect the process to be quite sensitive to local minima. In order to avoid such a problem, we can use an initial *guess* of the surface shape, which helps the minimization process converge to a global minimum and dramatically speeds up the matching process by reducing the size of the search space. In principle,

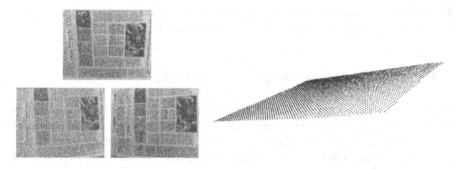

Fig. 3. Original views of the newspaper's page (glued to a planar surface) and 3D points reconstructed through area matching.

any method can be used for obtaining the initial surface. In our case we used the surface obtained through edge-matching [1,2], whose reliability is guaranteed by the accuracy of the camera model and the calibration procedure. As the result of the edge-matching is usually a sparse, though accurate, set of 3D points, such data is interpolated in order to generate the initial surface. We interpolated the 3D data by means of a modified and optimized version of the edge-preserving Discrete Smooth Interpolator (DSI) [16].

Some experiments of 3D scene reconstruction have been carried out on several test scenes. The first test presented in this paper concerns the measurement of the accuracy of the area matching using a flat object placed at about 1.2 m of distance from the camera system. The surface reconstruction resulted to be flat with 0.1 mm of standard deviation (see Fig. 3).

A second experiment concerned the 3D reconstruction of a tele-conferencing scene. The acquisition was made with a trinocular camera system at CCETT, France, within the ACTS "PANORAMA" Project (see Fig.4). No initial reconstruction was used for area matching. Instead, progressive-scan initialization was performed. The results of the area matching procedure are visible in Fig. 4. As we can see, the quality of the reconstruction greatly benefits from the fact that the geometric distortion is included in the model.

Fig. 4. One of the three original views of a conference scene (above) and two virtual views of the 3D points reconstructed through 3D area matching (below).

4. Motion Estimation through Line Matching

In order to be able to merge 3D data coming from different partial reconstructions, we need to accurately estimate the rigid motion that the acquisition system undergoes between two multi-view acquisitions. In order to do so, one could employ high-precision mechanical devices for positioning the camera system (or the object) before acquiring a multi-view. This *a-priori* solution of the ego-motion problem, however, is usually quite expensive and not very flexible. In alternative, one can perform detection and tracking of some image features throughout the acquisition process, and use the location of such features for estimating the camera motion. This last approach becomes particularly interesting when the features to be extracted are part of the scene to be reconstructed rather than being artificially added to it. Adding special *markers* to the imaged scene is, in fact, common practice in photogrammetry but, besides making the egomotion retrieval more invasive, it requires a certain expertise and slows down the acquisition process [8]. Conversely, natural point-like features that are already present in the scene are difficult to safely extract and accurately locate. Scene features that can be quite safely detected are, instead, luminance edges [6]. These features are more likely to be naturally present in the scene and rather easy to detect, which makes them good candidate features for egomotion estimation.

Our method is based on the analysis of 3D contours in the imaged scene. Having adopted a calibrated multi-ocular camera system [9,11], the estimation is entirely performed in the 3D space. In fact, all edges of each one of the multi-views are previously localized, matched and back-projected onto the object space [12]. Roughly speaking, the method searches for the rigid motion that best merges the sets of 3D edges that are extracted from each one of the multiple views.

After partitioning the 3D contours in lines and curves, we proceed as follows:

1. rough egomotion estimation from straight contours:
    - matching of straight contours
    - motion estimation through minimization of the distance between homologous contours
2. egomotion refinement using curved contours:
    - matching of curved contours
    - motion estimation through a minimization of the distance between homologous curved contours.

Notice that, as a first approximation of the egomotion is already available, the matching of curved contours is a rather simple operation compared with the matching of straight lines.

4.1 Egomotion from Straight Lines

Line matching in 3D space is performed through a hypothesize-and-test type of procedure [17]. The first step of this method consists of formulating hypotheses on the possible couplings by selecting all those that do not violate some rules of congruence based on a set of geometrical constraints. By doing so, we drastically reduce the search space over which to test for matching correctness. At this point we can proceed with an exhaustive search through the above reduced set of hypotheses and select the match that maximizes a matching quality index.

Once the matching process is complete, the egomotion estimation can be performed rather easily by searching for the rigid motion that minimizes an appropriate *merging cost* function between two sets of 3D lines that pertain two different partial reconstructions. Notice 3D contours are generally reconstructed as chains of segments whose length and fragmentation may vary quite drastically from multi-view to multi-view. We thus proceed by first determining the 3D line portions that best fit (through linear regression) the chains of fragments of edges that have been recognized as straight. Then instead of measuring the distances between extremal points of two segments, we measure the distance between the extremal points of one segment and the line that the other segment lies upon (see Fig. 5a).

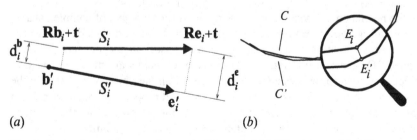

(a)   (b)

Fig. 5. Evaluation of the merging cost of two straight 3D contours (a). 3D curve matching: evaluation of the distance between two polylines (b).

Such distances are used for defining the merging cost as follows

$$C_s = \sum_{i=1}^{N} \left[\left(d_i^b \right)^2 + \left(d_i^e \right)^2 \right] .$$

In fact, the orientation of edges is usually less sensitive to fragmentation problems than their location in the 3D space [1,17].

4.2 Egomotion Refinement from Curved Contours

As already said above, curved contours are used for improving the accuracy of the egomotion's estimate. A matching process is still required but it is much simpler as we already have a first approximation of the camera motion, determined from straight edges. In fact, applying the pre-determined rigid motion to the set of curved edges, we can decide whether two curved edges are matched, depending on their global distance, which can be measured, with reference to Fig. 5a, as

$$d_g = \frac{1}{2}\left(d(C,C') + d(C',C) \right) , \qquad d(C,C') = \frac{1}{N}\sum_i d(E_i,C') = \frac{1}{N}\sum_i \left\| \overline{E_i E_i'} \right\|$$

The global cost function for motion refinement is of the form $C = C_s + kC_c$, where C_s and C_c are the merging costs associated to straight and curved contours, respectively, and k is weight for balancing the two contributes.

4.3 Examples of Application

The method has been extensively tested against convergence problems and has been applied to a series of trinocular acquisitions of real images in order to evaluate qualitatively and quantitatively the accuracy of the results and the speed of convergence. Furthermore, the performance of the proposed method has been compared with that of a previously studied method [2,8] based on point correspondences between artificially added markers. Quantitative results have been obtained by measuring the maximum thickness of the bundles of edges when superimposing different sets of them with the estimated motion parameters. The performance of the proposed method has been proven to be equal to or better than that of the point-based approach, resulting in a maximum bundle size of about 100 ppm in all tests (after merging all 3D edges coming from 20 multi-views).

In Fig. 6, the results on 3D data merging are reported for an object of complex shape, in both cases of egomotion estimated through point and line correspondences. In the first case the cost function is a rigidity constraint based on the distance between reconstructed 3D points of different 3D data sets. Such points are markers that have been artificially added to the scene (white dots placed on the object's support). In the second case the egomotion is computed with the method proposed in this paper. Even though no artificially added markers have been used for the estimation, the accuracy of the estimate is comparable with that obtained through point-matching.

5. Conclusions

In this paper we presented our global approach to accurate 3D reconstruction with a calibrated multi-camera system. In particular, we presented a simple and effective technique for calibrating CCD-based multi-camera acquisition systems. The proposed method was proven to be capable of highly-accurate results even when using very

Fig. 6. One of the original views of the object, fusion of all 3D edge sets through 3D point correspondences (added marks), fusion of all 3D edge sets through 3D contour matching (natural features).

simple calibration target-sets (with little or no *a-priori* information on it) and low-cost imaging devices, such as standard TV-resolution cameras connected to commercial frame-grabbers. We also showed our approach to adaptive calibration, which proved effective for keeping track of camera parameter drift through natural feature tracking.

We also proposed and illustrated a general and robust approach to the problem of close-range partial 3D reconstruction of objects from stereo-correspondences. The method is independent on the geometry of the acquisition system which could be a set of *n* cameras with strongly converging optical axes. The robustness of the approach can be mainly attributed to the physicality of the matching process, which is virtually performed in the 3D space. In fact, both 3D location and local orientation of the surface patches are estimated, so that the geometric distortion can be accounted for. The method takes into account the viewer-dependent radiometric distortion as well.

Finally, we presented a method for performing an accurate patchworking of the partial reconstructions, through 3D feature matching. The method, based on the best fusion of 3D curves, provides very accurate results even when using standard TV-resolution CCD cameras.

References

[1] N. Ayache, "Artificial vision for Mobile Robots", MIT Press, 1991.

[2] F. Pedersini, A. Sarti, S. Tubaro: "A Multi-view Trinocular System for Automatic 3D Object Modelling and Rendering". XVIII Int. Congress for Photogrammetry and Remote Sensing, 1996, Vienna, Austria.

[3] Y. Otha, T. Kanade, "Stereo by Intra- and Inter-Scanline Search Using Dynamic Programming", IEEE Trans. On PAMI, Vol. 7, N. 2, pp. 139-154, 1985.

[4] P. Pigazzini, F. Pedersini, A. Sarti, S. Tubaro: "3D Area Matching with Arbitrary Multiview Geometry". EURASIP Signal Processing: Image Communications. Special issue on *3D video technology*, early issues of 1998.

[5] F. Pedersini, A. Sarti, S. Tubaro: "Robust Area Matching". IEEE Intern. Conf. on Image Processing, 1997, October 26-29, 1997, Santa Barbara, CA, USA.

[6] F. Pedersini, A. Sarti, S. Tubaro: "Egomotion Estimation of a Multicamera System through Line Correspondence". IEEE ICIP, 1997, October 26-29, 1997, Santa Barbara, CA, USA.

[7] F. Pedersini, A. Sarti, S. Tubaro: "Automatic Surface Reconstruction of 3D Works of Art". International Conference on Electronic Imaging and the Visual Arts (EVA'97). March 19-25, 1997, Florence, Italy.

[8] F. Pedersini, A. Sarti, S. Tubaro: "3D Motion Estimation of a Trinocular System for a Full-3D Object Reconstruction". IEEE Intern. Conf. on Image Processing, September, 1996, Lausanne, Switzerland.

[9] R. Y. Tsai, "A Versatile Camera Calibration Technique for High-Accuracy 3D Machine Vision Metrology Using off-the-shelf TV Cameras and Lenses" - IEEE J. on Robotics and Automation, Vol. RA-3, No. 4, Aug. 1987, pp. 323-344.

[10] J. Weng, P. Cohen, M. Herniou, "Camera Calibration with Distortion Model and Accuracy Evaluation", *IEEE Trans. on PAMI*, Oct 1992, Vol. 14, No 10, 965-980.

[11] F. Pedersini, D. Pele, A. Sarti, S. Tubaro: "Calibration and Self-Calibration of Multi-Ocular Camera Systems". Intl. Workshop on Synthetic-Natural Hybrid Coding and Three-Dimensional (3D) Imaging (IWSNHC3DI'97). September 5-9 1997, Rhodes, Greece.

[12] F. Pedersini, S. Tubaro: , "Accurate 3D reconstruction from trinocular views through integration of improved edge-matching and area-matching techniques." *VIII European Signal Processing Conference*, September 10-13, 1996, Trieste, Italy

[13] L. Kitchen, A. Rosenfeld, "Gray-level corner detection", Pattern Recognition Letters, No. 1, 1982, pp. 95-102.

[14] G. Giraudon, R. Deriche "On corner and vertex detection", Proceedings Intl. Conf. on Computer Vision and Pattern Recognition, Maui, Hawaii, June 1991, pp. 650-655.

[15] K. Rohr, "Recognizing Corners by Fitting Parametric Models", Intl. J. of Computer Vision, Vol. 9, No. 3, 1992, pp. 213-230.

[16] J. Mallet: "Discrete Smooth Interpolation", ACM Tr. on Graphics, Vol. 8, No. 2, 1989, pp. 121-144.

[17] Z. Zhang, O.D. Faugeras: "3D dynamic scene analysis: a stereo based approach", Springer, 1992.

[18] F. Pedersini, A. Sarti, S. Tubaro: "Tracking Camera Calibration in Multi-Camera Sequences through Automatic Feature Detection and Matching". IX European Signal Processing Conference, September 8 - 11, 1998, Rhodes, Greece.

[19] L. Van Gool, A. Zisserman, "Automatic 3D model building from video sequences". European Tr. on Telecommunications, Vol. 8, No. 4, pp. 369-78, July-Aug. 1997.

Metric 3D Surface Reconstruction from Uncalibrated Image Sequences

Marc Pollefeys, Reinhard Koch, Maarten Vergauwen, and Luc Van Gool

K.U.Leuven, ESAT-PSI, Kard. Mercierlaan 94, B-3001 Heverlee, Belgium
firstname.lastname@esat.kuleuven.ac.be

Abstract. Modeling of 3D objects from image sequences is one of the challenging problems in computer vision and has been a research topic for many years. Important theoretical and algorithmic results were achieved that allow to extract even complex 3D scene models from images. One recent effort has been to reduce the amount of calibration and to avoid restrictions on the camera motion. In this contribution an approach is described which achieves this goal by combining state-of-the-art algorithms for uncalibrated projective reconstruction, self-calibration and dense correspondence matching.

1 Introduction

Obtaining 3D models from objects is an ongoing research topic in computer vision. A few years ago the main applications were robot guidance and visual inspection. Nowadays however the emphasis is shifting. There is more and more demand for 3D models in computer graphics, virtual reality and communication. This results in a change in emphasis for the requirements. The visual quality becomes one of the main points of attention.

The acquisition conditions and the technical expertise of the users in these new application domains can often not be matched with the requirements of existing systems. These require intricate calibration procedures every time the system is used. There is an important demand for flexibility in acquisition. Calibration procedures should be absent or restricted to a minimum.

Additionally, the existing systems are often build around specialized hardware (e.g. laser range finders or stereo rigs) resulting in a high cost for these systems. Many new applications however require robust low cost acquisition systems. This stimulates the use of consumer photo- or video cameras.

In this paper we present a system which retrieves a 3D surface model from a sequence of images taken with off-the-shelf consumer cameras. The user acquires the images by freely moving the camera around the object. Neither the camera motion nor the camera settings have to be known. The obtained 3D model is a scaled version of the original object (i.e. a *metric* reconstruction), and the surface albedo is obtained from the image sequence as well.

Other researchers have presented systems for extracting 3D shape and texture from image sequences acquired with a freely moving camera. The approach of

Reinhard Koch, Luc Van Gool (Eds.): SMILE '98, LNCS 1506, pp. 139–154, 1998.

Tomasi and Kanade [32] used an affine factorization method to extract 3D from image sequences. An important restriction of this system is the assumption of orthographic projection.

Another type of system starts from an approximate 3D model and camera poses and refines the model based on images (e.g. *Facade* proposed by Debevec et al. [5]). The advantage is that less images are required. On the other hand a preliminary model must be available and the geometry should not be too complex.

Our system uses full perspective cameras and does not require prior models. It combines state-of-the-art algorithms of different domains: *projective reconstruction, self-calibration* and *dense depth estimation*.

Projective Reconstruction: It has been shown by Faugeras [7] and Hartley [12] that a reconstruction up to an arbitrary projective transformation was possible from an uncalibrated image sequence. Since then a lot of effort has been put in reliably obtaining accurate estimates of the projective calibration of an image sequence. Robust algorithms were proposed to estimate the fundamental matrix from image pairs [33,36]. Based on this, an algorithm which sequentially retrieves the projective calibration of a complete image sequence has been developed [1]. A more recent version based on the trifocal tensor was presented in [9].

Self-Calibration: Since a projective calibration is not sufficient for many applications, researchers tried to find ways to automatically upgrade projective calibrations to metric (i.e. euclidean up to scale). Typically, it is assumed that the same camera is used throughout the sequence and that the intrinsic camera parameters are constant. This proved a difficult problem and many researchers have worked on it [8,22,35,13,25,34,15,26]. One of the main problems is that critical motion sequences exist for which self-calibration does not result in a unique solution [31]. We proposed a more pragmatic approach [27,28] which assumes that some parameters are (approximately) known but which allows others to vary. Therefore this approach can deal with zooming/focusing cameras. Others have proposed similar approaches [2,16].

Dense Depth Estimation: Since the calibration of the image sequence has been estimated we can use stereoscopic triangulation techniques between image correspondences to estimate depth. The difficult part in stereoscopic depth estimation is to find dense correspondence maps between the images. The correspondence problem is facilitated by exploiting constraints derived from the calibration and from some assumptions about the scene. We use an approach that combines local image correlation methods with a dynamic programming approach to constrain the correspondence search [21]. This technique was first proposed by Gimmel'Farb [10] and further developed by others [4,6,19].

The rest of the paper is organized as follows: In section 2 a general overview of the system is given. In the subsequent sections the different steps are explained in more detail: projective reconstruction (section 3), self-calibration (section 4), dense matching (section 5) and model generation (section 6). Section 7 concludes the paper.

2   Overview of the Method

The presented system gradually retrieves more information about the scene and the camera setup. The first step is to relate the different images. This is done pairwise by retrieving the epipolar geometry. An initial reconstruction is then made for the first two images of the sequence. For the subsequent images the camera pose is estimated in the projective frame defined by the first two cameras. For every additional image that is processed at this stage, the interest points corresponding to points in previous images are reconstructed, refined or corrected. Therefore it is not necessary that the initial points stay visible throughout the entire sequence. The result of this step is a reconstruction of typically a few hundred interest points. The reconstruction is only determined up to a projective transformation.

The next step is to restrict the ambiguity of the reconstruction to a metric one. In a projective reconstruction not only the scene, but also the camera is distorted. Since the algorithm deals with unknown scenes, it has no way of identifying this distortion in the reconstruction. Although the camera is also assumed to be unknown, some constraints on the intrinsic camera parameters (e.g. rectangular or square pixels, constant aspect ratio, principal point in the middle of the image, ...) can often still be assumed. A distortion on the camera mostly results in the violation of one or more of these constraints. A metric reconstruction/calibration is obtained by transforming the projective reconstruction until all the constraints on the cameras intrinsic parameters are satisfied.

At this point the system effectively disposes of a calibrated image sequence. The relative position and orientation of the camera is known for all the viewpoints. This calibration facilitates the search for corresponding points and allows us to use a stereo algorithm that was developed for a calibrated system. This step allows to find correspondences for most of the pixels in the images.

From these correspondences the distance from the points to the camera center can be obtained through triangulation. These results are refined and completed by combining the correspondences from multiple images.

A dense metric 3D surface model is obtained by approximating the depth map with a triangular wire frame. The texture is obtained from the images and mapped onto the surface.

In figure 1 an overview of the systems is given. It consists of independent modules which pass on the necessary information to the next modules. The first module computes the projective calibration of the sequence together with a sparse reconstruction. In the next module the metric calibration is computed from the projective camera matrices through self-calibration. Then dense correspondence maps are estimated. Finally all results are integrated in a textured 3D surface reconstruction of the scene under consideration.

Throughout the rest of the paper the different steps of the method will be explained in more detail. An image sequence of the Arenberg castle in Leuven will be used for illustration. Some of the images of this sequence can be seen in Figure 2. The full sequence consists of 24 images recorded with a video camera.

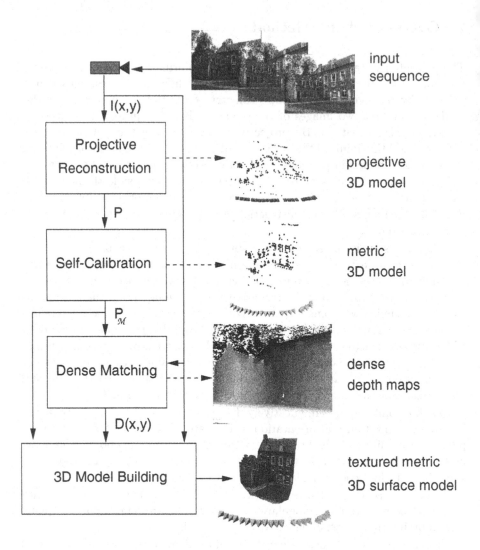

Fig. 1. Overview of the system: from the image sequence ($I(x,y)$) the projective reconstruction is computed; the projection matrices P are then passed on to the self-calibration module which delivers a metric calibration $P_{\mathcal{M}}$; the next module uses these to compute dense depth maps $D(x,y)$; all these results are assembled in the last module to yield a textured 3D surface model. On the right side the results of the different modules are shown: the preliminary reconstructions (both projective and metric) are represented by point clouds, the cameras are represented by little pyramids, the results of the dense matching are accumulated in dense depth maps (light means close and dark means far).

Fig. 2. Some images of the Arenberg castle sequence. This sequence is used throughout the paper to illustrate the different steps of the reconstruction system.

2.1 Notations

In this section some notations used in this paper are introduced. A detailed explanation of the basic concepts can be found in [23]. Projective geometry and homogeneous coordinates are used throughout this paper. Metric entities are indicated with a subscript $\mathcal{M}$.

The following equation is used to describe the perspective projection of the scene onto the images

$$m \propto \mathbf{P}M \tag{1}$$

where $\mathbf{P}$ is a 3×4 projection matrix describing the perspective projection process, $M = [XYZ\,1]^{\top}$ and $m = [x\,y\,1]^{\top}$ are vectors containing the homogeneous coordinates of the world points respectively image points. Note that $\propto$ will be used throughout this paper to indicate equality up to a non-zero scale factor. Indexes i and j will be used for points (e.g. M_i), indexes k and l for views (e.g. $\mathbf{P}_k$).

In the metric case the camera projection matrix factorizes as follows:

$$\mathbf{P}_{\mathcal{M}} = \mathbf{K}[\mathbf{R}\,|\text{-}\mathbf{R}t] \tag{2}$$

Here $(\mathbf{R}, t)$ denotes a rigid transformation (i.e. $\mathbf{R}$ is a rotation matrix and t is a translation vector) which indicate the position and orientation of the camera, while the upper triangular calibration matrix $\mathbf{K}$ encodes the intrinsic parameters of the camera:

$$\mathbf{K} = \begin{bmatrix} f_x & s & u_x \\ & f_y & u_y \\ & & 1 \end{bmatrix} \tag{3}$$

where f_x and f_y represent the focal length divided by the pixel width resp. height, (u_x, u_y) represents the principal point and s is a factor which is zero for rectangular pixels.

The following notations are used for the epipolar geometry: $\mathbf{F}_{kl}$ is the fundamental matrix for views k and l, e_{kl} is the epipole corresponding to this fundamental matrix in view l.

3   Projective Reconstruction

At first the images are completely unrelated. The only assumption is that the images form a sequence in which consecutive images do not differ too much. Therefore the local neighborhood of image points originating from the same scene point should look similar if images are close in the sequence. This allows for automatic matching algorithms to retrieve correspondences.

3.1   Relating the Images

It is not feasible to compare every pixel of one image with every pixel of the next image. It is therefore necessary to reduce the combinatorial complexity. In addition not all points are equally well suited for automatic matching. The local neighborhoods of some points contain a lot of intensity variation and are therefore easy to differentiate from others. An interest point detector (i.e. the Harris corner detector [11]) is used to select a certain number of such suited points. These points should be well located and indicate salient features that stay visible in consecutive images. Correspondences between these image points need to be established through a matching procedure.

Matches are determined through normalized cross-correlation of the intensity values of the local neighborhood. Since images are supposed not to differ too much, corresponding points can be expected to be found back in the same region of the image. Therefore at first only interest points which have similar positions are considered for matching. When two points are mutual best matches they are considered as potential correspondences.

Since the epipolar geometry describes the complete geometry relating two views, this is what should be retrieved. Computing it from the set of potential matches through least squares does in general not give satisfying results due to its sensitivity to outliers. Therefore a robust approach should be used. Several techniques have been proposed [33,36] based on robust statistics [29]. Our system incorporates the RANSAC (RANdom SAmpling Consesus) approach used by Torr [33]. Table 1 sketches this technique.

- repeat
  - take minimal sample (7 matches)
  - compute **F**
  - estimate $\%inliers$
  until $P_{OK}(\%inliers, \#trials) > 95\%$
- refine **F** (using all inliers)

Table 1. Robust estimation of the epipolar geometry from a set of matches containing outliers using RANSAC (P_{OK} indicates the probability that the epipolar geometry has been correctly estimated).

Once the epipolar geometry has been retrieved, one can start looking for more matches to refine this geometry. In this case the search region is restricted to a few pixels around the epipolar lines.

3.2   Initial Reconstruction

The two first images of the sequence are used to determine a reference frame. The world frame is aligned with the first camera. The second camera is chosen so that the epipolar geometry corresponds to the retrieved $\mathbf{F}_{12}$ (see [23]).

$$\begin{aligned} \mathbf{P}_1 &= [\quad\quad \mathbf{I}_{3\times 3} \quad\quad 0 \quad] \\ \mathbf{P}_2 &= [\ [e_{12}]_\times \mathbf{F}_{12} + e_{12} a^\top \ a_4 e_{12} \ ] \end{aligned} \quad\quad (4)$$

where $[e_{12}]_\times$ indicates the vector product with e_{12}. Equation 4 is not completely determined by the epipolar geometry (i.e. $\mathbf{F}_{12}$ and e_{12}), but has 4 more degrees of freedom (i.e. $a_i, i = 1 \ldots 4$). $a = [a_1 a_2 a_3]^\top$ determines the position of the plane at infinity and a_4 determines the global scale of the reconstruction. To avoid some problems during the reconstruction it is recommended to determine a in such a way that the plane at infinity does not cross the scene. Our implementation follows the quasi-Euclidean approach proposed in [1], but an alternative would be to use Hartley's cheirality [13] or oriented projective geometry [18]. Since there is no way to determine the global scale from the images, a_4 can arbitrarily be chosen to $a_4 = 1$.

Once the cameras have been fully determined the matches can be reconstructed through triangulation. The optimal method for this is given in [14]. This gives us a preliminary reconstruction.

3.3   Adding a View

For every additional view the pose towards the pre-existing reconstruction is determined, then the reconstruction is updated. This is illustrated in Figure 3.

The first steps consists of finding the epipolar geometry as described in Section 3.1. Then the matches which correspond to already reconstructed points are used to compute the projection matrix $\mathbf{P}_k$. This is done using a robust procedure similar to the one laid out in Table 1. In this case a minimal sample of 6 matches is needed to compute $\mathbf{P}_k$. Once $\mathbf{P}_k$ has been determined the projection of already reconstructed points can be predicted. This allows to find some additional matches to refine the estimation of $\mathbf{P}_k$. This means that the search space is gradually reduced from the full image to the epipolar line to the predicted projection of the point. This is illustrated in Figure 4.

Once the camera projection matrix has been determined the reconstruction is updated. This consists of refining, correcting or deleting already reconstructed points and initializing new points for new matches.

After this procedure has been repeated for all the images, one disposes of camera poses for all the views and the reconstruction of the interest points. In the further modules mainly the camera calibration is used. The reconstruction itself is used to obtain an estimate of the disparity range for the dense stereo matching.

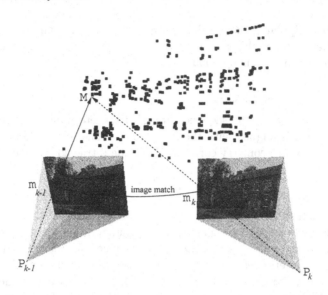

Fig. 3. Image matches (m_{k-1}, m_k) are found as described before. Since the image points, m_{k-1}, relate to object points, M_k, the pose for view k can be computed from the inferred matches (M, m_k).

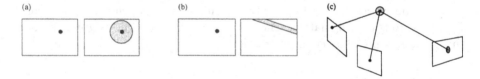

Fig. 4. (a) a priori search range, (b) search range along the epipolar line and (c) search range around the predicted position of the point.

4   Self-Calibration

The reconstruction obtained as described in the previous paragraph is only determined up to an arbitrary projective transformation. This might be sufficient for some robotics or inspection applications, but certainly not for visualization. In this section a technique to restrict this ambiguity to metric is described.

For a metric calibration the factorization of the camera projection matrices as in Equation 2 yields the physical parameters of the camera. A necessary condition for a metric reconstruction is therefore that constraints which exist on the intrinsic camera parameters are verified through this factorization.

To apply the following method to standard zooming/focusing cameras, some assumptions should be made. Often it can be assumed that pixels are rectangular or even square. If necessary (e.g. when only a short image sequence is at hand, when the projective calibration is not accurate enough or when the motion sequence is close to critical [31] without additional constraints), it can also be used that the principal point is close to the center of the image.

For the actual computations the absolute conic ω is used. This is an imaginary conic located in the plane at infinity Π_∞. Both entities are the only geometric entities which are in invariant under all Euclidean transformations. The plane at infinity and the absolute conic respectively encode the affine and metric properties of space. This means that when the position of Π_∞ is known in a projective framework, affine invariants can be measured. Since the absolute conic is invariant under Euclidean transformations its image only depends on the intrinsic camera parameters (focal length, ...) and not on the extrinsic camera parameters (camera pose). The following equation applies for the dual image of the absolute conic:

$$\omega_k^* \propto \mathbf{K}_k\mathbf{K}_k^\top \qquad (5)$$

Therefore constraints on the intrinsic camera parameters are readily translated to constraints on the dual image of the absolute conic. This image is obtained from the absolute conic through the following projection equation:

$$\omega_k^* \propto \mathbf{P}_k\Omega^*\mathbf{P}_k^\top \qquad (6)$$

where Ω^* is the dual absolute quadric which encodes both the absolute conic and its supporting plane, the plan at infinity. The constraints on ω_k^* can therefore be back-projected through this equation. The result is a set of constraints on the position of the absolute conic (and the plane at infinity).

Our systems first uses a linear method to obtain an approximate calibration. This calibration is then refined through a non-linear optimization step in a second phase.

4.1 Initial Calibration

To obtain a linear algorithm some assumptions have to be made. If the pixels are square and the principal point is in the middle of the image, the image can be transformed to obtain the following intrinsic camera parameters:

$$\mathbf{K}_k = \begin{bmatrix} f_k & 0 & 0 \\ & f_k & 0 \\ & & 1 \end{bmatrix} \qquad (7)$$

This simplifies Equation (6) as follows:

$$\lambda \begin{bmatrix} f_k^2 & 0 & 0 \\ 0 & f_k^2 & 0 \\ 0 & 0 & 1 \end{bmatrix} = \mathbf{P}_k \begin{bmatrix} c_1 & c_2 & c_3 & c_4 \\ c_2 & c_5 & c_6 & c_7 \\ c_3 & c_6 & c_8 & c_9 \\ c_4 & c_7 & c_9 & c_{10} \end{bmatrix} \mathbf{P}_k^\top \qquad (8)$$

with λ an explicit scale factor. From the left-hand side of Eq. (8) it can be seen that the following equations have to be satisfied:

$$\omega_k^{*(11)} = \omega_k^{*(22)}, \qquad (9)$$

$$\omega_k^{*(12)} = \omega_k^{*(13)} = \omega_k^{*(23)} = 0 \tag{10}$$

$$\omega_k^{*(21)} = \omega_k^{*(31)} = \omega_k^{*(32)} = 0 . \tag{11}$$

with $\omega_k^{*(ij)}$ representing the element on row i and column j of ω_k^*. Note that due to symmetry (10) and (11) result in identical equations. These constraints can thus be imposed on the right-hand side, yielding 4 independent linear equations in $c_i, i = 1 \dots 10$ for every image:

$$P_k^{(1)} \Omega^* P_k^{(1)^\top} = P_k^{(2)} \Omega^* P_k^{(2)^\top}$$

$$2 P_k^{(1)} \Omega^* P_k^{(2)^\top} = 0$$

$$2 P_k^{(1)} \Omega^* P_k^{(3)^\top} = 0$$

$$2 P_k^{(2)} \Omega^* P_k^{(3)^\top} = 0$$

with $P_k^{(j)}$ representing row j of $\mathbf{P}_k$ and Ω_* parameterized as in (8). The rank 3 constraint can be imposed by taking the closest rank 3 approximation (using SVD for example). This approach holds for sequences of 3 or more images. The special case of 2 images can also be dealt with, but with a slightly different approach. For more details see [28].

4.2   Refined Calibration

To refine the calibration Eq. (6) is used directly in a non-linear least squares criterion. In this case the user is free to specify the constraints which should be imposed. Every intrinsic parameter can be known, fixed or free. The dual image absolute conics ω_k^* should be parameterized in such a way that these constraints are enforced. For the absolute quadric Ω^* a parameterization should be used which takes into account the symmetry and the rank 3 constraint. Since Ω^* is only determined up to scale this leaves us with a minimum parameterization of 8 parameters. This can be done by putting $\Omega_{33}^* = 1$ and by calculating Ω_{44}^* from the rank 3 constraint. The following parameterization satisfies these requirements:

$$\Omega^* = \begin{bmatrix} \mathbf{KK}^\top & -\mathbf{KK}^\top a \\ -a^\top \mathbf{KK}^\top & a^\top \mathbf{KK}^\top a \end{bmatrix} . \tag{12}$$

Here a defines the position of the plane at infinity $\Pi_\infty = [a^\top \ 1]^\top$. In this case the transformation from projective to metric is particularly simple:

$$\mathbf{T}_{\mathcal{P} \to \mathcal{M}} = \begin{bmatrix} \mathbf{K}^{-1} & 0 \\ a^\top & 1 \end{bmatrix} \tag{13}$$

An approximate solution to these equations can be obtained through non-linear least squares. The following criterion should be minimized ($\|.\|_F$ is the Frobenius norm):

$$\min \sum_{i=1}^n \left\| \frac{\mathbf{K}_i \mathbf{K}_i^\top}{\|\mathbf{K}_i \mathbf{K}_i^\top\|_F} - \frac{\mathbf{P}_i \Omega^* \mathbf{P}_i^\top}{\|\mathbf{P}_i \Omega^* \mathbf{P}_i^\top\|_F} \right\|_F^2 . \tag{14}$$

5   Dense Depth Estimation

Only a few scene points are reconstructed from feature tracking. Obtaining a dense reconstruction could be achieved by interpolation, but in practice this does not yield satisfactory results. Small surface details would never be reconstructed in this way. Additionally, some important features are often missed during the corner matching and would therefore not appear in the reconstruction.

These problems can be avoided by using algorithms which estimate correspondences for almost every point in the images. At this point algorithms can be used which were developed for calibrated stereo rigs.

5.1   Rectification

Since we have computed the calibration between successive image pairs we can exploit the epipolar constraint that restricts the correspondence search to a 1-D search range. It is possible to re-map the image pair to standard geometry with the epipolar lines coinciding with the image scan lines [19]. The correspondence search is then reduced to a matching of the image points along each image scanline. This results in a dramatic increase of the computational efficiency of the algorithms by enabling several optimizations in the computations. The rectification procedure is illustrated in Figure 5. For some motions (i.e. when the epipole is located in the image) standard rectification based on planar homographies is not possible and a more advanced procedure should be used [30].

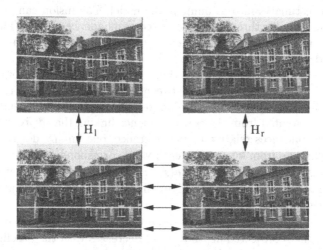

Fig. 5. Through the rectification process the image scan lines are brought into epipolar correspondence. This allows important gains in computational efficiency and simplification of the dense stereo matching algorithm.

5.2   Dense Stereo Matching

In addition to the epipolar geometry other constraints like preserving the order of neighboring pixels, bidirectional uniqueness of the match, and detection of occlusions can be exploited. These constraints are used to guide the correspondence towards the most probable scan-line match using a dynamic programming scheme [6].

For dense correspondence matching a disparity estimator based on the dynamic programming scheme of Cox *et al.* [4], is employed that incorporates the above mentioned constraints. It operates on rectified image pairs (I_k, I_l) where the epipolar lines coincide with image scan lines. The matcher searches at each pixel in image I_k for maximum normalized cross correlation in I_l by shifting a small measurement window (kernel size 5x5 to 7x7 pixel) along the corresponding scan line. The selected search step size ΔD (usually 1 pixel) determines the search resolution. Matching ambiguities are resolved by exploiting the ordering constraint in the dynamic programming approach [19]. The algorithm was further adapted to employ extended neighborhood relationships and a pyramidal estimation scheme to reliably deal with very large disparity ranges of over 50% of image size [6].

5.3   Multiview Matching

The pairwise disparity estimation allows to compute image to image correspondence between adjacent rectified image pairs, and independent depth estimates for each camera viewpoint. An optimal joint estimate is achieved by fusing all independent estimates into a common 3D model. The fusion can be performed in an economical way through controlled correspondence linking. The approach utilizes a flexible multi viewpoint scheme which combines the advantages of small baseline and wide baseline stereo [21].

Assume an image sequence with $k = 1 \rightarrow n$ images. Starting from a reference view point k the correspondences between adjacent images $(k + 1, k + 2, ..., n)$ and $(k - 1, k - 2, ..., 1)$ are linked in a chain. The depth for each reference image point m_k is computed from the correspondence linking that delivers two lists of image correspondences relative to the reference, one linking down from $k \rightarrow 1$ and one linking up from $k \rightarrow n$. For each valid corresponding point pair $(\mathbf{x_k}, \mathbf{x_l})$ we can triangulate a depth estimate $d(x_k, x_l)$ along S_{m_k} with e_l representing the depth uncertainty. The left part of Figure 6 visualizes the decreasing uncertainty interval during linking.

While the disparity measurement resolution ΔD in the image is kept constant (at 1 pixel), the reprojected depth error e_l decreases with the baseline. Outliers are detected by controlling the statistics of the depth estimate computed from the correspondences. All depth values that fall within the uncertainty interval around the mean depth estimate are treated as inliers. They are fused by a 1-D kalman filter to obtain an optimal mean depth estimate. Outliers are undetected correspondence failures and may be arbitrarily large. As threshold to detect the outliers we utilize the depth uncertainty interval e_l.

The result of this procedure is a very dense depth map. Most occlusion problems are avoided by linking correspondences from up and down the sequence. An example of such a very dense depth map is given in Figure 6.

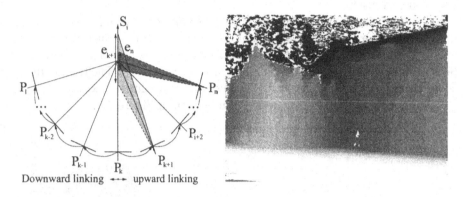

Fig. 6. Depth fusion and uncertainty reduction from correspondence linking (left), Resulting dense depth map (light means near and dark means far) (right).

6   Building the Model

The dense depth maps as computed by the correspondence linking must be approximated by a 3D surface representation suitable for visualization. So far each object point was treated independently. To achieve spatial coherence for a connected surface, the depth map is spatially interpolated using a parametric surface model. The boundaries of the objects to be modeled are computed through depth segmentation. In a first step, an object is defined as a connected region in space. Simple morphological filtering removes spurious and very small regions. We then employ a bounded thin plate model with a second order spline to smooth the surface and to interpolate small surface gaps in regions that could not be measured. If the object consist of dominant planar regions, the local surface normal may be exploited to segment the object into planar parts [20].

The spatially smoothed surface is then approximated by a triangular wireframe mesh to reduce geometric complexity and to tailor the model to the requirements of Computer Graphics visualization systems. The mesh triangulation currently utilizes the reference view only to build the model. The surface fusion from different view points to completely close the models remains to be implemented. Sometimes it is not possible to obtain a single metric framework for large objects like buildings since one may not be able to record images continuously around it. In that case the different frameworks have to be registered to each other. This will be done using available surface registration schemes [3].

Texture mapping onto the wire-frame model greatly enhances the realism of the models. As texture map one could take the reference image texture alone and map it to the surface model. However, this creates a bias towards the selected image and imaging artifacts like sensor noise, unwanted specular reflections or the shading of the particular image is directly transformed onto the object. A better choice is to fuse the texture from the image sequence in much the same way as depth fusion.

The viewpoint linking builds a controlled chain of correspondences that can be used for texture enhancement as well. The estimation of a robust mean texture will capture the static object only and the artifacts (e.g. specular reflections or pedestrians passing in front of a building) are suppressed [17]. The texture fusion could also be done on a finer grid, yielding a super resolution texture [24].

An example of the resulting model can be seen in Figure 7.

Fig. 7. 3D surface model obtained automatically from an uncalibrated image sequence, shaded (left), textured (right).

7   Conclusion

An automatic 3D scene modeling technique was discussed that is capable of building models from uncalibrated image sequences. The technique is able to extract metric 3D models without any prior knowledge about the scene or the camera. The calibration is obtained by assuming a rigid scene and some constraints on the intrinsic camera parameters (e.g. square pixels).

Work remains to be done to get more complete models by fusing the partial 3D reconstructions. This will also increase the accuracy of the models and eliminate artifacts at the occluding boundaries. For this we can rely on work already done for calibrated systems.

Acknowledgments

We would like to thank Andrew Zisserman and his team from Oxford for supplying us with robust projective reconstruction software. A specialization grant from the Flemish Institute for Scientific Research in Industry (IWT), the financial support from the EU ACTS project AC074 'VANGUARD' and the Belgian IUAP project 'IMechS' are also gratefully acknowledged.

References

1. P. Beardsley, P. Torr and A. Zisserman, 3D Model Acquisition from Extended Image Sequences. *Proc. European Conference on Computer Vision*, Cambridge, UK, vol.2, pp.683-695, 1996.
2. S. Bougnoux, From Projective to Euclidean Space Under any Practical Situation, a Criticism of Self-Calibration, In *Proc. International Conference on Computer Vision*, pp.790-796, Bombay, 1998.
3. Y. Chen and G. Medioni, Object Modeling by Registration of Multiple Range Images, In *Proc. IEEE International Conference on Robotics and Automation*, pp.2724-2729, Sacramento (CA), 1991.
4. I. Cox, S. Hingorani and S. Rao, A Maximum Likelihood Stereo Algorithm, *Computer Vision and Image Understanding*, Vol. 63, No. 3, May 1996.
5. P. Debevec, C. Taylor and J. Malik, Modeling and Rendering Architecture from Photographs: A Hybrid Geometry- and Image-Based Approach, In *Siggraph*, 1996.
6. L. Falkenhagen, Hierarchical Block-Based Disparity Estimation Considering Neighbourhood Constraints. In *Proc. International Workshop on SNHC and 3D Imaging*, Rhodes, Greece, 1997.
7. O. Faugeras, What can be seen in three dimensions with an uncalibrated stereo rig. In *Proc. European Conference on Computer Vision*, pp.563-578, 1992.
8. O. Faugeras, Q.-T. Luong and S. Maybank, Camera self-calibration: Theory and experiments, In *Proc. European Conference on Computer Vision*, pp.321-334, 1992.
9. A. Fitzgibbon and A. Zisserman, Automatic camera recovery for closed or open image sequences, In *Proc. European Conference on Computer Vision*, pp.311-326, Freiburg, 1998.
10. G. Gimel'farb, Symmetrical approach to the problem of automatic stereoscopic measurements in photogrammetry, Cybernetics, 1979, 15(20, 235-247; Consultants Bureau, N.Y.
11. C. Harris and M. Stephens, A combined corner and edge detector, in *Fourth Alvey Vision Conference*, pp.147-151, 1988.
12. R. Hartley, Estimation of relative camera positions for uncalibrated cameras. In *Proc. European Conference on Computer Vision*, pp.579-587, 1992.
13. R. Hartley, Euclidean reconstruction from uncalibrated views. In *Applications of invariance in Computer Vision*, LNCS 825, Springer-Verlag, pp.237-256, 1994.
14. R. Hartley and P. Sturm, Triangulation, *Computer Vision and Image Understanding*, 68(2):146-157, 1997.
15. A. Heyden and K. Åström, Euclidean Reconstruction from Constant Intrinsic Parameters In *Proc. International Conference on Pattern Recognition*, Vienna, Austria, pp.339-343, 1996.
16. A. Heyden, K. Åström, Euclidean Reconstruction from Image Sequences with Varying and Unknown Focal Length and Principal Point, In *Proc. IEEE Conference on Computer Vision and Pattern Recognition*, San Juan, Puerto Rico, 1997.

17. M. Irani and S. Peleg, Super resolution from image sequences, In *Proc. International Conference on Pattern Recognition*, Atlantic City, NJ, 1990.
18. S. Laveau, Géométrie d'un systeème de N caméras. Théorie, estimation et applications. Ph.D. thesis, Ecole Polytechnique, France, 1996.
19. R. Koch, Automatische Oberflachenmodellierung starrer dreidimensionaler Objekte aus stereoskopischen Rundum-Ansichten. *PhD thesis*, University of Hannover, Germany, 1996.
20. R. Koch, Surface Segmentation and Modeling from Stereoscopic Image Sequences, In *Proc. International Conference on Pattern Recognition*, Vienna, 1996.
21. R. Koch, M. Pollefeys and L. Van Gool, Multi Viewpoint Stereo from Uncalibrated Video Sequences, In *Proc. European Conference on Computer Vision*, Freiburg, Germany, 1998.
22. Q.-T. Luong and O. Faugeras, O. Self Calibration of a moving camera from point correspondences and fundamental matrices. In *Internation Journal of Computer Vision*, vol.22-3, 1997.
23. Moons, T. A Tutorial on Multi-View Relationships, In *Proc. SMILE workshop*, Freiburg, 1998.
24. E. Ofek, E. Shilat, A. Rappopport and M. Werman, Highlight and Reflection Independent Multiresolution Textures from Image Sequences. *IEEE Computer Graphics and Applications*, vol.17 (2), March-April 1997.
25. M. Pollefeys and L. Van Gool, A stratified approach to self-calibration. In *Proc. International Conference on Computer Vision and Pattern Recognition*, San Juan, Puerto Rico, pp.407-412, 1997.
26. M. Pollefeys and L. Van Gool, Self-calibration from the absolute conic on the plane at infinity, In *Proc. International Conference on Computer Analysis of Images and Patterns*, Kiel, Germany, pp. 175-182, 1997.
27. M. Pollefeys, R. Koch and L. Van Gool, Self-Calibration and Metric Reconstruction in spite of Varying and Unknown Internal Camera Parameters, In *Proc. International Conference on Computer Vision*, pp.90-95, Bombay, 1998.
28. M. Pollefeys, R. Koch and L. Van Gool, Self-Calibration and Metric Reconstruction in spite of Varying and Unknown Intrinsic Camera Parameters, to appear in IJCV.
29. P. Rousseeuw, *Robust Regression and Outlier Detection*, Wiley, New York, 1987.
30. S. Roy, J. Meunier and I. Cox, Cylindrical Rectification to Minimize Epipolar Distortion, In *Proc. IEEE Conference on Computer Vision and Pattern Recognition*, pp.393-399, 1997.
31. P. Sturm, Critical Motion Sequences for Monocular Self-Calibration and Uncalibrated Euclidean Reconstruction. In *Proc. International Conference on Computer Vision and Pattern Recognition*, San Juan, Puerto Rico, pp.1100-1105, 1997.
32. C. Tomasi and T. Kanade, Shape and motion from image streams under orthography: A factorization approach, *International Journal of Computer Vision*, 9(2):137-154, 1992.
33. P. Torr, Motion Segmentation and Outlier Detection, PhD Thesis, Dept. of Engineering Science, University of Oxford, 1995.
34. B. Triggs, The Absolute Quadric, In *Proc. International Conference on Computer Vision and Pattern Recognition*, San Juan, Puerto Rico, pp.609-614, 1997.
35. C. Zeller and O. Faugeras, Camera self-calibration from video sequences: the Kruppa equations revisited. INRIA, Sophia-Antipolis, France, Research Report 2793, 1996.
36. Z. Zhang, R. Deriche, O. Faugeras and Q.-T. Luong, A robust technique for matching two uncalibrated images through the recovery of the unknown epipolar geometry, *Artificial Intelligence Journal*, Vol.78, pp.87-119, October 1995.

Automatic 3D Model Construction for Turn-Table Sequences

Andrew W. Fitzgibbon, Geoff Cross, and Andrew Zisserman

Robotics Research Group, Department of Engineering Science,
University of Oxford, 19 Parks Road, Oxford OX1 3PJ, United Kingdom
{awf,geoff,az}@robots.ox.ac.uk
http://www.robots.ox.ac.uk/~vgg

Abstract. As virtual worlds demand ever more realistic 3D models, attention is being focussed on systems that can acquire graphical models from real objects. This paper describes a system which, given a sequence of images of an object rotating about a single axis, generates a textured 3D model fully automatically. In contrast to previous approaches, the technique described here requires no prior information about the cameras or scene, and does not require that the turntable angles be known (or even constant through the sequence).

From an analysis of the projective geometry of the situation, it is shown that the rotation angles may be determined unambiguously, and that camera calibration, camera positions and 3D structure may be determined to within a two parameter family. An algorithm has been implemented to compute this reconstruction fully automatically. The two parameter reconstruction ambiguity may be removed by specifying, for example, camera aspect ratio and parallel scene lines. Examples are presented on four turn-table sequences.

1 Introduction

Numerous graphics and computer vision papers have dealt with the construction of 3D solid models by volume intersection from multiple views. As pointed out by Ponce [19] the idea dates back to Baumgart [2] in 1974. Well engineered systems built on this idea have yielded 3D texture mapped graphical models of impressive quality [5, 19]. A good example is the system of Hannover [17] where, as is usual for such systems, the object is rotated on a turntable against a background which can easily be removed by image segmentation. Such systems are generally completely calibrated, i.e. the camera internal parameters, rotation angles, distance to the rotation axis etc are all accurately known.

In this paper we develop the projective geometry of single axis rotation and describe its automatic and optimal estimation from an image sequence with no other *a priori* information supplied. It is shown that 3D structure and cameras can be estimated (including auto-calibration) up to an overall two-parameter ambiguity. The angle of rotation between views is not ambiguous. This geometry is described in section 2, and an algorithm to automatically estimate this geometry from an image sequence is given in section 3.

Reinhard Koch, Luc Van Gool (Eds.): SMILE '98, LNCS 1506, pp. 155–170, 1998.
© Springer-Verlag Berlin Heidelberg 1998

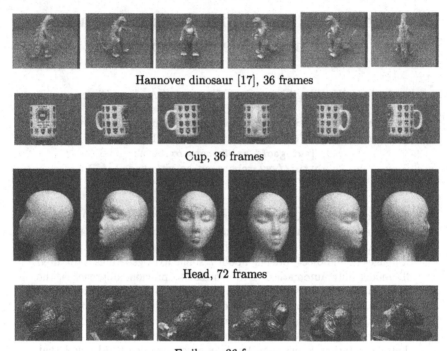

Hannover dinosaur [17], 36 frames

Cup, 36 frames

Head, 72 frames

Freiburg, 36 frames

Fig. 1. Some example sequences.

We then describe a modelling system based on this estimated geometry. The input is a turn-table image sequence, the output is the set of cameras and a 3D VRML texture mapped model of the object, with all processing automatic. Other than the estimation of the camera geometry, the system is much the same as the calibrated Hannover system, and involves: volume intersection; representation of the surface as a triangulated network; triangle grouping; and texture mapping. This is described in section 4. The output models are of equal quality to those of fully calibrated sequences—a fact demonstrated on a sequence supplied by Hannover and shown in figure 1.

General uncalibrated multiple-view geometry Before specializing to single axis rotation, consider first the general case of reconstruction from multiple pinhole cameras viewing a 3D scene [10]. 3D points X in the scene are represented as homogeneous 4-vectors $[X, Y, Z, 1]^\top$, while their 2D projections x are represented as homogeneous 3-vectors $[x, y, 1]^\top$. The action of each camera is represented by a 3×4 projection matrix P:

$$x_{ij} = P_i X_j$$

The m cameras are indicated by P_i while the n 3D points are X_j.

In the case where m different cameras view a scene, there is no relationship between the P_i. Therefore $11m$ parameters are required to specify all the cameras. When the cameras have identical internal parameters, such as when a camera is moved through a static scene without any change in focus or zoom, the internal parameters are constant over the sequence. This reduces the number of parameters required to specify the cameras from $11m$ to $6m + 5$.

Uncalibrated single-axis multiple-view geometry In the single-axis case, we shall see that the number of parameters is reduced to $m + 8$, and that estimation is relatively straightforward. It is worth contrasting the reduction in the number of parameters that occurs in this special motion case, with a popular alternative which is to reduce the number of parameters by approximating the perspective camera as a weak perspective camera [8, 18]. Such "affine" cameras are an approximation of the geometry, and under imaging conditions which typically apply in close-range model acquisition, this approximation can be quite poor. However, the advantage of this approximation is a simple, non-iterative estimation algorithm [23]. In contrast, specializing the motion to single axis is an exact model of the geometry, not an approximation, yet it admits a closed-form solution. Previous investigations of turn-table sequences [12, 20, 22] have not fully exploited the special motion to simplify camera recovery.

2   The Projective Geometry of Single Axis Motion

A single axis motion consists of a set of Euclidean actions on the world such that the relative motion between the scene and camera can be described by rotations about a single fixed axis. In the language of screw decompositions, any Euclidean action can be decomposed as a rotation about a screw axis (which is parallel to the Euclidean rotation axis) together with a translation along the screw axis. In the case of single axis motions there is zero translation along the screw axis, and the screw axes of each Euclidean action coincide.

There are many cases of this motion commonly occurring in computer vision applications. The most common, and the one that is used here, is the case of a static camera viewing an object rotating on a turntable. A second case is that of a camera rotating about a fixed axis. For example, imagine a QuickTime VR acquisition device where the camera is offset along its principal axis, so that it does not rotate about its centre. A third case is that of a camera viewing a rotating mirror.

It will be helpful in the following to consider that the object is fixed and that the camera rotates about it. The camera internal parameters are fixed. To aid visualisation, we assume that the rotation axis is vertical, so that the camera rotates in a horizontal plane.

We now describe the camera and image geometry arising from this constrained motion, particularly the fixed entities of the motion, which play an important rôle. It will be seen that the fundamental matrix, F, trifocal tensor $\mathcal{T}$ and camera matrices P all have additional properties, and that the multiple view tensors (F and $\mathcal{T}$) determine a two-parameter family of camera matrices. This ambiguity is removed using internal and external constraints.

2.1 3D Geometry

Under a single axis rotation the camera centre describes a circle in a horizontal plane π_h. The geometry is illustrated in figure 2. There are a number of geometric entities which are fixed under this motion, including:

- The (vertical) rotation axis denoted $\mathbf{L}_s$ ("s" for "screw" axis). This is a line of fixed points.
- The plane π_h, and indeed the pencil of horizontal planes. Each plane is fixed as a set.

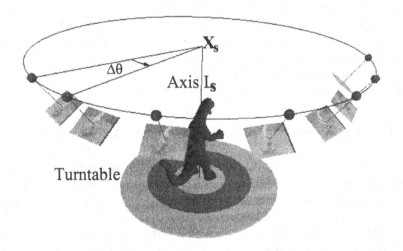

Fig. 2. 3D geometry. The cameras are indicated by their centres (spheres), and image planes. The point $\mathbf{X}_s$ is the intersection of the plane, π_h, containing the camera centres with the rotation axis $\mathbf{L}_s$.

2.2 Image Fixed Entities

The 3D fixed entities are *sequence invariants* since they are imaged at the same position in every view. Their images include:

- The line l_s which is the image of the rotation axis $\mathbf{L}_s$. Since points on $\mathbf{L}_s$ are fixed under the motion, their images are also fixed under the motion.
- The line l_h in which π_h intersects each image plane. It is the vanishing line of π_h (and indeed of all planes parallel to π_h).

- The point x_s which is the image of the fixed point X_s.
- The point v which is the vanishing point of the rotation axis.

These sequence invariants are illustrated schematically in Figure 3a, and the two fixed lines are illustrated in Figure 4 on a real sequence.

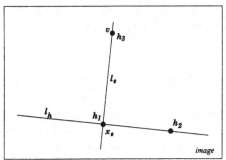 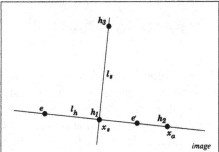

Fig. 3. (a) **Fixed image entities** over the sequence, and their relation to the columns h_i of H. (b) **Two-view entities**. The entities which can be determined from F and their relation to the columns of H. The symmetric part of F is a degenerate conic consisting of the two lines l_s and l_h. The anti- symmetric part is represented by the point x_a. Points x_s and x_a have fixed position over all view pairs. The position of the epipoles depends on the angle of rotation $\Delta\theta_i$ between views.

2.3 Camera Matrices

We have the freedom to choose the world coordinate system so that the rotation axis is aligned with the world z axis, and the first camera centre is at position t on the x axis. Thus the first camera may be written

$$P_0 = H[I \mid t]$$

where H is a homography representing the camera internal parameters and rotation about the camera centre, and $t = (t, 0, 0)^\top$. A rotation of the camera by θ about the z axis is achieved by post-multiplying P_0 by

$$\begin{bmatrix} R_Z(\theta) & \mathbf{0} \\ \mathbf{0}^\top & 1 \end{bmatrix}$$

yielding the camera $P_\theta = H[R_Z(\theta) \mid t]$. In detail, with h_i the columns of H:

$$P_\theta = \begin{bmatrix} h_1 & h_2 & h_3 \end{bmatrix} \begin{bmatrix} \cos\theta & \sin\theta & 0 & t \\ -\sin\theta & \cos\theta & 0 & 0 \\ 0 & 0 & 1 & 0 \end{bmatrix} \tag{1}$$

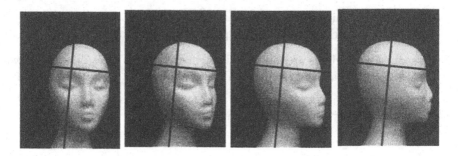

Fig. 4. Fixed image lines. The fixed image lines are shown overlaid on images from the head sequence. The almost vertical line is l_s, the horizontal line is l_h (see also figure 3a). The eyebrow of the mannequin, which is approximately coplanar with π_h, remains tangent to l_h as the object rotates. These fixed lines are automatically computed from the images using the algorithm of §3.

This division of the internal and external parameters means that H and t are fixed over the sequence, only the angle of rotation, θ_i, about the z axis varies for each camera P_i. Given this parametrization, the estimation problem can now be precisely stated: we seek the common matrix H and the angles θ_i in order to estimate the set of cameras P_i for the sequence. Thus a total of $8+m$ parameters must be estimated for m views, where 8 is the number of degrees of freedom of the homography H. Note, the magnitude of translation only determines the overall scaling and need not be considered further as we are interested only in a similarity reconstruction. The relative angle between views i and $i+1$ is denoted $\Delta\theta_i$.

We now relate the columns of H to the fixed image entities:

- x_s is the image of $\mathbf{X}_s = (0, 0, 0, 1)^\top$, so under any P_θ, $x_s = H(t, 0, 0)^\top = t h_1$.
- v is the image of the direction of the world z axis $(0, 0, 1, 0)^\top$, giving $v = h_3$.
- $l_s = h_1 \times h_3$.
- $l_h = h_1 \times h_2$.

These relations are shown in figure 3a. To see that l_s, the image of the z axis, is given by $l_s = h_1 \times h_3$, consider a general point on z, $(0, 0, u, v)^\top$. Its projection by any P_θ is $H(tv, 0, u)^\top = tv h_1 + u h_3$, a point on the line through h_1 and h_3. Similar consideration of a general point on π_h leads to $l_h = h_1 \times h_2$.

The columns of H are the vanishing points of an orthogonal triad of directions. This triad rotates with the camera such that these vanishing points are related to the fixed entities. h_2 is the vanishing point of the direction orthogonal to those corresponding to h_1 and h_3.

The procedure from here on is to determine the columns of H from the multiple view tensors (F, $\mathcal{T}$). We first consider the reconstruction ambiguity, where it will be seen that from the multiple view tensors (i.e. from image measurements alone) H is not determined uniquely, but is restricted to a two-parameter family.

2.4   Reconstruction Ambiguity

It is well known [6, 11] that if nothing is known of the calibration of 2 or more cameras, nor their relative placement, then the reconstruction of the scene and cameras is determined only up to an arbitrary projective transformation of 3-space. For if T is any 4×4 invertible matrix, representing a projective transformation of $\mathbb{P}^3$, then replacing points $\mathbf{X}_j$ by $T\mathbf{X}_j$ and cameras P_i by P_iT^{-1} does not change the image points since $x_{ij} = P_i\mathbf{X}_j = P_iT^{-1}T\mathbf{X}_j$.

In the case of single axis rotation we know that the cameras P_i have the restricted form (1), so we may ask the question: suppose we determine a reconstruction with a set of cameras of the form (1), how are these cameras related to the actual cameras?

To answer this question [16], consider the class of transformations T which preserve the form (1). Suppose we have two reconstructions with sets of cameras $P_i = H[R_Z(\theta_i) \mid t]$ and $P_i' = H'[R_Z(\theta_i') \mid t']$ of the correct form. Then, T is an admissible transformation if the sets of cameras are related as:

$$P_i' = H'[R_Z(\theta_i') \mid t'] = H[R_Z(\theta_i) \mid t]\, T \qquad \forall i \tag{2}$$

over at least 3 views (i.e. $m \geq 3$). We require that both H and H' are full rank 3×3 matrices independent of θ and θ', and $t = (t, 0, 0)^\top, t' = (t', 0, 0)^\top$. Since we are not concerned with the Euclidean transformation part of the ambiguity, T may be written as

$$T = \begin{bmatrix} U & 0 \\ a^\top & 1 \end{bmatrix}$$

where U is an upper triangular matrix. It can be shown that that (2) has a solution provided: $\theta_i' = \theta_i$ and

$$T = \begin{bmatrix} 1 & 0 & 0 & 0 \\ 0 & 1 & 0 & 0 \\ 0 & 0 & \alpha & 0 \\ 0 & 0 & \beta & 1 \end{bmatrix} \tag{3}$$

with α and β arbitrary scalars.

This shows: (i) from image measurements alone the camera matrices can be recovered only up to a two parameter ambiguity parametrized by α and β. Note that the angle θ is not ambiguous; (ii) the actual cameras lie in this two parameter family, so the reconstruction is also related to the actual cameras by (3); (iii) the matrix H is only determined up to this ambiguity. To see this, note that

$$P' = \begin{bmatrix} h_1 & h_2 & h_3 \end{bmatrix} \begin{bmatrix} \cos\theta & \sin\theta & 0 & t \\ -\sin\theta & \cos\theta & 0 & 0 \\ 0 & 0 & 1 & 0 \end{bmatrix} \begin{bmatrix} 1 & 0 & 0 & 0 \\ 0 & 1 & 0 & 0 \\ 0 & 0 & \alpha & 0 \\ 0 & 0 & \beta & 1 \end{bmatrix}$$

$$= \begin{bmatrix} h_1 & h_2 & h_3 \end{bmatrix} \begin{bmatrix} 1 & 0 & \beta t \\ 0 & 1 & 0 \\ 0 & 0 & \alpha \end{bmatrix} \begin{bmatrix} \cos\theta & \sin\theta & 0 & t \\ -\sin\theta & \cos\theta & 0 & 0 \\ 0 & 0 & 1 & 0 \end{bmatrix}$$

This means that the last column of H can only be determined to within a 2-parameter ambiguity from image measurements alone. We will see this ambiguity arising when computing H from F and $\mathcal{T}$ in the following sections, and return in section 2.7 to methods of resolving the ambiguity.

2.5   Two-View Geometry

The 2-view geometry of single axis rotation is identical to that of planar motion, for which many of the following properties of F have been derived [1, 4, 24]. In the planar motion case, however, the axis $\mathbf{L}_s$ varies between view pairs, i.e. it is not fixed over the sequence.

The fundamental matrix may be parametrized in terms of the fixed image lines and an image point $\boldsymbol{x}_a$ as

$$F = \mu \left[\boldsymbol{x}_a\right]_\times + \tan \frac{\Delta\theta}{2} \left(\boldsymbol{l}_s \boldsymbol{l}_h{}^\top + \boldsymbol{l}_h \boldsymbol{l}_s{}^\top\right) \quad \text{with} \quad \boldsymbol{x}_a{}^\top \boldsymbol{l}_h = 0$$

where the 3-vectors $\boldsymbol{x}_a, \boldsymbol{l}_h, \boldsymbol{l}_s$ are scaled to unit norm.

Once F is estimated from two view correspondences then the points $\boldsymbol{x}_a$ and $\boldsymbol{x}_s$ and lines $\boldsymbol{l}_s$ and $\boldsymbol{l}_h$ are known. Their relation to H is shown in figure 3b, and also can be read off from the expression for F in terms of H and $\Delta\theta$:

$$F = [\boldsymbol{h}_2]_\times - \frac{1}{(\det H)} \tan \frac{\Delta\theta}{2} \left((\boldsymbol{h}_1 \times \boldsymbol{h}_3)(\boldsymbol{h}_1 \times \boldsymbol{h}_2)^\top + (\boldsymbol{h}_1 \times \boldsymbol{h}_2)(\boldsymbol{h}_1 \times \boldsymbol{h}_3)^\top\right)$$

Taking account of the unknown scaling of the homogeneous 3-vectors, the columns of H are determined from F (i.e. the 2-view geometry), to within the 3-parameter family

$$H = [\boldsymbol{h}_1, \boldsymbol{h}_2, \boldsymbol{h}_3] = [\boldsymbol{x}_s, \mu \boldsymbol{x}_a, \nu \boldsymbol{x}_s + \omega \boldsymbol{d}] \tag{4}$$

parametrized by the as yet undetermined scalars μ, ν, and ω, where $\boldsymbol{d}$ is an (arbitrary) point on $\boldsymbol{l}_s$, which may be chosen as $\boldsymbol{d} = \boldsymbol{l}_s \times (0, 0, 1)^\top$. In detail the columns are determined by the following procedure:

1. Extract $\boldsymbol{x}_a$ from the antisymmetric part of F, $F - F^\top = [\boldsymbol{x}_a]_\times$.
2. Extract epipoles $\boldsymbol{e}$ and $\boldsymbol{e}'$, and compute $\boldsymbol{l}_h = \boldsymbol{e} \times \boldsymbol{e}'$.
3. Compute $\boldsymbol{l}_s = (2\boldsymbol{l}_h{}^\top \boldsymbol{l}_h I - \boldsymbol{l}_h \boldsymbol{l}_h{}^\top)(F + F^\top)\boldsymbol{l}_h$.
4. Compute $\boldsymbol{x}_s = \boldsymbol{l}_s \times \boldsymbol{l}_h$.
5. Set H according to (4).

Although the ratio k_i, where $\mu = k_i \tan \frac{\Delta\theta_i}{2}$ may be computed from F, the value of μ is unknown. This means that $\Delta\theta_i$ cannot be computed from two views.

2.6   Three View Geometry

From three views, it can be shown that the trifocal tensor may be written as a pencil of tensors, parametrized by μ:

$$\mathcal{T} = \mu^2 \mathcal{K} + \mathcal{K}'$$

where the elements of the tensors $\mathcal{K}$ and $\mathcal{K}'$ are computed from the two-view quantities k_i and $\mathtt{H}$. Thus, one three-view point correspondence allows μ, and hence the $\Delta\theta_i$, to be recovered uniquely. The only remaining ambiguity is in the third column h_3 of $\mathtt{H}$. As shown in section 2.4 this ambiguity cannot be reduced further by the single axis motion constraint alone.

2.7   Removing the Reconstruction Ambiguity

The reconstruction ambiguity of (3) is the following [25]: metric structure is recovered in planes perpendicular to the axis of rotation; there is an unknown 1D projective transformation along the axis. The ambiguity may be written:

$$\begin{pmatrix} x \\ y \\ z \end{pmatrix} \rightarrow \begin{pmatrix} x/(\beta'z+1) \\ y/(\beta'z+1) \\ \alpha'z/(\beta'z+1) \end{pmatrix}$$

Note that since metric structure is determined in planes perpendicular to the axis, the angle of rotation between views is known. Figure 5 illustrates this projective ambiguity.

Fig. 5. Projective ambiguity: With no information about the camera or scene, there is a 1D projective ambiguity in the z direction. Five models of the cup with different choices for h_3.

To this point no information on the internal calibration of the camera, or on the 3D shape of the object has been used. Internal constraints are provided, for example, by that fact that the image pixels have zero-skew, and known aspect ratio. Often the zero-skew constraint is not useful in practice because it does not resolve the ambiguity [26]. For example, if the image plane is parallel to the rotation axis then all members in the family of solutions for the calibration matrix will already satisfy the zero-skew constraint, so it does not provide any additional information.

It can be shown that specifying the aspect ratio places a quartic constraint on the parameters α, β.

The easiest method of resolution is to use a vanishing point in the scene to identify the plane at infinity (we already have the vanishing line of π_h), for example by identifying two or more parallel scene lines. This determines h_3 up to scale (i.e. the ratio $\alpha : \beta$), and the only remaining ambiguity is then a relative scaling of the z and plane directions:

$$\begin{pmatrix} X \\ Y \\ Z \end{pmatrix} \rightarrow \begin{pmatrix} X \\ Y \\ \alpha''Z \end{pmatrix}$$

Given h_3 up to scale, the internal aspect ratio then determines α and β uniquely (up to sign). Alternatively, the aspect ratio of the object can be used to resolve the ambiguity.

3   Estimation of Camera Matrices

This section describes the implementation of the algebra developed in the previous section. From a raw input sequence we wish to compute the P matrices and 3D point structure. We first summarize the algebraic procedure of the previous section, with the estimation steps then described in more detail below.

3.1   Algorithm Summary

Robust point tracks are computed *a priori* using our general-motion trifocal tensor based system [7].

1. For each pair of views fit the planar-motion fundamental matrix (eq. 4).
2. From one of the Fs determine H up to a 3-parameter ambiguity.[1]
3. From each T_i determine μ and the two angles $\Delta\theta_i$ and $\Delta\theta_{i+1}$.
4. Average μ over the sequence, and angles from overlapping triplets.
5. Bundle adjust, varying H, θ_i and 3D points X_j to minimize reprojection error $\sum_{i,j} d^2(x_{ij}, H[R_Z(\theta_i)|t]X_j)$.

3.2   Point Tracking

This is achieved by tracking interest points (Harris corners [9]) through the sequence. Tracking is easily achieved by our current general motion system [3, 7], based on the trifocal tensor. This functionality is used unchanged in the current system, although some speed improvements would certainly accrue if this process were also modified to make use of the specialized geometry. Example point tracks and track lifetimes are shown in figure 6. Typically, about 150 points are tracked in each image triplet, with 2000–3000 points appearing through a sequence.

3.3   F Estimation

The fundamental matrix is estimated by first fitting a general-motion F to the points. Then the symmetric part of F is truncated to rank 2, and decomposed to recover l_s and the epipoles. This provides a starting point for the special

---

[1] In the special case where the between-view angles $\Delta\theta_i$ are known to be identical, F is estimated from all 2-view correspondences (typically thousands). Then H is extracted from this F. Similarly T is fitted to all triplets.

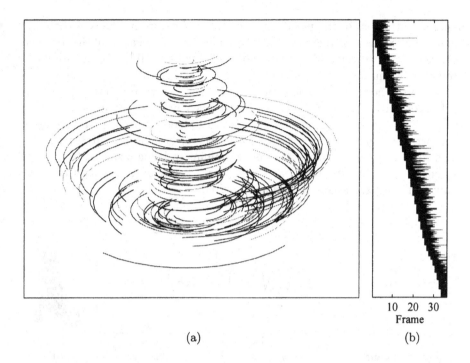

10 20 30
Frame
(b)

(a)

Fig. 6. (a) **Point tracks**: Some point tracks from the dinosaur sequence. For clarity, only the 200 tracks which survived for longer than 7 successive views are shown. In total, 3070 points were tracked for 3 or more views. (b) **Track lifetimes** for dinosaur sequence: Each horizontal bar corresponds to a single point track, extending from the first to last frame in which the point was seen. The measurement matrix is relatively sparse, and few points survived longer than 15 frames.

parametrized form (4), which is fitted by minimizing the distance of points to epipolar lines. The average number of point matches per view pair varied from 137 for the Head sequence to 399 for the Dinosaur. The average distance from points to epipolar lines is about 0.3 pixels.

3.4 $\mathcal{T}$ Estimation

The trifocal tensor is used only to determine μ from three views. From the special-form fundamental matrices for the views, the two tensors $\mathcal{K}$ and $\mathcal{K}'$ are computed. Then single point correspondences provide candidates for μ. The median of the candidates yields the estimate of μ for the triplet.

3.5 Bundle Adjustment

The two and three view geometry provides an (excellent) initial estimate for the camera matrices. In order to determine the maximum likelihood estimate, we assume that errors in the positions of the 2D points are normally distributed. An optimal estimate is then obtained by nonlinear minimization of the distances between the reprojected 3D points and the 2D corners [10]. Typical results for geometry estimation are shown in figure 7. These results are of comparable quality with those of [22] where the camera matrices were determined using a calibration pattern. Convergence is generally achieved in 8 iterations, reducing the RMS reprojection error from 0.3 pixels to 0.1 pixels. For 2000 points, compute time per iteration is of the order of 10 seconds on a 300MHz UltraSparc. The radius of convergence is large, the correct minimum being achieved from initial estimates where the θ_i are in error by up to a factor of 2, although of course many more iterations (about 100) are required.

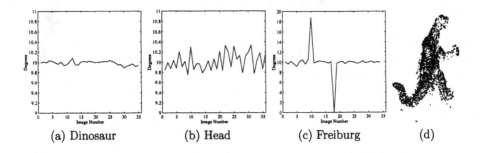

(a) Dinosaur   (b) Head   (c) Freiburg   (d)

Fig. 7. Geometry estimation. The graphs show the recovered angles between successive views for each of three sequences. (a) Object rotated by a mechanical turntable with a resolution of 1 millidegree. The RMS difference between the angle recovered by our algorithm and the nominal value is 40 millidegrees. This demonstrates the accuracy of the angle recovery. (b) (c) Turn-table rotated by hand. The angle increment is irregular and unknown *a priori*. Variation is up to 20° due to missing and repeated views. (d) 3D points for dinosaur sequence.

4   Space Carving and Surface Rendering

The object is computed as the intersection of the outline cones back-projected from all views. The outline in each image is determined by blue-screening. The surface of the object is determined very efficiently by an octree based algorithm.

Octree Growing The octree is initialised as a cube bounding the object, and is recursively subdivided to determine the surface. Each cube has one of three labels [21] depending on whether it lies entirely inside; entirely outside; or partially intersects the surface. The former two cases are not of interest, and the nodes are not subdivided. The subdividing is stopped at a preset depth. The label of a cube is determined by successively projecting it into each image in the sequence. An example of the octree "surface" developing is shown in figure 8.

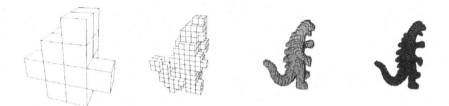

Fig. 8. Octree generation: the dinosaur octree is grown from a single bounding box. The images above show the octree after (*left* to *right*) 3, 5, 7 and 8 subdivisions, given 36 images of the dinosaur.

Surface Generation The standard marching cubes algorithm[15] provides an initial consistent surface which is then smoothed using a localised surface decimation algorithm. Examples are shown in figures 9 through 11.

Fig. 9. Texture-mapped dinosaur model. From 36 input images, a 256^3 resolution volumentric model was generated containing 34752 triangles.

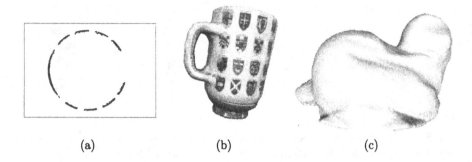

(a)   (b)   (c)

Fig. 10. (a) Top view of reconstructed cup points (no points were detected on the handle). RMS difference from a fitted cylinder is 0.004 of the diameter. (b) Texture-mapped cup model. (c) Shaded Freiburg model. The visual hull effect is apparent here, with too few views to penetrate to the object surface.

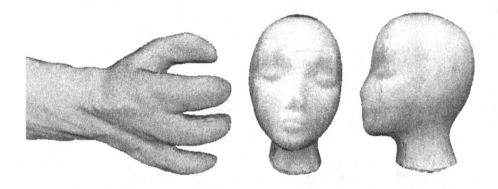

Fig. 11. Closeup: High-resolution model of dinosaur hand, showing the fine detail recoverable using volume intersection. **Head**: Texture-mapped model. The shades of grey indicate the view from which each texture was taken—for each triangle, the view in which it has largest visible area is chosen as the texture source.

5   Conclusions

This paper has demonstrated that uncalibrated structure recovery systems based on the single-axis motion constraint can produce models of equivalent quality to fully calibrated systems, making *a-priori* calibration and expensive control of the viewing environment unnecessary.

Also of interest are the results of volume intersection as a means of produc-ing fully 3D models of arbitrary topologies. Although the "visual hull" effect[14] might be expected to severely limit the range of models that can be acquired, the dinosaur and cup experiments (see especially Figure 11) show that surprisingly complex models can be acquired. However, it is on the model acquisition phase that most plans for future work are centred—given the excellent camera geometry, more advanced techniques [13] can be applied. Particularly, correlation of the surface texture is expected to allow true super-resolution texture mapping, and simultaneously get "inside" the visual hull.

Acknowledgements We are grateful for permission to use the dinosaur sequence supplied by the University of Hannover, and for financial support from EU ACTS Project Vanguard.

References

[1] M. Armstrong, A. Zisserman, and R. Hartley. Self-calibration from image triplets. In *Proc. ECCV*, LNCS 1064/5, pages 3–16. Springer-Verlag, 1996.

[2] B. G. Baumgart. *Geometric Modelling for Computer Vision*. PhD thesis, Standford University, Palo Alto, 1974.

[3] P. Beardsley, P. Torr, and A. Zisserman. 3D model acquisition from extended image sequences. In *Proc. ECCV*, LNCS 1064/1065, pages 683–695. Springer-Verlag, 1996.

[4] P. Beardsley and A. Zisserman. Affine calibration of mobile vehicles. In Mohr, R. and Chengke, W., editors, *Europe-China workshop on Geometrical Modelling and Invariants for Computer Vision*, pages 214–221. Xidan University Press, Xi'an, China, 1995.

[5] E. Boyer. Object models from contour sequences. In *Proc. ECCV*, pages 109–118, 1996.

[6] O. Faugeras. What can be seen in three dimensions with an uncalibrated stereo rig? In *Proc. ECCV*, LNCS 588, pages 563–578. Springer-Verlag, 1992.

[7] A. W. Fitzgibbon and A. Zisserman. Automatic camera recovery for closed or open image sequences. In *Proc. ECCV*, pages 311–326, 1998.

[8] C. J. Harris. Structure-from-motion under orthographic projection. In *Proc. ECCV*, pages 118–123, 1990.

[9] C. J. Harris and M. Stephens. A combined corner and edge detector. In *Alvey Vision Conf.*, pages 147–151, 1988.

[10] R. I. Hartley. Euclidean reconstruction from uncalibrated views. In J. Mundy, A. Zisserman, and D. Forsyth, editors, *Applications of Invariance in Computer Vision*, LNCS 825, pages 237–256. Springer-Verlag, 1994.

[11] R. I. Hartley, R. Gupta, and T. Chang. Stereo from uncalibrated cameras. In *Proc. CVPR*, 1992.

[12] S. B. Kang. Quasi-euclidean recovery from unknown but complete orbital motion. Technical Report CRL 97/10, Digital CRL, 1997.

[13] K. N. Kutalakos and S. M. Seitz. A theory of shape by space carving. Technical Report CSTR 692, University of Rochester, 1998.

[14] A. Laurentini. The visual hull concept for silhouette-based image understanding. *IEEE T-PAMI*, 16(2):150–162, Feb 1994.

[15] W. Lorensen and H. Cline. Marching cubes: A high resolution 3d surface construction algorithm. *ACM Computer Graphocs*, 21(24):163–169, July 1987.

[16] J. Mundy and A. Zisserman. Repeated structures: Image correspondence constraints and ambiguity of 3D reconstruction. In J. Mundy, A. Zisserman, and D. Forsyth, editors, *Applications of invariance in computer vision*, pages 89–106. Springer-Verlag, 1994.

[17] W. Niem and R. Buschmann. Automatic modelling of 3d natural objects from multiple views. In *European Workshop on Combined Real and Synthetic Image Processing for Broadcast and Video Production, Hamburg, Germany*, 1994.

[18] L. S. Shapiro, A. Zisserman, and M. Brady. 3d motion recovery via affine epipolar geometry. *IJCV*, 16(2):147–182, 1995.

[19] S. Sullivan and J. Ponce. Automatic model construction, pose estimation, and object recognition from photographs using triangular splines. In *Proc. ICCV*, 1998.

[20] R. Szeliski. Shape from rotation. In *Proc. CVPR*, pages 625–630, 1991.

[21] R. Szeliski. Rapid octree construction from image sequences. *CVGIP*, 58(1):23–32, July 1993.

[22] R. Szeliski and S. B. Kang. Recovering 3D shape and motion from image streams using non-linear least squares. Technical Report CRL 93/3, DEC Cambridge Research Lab, Mar 1993.

[23] C. Tomasi and T. Kanade. Shape and motion from image streams under orthography: A factorization approach. *IJCV*, 9(2):137–154, November 1992.

[24] T. Vieville and D. Lingrand. Using singular displacements for uncalibrated monocular vision systems. Technical Report 2678, I.N.R.I.A., 1995.

[25] A. Zisserman, P. Beardsley, and I. Reid. Metric calibration of a stereo rig. In *IEEE Workshop on Representation of Visual Scenes, Boston*, pages 93–100, 1995.

[26] A. Zisserman, D. Liebowitz, and M. Armstrong. Resolving ambiguities in autocalibration. *Phil. Trans. R. Soc. Lond. A*, 356:1193–1211, 1998.

Geometrically Constrained Structure from Motion: Points on Planes

Richard Szeliski and P. H. S. Torr

Microsoft Research, One Microsoft Way, Redmond, WA 98052, USA,
szeliski-philtorr@microsoft.com,
http://www.research.microsoft.com/research/vision/

Abstract. Structure from motion algorithms typically do not use external geometric constraints, e.g., the coplanarity of certain points or known orientations associated with such planes, until a final post-processing stage. In this paper, we show how such geometric constraints can be incorporated early on in the reconstruction process, thereby improving the quality of the estimates. The approaches we study include hallucinating extra point matches in planar regions, computing fundamental matrices directly from homographies, and applying coplanarity and other geometric constraints as part of the final bundle adjustment stage. Our experimental results indicate that the quality of the reconstruction can be significantly improved by the judicious use of geometric constraints.

1 Introduction

Structure from (image) motion algorithms attempt to simultaneously recover the 3D structure of a scene or object and the positions and orientations of the cameras used to photograph the scene. Algorithms for recovering structure and motion have many applications, such as the construction of 3D environments and pose localization for robot navigation and grasping, the automatic construction of 3D CAD models from photographs, and the creation of large photorealistic virtual environments.

Structure from motion is closely related to photogrammetry, where the 3D location of certain key *control points* is usually known, thereby allowing the recovery of camera pose prior to the estimation of shape through triangulation techniques. In structure from motion, however, very few constraints are usually placed (or assumed) on the geometric structure of the scene being analyzed. This has encouraged the development of mathematically elegant and general formulations and algorithms that can be applied in the absence of any prior knowledge.

In practice, however, structure from motion is often applied to scenes which contain strong geometric regularities. The man made world is full of planar structures such as floors, walls, and tabletops, many of which have known orientations e.g. horizontal, vertical or known relationships e.g. parallelism and perpendicularity. Even the natural world tends to have certain regularities, such as the generally vertical direction of tree growth, or the existence of relatively

Reinhard Koch, Luc Van Gool (Eds.): SMILE '98, LNCS 1506, pp. 171–186, 1998.

flat ground planes. A quick survey of many recent structure from motion papers indicates that the test data sets include some very strong regularities (mostly horizontal and vertical planes and lines) which are never exploited [22,2], except perhaps for a final global shape correction.

In this paper, we argue using external geometric knowledge can never decrease the quality of a reconstruction so long as this knowledge is applied in a statistically valid way. Rather than developing a single algorithm or methodology, we examine a number of different plausible ways to bring geometric constraints to bear, and then evaluate these empirically. In this way, we hope to elucidate where geometric constraints can be used effectively. Our experiments demonstrate that hallucinating additional correspondences in areas of known planar motion, and applying higher order constraints such as perpendicularities between planes, can lead to significantly better reconstruction.

After a brief review of related literature in Section 2, we present the basic imaging equations, develop the relationships between point positions in two views, and show how this reduces to a homography for the case of coplanar points (Section 3). In Section 4 we preview the three main approaches we will use to solve the structure from motion problem when subsets of points are known to lie on planes: augmenting planes with additional sample points before computing the fundamental matrix (Section 5); using homographies to directly compute the fundamental matrix (Section 6); using plane plus parallax techniques (Section 7); and performing global optimization (bundle adjustment) (Section 8). In Section 9 we discuss how additional knowledge about the planes (e.g., perpendicularity constraints) can be used to improve the solution. Section 10 presents our experimental setup . We close with a discussion of the results, and a list of potential extensions to our framework, including the important case of line data.

2 Previous Work

There has been a large amount of work on recovery of structure and motion from image sequences (A good introductory text book on the subject is [4]). However, relatively little work has been done on incorporating prior geometric knowledge (e.g., the coplanarity of points, or known feature orientations) directly into the reconstruction process.

There has been some work in exploiting the motion of one or more planes for recovering structure and motion. Luong and Faugeras [14] show how to directly compute a fundamental matrix from two or more of the homographies induced by the motions of planes within the image. This technique however is very noise sensitive. Plane plus parallax technique directly exploit a known dominant planar motion to compute the epipole(s) and perform a projective reconstruction [11,17,10]. However, none of these approaches incorporate the geometric constraints of coplanarity in a statistically optimal fashion.

3 General Problem Formulation

Structure from motion can be formulated as the recovery of a set of 3-D structure parameters $\{\mathbf{x}_i = (X_i, Y_i, Z_i)\}$ and time-varying motion parameters $\{(\mathbf{R}_k, \mathbf{t}_k)\}$ from a set of observed image features $\{\mathbf{u}_{ik} = (u_{ik}, v_{ik}, 1)\}$. In this section, we present the forward equations, i.e., the rigid body and perspective transformations which map 3-D points into 2-D image points. We also derive the *homography* (planar perspective transform) which relates two views of a planar point set.

To project the ith 3-D point $\mathbf{x}_i$ into the kth frame at location $\mathbf{u}_{ik}$, we write

$$\mathbf{u}_{ik} \sim \mathbf{V}_k \mathbf{R}_k (\mathbf{x}_i - \mathbf{t}_k), \tag{1}$$

where $\sim$ indicates equality up to a scale, $\mathbf{R}_k$ is the rotation matrix for camera k, $\mathbf{t}_k$ is the location of its optical center, and $\mathbf{V}_k$ is its projection matrix (usually assumed to be upper triangular or some simpler form, e.g., diagonal). In most cases, we will assume that $\mathbf{R}_0 = \mathbf{I}$ and $\mathbf{t}_0 = 0$, i.e., the first camera is at the world origin. The location of a 3D point corresponding to an observed image feature is

$$\mathbf{x}_i = w_{ik} \mathbf{R}_k^{-1} \mathbf{V}_k^{-1} \mathbf{u}_{ik} + \mathbf{t}_k, \tag{2}$$

where w_{ik} is an unknown scale factor.

It is useful to distinguish three cases, depending on the form of $\mathbf{V}_k$. If $\mathbf{V}_k$ is known, we have the *calibrated* image case. If $\mathbf{V}_k$ is unknown and general (upper triangular), we have the *uncalibrated* image case, from which we can only recover a *projective* reconstruction of world [4]. If some information about $\mathbf{V}_k$ is known (e.g., that it is temporally invariant, or that it has a reduced form), we can apply *self-calibration* techniques [7,12].

The motion of a point between two images k and l can thus be written as

$$\mathbf{u}_{ik} \sim \mathbf{V}_k \mathbf{R}_k (w_{il} \mathbf{R}_l^{-1} \mathbf{V}_l^{-1} \mathbf{u}_{il} + \mathbf{t}_l - \mathbf{t}_k) \sim \mathbf{H}_{kl}^\infty \mathbf{u}_{il} + w_{il}^{-1} \mathbf{e}_{kl}, \tag{3}$$

with $\mathbf{R}_{kl} = \mathbf{R}_k \mathbf{R}_l^{-1}$. The matrix $\mathbf{H}_{kl}^\infty = \mathbf{V}_k \mathbf{R}_{kl} \mathbf{V}_l^{-1}$ is the *homography* (planar perspective transform) which maps points at infinity $(w_{il}^{-1} = 0)$ from one image to the next, while $\mathbf{e}_{kl} = \mathbf{V}_k \mathbf{R}_k (\mathbf{t}_l - \mathbf{t}_k)$ is the *epipole* which is the vanishing point of the *residual parallax vectors* once this planar perspective motion has been subtracted (the epipole is also the image of camera k's center in camera l's image, as can be seen by setting $w_{il} \to 0$).

When the cameras are uncalibrated, i.e., the $\mathbf{V}_k$ can be arbitrary, the homography $\mathbf{H}_{kl}^\infty$ cannot be uniquely determined, i.e., we can add an arbitrary matrix of the form $\mathbf{e}_{kl} \mathbf{v}^T$ to $\mathbf{H}_{kl}^\infty$ and subtract a plane equation $\mathbf{v}^T \mathbf{u}_k$ from w_{il}^{-1} and still obtain the same result. More globally, the reconstructed 3D shape can only be determined up to an overall 3D global perspective transformation (*collineation*) [4,19].

The inter-image transfer equations have a simpler form when $\mathbf{x}$ is known to lie on a plane $\hat{\mathbf{n}}^T \mathbf{x} - d = 0$. In this case, we can compute w_{il} using

$$\hat{\mathbf{n}}^T \mathbf{x}_i - d = w_{il} \hat{\mathbf{n}}^T \mathbf{R}_l^{-1} \mathbf{V}_l^{-1} \mathbf{u}_{il} + \hat{\mathbf{n}}^T \mathbf{t}_l - d = 0,$$

or

$$w_{il}^{-1} = \hat{\mathbf{n}}^T \mathbf{R}_l^{-1} \mathbf{V}_l^{-1} \mathbf{u}_{il} / (d - \hat{\mathbf{n}}^T \mathbf{t}_l) = d_l^{-1} \hat{\mathbf{n}}^T \mathbf{R}_l^{-1} \mathbf{V}_l^{-1} \mathbf{u}_{il},$$

where $d_l = d - \hat{\mathbf{n}}^T \mathbf{t}_l$ is the distance of camera center l ($\mathbf{t}_l$) to the plane $(\hat{\mathbf{n}}, d)$. Substituting w_{il}^{-1} into (3) and multiplying through by d_l, we obtain [24]

$$\mathbf{u}_{ik} \sim (\mathbf{H}_{kl}^\infty + d_l^{-1} \mathbf{e}_{kl} \hat{\mathbf{n}}^T \mathbf{R}_l^{-1} \mathbf{V}_l^{-1}) \mathbf{u}_{il}. \tag{4}$$

Letting $\tilde{\mathbf{n}}_l = \mathbf{V}_l^{-T} \mathbf{R}_l \hat{\mathbf{n}}$ be the plane normal in the lth camera's (scaled) coordinate system, we see that the homography induced by the plane can be written as

$$\mathbf{H}_{kl} \sim \mathbf{H}_{kl}^\infty + d_l^{-1} \mathbf{e}_{kl} \tilde{\mathbf{n}}_l^T \tag{5}$$

i.e., it is very similar in form to the projective ambiguity which arises when using uncalibrated cameras (this also forms the basis of the plane plus parallax techniques discussed below).

4 Structure from Motion with Planes

In the remainder of this paper, we develop a number of techniques for recovering the structure and motion of a collection of points seen with 2 or more cameras. In addition to being given the estimated position of each point in two or more images, we also assume that some of the points are coplanar. We may also be given one or more image regions where the inter-frame homographies are known, but no explicit correspondences have been given.

Given this information, there are several ways we could proceed.

1. We can, of course, solve the problem ignoring our knowledge of coplanarity. This will serve as our reference algorithm against which we will compare all others.
2. We can hallucinate (additional) point matches based on the homographies which are either given directly or which can be computed between collections of coplanar points.
3. We can re-compute the 2D point locations so that the estimated or computed homographies are exactly satisfied.
4. We can use the homographies induced by the planes in the image to estimate the fundamental matrix, and thence structure.
5. We can use plane + parallax techniques to recover the camera geometry, and after that the projective 3D structure.
6. We can perform a global optimization (bundle adjustment), using the knowledge about coplanarity as additional constraints to be added to the solution.

To illustrate these algorithms, we initially use two simple data sets (Figure 1):

1. a collection of n points lying in a fronto-parallel plane with m points lying on a closer fronto-parallel plane;

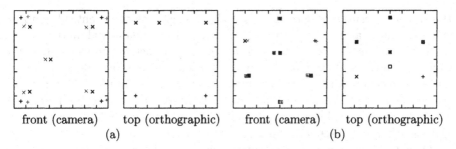

front (camera)   top (orthographic)   front (camera)   top (orthographic)
(a)   (b)

Fig. 1. Experimental datasets (front and top views): *Front view* shows the location of the points projected into image 1 (black symbol) and image 2 (grey symbol). *Top view* shows the relative 3d disposition of the points in orthographic projection from above. (a) $n = 5$ points lying on a plane with $m = 4$ points lying in front (b) $n = 4$ points on each face of a trihedral vertex. For our experiments, we use $t_0 = 6$ and rotate the data around the vertical axis through $10°$.

2. a trihedral vertex with n points on each of the three faces, with two of the points on each face being located along the common edge.

Although we could, we will not use data sets where homographies are directly given. Instead, we compute whatever homographies we need from the (noisy) 2D point measurements, and use these as inputs. A more detailed explanation of our data and methodology is given in Section 10.

5 Fundamental Matrices from Point Correspondences

Referring back to the basic two-frame transfer equation (3), we can pre-multiply both sides by $[\mathbf{e}_{kl}]_\times$, where $[\mathbf{v}]_\times$ is the matrix form of the cross-product operator with vector $\mathbf{v}$, to obtain

$$[\mathbf{e}_{kl}]_\times \mathbf{u}_{ik} \sim [\mathbf{e}_{kl}]_\times \mathbf{V}_k \mathbf{R}_{kl} \mathbf{V}_l^{-1} \mathbf{u}_{il}$$

(since $[\mathbf{e}_{kl}]_\times$ annihilates the $\mathbf{e}_{kl}$ vector on the right hand side). Pre-multiplying this by $\mathbf{u}_{ik}^T$, we observe that the left-hand side is 0 since the cross product matrix is skew symmetric, and hence

$$\mathbf{u}_{ik}^T \mathbf{F}_{kl} \mathbf{u}_{il} = 0, \tag{6}$$

where

$$\mathbf{F}_{kl} \sim [\mathbf{e}_{kl}]_\times \mathbf{V}_k \mathbf{R}_{kl} \mathbf{V}_l^{-1} = [\mathbf{e}_{kl}]_\times \mathbf{H}_{kl}^\infty \tag{7}$$

is called the *fundamental matrix* [4]. The fundamental matrix is of rank 2, since that is the rank of $[\mathbf{e}_{kl}]_\times$, and has seven degrees of freedom (the scale of $\mathbf{F}$ is arbitrary).

When the camera calibration is known, we can premultiply screen coordinates by $\mathbf{V}^{-1}$ (i.e., convert screen coordinates into Euclidean directions), and obtain the simpler *essential matrix*, $\mathbf{E} \sim [\mathbf{t}_{kl}]_\times \mathbf{R}_{kl}$, which has two identical non-zero singular values, and hence 5 degrees of freedom (the fundamental matrix has 7).

The *fundamental matrix* or *essential matrix* approach to two-frame structure from motion is one of the most widely used techniques for structure from motion, and some recent modifications have made this technique quite reliable in practice [23,25]. The essential matrix method was first developed for the calibrated image case [13]. This method was then generalized to the fundamental matrix approach [3,9], which can be used with uncalibrated cameras.

Once the fundamental (or essential) matrix has been computed, we can estimate $\mathbf{e}_{kl}$ [23,25], and then compute the desired homography $\mathbf{H}_{kl}^\infty = [\mathbf{e}_{kl}]_\times \mathbf{F}_{kl}$. The 3D location of each point can then be obtained by triangulation, and in our experiments, this can be compared to the known ground truth.

As mentioned earlier, when we know that certain points are coplanar, we can use this information in one of two ways: (1) hallucinate (additional) point matches based on the homographies; or (2) re-compute the 2D point locations so that the estimated or computed homographies are exactly satisfied.

5.1 Hallucinating Additional Correspondences

The first approach proves to be useful in data-poor situations, e.g., when we only have four points on a plane, and two points off the plane. By hallucinating additional correspondences, we can generate enough data (say, two additional points on the plane) to use a regular 8-point algorithm. If it helps for data poor situations, why not for other situations as well (say, eight points grouped onto two planes)? Eventually, of course, the new data must be redundant, but at what point? Methods which exploit homographies directly [14] (Section 6) indicate that there are six independent constraints available from a single homography. Is this so when the data is noisy?

Let's get a feel for how much additional points help by running some experiments. Table 1 shows the results of adding p hallucinated points per plane to both of our test data sets (bi-plane and trihedral),[1] and then running an 8-point algorithm to reconstruct the data [8,25]. For the initially underconstrained data sets ($n = 4, m = 2$ bi-plane and $n = 4$ trihedral), and even for the minimally constrained data sets ($n = 4, m = 4$ bi-plane), adding enough hallucinated points to get more than the minimum required 8 provides a dramatic improvement in the quality of the results. On the other hand, adding hallucinated points to data set which already have more than 8 points only gives a minor improvement. This suggests that having more than the minimal number of sample points is more important than fully exploiting all of the constraints available from our homographies.

---

[1] The $n = 6, m = 2$ and $n = 4, m = 2$ data sets actually only have a single plane for which a homography can be computed.

data set	n m p N	method	Euclidean	affine	co-planarity
plane + 2pts	4 2 2 8	"8 pt" **F**	0.0651	0.0130	0.0023
"	4 2 0 6	plane + ‖ax	0.0651	0.0130	0.0024
plane + 2pts †	6 2 0 8	"8 pt" **F**	0.1879	0.0430	0.0149
"	6 2 1 9	"	0.1482	0.0285	0.0158
"	6 2 0 8	plane + ‖ax	0.1185	0.0184	0.0105
2 ‖ planes †	4 4 0 8	"8 pt" **F**	0.1382	0.0335	0.0141
"	4 4 1 10	"	0.0858	0.0235	0.0128
"	4 4 2 12	"	0.0702	0.0200	0.0100
"	4 4 0 8	plane + ‖ax	0.1709	0.0395	0.0077
2 ‖ planes	5 5 0 10	"8 pt" **F**	0.0538	0.0226	0.0144
"	5 5 0 10	reproject	0.0484	0.0189	0.0114
"	5 5 0 10	**H → F**	0.5516	0.3698	0.0163
"	5 5 0 10	plane + ‖ax	0.0673	0.0189	0.0079
"	5 5 0 10	bundle adj.	0.0467	0.0170	0.0092
"	5 5 0 10	plane enf.	0.0392	0.0117	0.0000
"	5 5 0 10	plane constr.	0.0384	0.0081	0.0000
6 ‖ planes	4 4 0 24	"8 pt" **F**	0.0761	0.0234	0.0074
"	4 4 0 24	**H → F**	0.9459	0.7652	0.0088
"	4 4 0 24	plane + ‖ax	0.8145	0.5312	0.0078
tilted cube	4 4 1 10	"8 pt" **F**	0.1549	0.0307	0.0091
"	4 4 2 13	"	0.1301	0.0265	0.0076
"	4 4 0 7	**H → F**	0.1383	0.0237	0.0079
"	4 4 0 7	plane + ‖ax	0.2070	0.0411	0.0087
tilted cube	5 5 0 10	"8 pt" **F**	0.1460	0.0295	0.0110
"	5 5 1 13	"	0.1263	0.0256	0.0111
"	5 5 0 10	**H → F**	0.1014	0.0213	0.0093
"	5 5 0 10	plane + ‖ax	0.1657	0.0348	0.0107

† Randomized data point placement

Table 1. Reconstruction error for various methods of structure estimation. n and m are defined in Figure 1, p is the number of extra hallucinated points, and N is the total number of points. The Euclidean and affine reconstruction errors are for calibrated cameras. The coplanarity error measures the Euclidean distance of points to their best-fit plane (calibrated reconstruction).

5.2 Reprojecting Points Based on Homographies

A second approach to exploiting known coplanarity in the data set is to perturb the input 2D measurements such that they lie exactly on a homography. This seems like a plausible thing to do, e.g., projecting 3D points onto estimated planes is one way to "clean up" a 3D reconstruction. However, it is possible that this early application of domain knowledge may not be statistically optimal or even admissible. Let's explore this idea empirically.

The simplest way to perform this reprojection is to first compute homographies between a plane in the kth frame and the 0th frame, and to then project the points from the first frame into the kth frame using this homography. This is equivalent to assuming that the points in the first frame are noise-free. Another approach is to find $\mathbf{u}_{ik}^*$ such that they exactly satisfy the homographies and minimize the projected errors. Since the latter involves a complicated minimization, we have chosen to study the former, simpler idea. Methods to incorporate coplanarity as a hard constraint on the solution will be presented in Section 9.

Table 1 shows some results of reprojecting points in the second frame based on the computed homographies (row *reproject*). A slight decrease in error is visible, but this technique does not yield as dramatic improvements as hallucinating additional correspondences.

6   Fundamental Matrices from Homographies

Assuming that we are given (or can estimate) the inter-frame homographies associated with two or more planes in the scene, there is a more direct method for computing the fundamental matrix [14]. Recall from (5) that the homography associated with a plane $\hat{\mathbf{n}}^T \mathbf{x} - d = 0$ is $\mathbf{H}_{kl} \sim \mathbf{H}_{kl}^\infty + d_l^{-1} \mathbf{e}_{kl} \tilde{\mathbf{n}}^T$ and that the fundamental matrix (7) associated with the same configuration has the form $\mathbf{F}_{kl} \sim [\mathbf{e}_{kl}]_\times \mathbf{H}_{kl}^\infty$. The product

$$\mathbf{H}_{kl}^T \mathbf{F}_{kl} \sim \mathbf{H}_{kl}^{\infty T}[\mathbf{e}_{kl}]_\times \mathbf{H}_{kl}^\infty + d_l^{-1}\tilde{\mathbf{n}}\mathbf{e}_{kl}^T[\mathbf{e}_{kl}]_\times \mathbf{H}_{kl}^\infty = \mathbf{H}_{kl}^{\infty T}[\mathbf{e}_{kl}]_\times \mathbf{H}_{kl}^\infty$$

is skew symmetric, and hence

$$\mathbf{S} = \mathbf{H}_{kl}^T \mathbf{F}_{kl} + \mathbf{F}_{kl}^T \mathbf{H}_{kl} = 0. \tag{8}$$

Writing out these equations in terms of the entries h_{ij} and f_{ij} of $\mathbf{H}$ and $\mathbf{F}$ (we'll drop the kl frame subscripts) gives us

$$s_{ij} = \sum_k h_{ki} f_{kj} + f_{ki} h_{kj} = 0, \quad \forall (i,j). \tag{9}$$

Each known plane homography $\mathbf{H}$ contributes six independent constraints on $\mathbf{F}$, since the matrix $\mathbf{H}^T \mathbf{F} + \mathbf{F}^T \mathbf{H}$ is symmetric, and hence only has six degrees of freedom. Using two or more plane homographies, we can form enough equations to obtain a linear least squares problem in the entries in $\mathbf{F}$.

While this idea is quite simple, Luong and Faugeras [14] report that the technique is not very stable (it only yields improvements over a point-based technique for two planes). Can we deduce why this method performs poorly?

Instead of using (8) to solve for $\mathbf{F}$, what if we "hallucinate" point correspondences based on the known homographies. Say we pick an image point $\mathbf{u} = (u_0, u_1, u_2)$ and project it to $\mathbf{u}' = (v_0, v_1, v_2) = \mathbf{H}\mathbf{u}$, i.e., $v_k = \sum_i h_{ki} u_i$. The resulting constraint on $\mathbf{F}$ (6) has the form

$$\sum_{lj} v_k f_{kj} u_j = \sum_{ijk} f_{kj} h_{ki} u_i u_j = 0. \tag{10}$$

By choosing appropriate values for (u_0, u_1, u_2), we can obtain elements (or combinations of the elements) of the symmetric $\mathbf{S}$ matrix in (8). For example, when $\mathbf{u} = \delta_i$, we get $\sum_k f_{ki} h_{ki} = \frac{1}{2} s_{ii}$. Thus, three of the constraints used by [14] correspond to sampling the homography at points $(1,0,0),(0,1,0)$, and $(0,0,1)$, two of which lie at infinity! Similarly, for $\mathbf{u} = \delta_i + \delta_j, i \neq j$, we get $\sum_k f_{ki} h_{ki} + f_{ki} h_{kj} + f_{kj} h_{ki} + f_{kj} h_{kj} = \frac{1}{2} s_{ii} + \frac{1}{2} s_{jj} + s_{ij}$. Thus, the remaining three constraints used by [14] are linear combinations of constraints corresponding to three sample points, e.g., $(0,1,1)$, $(0,1,0)$, and $(0,0,1)$. Again, each constraint uses at least one sample point at infinity! This explains why the technique does not work so well. First, the homographies are sampled at locations where their predictive power is very weak (homographies are most accurate at predicting the correspondence *within* the area from which they were extracted). Second, the resulting sample and projected points are far from having the kind of nice unit distribution required for total least squares to work reasonably well.

To demonstrate the overall weakness of this approach, we show the reconstruction error using the method of [14] in Table 1. From these results, we can see that the approach is often significantly inferior to simply sampling the same homography with sample points in the interior of the region from which it was extracted. The six-plane data set (Figure 2) is representative of the kind of data used in [14], where they partitioned the image into regions and then scattered coplanar points within each region. For the trihedral data set, however, the homography-based method works quite well. To obtain comparable results using the point hallucination method, quite a few additional sample points need to be used. At the moment, we do not yet understand the discrepancy between the fronto-parallel and trihedral data set results. A plausible conjecture is that fronto-parallel data, whose "vanishing points" lie at far away from the optical center, are more poorly represented by an $\mathbf{H}$ matrix.

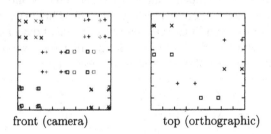

front (camera)   top (orthographic)

Fig. 2. Points clustered onto 6 fronto-parallel planes

7 Plane plus Parallax

Another traditional approach to exploiting one or more homographies between different views is to choose one homography as the *dominant motion*, and to compute the *residual parallax*, which should point at the epipole. Such *plane plus parallax* techniques [11,17] are usually used to recover a *projective* description of the world, although some work has related the projective depth (magnitude of the parallax) to Euclidean depth.

To compute the fundamental matrix, we choose one of the homographies, say the first one, and use it to warp all points from one from to the other. We then compute the epipole by minimizing the sum of squared triple products, $(\mathbf{x}_i, \mathbf{x}_i', \mathbf{e})^2$, where $\mathbf{x}_i$ and $\mathbf{x}_i$ are corresponding (after transfer by homography).[2] Once $\mathbf{e}$ has been determined, we can compute $\mathbf{F}_{kl}$.

Table 1 shows the results of using the plane plus parallax to recover the 3D structure for some of our data sets. The method works well when the points are mostly on the plane used for the homography ($n = 4$ or 6, $m = 2$), but not as well when the points are evenly distributed over several planes. This is not surprising. Plane plus parallax privileges one plane over all others, forcing the fundamental matrix to exactly match that homography. When the data is more evenly distributed, a point-based algorithm (with hallucination, if necessary) gives better results.

8 Global Optimization (Bundle Adjustment)

The final technique we examine in this paper is the one traditionally used by photogrammetrists, i.e., the simultaneous optimization of 3D point and camera placements by minimizing the squared error between estimated and measured image feature locations.

There are two general approaches to performing this optimization. The first interleaves structure and motion estimation stages [8]. This has the advantage that each point (or frame) reconstruction problem is decoupled from the other problems, thereby solving much smaller systems. The second approach simultaneously optimizes for structure and motion [19]. This usually requires fewer iterations, because the couplings between the two sets of data are made explicit, but requires the solution of larger systems. In this paper, we adopt the former approach. To reconstruct a 3D point location, we minimize

$$\sum_k \left(u_{ik} - \frac{\mathbf{p}_{k0}^T \tilde{\mathbf{x}}_i}{\mathbf{p}_{k2}^T \tilde{\mathbf{x}}_i} \right)^2 + \left(v_{ik} - \frac{\mathbf{p}_{k1}^T \tilde{\mathbf{x}}_i}{\mathbf{p}_{k2}^T \tilde{\mathbf{x}}_i} \right)^2 \tag{11}$$

where $\mathbf{p}_{kr}$ are the three rows of the *camera or projection matrix*

$$\mathbf{P}_k = \mathbf{V}_k[\mathbf{R}_k| - \mathbf{t}_k]$$

and $\tilde{\mathbf{x}}_i = [\mathbf{x}_i|1]$, i.e., the homogeneous representation of $\mathbf{x}_i$. As pointed out by [25], this is equivalent to solving the following overconstrained set of linear equations,

---

[2] The triple product measures the distance of $\mathbf{e}$ from the line passing through $\mathbf{x}_i$ and $\mathbf{x}_i'$, weighted by the length of this line segment.

$$D_{ik}^{-1}(\mathbf{p}_{k0} - u_{ik}\mathbf{p}_{k2})^T\tilde{\mathbf{x}}_i = 0 \tag{12}$$
$$D_{ik}^{-1}(\mathbf{p}_{k1} - v_{ik}\mathbf{p}_{k2})^T\tilde{\mathbf{x}}_i = 0,$$

where the weights are given by $D_{ik} = \mathbf{p}_{k2}^T\tilde{\mathbf{x}}_i$ (these are set to $D_{ik} = 1$ in the first iteration).[3] Notice that since these equations are homogeneous in $\tilde{\mathbf{x}}_i$, we solve this system by looking for the rightmost singular vector of the system of equations [6].

The same equations can be used to update our estimate of $\mathbf{P}_k$, by simply grouping equations with common k's into separate systems. When reconstructing a Euclidean ($\mathbf{V}_k[\mathbf{R}_k| - \mathbf{t}_k]$) description of motion, the estimation equations become more complicated. Here, applying a linearized least squares like the Levenberg-Marquardt algorithm is more fruitful. Let us assume the following updates

$$\mathbf{R}_k \leftarrow \mathbf{R}_k(\mathbf{I} + [\omega_k]_\times), \qquad \mathbf{t}_k \leftarrow \mathbf{t}_k + \delta\mathbf{t}_k. \tag{13}$$

We can compute the terms in

$$\mathbf{P}_k + \delta\mathbf{P}_k = \mathbf{V}_k[\mathbf{R}_k(\mathbf{I} + [\omega_k]_\times)| - (\mathbf{t}_k + \delta\mathbf{t}_k)] \tag{14}$$

as functions of $\mathbf{V}_k, \mathbf{R}_k, \mathbf{t}_k$, i.e., the Jacobian of the twelve entries in $\delta\mathbf{P}_k$ with respect to ω_k and $\delta\mathbf{t}_k$. We can then solve the system of equations

$$D_{ik}^{-1}\tilde{\mathbf{x}}_i^T(\delta\mathbf{p}_{k0} - \hat{u}_{ik}\delta\mathbf{p}_{k2}) = u_{ik} - \hat{u}_{ik} \tag{15}$$
$$D_{ik}^{-1}\tilde{\mathbf{x}}_i^T(\delta\mathbf{p}_{k1} - \hat{v}_{ik}\delta\mathbf{p}_{k2}) = v_{ik} - \hat{v}_{ik},$$

substituting the $\delta\mathbf{p}_k$ with their expansions in the unknowns $(\omega_k, \delta\mathbf{t}_k)$. The rotation and translation estimates can then be updated using (13), using Rodriguez's formula for the rotation matrix [1],

$$\mathbf{R} \leftarrow \mathbf{R}\left(\mathbf{I} + \sin\theta[\hat{\mathbf{n}}]_\times + (1 - \cos\theta)[\hat{\mathbf{n}}]_\times^2\right)$$

with $\theta = \|\omega\|$, $\hat{\mathbf{n}} = \omega/\theta$. A similar approach can be used to update the focal length, or other intrinsic calibration parameters, if desired.

The above discussion has assumed that each point can be solved for independently. What about points that are known to be coplanar? Here, we need to incorporate constraints of the form $\hat{\mathbf{n}}_p^T\mathbf{x}_i - d_p = 0, \{i \in \Pi_p\}$. Two approaches come to mind. The first is to alternate a plane estimation stage with the point reconstruction stage. The second is to simultaneously optimize the point positions and plane equations. We describe the former, since it is simpler to implement.

Fitting planes to a collection of 3D points is a classic total least squares problem [6]. After subtracting the centroid of the points, $\bar{\mathbf{x}}_p$, we compute the

---

[3] The Levenberg-Marquardt algorithm [15] leads to a slightly different set of equations

$$D_{ik}^{-1}(\mathbf{p}_{k0} - \hat{u}_{ik}\mathbf{p}_{k2})^T\delta\tilde{\mathbf{x}}_i = u_{ik} - \hat{u}_{ik},$$

where $\hat{u}_{ik}$ is the current estimate of u_{ik} and $\delta\tilde{\mathbf{x}}_i$ is the desired update to $\tilde{\mathbf{x}}_i$. In practice, the two methods perform about as well [25].

singular value decomposition of the resulting deviations, and choose the rightmost singular vector as the plane equation. We then set $d_p = \hat{\mathbf{n}}_p^T \bar{\mathbf{x}}_p$.

To enforce this hard constraint on the point reconstruction stage, we add the equation $\hat{\mathbf{n}}_p^T \mathbf{x}_i - d_p = 0$. to the system (13) as a linear constraint [6]. Since points may end up lying on several planes, we use the *method of weighting* approach to constrained least squares [6, p. 586], i.e., we add the constraints $\hat{\mathbf{n}}_p^T \mathbf{x}_i - d_p = 0$ to the set of equations for $\mathbf{x}_i$ with a large weight (currently $2^{60} \approx 10^{20}$).

Table 1 shows the results of applying bundle adjustment to the initial structure and motion estimates computed using an 8-point method. For fronto-parallel planes, bundle adjustment significantly reduces the reconstruction error. For the trihedral data set, it has little effect. Notice, however, the large discrepancy between the Euclidean and affine reconstruction errors for the trihedral data. This suggests that the major source of error is probably a *bas-relief ambiguity* [20], which is not removable even with a statistically optimal technique such as bundle adjustment. Enforcing coplanarity ("plane enf." in Table 1) does not significantly reduce the reconstruction error, although it is successful at reducing coplanarity error to 0 (which may be desirable to make the data appear less "wobbly").

9   Constraints on Planes

In addition to grouping points onto planes, we can apply additional constraints on the geometry of the planes themselves. For example, if we know that two or more planes are parallel, then we can compute a single normal vector for all the "coplanar" points after their individual centroids have been subtracted.

The line corresponding to method "plane constr." in Table 1 shows the result of applying a parallelism constraint to our fronto-parallel data set. The results are not all that different from not using the constraint.

If we know that certain planes are perpendicular, this too can be enforced during the normal computation stage. If two or three planes are known to be mutually orthogonal, we can concatenate the normals into a matrix, compute its SVD, replace the singular values with 1, and reconstitute the matrix.

Applying this idea to the trihedral data set as part of the bundle adjustment loop yields dramatically lower reconstruction errors (Table 1). Adding the perpendicularity constraint removes most of the bas-relief ambiguity (uncertainty) in the reconstruction, with the resulting reconstruction error being more closely tied to the triangulation error.

Lastly, if planes have explicitly known orientations (e.g., full constraints in the case of ground planes, or partial constraints in the case of vertical walls), these too can be incorporated. However, a global rotation and translation of coordinates may first have to be applied to the current estimate before these constraints can be enforced.

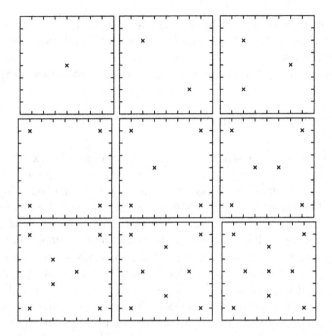

Fig. 3. Point layouts for $n = 1 \ldots 9$ points

10 Experiments

We have performed an extensive set of experiments to validate our algorithms and to test the relative merits of various approaches. Our experimental software first generates a 3D dataset in one of three possible configurations: a set of fronto-parallel planes filling the field of view (Figure 1a), a set of fronto-parallel planes in non-overlapping regions of the image (Figure 2), or a trihedral corner (Figure 1b). On each of the planes, we generate from 1 to 9 sample points, in the configurations shown in Figure 3.

The 3D configuration of points is projected onto the camera's image plane. For our current experiments, we rotate the data around the y axis in increments of 10°, and place the camera 6 units away from the data (the data itself fills a cube spanning $[-1, 1]^3$). We then generate 50 noise-corrupted versions of the projected points (for the experiments described in this paper, $\sigma = 0.2$ pixels, on a 200×200 image), and use these as inputs to the reconstruction algorithms. The *mean* RMS reconstruction error across all 50 trials is then reported.

The reconstruction errors are computed after first finding the best 3D mapping (Euclidean/similarity or affine) from the reconstructed data points onto the known ground truth points. The columns labeled "Euclidean" and "affine" in Table 1 measure the errors between data reconstructed using calibrated cameras and the ground truth after finding the best similarity and affine mappings. The coplanarity error is computed by finding the best 3D plane fit to each coplanar set of reconstructed points (calibrated camera), and then measuring the distances to the plane.

Table 1 is a representative sample from our more extensive set of experiments.

11 Discussion and Conclusions

In this paper, we have presented a number of techniques for exploiting the geometric knowledge typically available in structure from motion problems. In particular, we have focused on how to take advantage of known coplanarities in the data. Our techniques also enable us to directly exploit homographies between different regions of the image, when these are known. Of the techniques tried, hallucinating additional correspondences is simple to implement, and often yields a significant improvement in the results, especially in situations which are initially data-poor. Reprojecting the data to exactly fit the homography does not appear to significantly improve the results. Using homographies to directly estimate the fundamental matrix sometimes works, but also often fails dramatically; using hallucinated correspondences seems like a more prudent approach.

Bundle adjustment improves the results obtained with the 8-point algorithm, but often not by that much. Adding coplanarity as a hard constraint does not seem to make a significant difference in the accuracy of the reconstruction, although it does make the reconstruction look smoother. Adding parallelism as a geometric constraint does not seem to improve the results that much. On the other hand, adding perpendicularity constraints for the trihedral data set leads to a dramatic decrease in reconstruction error (most likely due to a reduction in the bas-relief ambiguity). As mentioned above, plane plus parallax works well when the points are mostly on the plane used for estimating the homography, but not as well when the points are evenly distributed over several planes.

These results suggest that adding hallucinated correspondences to planar grouping of points (or hallucinating correspondences in regions with known homographies) is a useful and powerful idea which improves structure from motion results with very little additional complexity. Similarly, geometric constraints (coplanarity, parallelism, and perpendicularity) can be added to the bundle adjustment stage with relatively little effort, and can provide significantly improved results.

11.1 Future Work

This paper has concentrated on the geometric constraints available from knowing that certain points are coplanar. Similar constraints are available for points which are known to be collinear. The situation, however, is often a little different: line matching algorithms often do not localize the endpoints of lines in each image, so there may be no initial points in correspondence, nor is it possible to hallucinate such correspondences prior to an actual reconstruction. However, exploiting known orientations for lines (e.g., vertical and horizontal), and geometric constraint between their orientations (parallelism and perpendicularity) is indeed possible, and can lead to algorithms which reconstruct a 3D scene from a single view.

In terms of points on planes, our current results could be extended in a number of directions. First, we have not yet explored the use of multi-frame algebraic approaches such as trilinear tensors [18]. Second, we have not explored multi-frame bundle adjustment techniques, nor have we explored the use of robust estimation techniques [23]. Hallucinating correspondences should be equally applicable to all three of these approaches. We would also like to better understand the differences in results obtained from fronto-parallel and oblique planes, and in general to anticipate the expected accuracy of results for various geometric configurations and camera motions.

References

1. N. Ayache. *Vision Stéréoscopique et Perception Multisensorielle*. InterEditions., 1989.
2. P. Beardsley, P. Torr, and A. Zisserman. 3D model acquisition from extended image sequences. In *ECCV'96*, volume 2, pages 683–695, 1996.
3. O. D. Faugeras. What can be seen in three dimensions with an uncalibrated stereo rig? In *ECCV'92*, pages 563–578, 1992.
4. O. Faugeras. *Three-dimensional computer vision: A geometric viewpoint*. MIT Press, 1993.
5. O. D. Faugeras and F. Lustman. Motion and structure from motion in a piecewise planar environment. *Int J Pattern Recognition and Artificial Intelligence*, 2(3):485–508, 1988.
6. G. Golub and C. F. Van Loan. *Matrix Computation, third edition*. The John Hopkins Univ Press, 1996.
7. R. I. Hartley. An algorithm for self calibration from several views. In *CVPR'94*, pages 908–912, 1994.
8. R. I. Hartley. In defense of the 8-point algorithm. *PAMI*, 19(6):580–593, 1997.
9. R. Hartley, R. Gupta, and T. Chang. Stereo from uncalibrated cameras. In *CVPR'93*, pages 489–494, 1993.
10. M. Irani, B. Rousso, and S. Peleg. Recovery of ego-motion using image stabilization. *PAMI*, 19(3):268–272, March 1997.
11. R. Kumar, P. Anandan, and K. Hanna. Direct recovery of shape from multiple views. In *ICPR'94*, volume A, pages 685–688, 1994.
12. Q.-T. Luong and O. D. Faugeras. Self-calibration of a moving camera from point correspondences and fundamental matrices. *IJCV*, 22(3):261–289, 1997.
13. H. C. Longuet-Higgins. A computer algorithm for reconstructing a scene from two projections. *Nature*, 293:133–135, 1981.
14. Q.-T. Luong and O. Faugeras. Determining the fundamental matrix with planes. In *CVPR'93*, volume 1, pages 489–494, 1993.
15. W. H. Press, B. P. Flannery, S. A. Teukolsky, and W. T. Vetterling. *Numerical Recipes in C*. Cambridge University Press, 1992.
16. M. E. Spetsakis and J. Y. Aloimonos. Optimal motion estimation. In *IEEE Workshop on Visual Motion*, pages 229–237, Irvine, California, March 1989.

17. H. S. Sawhney. 3D geometry from planar parallax. In *CVPR'94*, pages 929–934, 1994.
18. A. Shashua. Trilinearity in visual recognition by alignment. In *ECCV'94*, volume 1, pages 479–484, 1994. Springer-Verlag.
19. R. Szeliski and S. B. Kang. Recovering 3D shape and motion from image streams using nonlinear least squares. *Journal of Visual Communication and Image Representation*, 5(1):10–28, 1994.
20. R. Szeliski and S. B. Kang. Shape ambiguities in structure from motion. *PAMI*, 19(5):506–512, 1997.
21. R. Y. Tsai and T. S. Huang. Uniqueness and estimation of three-dimensional motion parameters of rigid objects with curved surfaces. *PAMI*, PAMI-6(1):13–27, 1984.
22. C. Tomasi and T. Kanade. Shape and motion from image streams under orthography: A factorization method. *IJCV*, 9(2):137–154, 1992.
23. P. H. S. Torr and D. W. Murray. A review of robust methods to estimate the fundamental matrix. *IJCV*, 24(3):271–300, 1997.
24. T. Viéville, C. Zeller, and L. Robert. Using collineations to compute motion and structure in an uncalibrated image sequence. *IJCV*, 20(3):213–242, 1996.
25. Z. Zhang. Determining the epipolar geometry and its uncertainty: A review. *International Journal of Computer Vision*, accepted 1997.

Euclidean and Affine Structure/Motion for Uncalibrated Cameras from Affine Shape and Subsidiary Information *

Gunnar Sparr

Dept. of Mathematics, Lund University/LTH,
P.O. Box 118, S-22100 Lund, Sweden
gunnar@maths.lth.se

Abstract. The paper deals with the structure–motion problem for un-calibrated cameras, in the case that subsidiary information is available, consisting e.g. in known coplanarities or parallelities among points in the scene, or known positions of some focal points (hand-eye calibration). Despite unknown camera calibrations, it is shown that in many instances the subsidiary information makes affine or even Euclidean reconstruction possible. A parametrization by affine shape and depth is used, providing a simple framework for the incorporation of apriori knowledge, and enabling the development of iterative, rapidly converging algorithms. Any number of points in any number of images are used in a uniform way, with equal priority, and independently of coordinate representations. Moreover, occlusions are allowed.

1 Introduction

The structure and motion problem is central for computer vision, dealing with the analysis of a 3D scene by means of a sequence of 2D images. It is often studied by epipolar geometry and multilinear constraints, cf. [2], [3], [4], [5], [6], [7]. [10], [11], [19], [21]. The present paper uses an alternative approach, based on the notions of affine shape and depth, developed in a series of papers [12], [13], [14], [15], [16], [17], [18].

Depending on the apriori information available, the structure and motion problem can be treated on different levels. In the case of uncalibrated cameras it is well known that only projective reconstruction is possible, cf. [2], [14]. Working with point configurations, we here consider the case when some affine or Euclidean knowledge about the scene or the camera locations is available, e.g. a number of occurences like 'two lines are parallel' or 'a line is parallel to a plane', in which case affine reconstruction can be achieved. When having in addition some sort of Euclidean information, like a city map in the case of pictures of a city scene, this may be strengthened to Euclidean reconstruction. Another

---

* The work has been supported by the ESPRIT reactive LTR project 21914, CUMULI, and by the Swedish Council for Engineering Sciences (TFR), project 95-64-222.

Reinhard Koch, Luc Van Gool (Eds.): SMILE '98, LNCS 1506, pp. 187–207, 1998.

situation considered is when the relative placement of at least five focal points are known, where is is shown that not only the projective but also the affine structure of the scene can be recovered. Again, having Euclidean information about the focal points, this can be strengthened to Euclidean reconstruction of the scene. The latter situation appears naturally in hand-eye calibration from pictures taken by a camera mounted on a moving robot arm, with registration of the motion parameters. It is also shown how to adjust a reconstruction to be consistent with coplanarity constraints for some set of points.

The notion of affine shape is well suited to handle these situations, theoretically as well as computationally. To gain robustness, numerical computations are based on a variational formulation, possible to exploit by linear algebraic methods. Data from any number of points in any number of images can be treated simultaneously, without preselection of reference points or images. In particular, there is no need to handle the numerically unstable situation of overdetermined systems of polynomial equations with uncertain coefficients.

The plan of the paper is as follows. In Section 2 a brief recapitulation of the notions of affine depth and shape and their use in single view geometry is given. Section 3 deals with multiple view geometry along the same lines. With this background, Section 4 presents algorithms for projective reconstruction. These are then extended in Section 5 to affine and Euclidean reconstruction in the case of subsidiary information. More details and discussions about the notions of affine shape and depth are given in a self-contained and independent Appendix.

2   Single View Geometry by Affine Shape and Depth

Let $\mathbf{A}^3$ denote the three-dimensional affine space, let Π' be a plane in $\mathbf{A}^3$, the *image plane*, and let Π be a subset of $\mathbf{A}^3$. By P_ϕ is meant the *perspective transformation* $\Pi \rightarrow \Pi'$ with *centre* ϕ. Here ϕ is allowed to be a point at infinity, in which case P_ϕ is a *parallel projection* in direction ϕ. Perspective transformations model the *pinhole camera*. If no metrical information is known or used, the camera is said to be *uncalibrated*.

The principal objects dealt with in this paper are *n-point configurations* $\mathcal{X}$, by which is meant ordered sets of points $\mathcal{X} = (X^1, \ldots, X^n)$, where $X^k \in \mathbf{A}^3$, $k = 1, \ldots, n$. Let $\rho_{\mathcal{X}}$ denote the *dimension* of $\mathcal{X}$, e.g. $\rho_{\mathcal{X}} = 3$ if $\mathcal{X}$ is a non-planar 3D-configuration. The set of n-point configurations of dimension ρ will be denoted $\mathcal{C}_{n,\rho}$.

In a series of papers [12], [13], [14], [15], the notions of *affine shape space* and *affine depth space* have been developed. The definitions and main properties are summarized below. For a somewhat more thorough presentation, see the accompanying appendix.

The following notation is used throughout the paper: If $\alpha = (\alpha_1, \ldots, \alpha_n)$, $\xi = (\xi_1, \ldots, \xi_n)$, let $\alpha\xi = (\alpha_1\xi_1, \ldots, \alpha_n\xi_n)$, and let $\overline{\alpha} = (1/\alpha_1, \ldots, 1/\alpha_n)$. Moreover, let $\Sigma_0 = \{\xi \in \mathbb{R}^n \mid \sum_1^n \xi_k = 0\}$.

- *Definition of affine shape and depth spaces.* Let x^k be the coordinate column vector of X^k with respect to an arbitrary affine basis, $k = 1, \ldots, n$. Then the *affine shape space* and the *affine depth space* are defined by

$$s(\mathcal{X}) = \mathcal{N}\begin{bmatrix} 1 & 1 & \cdots & 1 \\ x^1 & x^2 & \cdots & x^n \end{bmatrix} \quad \text{and} \quad d(\mathcal{X}) = \mathcal{R}_{\text{row}}\begin{bmatrix} 1 & 1 & \cdots & 1 \\ x^1 & x^2 & \cdots & x^n \end{bmatrix},$$

respectively, where $\mathcal{N}$ stands for nullspace, and $\mathcal{R}_{\text{row}}$ for rowspace. (Cf. Definition A.1 of the Appendix.)

- *Affine invariancy.* There exists an affine transformation $A : \mathcal{X} \longrightarrow \mathcal{X}'$ if and only if $s(\mathcal{X}) \subset s(\mathcal{X}')$, or, equivalently, $d(\mathcal{X}') \subset d(\mathcal{X})$. If $\mathcal{X}$ is restricted to planar configurations, then the inclusions are in fact equalities, $s(\mathcal{X}) = s(\mathcal{X}')$ and $d(\mathcal{X}') = d(\mathcal{X})$, respectively. In this case we also write $\mathcal{X} \overset{s}{=} \mathcal{X}'$. (Cf. Theorem A.1.)

- *Dimension.* The dimensions of the linear spaces $s(\mathcal{X})$ and $d(\mathcal{X})$ are related to the dimension of the configuration by $\dim s(\mathcal{X}) = n - \rho_{\mathcal{X}} - 1$ and $\dim d(\mathcal{X}) = \rho_{\mathcal{X}} + 1$, respectively. (Cf. Theorem A.2.)

- *Shape and depth theorem.* There exists a perspective transformation P such that $P(\mathcal{X}) \overset{s}{=} \mathcal{Y}$ with depth α if and only if $\alpha s(\mathcal{X}) \subset s(\mathcal{Y})$, or, equivalently, $\alpha d(\mathcal{Y}) \subset d(\mathcal{X})$. If $\mathcal{X}$ is restricted to planar configurations, then the inclusions are replaced by $\alpha s(\mathcal{X}) = s(\mathcal{Y})$ and $\alpha d(\mathcal{Y}) = d(\mathcal{X})$, respectively. (Cf. Theorem B.1.)

- *Definition of S- and D-matrices.* By an S-matrix of $\mathcal{X}$ is meant a matrix having $s(\mathcal{X})$ as column space. By a D-matrix is meant a matrix having $d(\mathcal{X})$ as row space. Passage between different S-matrix representations is performed by multiplication from the right by a non-singular matrix. (Cf. Definition A.2.)

- *Focal point theorem.* If $\alpha s(\mathcal{X}) \subset s(\mathcal{Y})$, then there exists a projection $P_\phi :$ $\mathcal{X} \longrightarrow \mathcal{Y}$ if and only if

$$\phi = \sum_{k=1}^{n} \overline{\alpha}_k \eta_k X^k \Big/ \sum_{k=1}^{n} \overline{\alpha}_k \eta_k \ ,$$

where $\eta \in s(\mathcal{Y}) \setminus \alpha s(\mathcal{X})$. The compound configuration $(\mathcal{X}, \phi)$ thus has an S-matrix

$$S_{(\mathcal{X},\phi)} = \begin{bmatrix} \text{diag}\,(\overline{\alpha}) S_{\mathcal{Y}} \\ -\overline{\alpha}^T S_{\mathcal{Y}} \end{bmatrix} .$$

(Cf. Theorem B.2.)

3   Multiple Views

3.1   Main Theorem

Suppose that $\mathcal{Y}^1, \ldots, \mathcal{Y}^m \in \mathcal{C}_{n,2}$ are projective images of one and the same configuration $\mathcal{X} \in \mathcal{C}_{n,3}$. The shape and depth theorem implies that $\alpha^1 s(\mathcal{X}) \subset s(\mathcal{Y}^1), \ldots, \alpha^m s(\mathcal{X}) \subset s(\mathcal{Y}^m)$, or, equivalently,

$$s(\mathcal{X}) \subset \overline{\alpha}^1 s(\mathcal{Y}^1) \quad , \ \ldots \ , \quad s(\mathcal{X}) \subset \overline{\alpha}^m s(\mathcal{Y}^m) \ , \quad \text{where } \alpha^1, \ldots, \alpha^m \in d(\mathcal{X}) \ .$$

From this the equivalence between the first two items in the following theorem follows. An analogous argument for the depth space yields the equivalence with the third item.

Theorem 1. Structure theorem. *Let $\mathcal{X} \in \mathcal{C}_{n,\rho}$. The following statements are equivalent:*

- *$\mathcal{Y}^i \in \mathcal{C}_{n,\rho-1}$ is a projective image of $\mathcal{X}$ with depth vector α^i, $i = 1,\ldots,m$, where not all projections are flat,*
- *$s(\mathcal{X}) = \overline{\alpha}^1 s(\mathcal{Y}^1) \bigcap \cdots \bigcap \overline{\alpha}^m s(\mathcal{Y}^m)$,*
- *$d(\mathcal{X}) = \alpha^1 d(\mathcal{Y}^1) + \ldots + \alpha^m d(\mathcal{Y}^m)$.*

First note the ambiguity in the last two items, consisting in that they remain valid after multiplication with any β in $d(\mathcal{X})$, giving rise to a new consistent reconstruction, with shape space $\beta s(\mathcal{X})$. This is the shape-depth formulation of the well-known projective reconstruction ambiguity, cf. [14]. Also note that since $\dim d(\mathcal{X}) = 4$, the ambiguity is governed by four independent components of β.

To indicate the usage of the theorem, consider the equivalence of the first two items in the case $m = 2$. First normalize by multiplying by $\beta = \alpha^1$, then put $q^2 = \alpha^2/\alpha^1$, and let $\mathcal{X}_\parallel$ denote the corresponding reconstructed object configuration. Here q^2 is called *kinetic depth*, and the notation $\mathcal{X}_\parallel$ comes from the fact that $\mathcal{Y}^1$ is formed by a parallel projection. The condition to fulfill is

$$s(\mathcal{X}_\parallel) = s(\mathcal{Y}^1) \bigcap \overline{q}^2 s(\mathcal{Y}^2) . \tag{1}$$

To analyze this condition, choose S-matrices $S_{\mathcal{Y}^1}$, $S_{\mathcal{Y}^2}$, and form the compound matrix

$$W_q(\mathcal{Y}^1, \mathcal{Y}^2) = \left[S_{\mathcal{Y}^1} \mid \mathrm{diag}(\overline{q}^1) S_{\mathcal{Y}^2} \right] .$$

A dimension argument yields that a necessary condition for (1) to be fulfilled is that

$$\dim \mathcal{N} W_q(\mathcal{Y}^1, \mathcal{Y}^2) = n - \rho - 1 \iff \mathrm{rank}\, W_q(\mathcal{Y}^1, \mathcal{Y}^2) = n - \rho + 1 .$$

One way to proceed is by forming polynomial equations from the vanishing of all subdeterminants of W_q of order $n - \rho$. For reasons that will be discussed in Section 3.3, we prefer another method, described in Section 4.1. However, once q^2 is determined, $\mathcal{X}_\parallel$ can be computed as the intersection space in (1), after which all other consistent reconstructions are obtained by multiplication with $\beta \in d(\mathcal{X}_\parallel)$. As remarked above, this gives a four parameter family of solutions to the reconstruction problem.

3.2   The Chasles Matrix

Next we combine Theorem 1 with the focal point theorem, to describe the interplay between structure and motion. By means of the S-matrices of the respective images and the depth vectors $\overline{\alpha}^1, \ldots, \overline{\alpha}^m$, a compound matrix, called the *Chasles matrix*, is formed

$$
C(\mathcal{Y}^1, \ldots, \mathcal{Y}^m; \overline{\alpha}^1, \ldots, \overline{\alpha}^m) =
\begin{bmatrix}
\text{diag}\,(\overline{\alpha}^1) S_{\mathcal{Y}^1} & \cdots & \text{diag}\,(\overline{\alpha}^m) S_{\mathcal{Y}^m} \\
-\overline{\alpha}^{1\,T} S_{\mathcal{Y}^1} & \cdots & 0 \\
0 & \cdots & 0 \\
\vdots & \cdots & \vdots \\
0 & \cdots & -\overline{\alpha}^{m\,T} S_{\mathcal{Y}^m}
\end{bmatrix} . \tag{2}
$$

Theorem 2. Structure and motion theorem. *Let $\mathcal{X} \in C_{n,\rho}$. The following statements are equivalent.*

- $\mathcal{Y}^i \in C_{n,\rho-1}$ *is a projective image of $\mathcal{X}$ with depth vector α^i, $i = 1, \ldots, m$, where not all projections are flat,*
- *the Chasles matrix $C(\mathcal{Y}^1, \ldots, \mathcal{Y}^m; \overline{\alpha}^1, \ldots, \overline{\alpha}^m)$ is an S-matrix of the compound configuration $(\mathcal{X}, \phi^1, \ldots, \phi^m)$.*

From this theorem it follows that a necessary and sufficient condition for geometric consistency is that the Chasles matrix has rank $m+n-4$. In particular, this means that when having fixed the locations of four of the $m + n$ points $X_1, \ldots, X_n, \phi^1, \ldots, \phi^m$, all the others are known too, as linear expressions in the four selected points. These expressions can be read out explicitly from the Chasles matrix, as illustrated by the following example.

Example 1. Let $\mathcal{Y}^1$ and $\mathcal{Y}^2$ be defined by their S-matrices

$$
S_{\mathcal{Y}^1} =
\begin{bmatrix}
8 & 8 \\
-4 & -1 \\
-1 & -4 \\
-3 & 0 \\
0 & -3
\end{bmatrix} , \quad
S_{\mathcal{Y}^2} =
\begin{bmatrix}
1 & 5 \\
-1 & 2 \\
1 & -4 \\
-1 & 0 \\
0 & -3
\end{bmatrix} .
$$

Then

$$
W_q(\mathcal{Y}^1, \mathcal{Y}^2) =
\begin{bmatrix}
8 & 8 & \overline{q}_1 & 5\overline{q}_1 \\
-4 & -1 & -\overline{q}_2 & 2\overline{q}_2 \\
-1 & -4 & \overline{q}_3 & -4\overline{q}_3 \\
-3 & 0 & -\overline{q}_4 & 0 \\
0 & -3 & 0 & -3\overline{q}_5
\end{bmatrix} .
$$

One verifies that if $\overline{q} = (3, 6, 9, 1, 2)$, then rank $W_q = 3$. According to (2), a Chasles matrix is obtained by enlarging W_q with two rows, in such a way that all column sums vanish:

$$
C(\mathcal{Y}^1, \mathcal{Y}^2, 1, q) =
\begin{bmatrix}
8 & 8 & 3 & 15 \\
-4 & -1 & -6 & 12 \\
-1 & -4 & 9 & -36 \\
-3 & 0 & -1 & 0 \\
0 & -3 & 0 & -6 \\
0 & 0 & 0 & 0 \\
0 & 0 & -5 & 15
\end{bmatrix} .
$$

Here the first five rows correspond to points of $\mathcal{X}$, while rows six and seven correspond to ϕ^1 and ϕ^2, respectively.

Another Chasles matrix is obtained by elimination of the ϕ^2-component in the fourth column:

$$C(\mathcal{Y}^1, \mathcal{Y}^2, 1, q) = \begin{bmatrix} 8 & 8 & 3 & 24 \\ -4 & -1 & -6 & -6 \\ -1 & -4 & 9 & -9 \\ -3 & 0 & -1 & -3 \\ 0 & -3 & 0 & -6 \\ 0 & 0 & 0 & 0 \\ 0 & 0 & -5 & 0 \end{bmatrix} .$$

From the fourth and third columns of C we read out that

$$s(\mathcal{X}_{\|}) = \text{linear hull} (8, -2, -3, -1, -2) \quad \text{and} \quad \phi^2 = \frac{1}{5}(3X_1 - 6X_2 + 9X_3 - X_4) .$$

Moreover, from the first column it follows that P^1 is a parallel projection in the direction

$$-4\overline{X_1 X_2} - \overline{X_1 X_3} - 3\overline{X_1 X_4} ,$$

which determines the point at infinity ϕ^1.

By this we have completely described one solution of the structure-motion problem. All other solutions are generated by letting $\overline{\alpha}^1$ run through $d(\mathcal{X}_{\|})$, i.e. the hyperplane $8\overline{\alpha}_1^1 - 2\overline{\alpha}_2^1 - 3\overline{\alpha}_3^1 - \overline{\alpha}_4^1 - 2\overline{\alpha}_5^1 = 0$, with four degrees of freedom. One example of such an $\overline{\alpha}^1$ is $(3, 3, 2, 6, 3)$. Then $\overline{\alpha}^2 = \overline{\alpha}^1 q = (9, 18, 18, 6, 6) \parallel (3, 6, 6, 2, 2)$, which gives the Chasles matrix

$$C(\mathcal{Y}^1, \mathcal{Y}^2, \alpha^1, \alpha^2) = \begin{bmatrix} 24 & 24 & 3 & 15 \\ -12 & -3 & -6 & 12 \\ -2 & -8 & 6 & -24 \\ -18 & 0 & -2 & 0 \\ 0 & -9 & 0 & -6 \\ 8 & -4 & 0 & 0 \\ 0 & 0 & -1 & 3 \end{bmatrix} .$$

After elimination of a ϕ^1-component of the first image, and a ϕ^2-component of the second, we obtain another Chasles matrix

$$C(\mathcal{Y}^1, \mathcal{Y}^2, \alpha^1, \alpha^2) = \begin{bmatrix} 24 & 72 & 3 & 24 \\ -12 & -18 & -6 & -6 \\ -2 & -18 & 6 & -6 \\ -18 & -18 & -2 & -6 \\ 0 & -18 & 0 & -6 \\ 8 & 0 & 0 & 0 \\ 0 & 0 & -1 & 0 \end{bmatrix} .$$

Now all characteristics of the structure–motion problem, the shape of $\mathcal{X}$ as well as the focal points, can be read out:

$$s(\mathcal{X}) = \text{linear hull} (4, -1, -1, -1, -1) ,$$
$$\phi^1 = -3X_1 + \tfrac{3}{2}X_2 + \tfrac{1}{4}X_3 + \tfrac{9}{2}X_4 ,$$
$$\phi^2 = 3X_1 - 6X_2 + 6X_3 - 2X_4 .$$

Note that columns two and four are parallel, and that both describe the shape of $\mathcal{X}$. This is what could be expected from the fact that the object configuration has not changed between the imaging instants. Also note that $\alpha^1 s(\mathcal{X}) = s(\mathcal{X}_{\parallel})$, in accordance with the discussion above.

3.3 Relation to Fundamental Matrices and Multilinear Forms

To fix the ideas, consider the case of 5-point configurations, and choose S-matrices so that

$$
W_q(\mathcal{Y}^1, \mathcal{Y}^2) = \begin{bmatrix} \eta_{11}^1 & \eta_{12}^1 & \bar{q}_1\eta_{11}^2 & \bar{q}_1\eta_{12}^2 \\ \eta_{21}^1 & \eta_{22}^1 & \bar{q}_2\eta_{21}^2 & \bar{q}_2\eta_{22}^2 \\ \eta_{31}^1 & \eta_{32}^1 & \bar{q}_3\eta_{31}^2 & \bar{q}_3\eta_{32}^2 \\ -1 & 0 & -\bar{q}_4 & 0 \\ 0 & -1 & 0 & -\bar{q}_5 \end{bmatrix} .
$$

By the discussion after Theorem 1, the necessary and sufficient condition for geometric consistency is rank $W_q = 5 - 4 + 2 = 3$, or, equivalently, that all 4×4-subdeterminants of W_q vanish. Consider for instance the subdeterminant obtained from the rows $1, 2, 3, 4$. Put $\zeta^1 = [\eta_{12}^1 \ \eta_{22}^1 \ \eta_{32}^1]^T$, $\zeta^2 = [\eta_{12}^2 \ \eta_{22}^2 \ \eta_{32}^2]^T$. It is readily verified that the subdeterminant condition can be written

$$
\zeta^{1^T} \Phi \zeta^2 = 0 \quad \text{with} \quad \Phi = \begin{bmatrix} 0 & B_1 & -B_2 \\ -B_1 & 0 & B_3 \\ B_2 & -B_3 & 0 \end{bmatrix} \operatorname{diag}(\bar{q}_1, \bar{q}_2, \bar{q}_3) ,
$$

and

$$
B_1 = \begin{vmatrix} \eta_{31}^1 & \bar{q}_3\eta_{31}^2 \\ \eta_{41}^1 & \bar{q}_4\eta_{41}^2 \end{vmatrix} , \quad B_2 = \begin{vmatrix} \eta_{21}^1 & \bar{q}_2\eta_{21}^2 \\ \eta_{41}^1 & \bar{q}_4\eta_{41}^2 \end{vmatrix} , \quad B_3 = \begin{vmatrix} \eta_{11}^1 & \bar{q}_1\eta_{11}^2 \\ \eta_{41}^1 & \bar{q}_4\eta_{41}^2 \end{vmatrix} .
$$

This shows that $\zeta^{1^T} \Phi \zeta^2 = 0$ is a necessary condition for the points ζ^1 and ζ^2 in the respective images to match. This is the classical epipolar constraint, cf. [2], and the matrix Φ is the fundamental matrix with respect to this particular choice of frames. The factorization of Φ was discovered in [6], in a slightly different setting, where it was called the *reduced fundamental matrix*. In an analogous way, trilinear and multilinear forms appear by taking subdeterminants of W_q when $m > 2$.

In the case of exact data, the statement that W_q has rank 3 is equivalent to the vanishing of a number of appropriately chosen subdeterminants, some of which can be interpreted as fundamental matrices. However, using such a finite family of algebraic conditions in the presence of noise, there is no longer any guarantee for the fulfillment of the rank condition. The same objection remains in the case of multilinear forms, and depicts a drawback of algorithms based on fundamental and multilinear forms. Another disadvantage is the coordinate dependency, which may require rules for coordinate normalization.

All these problems are avoided by working with the matrix W_q and the Chasles matrix, where, loosely speaking, simultaneous and uniform averaging is done over all conceivable constraints. One is lead to a viewpoint, where there is nothing special with the epipolar constraint compared to the other constraints that can be drawn from Theorem 1, except that contrary to most of the others, the epipolar constraint has a nice geometric interpretation.

3.4 Proximity Measures

Intending to work with linear algebraic methods instead of polynomial equations, a quantitative tool for comparison of the correlation of linear subspaces is needed. In fact, the shape and depth theorem (single view) and the structure theorem (multiple views) both make assertments about the intersection of linear subspaces. In the single view case, the condition is that the intersection space of $as(\mathcal{X})$ and $s(\mathcal{Y})$ coincides with $as(\mathcal{X})$, and in the multiple view case, the condition is that the $n-3$-dimensional subspaces $s(\mathcal{Y}^1), \ldots, s(\mathcal{Y}^m)$ intersect in an $n-4$-dimensional subspace. This leads to the formulation of the

> General problem: Measure the rate of c-dimensional coincidence between linear subspaces $V_1, \ldots, V_m$ of $\mathbb{R}^n$.

To construct such a measure, let P_V denote the orthogonal projection matrix onto V. Then there is a chain of equivalences,

$$x \in V_1 \cap \ldots \cap V_m \iff \tfrac{1}{m}(P_{V_1}x + \ldots + P_{V_m}x) = x \iff$$

$$x \text{ eigenvector with eigenvalue 1 of } M = \tfrac{1}{m}(P_{V_1} + \ldots + P_{V_m}) .$$

It follows that $V_1, \ldots, V_m$ intersect in a c-dimensional subspace if and only if the eigenspace corresponding to the eigenvalue 1 of M has dimension c. Hence the matrix $I - M$ has rank deficiency c. A natural measure of this rank deficiency is the c:th smallest eigenvalue of $I - M$. An equivalent choice, more suitable for convergence studies of the algorithms below, is the following *proximity measure*:

$$\pi(V_1, \ldots, V_m) = (\sum_{k=1}^{c} \lambda_k^2)^{1/2} \text{ where } \lambda_1 \leq \ldots \leq \lambda_n \text{ are eigenvalues of } I - M .$$

In connection with single and multiple view geometry, as described by the shape and depth theorem and the structure theorem, $V = s(\mathcal{Y})$ for some $\mathcal{Y}$. Taking an S-matrix for $\mathcal{Y}$ with orthogonal columns, the projection matrix can be written SS^T. Using these theorems, a complication is the unknown depth parameters that appear. Violating slightly the orthogonality claim, in the case of single views below we work with the matrix

$$M = \frac{1}{2}(\Delta S_{\mathcal{X}} S_{\mathcal{X}}^T \Delta + S_{\mathcal{Y}} S_{\mathcal{Y}}^T) \quad \text{with} \quad \Delta = \operatorname{diag} \alpha ,$$

and in the case of multiple views, with the matrix

$$M = \frac{1}{m}(S_{\mathcal{Y}_1} S_{\mathcal{Y}_1}^T + Q_2 S_{\mathcal{Y}_2} S_{\mathcal{Y}_2}^T Q_2 + \ldots + Q_m S_{\mathcal{Y}_m} S_{\mathcal{Y}_m}^T Q_m) ,$$

with $Q_i = \operatorname{diag}(q^i)$, $i = 1, \ldots, m$. An analogous construction can be done with depth spaces instead of shape spaces, cf. [8].

4   Algorithms for Projective Reconstruction

4.1   Complete Data, No Occlusions

By the discussion above, the problem is to determine kinetic depth vectors q so that the m-image analogue of (1) is fulfilled for some $\mathcal{X}_{\parallel}$. This can be done by the following algorithm, introduced in [18]. A dual version, using depth instead of shape spaces, leads to factorization methods generalizing the one of [20], cf. [8]. The algorithm reads:

1. take $q^i = \mathbf{1}$ for $i = 1, \dots, m$,
2. compute an estimate of $\mathcal{X}$ by means of multiple view proximity,
3. knowing an estimate of $\mathcal{X}$, compute for each image i an estimate of the kinetic depth vector α^i by means of single view proximity, and form the corresponding kinetic depth vector q^i,
4. goto 2 or STOP, according to some criterion.

It can be shown that the sequence formed by the successively computed values of the proximity measure, $(\pi_k)_1^\infty$, decreases and convergences to a local minimum of π, considered as a function of $q^1, \dots, q^m$. Also the successively computed kinetic depth values and reconstruction estimates converge. In the case of exact data, and sufficiently many images and points, there is a unique minimum, corresponding to the true values of kinetic depth and the true object configuration $\mathcal{X}$. Empirically, the algorithm convergences very rapidly, in 10–20 iterations.

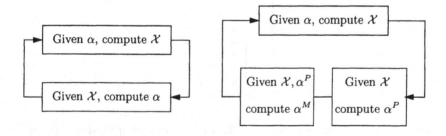

Fig. 1. Left loop: algorithm of Section 4.1. Right loop: algorithm of Section 4.2.

The convergence can be proved by observing that the minimization problem hidden in the proximity measure can be formulated

$$\pi = \inf_{q^2, \dots, q^m} \inf_P ||M(q^2, \dots, q^m) - P||_{\text{Frob}}$$

where P runs through the orthogonal projection matrices of rank $n - 4$. This minimization problem can be studied by classical analytical methods.

4.2 Missing Data, Occlusions

The algorithm above can easily be modified to handle also the the situation of missing data, i.e. when not all points are visible in all images. In this case the second step of the algorithm in Section 4.1 is divided into two:

3′ knowing an estimate of $\mathcal{X}$, compute by means of single view proximity for each image i a depth vector $\alpha^{P,i}$ corresponding to points present in image i,

3″ compute for each image i the depth vector $\alpha^{M,i}$ corresponding to the missing points, using that the total depth vector $\alpha^i \in d(\mathcal{X})$.

   The algorithms have been tested on images of a London scene, provided by Fraunhofer IGD within the CUMULI project. Six images have been used, taken at different locations on the river bank of the Thames. Forty points were manually detected in the images, where due to occlusions about 20 % of data was missing. The outcome is illustrated in Figure 2 and Figure 3, left diagram.

5   Using Subsidiary Information

5.1 Coplanarities

In man-made scenes, one often knows apriori that certain points are coplanar. The formalism of affine shape is well adapted to this situation. Suppose for instance that the first four points are coplanar. Then $s(\mathcal{X})$ contains an element where all components except the first four vanish (cf. *(i)* in Example A.1). Hence, for a given S-matrix, there is a column vector z such that

$$
\begin{bmatrix} \times \\ \times \\ \times \\ \times \\ 0 \\ \vdots \\ 0 \end{bmatrix} = \underbrace{\begin{pmatrix} \times & \cdots & \times \\ \times & \cdots & \times \\ \times & \cdots & \times \\ \times & \cdots & \times \\ \times & \cdots & \times \\ \vdots & \ddots & \vdots \\ \times & \cdots & \times \end{pmatrix}}_{S_{\mathcal{X}}} z \; .
$$

   In case of non-exact data, this can't be expected to be fulfilled exactly. However, by a least square argument, the S-matrix can easily be adjusted to fulfill one or several coplanarity conditions. For instance, in the situation above, let ξ be the element in $s(\mathcal{X})$ that is closest to the linear space U consisting of vectors with vanishing components $5, \ldots, n$, and let ξ' be the projection of ξ on U. Let $\xi^{\perp}$ be the orthogonal complement of ξ in $s(\mathcal{X})$. Then $\xi' \oplus \xi^{\perp}$ is the subspace of Σ_0 that is closest to $s(\mathcal{X})$ in proximity measure π. It is shape space of some configuration $\mathcal{X}'$, obeying the coplanarity constraint. In the same way, multiple coplanarity constraints can be handled.

   This leads to an algorithm, illustrated by the left hand loop in Figure 4, yielding projective reconstruction of an object fulfilling a family of coplanarity constraints.

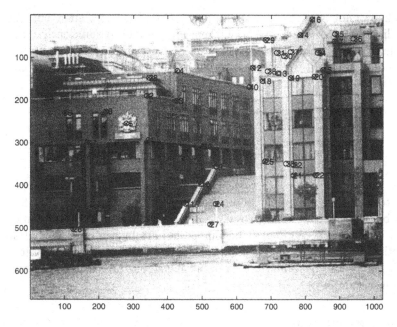

Fig. 2. Two of the six images used of a London scene. The symbols × denote the point configuration used, consisting of 40 points, with lots of occlusions. The circle symbols denote backprojection of reconstructed points, as if the scene had been transparent.

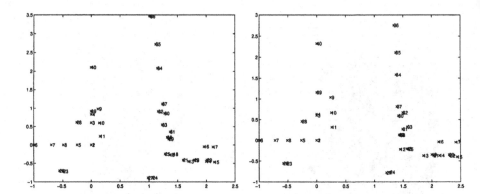

Fig. 3. Bird-eye perspectivities of the London scene, with placement of four points on the left building according to a city map. Left image: Projective reconstruction without using subsidiary information. Right image: Affine reconstruction, corrected for coplanarities given by the walls, and parallelities given by roofs, walls, windows and ground.

5.2   Parallelity

Often one knows not only that certain points A, B, C, D are coplanar, but also that some lines AB and CD connecting them are parallel. If sufficiently many such parallelities are known, the projective reconstruction can be strengthened to an affine one. In fact, it is easily seen that (cf. *(ii)* in Example A.1) $AB \parallel CD$ if and only if

$$\begin{bmatrix} a \\ -a \\ b \\ -b \\ 0 \\ \vdots \\ 0 \end{bmatrix} \in \beta s(\mathcal{X}_{\parallel}) \quad \text{for some} \quad a, b \, .$$

This leads to a linear system of equations in β, from which the depth in the first image can be determined, yielding an affine reconstruction of the object configuration $\mathcal{X}$. If Euclidean coordinates of four points are known, then Euclidean reconstruction of the whole configuration is achieved. An algorithm is described by the left hand loop in Figure 4. The performance on the London images is illustrated in Figure 3, right diagram.

5.3   Known Focii Locations

By means of Theorem 2 it is also possible to use the affine shape formalism to make Euclidean hand-eye calibration, even in the case of uncalibrated cameras, provided that the focal points are known. In fact, knowing the affine shape of the configuration formed by five or more focal points, from the Chasles matrix the

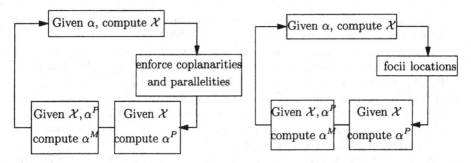

Fig. 4. Left loop: algorithm of Section 5.1 and 5.2. Right loop: algorithm of Secion 5.3.

depth in the first image can be computed, cf. [9], by iterative solving of linear systems of equations. This is done by a similar argument as the one behind the algorithm in Section 5.1, and yields an affine reconstruction. When knowing Euclidean coordinates for the focal points, from the Chasles matrix also the location of all objects points can be computed, yielding Euclidean reconstruction. An algorithm is described by the right hand loop in Figure 4. Figure 5 illustrates the typical performance of the algorithm on simulated data, in a situation where the focal points are densely distributed far away from the object. It is interesting to note that the impact of image noise mainly consists in a translation of the object along the ray of sight, while its shape is preserved to a large extent.

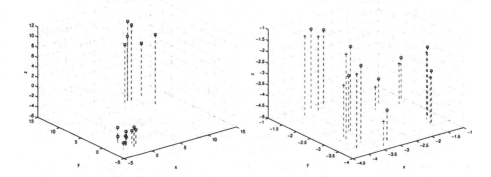

Fig. 5. Left diagram depicts focal points by squares and object points by circles. Right diagrams depicts true object points by circles and reconstructed points by crosses, in the presence of image noise.

References

1. Carlsson, S.: The Double Algebra: An Effective Tool for Computing Invariants in Computer Vision. Applications of Invariance in Computer Vision, Springer Verlag, Lecture Notes in Computer Science **825** (1992) 145-164

2. Faugeras, O.D.: Three Dimensional Computer Vision, A Geometric Viewpoint. The MIT Press, Cambridge, Massachusetts, London (1993)

3. Faugeras, O.D. and Mourrain, B.: On the geometry and algebra of the point and line correspondences between n images, Proc. 5th ICCV, Cambridge, Massachusetts, IEEE Computer Society Press (1995) 951-956

4. Hartley, R. and Gupta, R. and Chang, T.: Stereo from uncalibrated cameras. Proc. IEEE Conf. on Computer vision and Pattern Recognition (1992) 761-764

5. Heyden, A.: Geometry and Algebra of Multiple Projective Transformations. PhD thesis, Dept of Mathematics, Lund (1995)

6. Heyden, A.: Reconstruction from Image Sequences by means of Relative Depths. Proc. 5th ICCV, Cambridge, Massachusetts, IEEE Computer Society Press (1995) 1058-1063

7. Heyden, A. and Åström, K.: A Canonical Framework for Sequences of Images. IEEE Workshop on Representation of Visual Scenes, IEEE Computer Society Press (1995)

8. Heyden, A.: Projective Structure and motion from image sequences using subspace methods. Proc. 10th Scandinavean Conference on Computer Vision (1997 963-968

9. Lindström, P.: Computation of geometric structure from an uncalibrated camera on a robot arm. ISRN LUTFD2/TFMA–98/7003–SE, Dept. of Mathematics, Lund (1998)

10. Shashua, A.: Trilinearity in Visual Recognition by Alignment. Computer Vision - ECCV94, Springer Verlag, Lecture Notes in Computer Vision **801** (1994) 479-484

11. Shashua, A.: Algebraic functions for recognition. IEEE Trans. Pattern Anal. Machine Intell. **17:8** (1995)

12. Sparr, G.: Projective invariants for affine shapes of point configurations. ESPRIT/DARPA Invariants Workshop, Reykjavik (1991)

13. Sparr, G: Depth computations from polyhedral images. Image and Vision Computing **10:10** (1992) 683-688

14. Sparr, G.: An algebraic/analytic method for reconstruction from image correspondences. In Theory & Applications of Image Analysis, Machine Perception Artificial Intelligence, World Scientific Publishing Co (Selected papers from SCIA'91) **2** (1992) 87-98

15. Sparr, A. and Sparr, G.: On a theorem of M. Chasles. Dept. of Mathematics, Lund, ISRN LUTFD2/TFMA–7001–SE (1993)

16. Sparr, G.: A common framework for kinetic depth, motion and reconstruction. Computer Vision – ECCV'94, Springer Verlag, Lecture Notes in Computer Science, Lecture Notes in Computer Science **801** (1994) 471-482

17. Sparr, G.: Structure and motion from kinetic depth. Dept. of Mathematics, Lund, ISRN LUTFD2/TFMA–95/7016–SE (Lecture notes from Sophus Lie symposium on Computer Vision, Nordfjordeid) (1995)

18. Sparr, G.: Simultaneous reconstruction of scene structure and camera locations from uncalibrated image sequences. Proc. ICPR'96 (1996) A328-333

19. Spetsakis, M. and Aloimonos, Y.: A unified theory of structure from motion. DARPA IU Workshop (1990) 271-283

20. Tomasi, C. and Kanade, T.: Shape and motion from image streams under orthography: A factorization method. Int. Journal of Computer Vision, **9:2** (1992) 137-154

21. Triggs, B.: Matching Constraints and the Joint Image. Proc. 5th ICCV, Cambridge, Massachusetts, IEEE Computer Society Press (1995) 338-343

Appendix

A   Affine Shape and Depth

In this section, a brief recapitulation of the definitions and the basic properties of affine shape and depth spaces is given. For more details and proofs, see [12], [13], [14], [15], [16], [17], [18].

A.1   Subspace Formulation

Let $\mathbf{A}^d$ denote an affine space of dimension d, where the cases $d = 2$ and $d = 3$ are of particular interest. In our approach, the primitive objects are not individual points of $\mathbf{A}^d$, but *point configurations*,

$$\mathcal{X} = (X^1, \dots, X^n), \quad \text{where} \quad X^k \in \mathbf{A}^d, \ k = 1, \dots, n .$$

By the *dimension* $\rho_{\mathcal{X}}$ of $\mathcal{X}$ is meant the dimension of the smallest affine subspace containing $\mathcal{X}$. Let the set of n-point configurations of dimension ρ be denoted $\mathcal{C}_{n,\rho}$. For instance, $\mathcal{C}_{n,2}$ consists of n-point configurations in $\mathbf{A}^3$ which are planar but not linear.

The main idea of the approach of affine shape is to peel off any dependency of the coordinatization of $\mathbf{A}^d$ on the parametrization of $\mathcal{C}_{n,\rho}$. To construct such a parametrization, consider two different coordinate representations x and $\bar{x}$ on $\mathbf{A}^d$. Here $\bar{x} = Bx + b$, where B is a non-singular $d \times d$-matrix, and b is a column matrix. For a given configuration $\mathcal{X}$, to the respective coordinate representations we associate matrices with the coordinate vectors as columns, but augmented with a row of ones,

$$X_a = \begin{bmatrix} x^1 & \cdots & x^n \\ 1 & \cdots & 1 \end{bmatrix}, \quad \bar{X}_a = \begin{bmatrix} \bar{x}^1 & \cdots & \bar{x}^n \\ 1 & \cdots & 1 \end{bmatrix} .$$

Then

$$\bar{X}_a = A X_a \quad \text{with} \quad A = \begin{bmatrix} B & b \\ 0 & 1 \end{bmatrix} . \tag{1}$$

In this way, the set of augmented coordinate matrices is partitioned into equivalence classes, each of which can be identified with one particular point configuration. The problem is to label these equivalence classes. This is done by means of the two consequences of (1):

$$\mathcal{N}(\bar{X}_a) = \mathcal{N}(X_a) , \quad \mathcal{R}_{\text{row}}(\bar{X}_a) = \mathcal{R}_{\text{row}}(X_a) ,$$

where $\mathcal{N}$ stands for 'nullspace' (column) and $\mathcal{R}_{\text{row}}$ for 'row space'. We have seen that these linear subspaces discriminate between point configurations. On the other hand, one readily verifies that if $\mathcal{N}(\bar{X}) = \mathcal{N}(X)$ or $\mathcal{R}_{\text{row}}(\bar{X}) = \mathcal{R}_{\text{row}}(X)$, then there exists an affine transformation A such that $\bar{X}_a = A X_a$. This shows that the linear subspaces $\mathcal{N}(X_a)$ and $\mathcal{R}_{\text{row}}(X_a)$ stand in a one-one correspondence with the set of point configurations. Since they are independent of the coordinatization of $\mathbf{A}^d$, the following definition makes sense.

Definition A.1. *Let X_a be an augmented coordinate matrix for $\mathcal{X} \in C_{n,\rho}$ with respect to some coordinate system. Then*

the affine shape space of $\mathcal{X}$, denoted $s(\mathcal{X})$, is defined by $s(\mathcal{X}) = \mathcal{N}(X_a)$,
the affine depth space of $\mathcal{X}$, denoted $d(\mathcal{X})$, is defined by $d(\mathcal{X}) = \mathcal{R}_{\mathrm{row}}(X_a)$.

Often we use abbreviated denominations, saying e.g. 'affine shape', 'shape space' or simply 'shape' instead of 'affine shape space', analogously for depth. The denomination 'affine depth' will be motivated in Remark 1 below. Affine shape also has an interpretation in terms of barycentric coordinates, cf. e.g. [13].

The discussion above is summarized in the following theorem, saying that affine shape and affine depth are complete affine invariants.

Theorem A.1. *Let $\mathcal{X}, \overline{\mathcal{X}} \in C_{n,\rho}$. The following statements are equivalent:*

- *$\mathcal{X}$ and $\overline{\mathcal{X}}$ can be mapped onto each other by an affine transformation,*
- *$s(\overline{\mathcal{X}}) = s(\mathcal{X})$,*
- *$d(\overline{\mathcal{X}}) = d(\mathcal{X})$.*

To continue, some further notations are needed. Let

$$\Sigma_0 = \{\xi \in (\xi_1, \dots, \xi_n) \in \mathbb{R}^n \mid \sum_{k=1}^{n} \xi_k = 0\},$$

and let a multiplication on $\mathbf{R}^n$ be defined by

$$\alpha\xi = (\alpha_1\xi_1, \dots, \alpha_n\xi_n) \quad \text{if} \quad \alpha = (\alpha_1, \dots, \alpha_n), \ \xi = (\xi_1, \dots, \xi_n).$$

In the same way, division ξ/α is defined by componentwise division, provided that $\alpha_i \neq 0$, $i = 1, \dots, n$. We use the notation $\overline{\alpha} = 1/\alpha$, where $\mathbf{1} = (1, \dots, 1) \in \mathbf{R}^n$. Finally, for the situation in Theorem A.1 we use the notation

$$\overline{\mathcal{X}} \overset{s}{=} \mathcal{X} \iff \overline{\mathcal{X}} \text{ and } \mathcal{X} \text{ have equal shape}.$$

The following example is crucial for some common kinds of subsidiary information. It shows that shape spaces mirror a lot of qualitative information about point configurations.

Example A.1.

(i) Let $\mathcal{X} = (X^1, \dots, X^n)$. Then the sub-configuration $(X^{k_1}, X^{k_2}, X^{k_3}, X^{k_4})$ is planar if and only if

$$\xi_{k_1} X^{k_1} + \dots + \xi_{k_4} X^{k_4} = 0 \quad \text{with} \quad \xi_{k_1} + \dots + \xi_{k_4} = 0.$$

Hence $s(\mathcal{X})$ contains an element $\xi = (\xi_1, \dots, \xi_n)$ where all components except $\xi_{k_1}, \dots, \xi_{k_4}$ vanish.

(ii) One readily verifies that in (i), the vectors $\overline{X^{k_1} X^{k_2}}$ and $\overline{X^{k_3} X^{k_4}}$ are parallel if and only if $\xi_{k_1} = -\xi_{k_2}, \xi_{k_3} = -\xi_{k_4}$. In particular, $(X^{k_1}, X^{k_2}, X^{k_3}, X^{k_4})$ forms a parallelogram if and only if $\pm\xi_{k_1} = \pm\xi_{k_2} = \pm\xi_{k_3} = \pm\xi_{k_4}$, with two positive and two negative signs.

(iii) It can be shown that the vector $\overline{X^{k_1} X^{k_2}}$ is parallel to the plane spanned by the points $X^{k_3}, X^{k_4}, X^{k_5}$ if and only if $s(\mathcal{X})$ contains an element $\xi = (\xi_1, \dots, \xi_n)$, where all components except $\xi_{k_1}, \dots, \xi_{k_5}$ vanish and $\xi_{k_1} = -\xi_{k_2}$.

Theorem A.2. *Let* $\mathcal{X} \in C_{n,\rho}$. *Then*

- *the affine shape space fulfills*
  - $\dim s(\mathcal{X}) = n - \rho - 1$,
  - $s(\mathcal{X}) \subset \Sigma_0$,
- *the affine depth space fulfills*
  - $\dim d(\mathcal{X}) = \rho + 1$,
  - $\mathbf{1} = (1, \ldots, 1) \in d(\mathcal{X})$,
- *the affine shape and depth spaces are connected by*
  - $d(\mathcal{X})s(\mathcal{X}) = 0$,
  - $s(\mathcal{X}) \oplus d(\mathcal{X}) = \mathbb{R}^n$.

The theorem says that the generic dimension of $s(\mathcal{X})$ is $n - 3$ for 2D-configurations, and $n - 4$ for 3D-configurations. In the same way, the generic dimension of $d(\mathcal{X})$ is 3 for 2D-configurations and 4 for 3D-configurations.

By the last item, the shape and depth spaces of an n-point configuration are orthogonal complements of each other in $\mathbb{R}^n$, $s(\mathcal{X})^0 = d(\mathcal{X})$, $d(\mathcal{X})^0 = s(\mathcal{X})$. Although this makes one of them seem superfluous, it is practical to use them in parallel since they embody different aspects of the geometry, with shape space directed on point configurations and depth spaces on transformations.

The following theorem generalizes Theorem A.1 to non-singular transformations, typically from 3D to 2D.

Theorem A.3. *Let* $\mathcal{X} \in C_{n,\rho}$ *and* $\overline{\mathcal{X}} \in C_{n,\rho-1}$. *The following statements are equivalent:*

- $\mathcal{X}$ *can be mapped onto* $\overline{\mathcal{X}}$ *by an affine transformation,*
- $s(\mathcal{X}) \subset s(\overline{\mathcal{X}})$,
- $d(\overline{\mathcal{X}}) \subset d(\mathcal{X})$.

A.2   Matrix Formulation

To make numerical computations, matrix representations of the linear spaces $s(\mathcal{X})$ and $d(\mathcal{X})$ are needed.

Definition A.2. *Let* $\mathcal{X} \in C_{n,\rho}$. *Then*

- *by an S-matrix of* $\mathcal{X}$ *is meant a matrix with column space* $s(\mathcal{X})$,
- *by a D-matrix of* $\mathcal{X}$ *is meant a matrix with row space* $d(\mathcal{X})$.

Note that X_a is a D-matrix of $\mathcal{X}$. The following example illustrates some typical computations with S-matrices.

Example A.2. Let

$$S = \begin{bmatrix} 2 & 1 & 4 \\ -2 & 1 & 0 \\ 0 & -2 & -4 \\ 2 & 0 & 2 \\ -1 & -1 & -2 \\ -1 & 1 & 0 \end{bmatrix}.$$

We claim that this is an S-matrix of some configuration $\mathcal{X} \in C_{6,2}$. In view of Theorem A.2, first note that the matrix fulfills the necessary conditions of having rank 3 and vanishing column sums. The column space is unaffected by multiplication from the right by a non-singular matrix. In particular, using the inverse of the submatrix of S formed by the rows 3, 4 and 5, we obtain a new matrix with the same column space,

$$
-\begin{bmatrix} 2 & 1 & 4 \\ -2 & 1 & 0 \\ 0 & -2 & -4 \\ 2 & 0 & 2 \\ -1 & -1 & -2 \\ -1 & 1 & 0 \end{bmatrix} \begin{bmatrix} 0 & -2 & -4 \\ 2 & 0 & 2 \\ -1 & -1 & -2 \end{bmatrix}^{-1} = \begin{bmatrix} \frac{1}{2} & -1 & 0 \\ \frac{1}{2} & 1 & 0 \\ -1 & 0 & 0 \\ 0 & -1 & 0 \\ 0 & 0 & -1 \\ 0 & 1 & 1 \end{bmatrix} .
$$

The corresponding elements of the columns of the matrix on the right hand side provide the barycentric coordinate representations for the points X^3, X^4 and X^5, respectively, with respect to the affine frame X^1, X^2, X^6. Here in fact more can be said. Thus the first column says that,

$$
X^3 = \frac{1}{2}X^1 + \frac{1}{2}X^2 ,
$$

which means that X^1, X^2, X^3 are collinear, and that X^3 is the centroid of X^1 and X^2. The second column says that

$$
-X^1 + X^2 - X^3 + X^4 = 0 ,
$$

which means that X^1, X^2, X^3, X^4 are vertices of a parallelogram. Finally, the third column says that

$$
-X^5 + X^6 = 0 ,
$$

i.e. that the points X^5 and X^6 coincide.

So far, we have avoided 'points at infinity'. The following example illustrates how they can be treated within the framework of affine shape.

Example A.3. Let X^1, X^2, X^3 be three fixed points, and let X^4 be defined by

$$
\overline{X^1 X^4} = w\xi_2 \overline{X^1 X^2} + w\xi_3 \overline{X^1 X^3} . \tag{2}
$$

Then $s(\mathcal{X})$ is a one-dimensional subspace of $\mathbb{R}^4$, generated by the vector $(1 - w\xi_2 - w\xi_3, w\xi_2, w\xi_3, -1)$. Letting $w \longrightarrow \infty$, by (2) we are led to interpret X^4 as the point at infinity in the direction $\xi_2 \overline{X^1 X^2} + \xi_3 \overline{X^1 X^3}$. Taking limits also of $s(\mathcal{X})$, where $\mathcal{X} = (X^1, \ldots, X^4)$, one finds that

$$
s(\mathcal{X}) = \{(\xi_1, \xi_2, \xi_3, 0) \quad \text{with} \quad \xi_1 + \xi_2 + \xi_3 = 0\} .
$$

A.3 Relation to Grassman Manifolds

During the last few years, Grassman-Cayley and exteriour algebra has attracted some attention in computer vision, cf. e.g. [1]. The discussion below aims at explaining the place of affine shape and depth in this context.

By Theorem A.2, every point configurations $\mathcal{X}$ obeys the inclusion $s(\mathcal{X}) \subset \Sigma_0$. Conversely, every linear subspace U of Σ_0 is shape space for some point configuration. In fact, if $\dim U = \sigma$, in the same way as in Example A.2 it is seen that $U = s(\mathcal{X})$ for some configuration $\mathcal{X}$ of dimension $\rho_\mathcal{X} = n - \sigma - 1$. By Theorem A.3 we thus have a one-to-one correspondence between linear subspaces of Σ_0 and point configurations modulo affine transformations,

$$\mathcal{C}_{n,\rho}/\mathrm{aff} \cong G(\Sigma_0, n - \rho - 1) \ ,$$

where $G(\Sigma_0, d)$ denotes the Grassman manifold consisting of all d-dimensional linear subspaces of $\Sigma_0 \subset \mathbf{R}^n$.

The connection to Grassman algebra can be made more precise. For instance, let $\mathcal{X}$ be a planar 4-point configuration, with an augmented coordinate matrix X_a. By definition, the S-matrix, which in this case only has one column, is obtained by solving for the nullspace of X_a. Cramer's rule yields the components

$$\xi_{ijk} = \det \begin{bmatrix} x_i & x_j & x_k \\ 1 & 1 & 1 \end{bmatrix} \ . \tag{3}$$

These are recognized as Plücker coordinates of the subspace $s(\mathcal{X})$ in $\mathbb{R}^4$. The same holds true for bigger configurations. For instance, if $\mathcal{X}$ is a 5-point configuration, then all $\times$:es in the S-matrix

$$S_\mathcal{X} = \begin{bmatrix} \times & \times \\ \times & \times \\ \times & \times \\ \times & 0 \\ 0 & \times \end{bmatrix}$$

are Plücker coordinates for $s(\mathcal{X})$.

From this we learn that in uncalibrated camera geometry, it is only parameters of the form (3) that matter. In fact, regardless of the choice of coordinate system, image data organize themselves into such packages. An important feature of the approach by affine shape is that the array structure of the S-matrix adds further geometric information, compared to the Plücker coordinates alone.

B   Projective Transformations and Spaces

B.1   Background

By a *perspective transformation* $P : \mathbf{A}^3 \longrightarrow \mathbf{A}^2$ with *focus* ϕ and image plane Π is meant a transformation such that every point $X \in \mathbf{A}^3$ is mapped to the point of intersection of Π and the line ϕX. Perspective transformations are used to model the *pinhole camera*. Whenever the focus is of interest, the notation P_ϕ will be used.

To deal with perspective transformations and their compositions, the *projective* transformations, to get a coherent theory one has to adjoin *points at infinity* to the ambient affine space. As described in Example A.3, such points can be interpreted as directions in $\mathbf{A}^3$. This gives a model for the *d-dimensional projective space* $\mathbf{P}^d$. If ϕ is a point at infinity, then P_ϕ is a *parallel projection* in the direction described by ϕ.

If $Y = P_\phi(X)$, then $\overline{\phi X} = \alpha \overline{\phi Y}$ for some α, called the *depth* of X with respect to Y. If ϕ is a point at infinity, the depth is by definition 1. If a configuration $\mathcal{X}$ is mapped onto a configuration $\mathcal{Y}$ by a perspective transformation, and the depth of X^k with respect to Y^k is α_k, $k = 1, \ldots, n$, then the vector $\alpha = (\alpha_1, \ldots, \alpha_n) \in \mathbf{R}^n$ is called the *depth vector* of $\mathcal{X}$ with respect to $\mathcal{Y}$.

B.2   Shape, Depth, and Projective Transformations

The following theorem gives a complete description of the single view geometry.

Theorem B.1. Shape and depth theorem.

(i) If $\mathcal{X}, \mathcal{Y} \in C_{n,\rho}$, then the following statements are equivalent:
- *there exists a perspective transformation P, such that $P(\mathcal{X}) \overset{s}{=} \mathcal{Y}$ with depth vector α,*
- *$\alpha s(\mathcal{X}) = s(\mathcal{Y})$,*
- *$\alpha d(\mathcal{Y}) = d(\mathcal{X})$.*

(ii) If $\mathcal{X} \in C_{n,\rho}$, $\mathcal{Y} \in C_{n,\rho-1}$, then the following statements are equivalent:
- *there exists a perspective transformation P, such that $P(\mathcal{X}) \overset{s}{=} \mathcal{Y}$ with depth vector α,*
- *$\alpha s(\mathcal{X}) \subset s(\mathcal{Y})$,*
- *$\alpha d(\mathcal{Y}) \subset d(\mathcal{X})$.*

Remark 1. Now the terminology 'affine depth space' can be motivated, giving the answer to the question: Which depths can occur in conjunction with $\mathcal{X}$? From Theorem B.1 and the fact that every subspace of Σ_0 is a shape space, it follows that α is the depth of a perspective mapping acting on $\mathcal{X}$ if and only if $\alpha s(\mathcal{X}) \subset \Sigma_0$, i.e. $\alpha \in s(\mathcal{X})^0$. Since, by Theorem A.2, $s(\mathcal{X})^0 = d(\mathcal{X})$, the name 'depth space' for $d(\mathcal{X})$ is adequate.

B.3   Location of Focal Point

By Theorem B.1, there exists a projective transformation from 3D to 2D, $P_\phi : \mathcal{X} \rightarrow \mathcal{Y}$, with depth α, if and only if there holds a strict inclusion between linear subspaces, $\alpha s(\mathcal{X}) \subset s(\mathcal{Y})$. According to the following theorem, there is a one-to-one correspondence between ϕ and the set-difference $s(\mathcal{Y}) \setminus \alpha s(\mathcal{X})$, and it is possible to express ϕ in terms of $\mathcal{X}$ by an explicit formula. In formulating the theorem, a degenerate case called 'flat projection' has to be singled out, for details see [17]. If $\mathcal{X}$ is an n-point configuration and ϕ a point, then $(\mathcal{X}, \phi)$ denotes the $n+1$-point configuration formed by adjoining ϕ as an $n+1$:th point after the points of $\mathcal{X}$.

Theorem B.2. Focal point theorem. *Suppose that* $\alpha s(\mathcal{X}) \subset s(\mathcal{Y})$, *where* $\alpha \in \mathbb{R}^n$, $\mathcal{X} \in \mathcal{C}_{n,\rho}$, *and* $\mathcal{Y} \in \mathcal{C}_{n,\rho-1}$. *Then* $\mathcal{Y} = P_\phi(\mathcal{Y})$ *with a non-flat projection* P_ϕ *if and only if*

$$\phi = \sum_{k=1}^n \overline{\alpha}_k \eta_k X_k / \sum_{k=1}^n \overline{\alpha}_k \eta_k , \tag{4}$$

with $\eta \in s(\mathcal{Y}) \setminus \alpha s(\mathcal{X})$. *Analogously when* ϕ *is a point at infinity. In either case, the compound configuration* $(\mathcal{X}, \phi)$ *has an S-matrix*

$$S_{(\mathcal{X},\phi)} = \begin{bmatrix} \operatorname{diag}(\overline{\alpha}) S_y \\ -\overline{\alpha}^T S_y \end{bmatrix} . \tag{5}$$

B.4   Depth, Shape, and Camera Matrices

With x, y denoting object and image coordinates, respectively, the *camera matrix* P fulfills $P \begin{bmatrix} x \\ 1 \end{bmatrix} = \lambda \begin{bmatrix} y \\ 1 \end{bmatrix}$. For point configurations, it follows that

$$P X_a = Y_a \Lambda , \quad \text{with} \quad \Lambda = \operatorname{diag}(\lambda_1, \ldots, \lambda_n) .$$

The camera matrix of course depends on the coordinate systems used for the scene and the images.

From the equation $P X_a = Y_a \Lambda$ one reads out that each row of $Y_a \Lambda$ is a linear combination of the rows of X_a, with coefficients from P. It follows that $\lambda d(\mathcal{Y}) \subset d(\mathcal{X})$, where $\lambda = (\lambda_1, \ldots, \lambda_n)$. Conversely, if $\lambda d(\mathcal{Y}) \subset d(\mathcal{X})$ it can be shown that there exists a matrix P such that $P X_a = Y_a \Lambda$. This depicts the connection between camera matrices and depth and shape spaces, and that $\lambda = \alpha$ is the depth vector of the camera transformation.

Working with camera matrices, it is well known that the focus is obtained as the nullspace of the camera matrix. Theorem B.2 gives a novel characterization, having the advantage of providing an explicit formula for the focal point in terms of the object $\mathcal{X}$. To see the connection, take $\eta \in s(\mathcal{Y})$. From $P X_a \Lambda^{-1} = Y_a$, it follows that $P X_a \Lambda^{-1} \eta = Y_a \eta = 0$, which shows that $X_a \Lambda^{-1} \eta$ belongs to the nullspace of P, and thus is a focal point.

From Ordinal to Euclidean Reconstruction with Partial Scene Calibration

Daphna Weinshall[1], P. Anandan[2], and Michal Irani[3]*

[1] Institute of Computer Science Hebrew University 91904 Jerusalem, Israel
daphna@cs.huji.ac.il
[2] Microsoft Research, One Microsoft Way, Redmond, WA 98052, USA
anandan@microsoft.com,
[3] Dept. of Applied Math and CS, The Weizmann Inst. of Science, Rehovot, Israel
irani@wisdom.weizmann.ac.il

Abstract. Since uncalibrated images permit only projective reconstruction, metric information requires either camera or scene calibration. We propose a stratified approach to projective reconstruction, in which gradual increase in *domain* information for scene calibration leads to gradual increase in $3D$ information. Our scheme includes the following steps: (1) Register the images with respect to a reference plane; this can be done using limited scene information, e.g., the knowledge that two pairs of lines on the plane are parallel. We show that this calibration is sufficient for ordinal reconstruction - sorting the points by their height over the reference plane. (2) If available, use the relative height of two additional out-of-plane points to compute the height of the remaining points up to constant scaling. Our scheme is based on the dual epipolar geometry in the reference frame, which we develop below. We show good results with five sequences of real images, using mostly scene calibration that can be inferred directly from the images themselves.

1 Introduction

Given multiple images, stratified $3D$ reconstruction can be obtained depending on the available camera and scene calibration. In general uncalibrated images permit only projective reconstruction [6], which is of limited use; for example, we cannot determine from projective structure which part of the object is in front of the other. Its topological nature makes this representation useful primarily for verification, e.g., object recognition; for most other applications some scene or camera calibration is needed.

With calibrated cameras, or if self calibration is possible (when the same camera with partially fixed internal parameters is used to obtain all the images), Euclidean reconstruction can be obtained [9,17]. Alternatively, active vision techniques, based on imposing constraints on the viewing geometry and/or

---

* MI and DW are supported in part by DARPA through ARL Contract DAAL01-97-K-0101. This research was done while DW was on sabbatical at NECI Princeton.

Reinhard Koch, Luc Van Gool (Eds.): SMILE '98, LNCS 1506, pp. 208–223, 1998.
© Springer-Verlag Berlin Heidelberg 1998

the camera motion, can be used. Such externally imposed constraints may simplify the problem enough to permit affine or Euclidean reconstruction, e.g., [21] (see also [22]). However, active vision techniques cannot be universally applied, and in particular they are of little help when the sequence of images is already given (such as the case with video analysis). Similarly, techniques which obtain Euclidean reconstruction using self camera calibration cannot be used with just any sequence unless it is known that some of the internal parameters of the camera taking the sequence were kept fixed or are known.

The alternative to active vision and self camera calibration is to use scene calibration. Thus projective reconstruction can be turned into Euclidean reconstruction if the $3D$ coordinates of five points are given [14]. Computing Euclidean reconstruction from affine reconstruction requires that the $3D$ coordinates of four points are given. These results were used to formulate a stratified approach to reconstruction, characterized by invariance to increasingly smaller groups of transformations in $\mathcal{R}^3$: projective, affine and similarity (scaled Euclidean) [7]. The usefulness of techniques using scene calibration is limited to cases when the needed $3D$ information is available. Unlike the case with camera calibration and active vision, there are no results on partial scene calibration which could give partial metric information.

Our approach fills in this gap (a related approach is independently described in [5]); we investigate partial scene calibration which can be used to obtain some metric information from uncalibrated images. Unlike previous approaches using scene calibration, in which the $3D$ information had to be given a-priori, we make use of scene information that can be inferred automatically from images, such as that lines are parallel. This information only permits ordinal reconstruction in our scheme. In addition, in order to achieve affine reconstruction we need to know the relative height of one $3D$ point; this requirement still seems easier to meet than the knowledge of the $3D$ coordinates of five $3D$ points, as required in [14].

More specifically, we compute non-invariant reconstruction in a special coordinate system. This coordinate system is defined relative to a physical (real or virtual) planar surface in the scene. The projection of the scene points onto an input camera image is decomposed into two stages: (i) the projection of each scene point through the focal-point of the camera onto the *reference plane*, and (ii) the re-projection of the reference plane image onto the camera image plane. The projection from $3D$ to the reference plane depends only on the $3D$ positions of the scene points and the focal-point of the camera. All effects of the camera's internal calibration and the orientation of the image plane are folded into the re-projection step, which is captured by a homography between the reference plane and the camera image plane.

The reconstruction of the $3D$ scene is done relative to the reference plane, within a Cartesian coordinate system whose $X - Y$ axes span the reference plane, and whose Z direction is perpendicular to it. Given multiple images of the same scene, the homography relating each image to the reference plane is determined by specifying a few pieces of geometric information about the reference plane. This homography is then applied to each camera image to determine the corresponding reference-plane image. The "Height" (Z) of each scene point is determined by analyzing the disparity between the positions of each scene point on the multiple reference plane images[1]. The basic relationships associated with multi-view parallax geometry (with respect to a reference plane) are described in our recent paper [1]. However, while [1] focuses on the geometric relationships and elaborated on one application (namely "new view synthesis"), the present paper focuses on the use of this framework for stratified reconstruction, based on partial scene calibration.

The specification of the geometric information about the reference plane amounts to "registering" the reference plane. Such registration, with no 3D calibration, is sufficient to determine whether points lie on the same side of the plane [16]. Here we show that ordinal information about the 3D scene can be obtained even with very little scene calibration data, e.g., we can compute height ordering with respect to a plane from knowing (or guessing) the existence of two pairs of parallel lines on the plane; we call this **ordinal reconstruction** (cf. [12]). By providing additional *domain-information* (e.g., heights of one or two out-of-plane points), we can gradually obtain more metric 3D information, achieving affine and Euclidean reconstruction.

2 Geometry on the Reference Plane

The perspective projection of a point P_i in space to an image plane can be written as $p_{it} = M_t P_i$, where p_{it} and P_i are the point homogeneous coordinates in 2D and 3D respectively, and M_t is the 3×4 projection matrix describing the camera t. M_t depends on the orientation of the image plane and the location of the camera center P_t.

Here we break down the projection into 2 operations: the projection of the 3D world onto a 2D reference plane Π through the focal-point P_t, followed by a 2D projective transformation (homography) which maps the reference plane Π to the image plane of camera t.

Our purpose in this paper is to use this decomposition for the gradual reconstruction of the 3D scene relative to Π. The key idea in this paper is that by analyzing the images formed by projecting the scene through each camera center onto the reference plane Π, we vastly simplify the problem of 3D reconstruction. As explained in Section 3, the reference plane images from each camera view are obtained by registering each image to a pre-defined (affine or Cartesian) coordinate system on the reference plane.

2.1 Reference Plane Coordinate System

Let Π denote a (real or virtual) planar surface in the scene. We call Π the "reference plane". We define a 3D Cartesian coordinate system whose $X - Y$

---

[1] A related approach called "plane+parallax" was taken in [13,18], but there 3D reconstruction was relative to the coordinate systems of both the reference plane and a reference image.

axes span the reference plane Π, and the Z direction is perpendicular to Π. We call this system the "reference plane coordinate system".

An object, composed of n points in $3D$ space, is represented in the reference plane coordinate system by the **shape matrix P**, the following $4 \times n$ matrix:

$$\mathbf{P} = \begin{bmatrix} 0 \ a_1 \ a_2 \ a_3 \ a_4 & X_i \ X_{i+1} \\ 0 \ b_1 \ b_2 \ b_3 \ b_4 & \cdots \ Y_i \ Y_{i+1} \ \cdots \\ 1 \ 0 \ 0 \ 0 \ 0 & Z_i \ Z_{i+1} \\ 0 \ 1 \ 1 \ 1 \ 1 & W_i \ W_{i+1} \end{bmatrix} \tag{1}$$

Columns $[a_i \ b_i \ 0 \ 1]$ are the coordinates of points on the reference plane Π, $[0 \ 0 \ 1 \ 0]$ is a point at ∞ on the line through the origin which is perpendicular to the reference plane, and columns $[X_i \ Y_i \ Z_i \ W_i]^T$ are the coordinates of general points P_i on the object.

Every object can be represented this way; but the representation is *not* unique - a transformation from another projective coordinate system to this particular one is determined only up to an independent scaling of the Z axis. This ambiguity comes about because the standard projective basis requires that no four points are co-planar, whereas the basis of our system includes a plane. We need not worry about this ambiguity in the following derivations, however, because all quantities of interest involve ratios of Z values.

2.2 Projection on the Reference Plane

The $3D$ scene points are first projected onto the reference plane Π through the focal-point P_t of the camera. This forms a "virtual" image on Π. We refer to this image as the "reference-plane" image.

Corresponding to the object-shape matrix P defined in (1) and camera t, we define the following matrix $\mathbf{p_t}$ of reference-image points:

$$\mathbf{p_t} = \begin{bmatrix} \alpha_t \ a_1 \ a_2 \ a_3 \ a_4 & x_{it} \ x_{(i+1)t} \\ \beta_t \ b_1 \ b_2 \ b_3 \ b_4 & \cdots \ y_{it} \ y_{(i+1)t} \ \cdots \\ \gamma_t \ 1 \ 1 \ 1 \ 1 & w_{it} \ w_{(i+1)t} \end{bmatrix}$$

Note that the first two coordinates of the points $1, \dots 4$, which are physically located on the reference plane Π, are the same as the corresponding coordinates in their $3D$ representation. This is a direct consequence of our choice of the coordinate system for the $3D$ representation.

As explained before, the coordinates of the image points in the "original" input images are obtained by applying a $2D$ projective transformation to the corresponding reference plane images. That is, $\mathbf{q_t} = H_t \mathbf{p_t}$, where $\mathbf{q_t}$ is the "image matrix" corresponding to the original image t, and H_t is the $2D$ projective transformation (3×3 matrix) that relates the reference plane to the image plane of camera t.

As will become clear later, our *stratified* approach to $3D$ reconstruction does not require that the reference plane image coordinates be completely known. It is sufficient to specify them up to $2D$ affine deformation of the reference plane Π. Thus, it is sufficient to specify $\hat{\mathbf{p}}_\mathbf{t} = G_t \mathbf{p_t}$ where $G_t = \begin{bmatrix} g_{11} & g_{12} & g_{13} \\ g_{21} & g_{22} & g_{23} \\ 0 & 0 & 1 \end{bmatrix}$ denotes the (possibly unknown) affine transformation of the reference plane. In the remainder of this paper, we call $\mathbf{p_t}$ the "fully normalized" reference plane image, and $\hat{\mathbf{p}}_\mathbf{t}$ the "affine normalized" reference plane image.

If image $\mathbf{p_t}$ is fully normalized, it can be shown (or, more easily, verified) that the projection matrix M_t associated with it is:

$$M_t = \begin{bmatrix} \delta_t & 0 & \alpha_t & 0 \\ 0 & \delta_t & \beta_t & 0 \\ 0 & 0 & \gamma_t & \delta_t \end{bmatrix}$$

We impose the constraint that the focal point of the camera cannot be possibly seen in the (reference-plane) image; thus it is the null vector of M_t. We denote the $3D$ coordinates of the focal point P_t of the camera t by $[X_t \ Y_t \ Z_t \ W_t]$, then

$$\begin{bmatrix} 0 \\ 0 \\ 0 \end{bmatrix} \propto \begin{bmatrix} \delta_t & 0 & \alpha_t & 0 \\ 0 & \delta_t & \beta_t & 0 \\ 0 & 0 & \gamma_t & \delta_t \end{bmatrix} \cdot \begin{bmatrix} X_t \\ Y_t \\ Z_t \\ W_t \end{bmatrix} \implies \begin{cases} 0 = \delta_t X_t + \alpha_t Z_t \\ 0 = \delta_t Y_t + \beta_t Z_t \\ 0 = \delta_t W_t + \gamma_t Z_t \end{cases}$$

and the solution is:

$$[\delta_t \ \alpha_t \ \beta_t \ \gamma_t] \propto [-Z_t \ X_t \ Y_t \ W_t]$$

The normalized reference-plane image $\mathbf{p_t}$ is therefore obtained by the following projection:

$$\mathbf{p_t} \propto \begin{bmatrix} -Z_t & 0 & X_t & 0 \\ 0 & -Z_t & Y_t & 0 \\ 0 & 0 & W_t & -Z_t \end{bmatrix} \mathbf{P}$$

Let $p_{it} = [x_{it} \ y_{it} \ w_{it}]^T$ denote the reference-plane image position of the object point P_i projected through the camera focal-point P_t (onto Π). Then:

$$p_{it} = \begin{bmatrix} x_{it} \\ y_{it} \\ w_{it} \end{bmatrix} \propto \begin{bmatrix} -Z_t & 0 & X_t & 0 \\ 0 & -Z_t & Y_t & 0 \\ 0 & 0 & W_t & -Z_t \end{bmatrix} \begin{bmatrix} X_i \\ Y_i \\ Z_i \\ W_i \end{bmatrix} \qquad (2)$$

Observe that each point on the reference-plane image imposes 2 constraints relating to the coordinates of the object point P_i and the camera center P_t, which follow immediately from (2):

$$\frac{x_{it}}{w_{it}} = \frac{-Z_t X_i + X_t Z_i}{-Z_t W_i + W_t Z_i}, \qquad \frac{y_{it}}{w_{it}} = \frac{-Z_t Y_i + Y_t Z_i}{-Z_t W_i + W_t Z_i} \qquad (3)$$

In this equation, the $3D$ coordinates of the $3D$ point P_i and the focal point P_t of camera t are **dual**: the focal point of the camera $[X_t \ Y_t \ Z_t \ W_t]$ is interchangeable with the $3D$ point $[X_i \ Y_i \ Z_i \ W_i]$.

From (3) we get the epipolar and dual-epipolar geometry on the reference plane.

2.3 Epipolar Geometry on the Reference Plane

The epipolar geometry is obtained by the elimination of the $3D$ point coordinates from (3). In the following derivation we follow the method described in [8]. First, we rewrite (3) and note that each camera t imposes 2 constraints on the $3D$ point coordinates

$$\begin{pmatrix} w_{it}Z_t & 0 & (x_{it}W_t - w_{it}X_t) & -x_{it}Z_t \\ 0 & w_{it}Z_t & (y_{it}W_t - w_{it}Y_t) & -y_{it}Z_t \end{pmatrix} \begin{bmatrix} X_i \\ Y_i \\ Z_i \\ W_i \end{bmatrix} = 0$$

Two cameras (e.g., t and s) give 4 constraints. Since they have a non-trivial solution $[X_i \; Y_i \; Z_i \; W_i]$, the determinant of their matrix must equal 0. This yields a relation between the focal points $P_t = [X_t \; Y_t \; Z_t \; W_t]$ and $P_s = [X_s \; Y_s \; P_{it} = [x_{it} \; y_{it} \; w_{it}]$ and $p_{is} = [x_{is} \; y_{is} \; w_{is}]$ of the point P_i in the two corresponding reference-plane images. This relation can be rewritten as:

$$p_{it}^T F_{ts} \, p_{is} = 0, \quad F_{ts} = \begin{bmatrix} 0 & Z_sW_t - Z_tW_s & -Z_sY_t + Z_tY_s \\ -Z_sW_t + Z_tW_s & 0 & Z_sX_t - Z_tX_s \\ Z_sY_t - Z_tY_s & -Z_sX_t + Z_tX_s & 0 \end{bmatrix} \quad (4)$$

and F_{ts} is the "fundamental" matrix.

(4) gives the **epipolar geometry** *on the reference plane*—a relation between the coordinates of point P_i in the reference-plane image from camera t to its coordinates in the reference-plane image from camera s. The "fundamental matrix" F_{ts} is anti-symmetric, with essentially 3 unknowns: $(Z_sX_t - Z_tX_s)$, $(Z_sY_t - Z_tY_s)$ and $(Z_sW_t - Z_tW_s)$. We also observe that these are the coordinates of the point p_{ts}, which can be obtained by substituting the object point P_i by the camera-center P_s in (2). Thus, p_{ts}, which determines the fundamental matrix F_{ts}, is the projection of the focal point P_s through P_t on the reference plane—in other words, p_{ts} is the *epipole*.

The two epipoles, p_{st} and p_{ts}, are the same on the reference plane; they are defined by the intersection of the line going through the focal points of the two cameras and the reference plane. Thus the epipolar geometry on both image s and image t, when mapped to the reference plane, is the same. This remains true even if the images are not normalized at all, that is, they are aligned with the reference plane up to some homography only.

2.4 Dual Geometry on Reference Plane

The dual epipolar geometry is obtained by eliminating the coordinates of the camera's focal point from (3). Once again, we first rewrite (3) so that each point P_i imposes 2 constraints on the coordinates of the focal point of the camera t:

$$\begin{pmatrix} w_{it}Z_i & 0 & (x_{it}W_i - w_{it}X_i) & -x_{it}Z_i \\ 0 & w_{it}Z_i & (y_{it}W_i - w_{it}Y_i) & -y_{it}Z_i \end{pmatrix} \begin{bmatrix} X_t \\ Y_t \\ Z_t \\ W_t \end{bmatrix} = 0$$

Two points give 4 constraints, which have a non-trivial solution. Following the same reasoning as before for points P_i, P_j, we get a relation between the $3D$ coordinates of the two points $[X_i \ Y_i \ Z_i \ W_i], [X_j \ Y_j \ Z_j \ W_j]$, and the image coordinates p_{it}, p_{jt} of the points in image t. This relation can be rewritten as

$$p_{it}^T \ G_{ij} \ p_{jt}, \quad G_{ij} = \begin{bmatrix} 0 & Z_j W_i - Z_i W_j & -Z_j Y_i + Z_i Y_j \\ -Z_j W_i + Z_i W_j & 0 & Z_j X_i - Z_i X_j \\ Z_j Y_i - Z_i Y_j & -Z_j X_i + Z_i X_j & 0 \end{bmatrix} \quad (5)$$

and G_{ij} is the **dual** "fundamental" matrix.

Similar to the case of the fundamental matrix F, the *dual* fundamental Matrix G is determined by the coordinates of the **dual** epipole p_{ij} [10], which is obtained by projecting the scene point P_i through P_j onto the reference plane. These dual relations are similar to those previously described in [3,20,4], where they were derived with respect to the quantities from the actual image points; here the dual relations are derived in the context of the reference-plane images.

2.5   Using Affine Normalization

When the homography H_t between the actual *observed* image $\mathbf{q}_t$ and the corresponding virtual image $\mathbf{p}_t$ on the reference plane is *completely* determined by the given scene calibration data, then for each point in the observed imagei we can compute the corresponding reference-image point coordinates $p_{it} = H_t^{-1} q_{it}$. These quantities can then be used in the constraints derived above. However, if the homography is known only up to a $2D$ affine transformation G_t of Π, then we can use the affine normalized coordinates $\widehat{p_{it}} = G_t p_{it}$.

If we replace p_{it} by $\widehat{p}_{it}$ in all the derivations above, everything remains true but with respect to a different $3D$ coordinate system: the $3D$ point coordinates are now taken with respect to a $3D$ coordinate system where the $X - Y$ plane is transformed by the same affine transformation G_t. The coordinates of point P_i in this new coordinate system are $[X_i', Y_i', \alpha Z_i, W_i]$, where X_i', Y_i' are obtained from X_i, Y_i by G_t, and α is some scale factor. Thus when using image coordinates from $\widehat{p}_t$, we can still use all the expressions developed in Section 2.2, noting to replace (X_i, Y_i) by (X_i', Y_i').

3   Stratified Reconstruction

In this section we show how the relations established in Section 2 between the image positions of scene points on the reference plane can be used to recover $3D$ information about the scene with very little scene information. We will describe an approach in which gradual increase in *domain* information for scene calibration leads to gradually increasing $3D$ information.

Registering the Input Images to the Reference Plane Π: As mentioned in Section 1 our approach is based on registering each input image to a pre-specified affine or Cartesian coordinate system on the reference plane. For practical reasons, we do this in three stages: (i) determine the homography H_{st} between each image "s" in the sequence and an arbitrarily selected reference image "t" from the same sequence, (ii) specify or infer the domain information needed to register the reference image t to the reference plane Π; based on this specification determine the $2D$ transformation $H_{t\pi}$ that aligns image t with Π, and (iii) concatenate H_{st} and $H_{t\pi}$ to determine the transformation $H_{s\pi}$ that registers s with Π. We refer to this process of registering the images to the reference plane as "registering the reference plane".

Affine vs. Euclidean Normalization: As noted in Section 2.5, if the positions of the image points on the reference plane Π are known only up to a $2D$ affine transformation of Π, it only affects the X and Y coordinates of the $3D$ scene points. The Z component is not affected by the unknown $2D$ affine transformation G_t. Here the minimal scene calibration required for some $3D$ inference should be sufficient for the registration of the reference plane up to an affine transformation.

$3D$ **Reconstruction from the Dual Epipolar Geometry:** (5) establishes the relationship between reference-plane image positions of two points in one view and the dual Fundamental matrix G, which in turn depends on the coordinates of the dual-epipole. Since this equation is homogeneous, it can be divided by an arbitrary scale factor. In particular, we can divide (5) by $Z_i Z_j$ and obtain a new form for G, which depends on the *scaled* homogeneous coordinates of the dual-epipole

$$p_{ij} \overset{\text{def}}{=} [\frac{X_j}{Z_j} - \frac{X_i}{Z_i}, \frac{Y_j}{Z_j} - \frac{Y_i}{Z_i}, \frac{W_j}{Z_j} - \frac{W_i}{Z_i}]. \tag{6}$$

(5) provides one constraint on these 3 variables. Looking separately at the pairs of $3D$ points $\{P_i, P_j\}$, $\{P_i, P_k\}$, $\{P_j, P_k\}$, we get from each image 3 constraints on the 9 homogeneous coordinates of the three dual-epipoles p_{ij}, p_{jk} and p_{ki}. Thus, 2 images $t = 1, 2$ give 6 homogeneous constraints on these 9 variables. In addition, it can be easily verified from (6) that $p_{ij} + p_{jk} + p_{ki} = 0$ which gives 3 more constraints. Taken together these 9 homogeneous constraints are sufficient to compute the coordinates of the three dual-epipoles up to a single scale factor.

Note that each additional image provides 3 more homogeneous constraints on the same 9 variables. Thus, if given more than 2 images, the computation of the dual epipoles requires the solution of an over-determined linear system of equations; such system can be solved in a least-squares sense using standard tools such as SVD.

Of particular interest is the third coordinate of the dual-epipoles. Assuming, w.l.o.g, $W_i = 1$, the third coordinate of the three dual-epipoles are: $(\frac{1}{Z_i} - \frac{1}{Z_j}), (\frac{1}{Z_j} - \frac{1}{Z_k}), (\frac{1}{Z_k} - \frac{1}{Z_i})$. Since we can compute these quantities only up to a scale factor, we can only determine their ratios. We arbitrarily select two out-of-plane points as "reference points" and denote them by indices 1 and 2. Then for any other point i we can compute

$$u_i = (\frac{1}{Z_i} - \frac{1}{Z_1})/(\frac{1}{Z_2} - \frac{1}{Z_1}) \implies Z_i = \frac{Z_1}{1 + \alpha u_i} \qquad (7)$$

where $\alpha = \frac{Z_1}{Z_2} - 1$.

Stratified Reconstruction: (7) can be used to compute the height of points relative to the reference plane Π. With increasing amount of scene information we get increasing specificity:

Ordinal reconstruction: from (7) it follows that u_i is monotonically related to the height Z_i. Hence, given only the knowledge whether α is positive or negative, the ordering of the height of all other points relative to Π can be determined without *any additional information*. This type of 3D information is useful in a number of visual reasoning tasks such as navigation and grasping, in order to determine potential obstructions or provide micro-management control commands.

Affine reconstruction: if the ratio (Z_2/Z_1) is given, α can be determined, and the height of all other scene points relative to Π can be determined up to an unknown scale factor.

Absolute depth: if, in addition, the height of Z_1 is known, then the absolute height of all points relative to Π can be determined.

Euclidean reconstruction: the remaining elements of the dual epipoles can be used to compute the X and Y coordinates of the object points. Given the height of Z_1, Z_2, the X, Y coordinates can be determined up to image translation. Given (X_1, Y_1), (X_i, Y_i) can be determined absolutely.

4   Experiments

We compute the stratified reconstruction using four sequences of real images. In the first three cases, corners were automatically extracted (see Fig 1b) and then automatically tracked over the sequence; for comparison we were given all the 3D coordinates of the points. In the last two sequences, a reference plane in the scene was stabilized first, then a dense parallax flow field was recovered [10,13]. The reconstruction was then based on this parallax data. In this case, the images were obtained using a hand-held video camera in a casual manner, without making controled measurements of the camera or scene parameters.

4.1   Medium Depth Sequence

An object (box) 15cm wide at about 60cm from the camera (Fig 1a) was photographed from 5 different points of view. First, we affine-normalized all the images: using two identified pairs of parallel lines (e.g., the sides on one of the

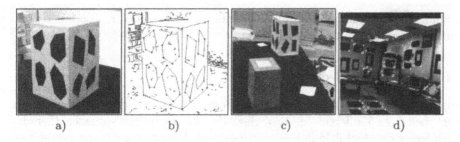

Fig. 1. a) one frame from the medium depth sequence; b) corners extracted from a);
c) one frame from the large depth sequence; d) one frame from the lab sequence.

faces of the box), we applied a 2D homography which made the two lines parallel
in the image and confined to the same image position in all the frames. We then
arbitrarily selected two out-of-plane points as reference points, and computed
the dual-epipole between them, as well as the dual-epipole between each of the
other data points and the two reference points. The dual-epipoles were computed by using all the 5 frames and a least-squares solution to (5). Using these
dual-epipoles, we computed ordinal reconstruction as described in Section 3. The
results - each computed u_i value vs. the real u_i value - are shown in Table 1.

u_i est.	u_i act.	u_i est.	u_i act.	u_i est.	u_i act.	Z_i est.	Z_i act.
12.9521	12.6736*	0.5658	0.5729	-0.5205	-0.5166	0.8827	0.9
8.5741	6.4453	0.3900	0.4712*	-0.4302	-0.5292	3.1798	3.2
7.7989	6.2027	0.0666	0.3356	-0.5136	-0.5456*	5.0657	5.1
2.5462	3.1829	0.1853	0.2679	-0.1878	-0.5576	6.5621	6.3
2.4668	2.4414*	0.0527	0.2170	-0.5954	-0.5844	7.3215	7.5
2.0456	2.3201	0.1875	0.1458*	-0.6176	-0.6407	8.7334	9.15
2.2506	1.9965	0.0972	0.0096	-0.6576	-0.6473*	12.2156	12.6
1.4493	1.9965	0.0341	-0.0188	-0.7028	-0.7083	14.1592	14
0.9668	0.9498*	-0.1484	-0.1468	-0.7537	-0.7083		
0.9641	0.8550	-0.0954	-0.1622*	-0.8160	-0.7083		
0.6754	0.6091	-0.4950	-0.5036				

Table 1. The estimated vs. actual reconstructed 3D data, ordinal (u_i) and Euclidean
(Z_i), for the Medium Depth Sequence. For conciseness, the height Z_i is only shown for
every fourth point, and the corresponding ordinal values are marked by *.

Given the heights of the two reference points, we can continue further and
transform the ordinal reconstruction into Euclidean reconstruction by computing
the actual height Z_i at each point. The results - some of the computed Z_i vs.
the actual Z_i - are shown in Table 1.

Looking closely at these results, clearly the ordinal reconstruction by u_i is
accurate at most of the points, with only a few points close in height switched

around. The heights are also quite accurate for most points, as the few representative heights in Table 1 show.

4.2 Large Depth Sequence

Objects spanning 60cm at about 60cm from the camera (Fig 1c) were photographed from 5 different points of view. Unlike the previous sequence, there is much larger depth of field in this sequence, and thus there are larger projective distortions. Such distortions make metric reconstruction difficult. Once again, we first affine-normalized all the images and followed a procedure similar to the previous experiment to recover ordinal height (u_i) for 24 tracked points. The estimated vs. the actual $3D$ data are shown in Table 2.

u_i est.	u_i act.	u_i est.	u_i act.	u_i est.	u_i act.	Z_i est.	Z_i act.
0.0077	0*	3.8829	3.7841*	1.4512	1.3885*	-20.4185	-20
-0.1529	-0.3068	2.4482	2.5179	1.3658	1.3817	-0.2296	0
-0.167	-0.3068	2.4848	2.402	1.1322	1.1103	2.138	2.2
-2.4833	-3.079	2.6841	2.25	1.1175	1.1103	4.1373	4.4
-32.2960	∞*	2.1878	2.0795*	1.2088	1.0893*	6.9691	7.4
15.8281	∞	1.7263	1.6045	1.072	1.0568	8.9946	10.5
10.8487	8.2697	1.6723	1.6045	1.0901	1		
8.4828	6.3750	1.4574	1.4024	1.089	1		

Table 2. Estimated vs. Actual $3D$ Data, ordinal (u_i) and Euclidean (Z_i), for the Large Depth Sequence. For conciseness, the height Z_i is only shown for every fourth point, and the corresponding ordinal values are marked by *.

Given the heights of the 2 reference points, we can continue further and transform the ordinal reconstruction into Euclidean reconstruction by computing the actual height Z_i at each point. The results - the computed Z_i vs. the actual Z_i - are shown in Table 2.

Here, too, the ordinal reconstruction by u_i is almost always accurate. Of the 30 features, only 3 pairs of neighbors in height were swapped with each other (their height was 4 vs. 3.5, 11 vs. 12 and 10.2 vs. 10.5). The Z values are still good, but less accurate when compared with the previous experiment.

4.3 Lab Sequence

This sequence includes 16 images of a robotic laboratory, obtained by rotating a robot arm $120°$ (one frame is shown in Fig. 1d). 32 corner-like points were tracked. This sequence has the largest depth of field - the depth values of the points in the first frame (relative to the camera) ranged from 13 to 33 feet. Moreover, a wide-lens camera was used, causing distortions at the periphery which were not compensated for. This is therefore the most difficult sequence so far. Once again, following the same procedure as in the other two experiments,

Z_i est.	Z_i act.	Z_i est.	Z_i act.	Z_i est.	Z_i act.	Z_i est.	Z_i act.	Z_i est.	Z_i act.
0.2045	-0.3386	9.4100	5.6942	8.3978	10.0444	9.2478	11.4074	15.3879	15.8765
-0.2048	0.3409	7.1877	6.4347	9.0416	10.0446	9.3495	12.1890	16.1396	16.5352
2.2095	1.1965	9.4263	9.3823	9.1713	10.9708	9.2442	13.6701	17.4406	16.6093
8.5974	1.5249	9.1724	9.4161	9.5846	10.9993	13.2664	13.9289	13.6005	16.6761
8.1943	2.8690	9.9265	9.4161	9.9490	11.2723	16.5506	14.6616	16.5688	17.5328

Table 3. Estimated vs. Actual Heights for the Lab Sequence.

we estimated ordinal and Euclidean reconstruction in 25 points. The estimated Z_i vs. actual Z_i for these points are shown in Table 3.

Note that although there are gross errors for some points, the computed height in most points is fairly close to their true height.

4.4 Dense Height Maps

The previous three examples gave quantitative illustrations of stratified reconstruction at a sparse set of points in the scene. Here we include two examples of dense reconstruction of ordinal heights. In both cases, the images were acquired using a hand-held video camera. No quantitative information about the scene structure, the camera imaging parameters, or its motion were available.

Given two input images, we used the method described in [19] to first estimate the homography that aligns a dominant planar surface in the scene between the two images. The residual parallax displacements between the points were then computed using the method described in [13]. These displacements were used as input for the stratified reconstruction of the scene.

The first example uses the "Toys" image sequence previously used in [11], see Figure 2a. The scene consists of a few toys standing on a rug.

In order to register the images to the reference plane (*upto 2D affine transformation*), we used the following approach. Using commonly available image manipulations tools on a PC, we drew two pairs of lines on the reference image, that were visually judged to be parallel to the "grooves" of the rug. These are shown as grey lines painted on the carpet in Figure 2a. Note that the vertical pair in particular is not parallel in the image itself, although it represents parallel lines on the rug. We then interactively warped the images (using homographies) until the lines appeared parallel in the image. Any of a family of homographies that are equivalent upto a 2D affine transformation is sufficient for this purpose. We arbitrarily picked one to achieve the intended effect. The result of this process is shown in Figure 2b.

We then computed the ordinal height u_i (see (7)) using the parallax displacements (also appropriately warped to reflect the projection onto the reference plane). However, since $u_i = \infty$ for points on the reference plane itself (i.e., when $Z_i = 0$ in (7)), we display $\frac{1}{u_i}$ in Figure 2c. As evident from this image, the points on the rug are dark (corresponding to an ordinal height of 0); also, a gradual

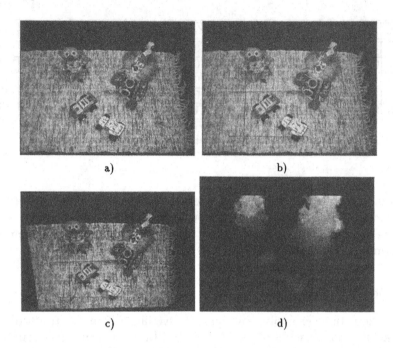

Fig. 2. a) one frame from the toys sequence; b) same image as (a) but with lines drawn on it (see text); c) the result of projecting (b) onto the reference plane (the rug); d) ordinal height.

increase in height along the two dominant objects is noticeable. Since we did not have the actual heights of any of the objects in the scene, we stopped at this stage of our stratified reconstruction.

The second example uses a new sequence, which we will refer to as the "Doll" sequence (see Figure 3a). In this case, the carpet and the floor constituted the reference plane. The grid lines on the carpet and the floor served as the basis for registering the images to the reference plane. As in the case of the "Toys" example, we interactively warped the images until these lines appeared parallel in the image, and arbitrarily picked one homography that achieved this effect. Once again, we display $\frac{1}{u_i}$ in Figure 3c.

Note that in both these examples, even with the minimal calibration (two sets of parallel lines) we obtain a reconstruction that looks qualitatively consistent with the actual structure of the scene. As noted earlier, this would be useful in a number of visual reasoning tasks, such as navigation and grasping.

4.5 Discussion

The computation of height (a *metric* quantity) relative to the reference plane consistently gave good results while using noisy sequences with large perspective distortions. The algorithm is fast, robust and easy to implement since it only solves a linear system of equations. Height was computed with minimal scene

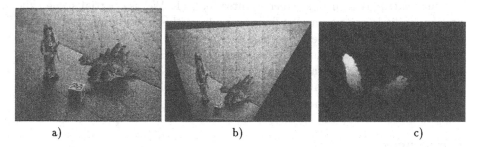

a)   b)   c)

Fig. 3. a) one frame from the doll sequence; b) the result of projecting (a) onto the reference plane (the rug); c) ordinal height.

calibration: (i) **ordinal reconstruction** required knowledge of the reference frame up to affine transformation - 2 degrees of freedom[2], and (ii) **exact height** required knowledge of the height of two points not on the reference plane - 2 additional d.o.f. Thus we used 2-4 d.o.f. of scene calibration information, much less than required by other reconstruction algorithms which use scene calibration.

For example, the scene calibration needed by the reconstruction algorithm described in [14] includes the specification of the $3D$ coordinates of 5 reference points (supplied by an oracle) - 15 d.o.f. We used this method in [2] to accomplish reconstruction with the first two sequences described above. Although this computation relied on 15, rather than 4, pre-determined pieces of calibration data, and involved a complex non-linear algorithm, the reconstruction results in [2] are no better than our results here (e.g., a relative error of about $5\% - 10\%$ per datapoint using the second sequence).

5   Summary

Since uncalibrated images only permit projective reconstruction, no metric information (such as relative depth) can be deduced without some calibration, either camera calibration (external and internal parameters of the camera) or scene calibration (the $3D$ affine or Euclidean coordinates of some $3D$ landmarks). Camera calibration, however, is not always possible: it requires a partially fixed camera (unsuitable, e.g., if the images are taken by many cameras) or some control over the camera motion (unsuitable, e.g., with video data). Scene calibration requires a priori knowledge of known $3D$ points, and is typically employed after the projective reconstruction; therefore it is typically ill-advised to use directly a least squares linear reconstruction algorithm as we do here, since there is no suitable least squares error in $3D$ projective space.

---

[2] The $2D$ affine transformation G_t has 6 degrees of freedom, whereas a general $2D$ projective transformation (homography) has 8 d.o.f.; thus $2D$ affine plane calibration requires the specification of 2 d.o.f.

Our contribution in this paper is three fold: (1) We use partial scene calibration, as little as two parallel lines on a plane; this information need not be given a priori, and can be inferred from the images directly. (2) We perform the calibration prior to the reconstruction; this allows the use of a robust least squares structure computation from many frames. (3) We obtain a hierarchy of intermediate representations, from ordinal to Euclidean, which increasingly depend on the amount of scene calibration available.

References

1. M. Irani, P. Anandan, and D. Weinshall. From Reference Frames to Reference Planes: Multi-view Parallax Geometry and Applications In *Proc. 5th ECCV*, Freiburg, Germany, June 1998.
2. B. Boufama, D. Weinshall, and M. Werman. Shape from motion algorithms: a comparative analysis of scaled orthography and perspective. In *Proc. 3rd ECCV*, pages 199–204, Stockholm, Sweden, 1994.
3. S. Carlsson. Duality of reconstruction and positioning from projective views. In *Workshop on Representations of Visual Scenes*, 1995.
4. S. Carlsson and D. Weinshall. Dual Computation of Projective Shape and Camera Positions from Multiple Images. *IJCV*, 27(3), 1998.
5. A. Criminisi, I. Reid, and A. Zisserman. Duality, rigidity, and planar parallax. In *Proc. 5th ECCV*, Freiburg, Germany, June 1998.
6. O.D. Faugeras. What can be seen in three dimensions with an uncalibrated stereo rig? In *Proc. 1st ECCV*, pages 563–578, Santa Margarita Ligure, May 1992.
7. O.D. Faugeras. Stratification of three-dimensional vision:projective, affine and metric representations. JOSA, 12(3):465-484, March 1995.
8. O. Faugeras and B. Mourrain. On the geometry and algebra of the point and line correspondences between N images. In *Proc. ECW*. Xidian University Press, 1995.
9. Richard Hartley. Euclidean Reconstruction from Uncalibrated Views. In *Applications of Invariance in Computer Vision*, J.L. Mundy, D. Forsyth, and A. Zisserman (Eds.), Springer-Verlag, 1993.
10. M. Irani and P. Anandan. Parallax geometry of pairs of points for 3D scene analysis. In *Proc. 3rd ECCV*, Cambridge, UK, April 1996.
11. M. Irani and P. Anandan. A unified approach to moving object detection in 2D and 3D scenes. *IEEE Trans. on PAMI*, in press.
12. J. J. Koenderink and A. J. van Doorn. Affine structure from motion. *JOSA*, 8(2):377–385, 1991.
13. R. Kumar, P. Anandan, and K. Hanna. Direct recovery of shape from multiple views: a parallax based approach. In *Proc 12th ICPR*, 1994.
14. R. Mohr, , L. Quan, F. Veillon, and B. Boufama. Relative 3D reconstruction using multiple uncalibrated images. RT 84–IMAG–12 LIFIA, Uni. of Grenoble, 1992.
15. H. S. Sawhney, J. Oliensis, and A. R. Hanson. Description and reconstruction from image trajectories of rotational motion. In *Proc. 3rd ICCV*, Osaka, Japan, 1990.
16. L. Robert and O.D. Faugeras. Relative 3D Positioning and 3D Convex Hull Computation from a Weakly Calibrated Stereo Pair. J. Imaging and Vision Compting, 13(3), 1995.
17. M. Pollyfeys, R. Koch, and L. van Gool. Self-calibration and Metric Reconstruction in Spite of Varying and Unknown Internal Camera Parameters. In *Proc. 6th ICCV*, Mumbai, India, January 1998.

18. A. Shashua and N. Navab. Relative affine structure: Theory and application to 3D reconstruction from perspective views. In *Proc. CVPR*:483–489, Seattle, 1994.
19. R. Szeliski and H. Shum. Creating full view panoramic mosaics and texture-mapped models. In *Proc. SIGGRAPH 97*, pp. 251-258, Los Angels, 1997.
20. D. Weinshall, M.Werman, and A. Shashua. Shape Tensors for Efficient and Learnable Indexing. In *Workshop on Representations of Visual Scenes*, 1995.
21. A. Zisserman. Active Visual Navigation using Non-Metric Structure. In *Proc. 5th ICCV*, Boston, USA, 1995.
22. Z. Zhang, R. Weiss and A. Hanson. Obstacle Detection Using Qualitative and Quantitative 3D Reconstruction. In *IEEE PAMI*, 19(2):15-26, January 1997.

Imposing Euclidean Constraints During Self-Calibration Processes

Didier Bondyfalat and Sylvain Bougnoux

INRIA, 2004 route des Lucioles, BP 93
F-06902 Sophia-Antipolis Cedex
first.last@sophia.inria.fr

Abstract. Using Euclidean constraints to model large 3D environments is made possible. This has been a challenging issue for many years. Using such knowledge not only enlarges the number of feasible cases, but it also provides perfect results, unreachable formerly. We deal with a limited set of constraints composed of incidence relations, parallelism, and orthogonality. This knowledge is given manually, processed through a geometric reasoning system, and used during what we call a constraint bundle adjustment. Results are very encouraging, even though the computational time may be prohibitive.

Keywords: Geometric Reasoning, Self-Calibration, Euclidean Constraints.

1 Introduction

Modeling large 3D environments has been a major challenging question for the past decades. Many approaches have been tried, using technologies from Photogrammetry [8], Laser-Range Metrology [9], and Computer Vision [7]. Building a system that will automatically model a 3D environment under every circumstance is for the time being far from being realized. Many results have already been obtained [12, 2, 10, 6]. But, though for some applications they may seem quite acceptable, they are always computed up to sensor accuracy. To reach absolute accuracy, measurement must become certitude or knowledge. For instance, even if you measure 2 planes as being parallel, they are not parallel mathematically speaking until you impose them to be so. So the idea of using knowledge of the environment to both stretch the feasible cases, and to reach absolute accuracy, is very appealing. However, it is a very difficult task to use such information, and very little has been done on the subject.

In Computer Vision, we use self-calibration techniques to estimate both the scene and the camera parameters. Those techniques have proved difficult because small perturbations in the 3D space infer bigger perturbations in the calibration[1]. Thus, to cancel out 3D perturbations, we want to impose Euclidean constraints on a reconstruction, and accordingly, adjust the calibration. So we need a set of images with extracted features such as points, segments, lines, and planes. Those features have to be matched among the image sequence, and a

Reinhard Koch, Luc Van Gool (Eds.): SMILE '98, LNCS 1506, pp. 224–235, 1998.
© Springer-Verlag Berlin Heidelberg 1998

calibration must be estimated. We then want to use Euclidean constraints such as:

- incidence constraints, *e.g.* points belong to lines or planes; lines belong to planes
- parallelism of lines or planes
- orthogonality of lines or planes

We teach our system such constraints manually.

In the following we explain what we can do with such knowledges. First, we introduce the Ritt-Wu's method, a technique for automatically proving geometry theorems. Second, we show how this method can be use to find a minimal parametrization of the scene. Third, we introduce our constraint bundle adjustment. Lastly, results are shown for a real situation.

2 Geometry and Symbolic Algebra Computation

2.1 An Introduction to the Ritt-Wu's Method

The Ritt-Wu's method [14] [13] [3] is a technique to prove geometric theorems automatically. This method has already proved more than five hundred non-trivial theorems [4]. A geometric theorem is composed of a set of hypotheses (geometric configuration) and a set of conclusions. The hypotheses are defined with a set of geometric primitives (*e.g.* points, lines, planes, ...) and a set of geometric constraints (*e.g.* incidence relations, parallelism, orthogonality, ...). A conclusion for such a theorem is a geometric constraint. To deal with geometric primitives, we must express the geometry in an algebraic notation. One possible way to do this, is to choose a coordinate system of the space.

In this case, the geometric primitives are defined by several parameters and the geometric properties by some polynomial equations in those parameters. A geometric configuration can thus be seen like a set of variables (the parameters of the 3D primitives) and a system of polynomial equations (the geometric constraints). Roughly speaking, a geometric configuration is an algebraic manifold [5].

More precisely, a geometric configuration might also have degenerate conditions. For example, if we look at the median theorem:

> Let ABC be a triangle. Let B', C' be the midpoints of AC, AB respectively. Let G be the intersection of the lines BB', CC'. Then, the point of intersection of the lines AG, BC is the midpoint of BC.

Obviously, if the points A, B, and C are collinear, the theorem is false. The equation, $det(A, B, C) = 0$ represents a degenerate condition. The set of degenerate conditions also defined a manifold. Thus, a geometric configuration is represented, by the manifold defined by the geometric properties, excluding the manifold defined by the degenerate conditions.

Therefore, in order to prove a theorem, we must:

- find the manifold of hypotheses H defined by the geometric constraints.
- find the manifold of degenerate conditions D.
- represent the conclusion of the theorem as a set of polynomial equations C.

Then, the theorem is true if and only if the equations of C are satisfied on H excluding D.

We can decompose the proving of a theorem in 2 problems. First, we must insure that a polynomial of C vanishes on the manifold H. Second, we must find the manifold of degenerate conditions.

Now, let's focus on the first problem. We call PS a polynomial system defining the manifold H, and P a polynomial of C. In the particular case where all the polynomials of PS, and P, are linear, the solution is trivial. One way of solving this problem consists of solving the system PS (by a triangular form of PS) and substituting this result into the polynomial P. After substitution, P is zero if and only if P vanishes on the manifold H. In the general case, Ritt and Wu introduced: the notion of ascending chains (triangular forms of polynomial systems), the notion of pseudo-division (in the linear case, pseudo-division is substitution), and the notion of a characteristic set CS of PS. The interesting properties of CS are:

- CS is an ascending chains (i.e. a triangular form of a polynomial system).
- If P vanishes on H, the result of pseudo-division of P by CS is zero.
- Conversely, if H is an irreducible manifold, and if the result of pseudo-division of P by CS is zero, then P vanishes on H.

In other words, a characteristic set is a means of verifying that P vanishes on the manifold H. Ritt and Wu also gave an algorithm for computing a characteristic set automatically [14], which is out of the scope of this article.

Now, let's focus on the second problem. Let's call the leading coefficient of a polynomial P, the polynomial coefficient associated to the highest degree of P considered as a polynomial in its highest variable. During the computation of a characteristic set, the leading coefficients of the polynomials of the characteristic set must sometimes be tested to be different from zero. Ritt and Wu showed that the leading coefficients, when vanishing, describe the degenerate conditions.

We can now prove a theorem. Let T be a theorem. If the manifold defined by the hypotheses H of T is irreducible, then the Ritt-Wu's method can prove the theorem T. If H is reducible, then the Ritt-Wu's method is not sufficient, and we have to used the complete Wu's method (we do not describe this method in this paper) [14]. Fortunately, in almost every case, the manifold H is irreducible and the Ritt-Wu's method is sufficient. In the other cases, the coordinate system is not adapted to the geometric configuration, or at least one primitive of the geometric configuration is not completely determined.

2.2   Constraints and Parametrization of a Geometric Model

A geometric model is defined by a set of primitives (e.g. points, lines and planes) and a set of constraints among those primitives. Let M be a geometric model. Choosing a coordinate system allows us to give a parametrization of M as follows:

– Each point is given three parameters (the coordinates).
– Each line is given six parameters (two points).
– Each plane is given three parameters (the coefficients of the equation, normalizing the constant term to 1, which is possible if the plane does not go through the origin of the coordinate system[1]).

The Ritt-Wu's method does not restrict the choice of geometry (Projective, Affine or Euclidean) nor the choice of constraints. This technique works with anything which can be written as polynomial equations. In this paper, we use only incidence, parallel, and orthogonal constraints. With such a limited set of constraints, it is easy to compute the polynomial equations which represent a geometric constraint automatically. For example, we represent the orthogonality between 2 planes $P'(n, 1)$ and $P'(n', 1)$, by the polynomial equation :

$$n \cdot n' = 0$$

It can be seen that all our constraints are linear with respect to each parameter taken individually. For instance, $n_x n'_x + n_y n'_y + n_z n'_z = 0$ is linear in all its parameters $\{n_x, n_y, n_z, n'_x, n'_y, n'_z\}$.

Now, for the model M, we have: a full parametrization of the primitives X, a set of polynomial equations PS representing the constraints, and H the manifold defined by PS. Remembering that a characteristic set CS of PS is a triangular form of a polynomial system, it is possible to separate the set of parameters into 2 parts. The first one X_c, is the set of the leading parameters (the highest variable) in each polynomial in CS. The second one X_m, is the set of the other parameters (table 1). In the following, we note $\tilde{Y}$ the set of numerical values of a

$$f_1 \in K[X_m, x_1]$$
$$f_2 \in K[X_m, x_1, x_2]$$
$$\vdots \quad \vdots \quad \vdots \qquad \ddots$$
$$f_n \in K[X_m, x_1, x_2, \cdots, x_n]$$

where $X_c = \{x_1, x_2, \cdots, x_n\}$.

Table 1. A triangular polynomial system.

set of parameters Y. The theory of characteristic sets [14] [4] [13] assumes that:

– The knowledge of $\tilde{X}_m$ (the values of the parameters of X_m) allows us to infer $\tilde{X}$. More precisely, there exists an order on the parameters of X_c which allows us to evaluate any parameter from the knowledge of the parameters which come before it. Roughly speaking, we compute each parameter by a back-substitution over CS.
– The knowledge of $\tilde{X}_m$ infer a finite number of evaluations of $\tilde{X}$. This tells us that the number of parameters in X_m is minimal.

---

[1] this is always made possible by moving the origin.

- The number of parameters of X_m is equal to the dimension of an undegenerated component of H.

When computing $\tilde{X}$, the back-substitution may lead us to solve polynomials with degree greater than 1, which obviously have several roots. Thus $\tilde{X}$ may not be defined uniquely.

In our case, PS is linear in each parameter. Moreover, it is possible to show that H has only one undegenerated component [11]. As a consequence, with such a limited set of constraints, we are able to : in one hand give a minimal parametrization of the model M, and in the other hand give a finite set of possible values for every parameter of M.

3   Algorithm

Defining a minimal parametrization is equivalent to defining a mapping from the 3D space to a set of values. The problem is to go the other way, *i.e.* from the set of minimal parameters, we need to infer the 3D location of all our 3D primitives. This inverse mapping is not straightforward as some equations may provide several solutions. Each time we compute a value of a parameter from an implicit equation, if the equation has different solutions, we need to choose the one that corresponds to a suitable 3D interpretation. More precisely, as we start from an initialization, at each step we have an estimation of any primitive location. Thus, we can choose during ambiguous cases, the closest solution to the current estimation. Doing so, we define the inverse mapping that produces from the minimal parametrization, the 3D location of all primitives.

We can now adjust the parametrization from the images and thus define our constrained bundle adjustment. In fact, from a current minimal parametrization $\tilde{X}_m$, we can infer $\tilde{X}$ which encodes the 3D coordinates of all primitives P. Then, using the current calibration parameters X_{cam}, we can defined p_i^j as the projection in image j of the primitive P_i, *i.e.* $p_i^j = proj^j(P_i)$. We can now compare, using an image distance d, a primitive defined originally in image j, $\tilde{p}_i^j$, with its projected counterpart p_i^j. Noting as P_{ind} the set of indices describing the set of primitives and as I_{ind} the set of indices describing the set of images, we thus defined a cost function:

$$\mathcal{C}(X_{cam}, \tilde{X}_m) = \sum_{i \in P_{ind}, j \in I_{ind}} d(\tilde{p}_i^j, proj^j(P_i)) \tag{1}$$

With such a cost function we can define a constraint bundle adjustment. In fact, in order to get a calibration and a constraint reconstruction, we minimize the cost function (1) over the camera parameters and the minimal parametrization of the scene:

$$\min_{X_{cam}, \tilde{X}_m} \mathcal{C}(X_{cam}, \tilde{X}_m)$$

4   Experiment

We start from a reconstruction estimated by TotalCalib[2]. This reconstruction (fig 1) comes from a self-calibration process, *i.e.* in particular, we do not have any knowledge of the scene. Meanwhile, from our comprehension of the

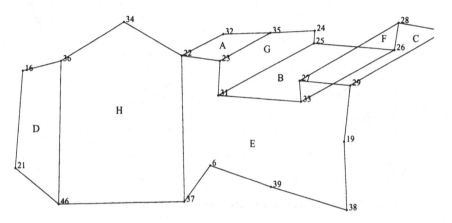

Fig. 1. 'La place des Arcades'

scene, we think that some Euclidean constraints have to be respected. In fact, the scene being made of buildings, some plans of the scene are parallel, others are orthogonal, and some points belong to some plans... Here is an orthographic top view (fig 2) of the estimated structure of the scene without imposing any knowledge.

This particular scene can be structured with 7 planes (A,B,C,D,E,F,G,H), where A is defined with 4 points (22,23,32,35), B with 4 points (25,26,31,33),..., up to H which is defined with 5 points (22,34,36,37,46). We want to impose: first, that all points belong to their respective planes; second, that A, B, and C are rectangle; third, that the following Euclidean constraints are respected:

$$\begin{cases} A\|B\|C \\ D\|E \\ F\|G\|H \\ A \perp G \\ D \perp H \end{cases}$$

Tables (2,3) summarize the values of the Euclidean constraints after the self-calibration process. In particular, table 2 shows the distances (in percentage of the size of the scene) of all points to the planes to which they belong. Table 3 shows the angles between normals of planes, *i.e.* the angle should be 0.0 for parallel planes and 90.0 for orthogonal planes.

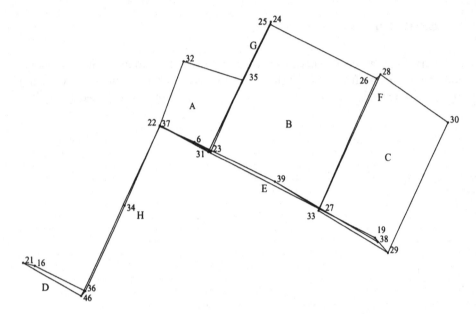

Fig. 2. 'La place des Arcades' seen from above

This scene, being made of 22 points, has 66 (3*22) parameters or degrees of freedom. Imposing the Euclidean constraints makes the number of parameters come down to 41. Now, running a constraint bundle adjustment on the calibration parameters and the 41 parameters of the scene gives us a reconstruction (figs 3,4) with Euclidean constraints perfectly satisfied! The final residual after the second bundle adjustment is $1.21 pixel$, versus $0.61 pixel$ for the first one. As the 2D points are defined up to pixel accuracy above images, the small residual values mean that we gain the major improvement of imposing 3D constraints without perturbing too much the calibration.

5   Conclusion

Using Euclidean constraints, generally speaking, is a very difficult problem. Here, with a limited set of constraints and the use of a powerful algebraic theory, we can obtain perfect modeling results. Unfortunately, extending the set of constraints, to known distances for instance, may be very difficult because it induces solving polynomial systems of much higher degrees. Theoretically, when using more constraint types, the existence of a minimal parametrization is not guaranteed anymore. Moreover, though the theory of the characteristic set is a powerful tool, using it requires a lot of resources, which for the time being, becomes too much on larger environments.

	A	B	C	D	E	F	G	H
6					0.30			
16				0.54				
19					2.17			
21				0.46				
22	0.98				0.10			0.83
23	0.85				1.28		1.17	
24							0.14	
25		0.15					0.77	
26		0.15				0.31		
27			0.20		0.09	0.35		
28			0.20			0.30		
29			0.21		3.99			
30			0.21					
31		0.14			0.73		0.66	
32	0.91							
33		0.14			1.69	0.37		
34								0.49
35	0.79						1.14	
36				0.39				0.21
37					2.94			0.55
38					1.13			
39					3.36			
46				0.30				0.43

Table 2. Distances(%) between Points and Planes

	A	B	C	D	E	F	G	H
A		1.46	2.84			87.5	90.08	90.2
B			1.41			87.0	89.5	89.6
C						86.1	88.6	88.8
D					2.9	87.7	89.5	89.2
E						87.9	89.6	89.3
F							2.73	2.75
G								0.38

Table 3. Angles(in degree) of Planes

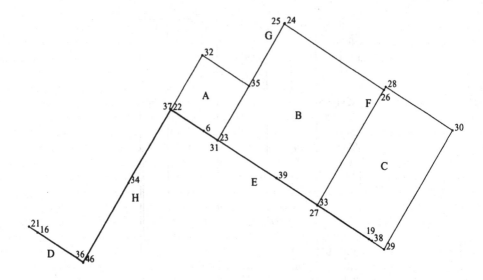

Fig. 3. 'La place des Arcades' seen from above, imposing constraints

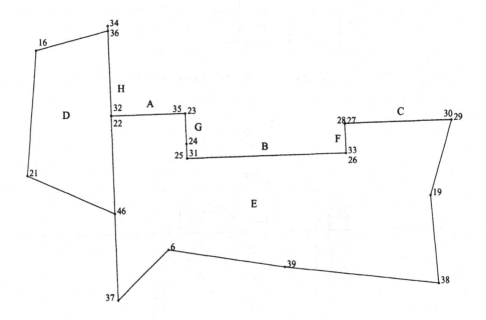

Fig. 4. 'La place des Arcades' imposing constraints

6 Appendix

We illustrate the Ritt-Wu's method with the following example.

Simpson's theorem: Lets ABC be a triangle and C its circumscribed. Let D be a point on C. Lets E, F, and G be the images of D by the respective perpendicular projections on the sides BC, CA, and AB. Then E, F, and G are collinear.

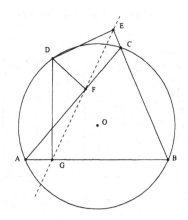

Proof:
We give coordinates to the points $A = (0,0)$, $B = (u_1, 0)$, $C = (u_2, u_3)$, $O = (x_1, x_2)$, $D = (x_3, u_4)$, $E = (x_5, x_4)$, $F = (x_7, x_6)$ and $G = (x_3, 0)$.

We represent the hypotheses by a set of polynomial equations PS:

$$
\begin{array}{lll}
OA = OC & \Longleftrightarrow & h_1 = 2u_2 x_2 + 2u_3 x_1 - u_3^2 - u_2^2 = 0 \\
OA = OB & \Longleftrightarrow & h_2 = 2u_1 x_2 - u_1^2 = 0 \\
OA = OD & \Longleftrightarrow & h_3 = -x_3^2 + 2x_2 x_3 + 2u_4 x_1 - u_4^2 = 0 \\
(DF), (AC) \text{ perpendicular} & \Longleftrightarrow & h_4 = u_2 x_7 + u_3 x_6 - u_2 x_3 - u_3 u_4 = 0 \\
(DE), (BC) \text{ perpendicular} & \Longleftrightarrow & h_5 = (u_2 - u_1)x_5 + u_3 x_4 + (u_1 - u_2)x_3 - u_3 u_4 = 0 \\
F, A, C \text{ collinear} & \Longleftrightarrow & h_6 = u_3 x_7 - u_2 x_6 = 0 \\
E, B, C \text{ collinear} & \Longleftrightarrow & h_7 = u_3 x_5 + (-u_2 + u_1)x_4 - u_1 u_3 = 0
\end{array}
$$

Now, We compute a characteristic set CS of PS by Ritt-Wu's method:

$$
\begin{aligned}
f1 &= -2(u_1 u_2)x_1 + u_1(u_3^2 + u_2^2 - u_1 u_2) \\
f2 &= 2(u_1)x_2 - u_1^2 \\
f3 &= -(u_1 u_3)x_3^2 + u_1^2 u_3 x_3 + u_1 u_4(u_2^2 + u_3^2 - u_1 u_2) \\
f4 &= -((u_1 - u_2)^2 + u_3^2)x_4 + (u_2 - u_1)u_3 x_3 + u_3(u_1^2 - u_1 u_2 + u_3 u_4) \\
f5 &= u_3((u_1 - u_2)^2 + u_3^2)x_5 - u_3(u_1 - u_2)^2 x_3 + u_1 u_3^2 u_4 - u_1 u_3^3 - u_2 u_3^2 u_4 \\
f6 &= (u_2^2 + u_3^2)x_6 - u_3 u_2 x_3 - u_3^2 u_4 \\
f7 &= u_3(u_2^2 + u_3^2)x_7 - u_2^2 u_3 x_3 - u_2 u_3^2 u_4
\end{aligned}
$$

	u_1	u_2	u_3	u_4	x_1	x_2	x_3	x_4	x_5	x_6	x_7
h_1		o	o		o	o					
h_2	o					o					
h_3			o	o	o	o					
h_4		o	o	o		o				o	o
h_5	o	o	o	o			o	o	o		
h_6		o	o							o	o
h_7	o	o	o					o	o		

Table 4. The distribution of the variables in the polynomial equations PS.

	u_1	u_2	u_3	u_4	x_1	x_2	x_3	x_4	x_5	x_6	x_7
f_1	o	o	o		o						
f_2	o					o					
f_3	o	o	o	o			o				
f_4	o	o	o	o			o	o			
f_5	o	o	o	o			o		o		
f_6		o	o				o			o	
f_7		o	o	o			o				o

Table 5. The distribution of the variables in the polynomial equations CS.

The conclusion, E, F, and G are *collinear*, is represented by:

$$g = x_4 x_7 + (x_3 - x_5)x_6 - x_3 x_4 = 0.$$

Now, as the result of pseudo-division of g by CS is zero, the Simpson's Theorem is true. Moreover, it also provides us with the following degenerate conditions:

$$u_1 u_3 = 0 \qquad \Longleftrightarrow A = B \text{ or } A, B \text{ and, } C \text{ are collinear}$$
$$u_1 = 0 \qquad \Longleftrightarrow A = B$$
$$(u_1 - u_2)^2 + u_3^2 = 0 \qquad \Longleftrightarrow B = C$$
$$u_3((u_1 - u_2)^2 + u_3^2) = 0 \Longleftrightarrow A, B \text{ and, } C \text{ are collinear or } B = C$$
$$u_3^2 + u_2^2 = 0 \qquad \Longleftrightarrow A = C$$
$$u_3(u_3^2 + u_2^2) = 0 \qquad \Longleftrightarrow A = C \text{ or } A, B \text{ and, } C \text{ are collinear}$$

References

[1] Sylvain Bougnoux. From projective to euclidean space under any practical situation, a criticism of self-calibration. In *International Conference on Computer Vision*, pages 790–796, 1998.

[2] Sylvain Bougnoux and Luc Robert. Totalcalib: a fast and reliable system for off-line calibration of images sequences. In *Proceedings of the International Conference on*, June 1997. The Demo Session.

[3] Shang-Ching Chou and Xio-Shan Gao. Ritt-wu's decomposition algorithm and geometry theorem proving. In *Proc. CADE-10*, pages 202–220, Kaiserslautern, Germany, 1990.

[4] Shang-Ching Chou, William F. Schelter, and Jin-Gen Tang. *Characteristic Sets and Gröbner Bases in Geometry Theorem Proving*. Springer, 1989.

[5] D. Cox, J. Little, and D. O'Shea. *Ideals, Varieties and Algorithms*. Undergraduate texts in mathematics. Springer, 1992.

[6] P.E. Debevec, C.J. Taylor, and J. Malik. Modeling and rendering architecture from photographs: a hybrid geometry- and image-based approach. In *SIGGRAPH*, pages 11–20, 1996.

[7] O. Faugeras. *Three-Dimensional Computer Vision: a Geometric Viewpoint*. MIT Press, 1993.

[8] Armin Gruen and Horst A. Beyer. System calibration through self-calibration. In *Proceedings of the Workshop on Calibration and Orientation of Cameras in Computer Vision*, Washington D.C., August 1992.

[9] M. Hebert and E. Krotkov. 3D measurements from imaging laser radars. *Image and Vision Computing*, 10(3), April 1992.

[10] F. Leymarie, A. de la Fortelle, J. Koenderink, A. Kappers, M. Stavridi, B. van Ginneken, S. Muller, S. Krake, O. Faugeras, L. Robert, C. Gauclin, S. Laveau, and C. Zeller. Realise: Reconstruction of reality from image sequences. In P.Delogne, editor, *International Conference on Image Processing*, volume 3, pages 651–654, 1996.

[11] Bernard Mourrain. Géométrie et interétation générique: un algorithme. *comptes-rendus du congrès M.E.G.A-90*, pages 363–377, 1990.

[12] M. Pollefeys, R. Koch, and L. Van Gool. Self-calibration and metric reconstruction in spite of varying and unknown internal camera parameters. In *International Conference on Computer Vision*, pages 90–95, 1998.

[13] Dongming. Wang and Xiaofan. Jin. *Mechanical Theorem Proving in Geometries*. Texts and Monographie in Symbolic Computation. Springer, 1994.

[14] Wen-tsün Wu. Basic principles of mechanical theorem proving in elementary geometries. *Journal of automated Reasoning*, 2:221–252, 1986.

Interactive 3D Modeling from Multiple Images Using Scene Regularities

Heung-Yeung Shum[1], Richard Szeliski[1], Simon Baker[2], Mei Han[3], and P. Anandan[1]

[1] Microsoft Research
[2] Columbia University
[3] Carnegie Mellon University
http://www.research.microsoft.com/research/vision/

Abstract. We present some recent progress in designing and implementing two interactive image-based 3D modeling systems.

The first system constructs 3D models from a collection of panoramic image mosaics. A panoramic mosaic consists of a set of images taken around the same viewpoint, and a camera matrix associated with each input image. The user first interactively specifies features such as points, lines, and planes. Our system recovers the camera pose for each mosaic from known line directions and reference points. It then constructs the 3D model using all available geometrical constraints.

The second system extracts structure from stereo by representing the scene as a collection of approximately planar layers. The user first interactively segments the images into corresponding planar regions. Our system recovers a composite mosaic for each layer, estimates the plane equation for the layer, and optionally recovers the camera locations as well as out-of-plane displacements.

By taking advantage of known scene regularities, our interactive systems avoid difficult feature correspondence problems that occur in traditional automatic modeling systems. They also shift the interactive high-level structural model specification stage to precede (or intermix with) the 3D geometry recovery. They are thus able to extract accurate wire frame and texture-mapped 3D models from multiple image sequences.

1 Introduction

A lot of progress has been made recently in developing automated techniques for 3D scene reconstruction from multiple images, both with calibrated and uncalibrated cameras [13, 24, 12, 31, 2, 14, 4, 26, 39]. Unfortunately, the results from many automated modeling systems are disappointing due to the complexity of real scenes and the fragility of fully automated vision techniques. Part of the reason stems from the accurate and robust correspondences required by many computer vision techniques such as stereo and structure from motion. Moreover, such correspondences may not be available in regions of the scene that are untextured.

Reinhard Koch, Luc Van Gool (Eds.): SMILE '98, LNCS 1506, pp. 236–252, 1998.

Automated techniques often require manual clean-up and post-processing to segment the scene into coherent objects and surfaces, or to triangulate sparse point matches [2]. They may also be required to enforce geometric constraints such as known orientations of surfaces. For instance, building interiors and exteriors provide vertical and horizontal lines and parallel and perpendicular planes. In this paper, we attack the 3D modeling problem from the other side: we specify some geometric knowledge ahead of time (e.g., known orientations of lines, co-planarity of points, initial scene segmentations), and use these constraints to guide our matching and reconstruction algorithms.

The idea of using geometric constraints has previously been exploited in several interactive modeling systems. For example, PhotoModeler [25] is a commecial product which constructs 3D models from several images, using photogrammetry techniques and manually specified points. The TotalCalib system, on the other hand, estimates the fundamental matrix from a few hand-matched points, and then predicts and verifies other potential matching points [8]. The Facade system exploits the known rectahedral structure of building exteriors to directly recover solid 3D models (blocks) from multiple images [11].

This paper presents two interactive (semi-automated) systems for recovering 3D models of large-scale environments from multiple images. Our first system uses one or more panoramic image mosaics, i.e., collections of images taken from the same viewpoint that have been registered together[32]. Panoramas offer several advantages over regular images. First, we can decouple the modeling problem into a zero baseline problem (building panoramas from images taken with rotating camera) and a wide baseline stereo or structure from motion problem (recovering 3D model from one or more panoramas). Second, the intrinsic camera calibrations are recovered as part of the panorama construction [16]. Due to recent advances, it is now possible to construct panoramas even with hand-held cameras [36].

Unlike previous work on 3D reconstruction from multiple panoramas [23, 20], our 3D modeling system exploits important regularities present in the environment, such as walls with known orientations. Fortunately, the man-made world is full of constraints such as parallel lines, lines with known directions, planes with lines and points on them. Using these constraints, we can construct a fairly complex 3D model from a single panorama (or even a wide-angle photograph), and easily handle large co-planar untexture regions such as walls. Using multiple panoramas, more complete and accurate 3D models can be constructed.

Multiple-image stereo matching can be used to recover a more detailed description of surface shape than can be obtained by simply triangulating matched feature points [26]. Unfortunately, stereo fails in regions without texture. A simple depth map also cannot capture the full complexity of a large-scale environment. Methods for overcoming this limitation include volumetric stereo techniques [29, 35] and model-based stereo [11].

In this paper, we propose a different approach—extending the concept of layered motion estimates [42, 43] and "shallow" objects [27] to true multi-image stereo matching. Our second interactive modeling system reconstructs the 3D scene as a collection of approximately planar layers, each of which has an explicit 3D plane equation, a color image with per-pixel opacity, and optionally a per-pixel out-of-plane displacement[3]. This representation allows us to account for inter-surface occlusions, which traditional stereo systems have trouble modeling correctly.

2 3D Modeling from Panoramas

2.1 Interactive Modeling System

Our modeling system uses one or more panoramas. For each panorama, we draw points, lines, and planes, set appropriate properties for them, and then recover the 3D model. These steps can be repeated in any order to refine or modify the model. The modeling system attempts to satisfy all possible constraints in a consistent and coherent way.

Three coordinate systems are used in our work. The first is the world coordinate system where the 3D model geometry is defined. The second is the "2D" camera coordinate system (panorama coordinates). The third is the screen coordinate system where zoom and rotation (pan and tilt, but no roll) are applied to facilitate user interaction. While each panorama has a single 2D coordinate system, several views of a given panorama can be open simultaneously, each with its own screen coordinate system.

We represent the 3D model by a set of points, lines and planes. Each point is represented by its 3D coordinate $\mathbf{x}$. Each line is represented by its line direction $\mathbf{m}$ and points on the line. Each plane is defined by $(\mathbf{n}, d)$ where $\mathbf{n}$ is the normal, d is the distance to the origin, and $\mathbf{n} \cdot \mathbf{x} + d = 0$ or $(\mathbf{n}, d) \cdot (\mathbf{x}, 1) = 0$. A plane typically includes several vertices and lines.

Each 2D model consists of a set of 2D points and lines extracted from a panorama. A panorama consists of a collection of images and their associated transformations. A 2D point $\tilde{\mathbf{x}}$ (i.e., on a panorama) represents a ray going through the 2D model origin (i.e., camera optical center).[1] Likewise, a 2D line (represented by its line direction $\tilde{\mathbf{m}}$) lies on the "line projection plane" (with normal $\tilde{\mathbf{n}}_p$) which passes through the line and 2D model origin.[2]

2.2 Modeling Steps

Many constraints exist in real scenes. For example, we may have known quantities like points, lines, and planes. Or we may have known relationships such as parallel and vertical lines and planes, points on a line or a plane. With multiple panoramas, we have more constraints from corresponding points, lines, and planes.

---

[1] We use the notation $\tilde{\mathbf{x}}$ for a 2D point, $\mathbf{x}$ for a 3D point, and $\hat{\mathbf{x}}$ for a 3D point whose position is known. Likewise for line directions, plane normals, etc..

[2] If a pixel has the screen coordinate $(u, v, 1)$, its 2D point on the panorama is represented by (u, v, f) where f is the focal length.

Some of these constraints are bilinear. For example, a point on a plane is a bilinear constraint in both the point location and the plane normal. However, plane normals and line directions can be recovered without knowing plane distance and points. Thus, in our system we decouple the modeling process into several linear steps: (a) recovering camera orientations ($\mathbf{R}$) from known line directions; (b) recovering camera translations ($\mathbf{t}$) from known points; (c) estimating plane normals ($\mathbf{n}$) and line directions ($\mathbf{m}$); (d) estimating plane distances (d), vertex positions ($\mathbf{x}$). These steps are explained in detail in the next sections.

2.3   Recovering Camera Pose

The camera poses describe the relationship between the 2D models (panorama coordinate systems) and the 3D model (world coordinate system).

To recover the camera rotation, we use lines with known directions. For example, one can easily draw several vertical lines at the intersections of walls and mark them to be parallel to the Z axis of the world coordinate system. Given at least two vertical lines and a horizontal line, or two sets of parallel lines of known directions, the camera matrix can be recovered. This is achieved by computing vanishing points for the parallel lines, and using these to constrain the rotation matrix. If more than 2 vanishing points are available, a least squares solution can be found for $\mathbf{R}$.

To recover the translation, observe that a point on a 2D model (panorama) represents a ray from the camera origin through the pixel on the image,

$$(\mathbf{x} - \mathbf{t}) \times \mathbf{R}^T \tilde{\mathbf{x}} = 0. \tag{1}$$

This is equivalent to

$$(\mathbf{x} - \mathbf{t}) \cdot (\mathbf{R}^T \tilde{\mathbf{p}}_j) = 0, j = 0, 1, 2, \tag{2}$$

where $\tilde{\mathbf{p}}_0 = (-x_2, x_1, 0)$, $\tilde{\mathbf{p}}_1 = (-x_3, 0, x_1)$ and $\tilde{\mathbf{p}}_2 = (0, -x_3, x_2)$ are three directions perpendicular to the ray $\tilde{\mathbf{x}} = (x_1, x_2, x_3)$. Note that only two of the three constraints are linearly independent.[3] Thus, camera translation $\mathbf{t}$ can be recovered as a linear least-squares problem if we have two or more given points. Given a single known point, $\mathbf{t}$ can be recovered only up to a scale. In practice, it is convenient to fix a few points in 3D model, such as the origin $(0, 0, 0)$. These given points are also used to eliminate the ambiguities in recovering camera pose.

For a single panorama, the translation $\mathbf{t}$ is set to zero if no point in 3D model is given. This implies that the camera coordinate coincides with the 3D model coordinate.

2.4   Estimating Plane Normals

Once we have camera pose, we can recover the scene geometry. Because of the bilinear nature of some constraints (such as points on planes), we recover plane

---

[3]   The third constraint with minimum $\|\tilde{\mathbf{p}}_i\|^2$ is eliminated.

normals ($\mathbf{n}$) before solving for plane distances (d) and points ($\mathbf{x}$). If a normal is given (north, south, up, down, etc.), it can be enforced as a hard constraint. Otherwise, we compute the plane normal $\mathbf{n}$ by finding two line directions on the plane.

If we draw two pairs of parallel lines (a parallelogram) on a plane, we can recover the plane normal. Because $\mathbf{R}$ has been estimated, and we know how to compute a line direction (i.e., the vanishing point $\tilde{\mathbf{m}}$) from two parallel lines, we obtain $\mathbf{m} = \mathbf{R}^T \tilde{\mathbf{m}}$. From two line directions $\mathbf{m}_1$ and $\mathbf{m}_2$ on a plane, the plane normal can be computed as $\mathbf{n} = \mathbf{m}_1 \times \mathbf{m}_2$.

In general, the line direction recovery problem can be formulated as a standard minimum eigenvector problem. Because each "line projection plane" is perpendicular to the line (i.e., $\tilde{\mathbf{n}}_{pi} \cdot \tilde{\mathbf{m}} = 0$), we want to minimize

$$e = \sum_i (\tilde{\mathbf{n}}_{pi} \cdot \tilde{\mathbf{m}})^2 = \tilde{\mathbf{m}}^T (\sum_i \tilde{\mathbf{n}}_{pi} \tilde{\mathbf{n}}_{pi}^T) \tilde{\mathbf{m}}. \tag{3}$$

This is equivalent to finding the vanishing point of the lines [9]. The advantage of the above formulation is that the sign ambiguity of $\tilde{\mathbf{n}}_{pi}$ can be ignored. When only two parallel lines are given, the solution is simply the cross product of two line projection plane normals.

Using the techniques described above, we can therefore recover the surface orientation of an arbitrary plane (e.g., tilted ceiling) provided either we can draw a parallelogram (or a 3-sided rectangle) on the plane.

2.5   Estimating the 3D Model

Given camera pose, line directions, and plane normals, recovering plane distances (d), 3D points ($\mathbf{x}$), and camera translation $\mathbf{t}$ (if desired), can be formulated as a linear system consisting of all possible constraints. By separating hard constraints from soft ones, we obtain a least-squares system with equality constraints. Intuitively, the difference between soft and hard constraints is their weights in the least-squares formulation. Soft constraints have unit weights, while hard constraints have very large weights [15].

Some constraints (e.g., a point is known) are inherently hard, therefore equality constraints. Some constraints (e.g., a feature location on a 2D model or panorama) are most appropriate as soft constraints because they are based on noisy image measurements. Take a point on a plane for an example. If the plane normal $\hat{\mathbf{n}}_k$ is given, we consider the constraint ($\mathbf{x}_i \cdot \hat{\mathbf{n}}_k + d_k = 0$) as hard. We use the notations $\hat{\mathbf{m}}$ and $\hat{\mathbf{n}}$ to represent the given line direction $\mathbf{m}$ and plane normal $\mathbf{n}$, respectively. This implies that the point has to be on the plane, only its location can be adjusted. On the other hand, if the plane normal $\mathbf{n}_k$ is estimated, we consider the constraint ($\mathbf{x}_i \cdot \mathbf{n}_k + d_k = 0$) as soft. This could lead to an estimated point that is not on the plane at all. So why not make the constraint ($\mathbf{x}_i \cdot \mathbf{n}_k + d_k = 0$) hard as well?

The reason is that we may end up with a very bad model if some of the estimated normals have large errors. Too many hard constraints could conflict with one another or make other soft constraints insignificant. To satisfy all possible constraints, we formulate our modeling process as an equality-constrained least-squares problem. In other words, we would like to solve the linear system (soft constraints) $\mathbf{Ax} = \mathbf{b}$ subject to (hard constraints) $\mathbf{Cx} = \mathbf{q}$ where $\mathbf{A}$ is $m \times n$, $\mathbf{C}$ is $p \times n$. A solution to the above problem is to use the QR factorization [15].

Before we can apply the equality-constrained linear system solver, we must check whether the linear system formed by all constraints is solvable. In general, the system may consist of several subsystems (connected components) which can be solved independently. For example, when modeling a room with a computer monitor floating in the space not connected with any wall, ceiling or floor, we may have a system with two connected components. To find all connected components, we use depth first search to step through the linear system. For each connected components we check that: (a) the number of equations (including both hard and soft constraints) is no fewer than the number of unknowns; (b) the right hand side is a non-zero vector, i.e., has some minimal ground truth data; (c) the hard constraints are consistent. If any of the above is not satisfied, the system is declared unsolvable, and a warning message is then generated to indicate which set of unknowns cannot be recovered.

3   3D Modeling Using Layered Stereo

3.1   Overview of Layered Stereo Approach

Our second 3D modeling system interactively extracts structure as a collection of 3D (quasi-) planar layers from multiple images. The basic concepts of the layered stereo approach are illustrated in Figure 1. Assume that we are given as input K images $I_1(\mathbf{u}_1), I_2(\mathbf{u}_2), \ldots, I_K(\mathbf{u}_K)^4$ captured by K cameras with camera matrices $\mathbf{P}_1, \mathbf{P}_2, \ldots, \mathbf{P}_K$. In what follows, we will drop the image coordinates $\mathbf{u}_k$ unless they are needed to explain a warping operation explicitly. Our hypothesis is that we can reconstruct the world as a collection of L approximately planar layers. Following [7], we denote a layer "sprite" image by $L_l(\mathbf{u}_l) = (\alpha_l \cdot r_l, \alpha_l \cdot g_l, \alpha_l \cdot b_l, \alpha_l)$, where $r_l = r_l(\mathbf{u}_l)$ is the red band, $g_l = g_l(\mathbf{u}_l)$ is the green band, $b_l = b_l(\mathbf{u}_l)$ is the blue band, and $\alpha_l = \alpha_l(\mathbf{u}_l)$ is the opacity of pixel $\mathbf{u}_l$.[5] We also associate with each layer a homogeneous vector $\mathbf{n}_l$ which defines the plane equation of the layer via $\mathbf{n}_l^T \mathbf{x} = 0$, and optionally a per-pixel residual depth offset $Z_l(\mathbf{u}_l)$.

A number of automatic techniques have been developed to initialize the layers, e.g, merging [42, 28, 6], splitting [18, 28], color segmentation [1] and plane fitting to a recovered depth map. In our system, we interactively initialize the layers because we wish to focus initially on techniques for creating composite (mosaic) sprites from multiple images, estimating the sprite plane equations,

---

[4] We use homogeneous coordinates in this section for both 3D world coordinates $\mathbf{x} = (x, y, z, 1)^T$ and for 2D image coordinates $\mathbf{u} = (u, v, 1)^T$.

[5] The terminology comes from computer graphics, where sprites are used to quickly (re-)render scenes composed of many objects [38].

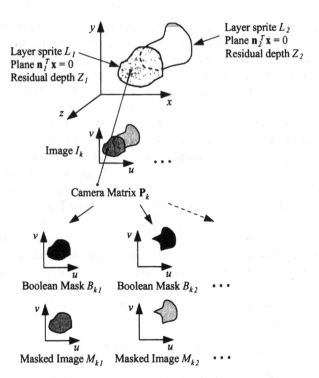

Fig. 1. Suppose K images I_k are captured by K cameras $\mathbf{P}_k$. We assume the scene can be represented by L sprite images L_l on planes $\mathbf{n}_l^T \mathbf{x} = 0$ with depth offsets Z_l. The boolean masks B_{kl} denote the pixels in image I_k from layer L_l and the masked images $M_{kl} = B_{kl} \cdot I_k$.

and refining layer assignments. We plan to incorporate automated initialization techniques later.

The input consists of a collection of images I_k taken with known camera matrices $\mathbf{P}_k$. The camera matrices can be estimated when they are not known *a priori*, either using traditional structure from motion [12, 4, 26], or directly from the homographies relating sprites in different images [22, 37]. Our goal is to estimate the layer sprites L_l, the plane vectors $\mathbf{n}_l$, and the residual depths Z_l.

Our approach can be subdivided into a number of steps where we estimate each of L_l, $\mathbf{n}_l$, and Z_l in turn. To compute these quantities, we use auxiliary boolean mask images B_{kl}. The boolean masks B_{kl} denote the pixels in image I_k which are images of points in layer L_l. Since we are assuming boolean opacities, $B_{kl} = 1$ if and only if L_l is the front-most layer which is opaque at that pixel in image I_k. Hence, in addition to L_l, $\mathbf{n}_l$, and Z_l, we also need to estimate the boolean masks B_{kl}. Once we have estimated these masks, we can compute masked input images $M_{kl} = B_{kl} \cdot I_k$ (see Figure 1).

Given any three of L_l, $\mathbf{n}_l$, Z_l, and B_{kl}, there are techniques for estimating the remaining one. Our algorithm therefore consists of first initializing these quantities. Then, we iteratively estimate each of theses quantities in turn fixing the other three.

3.2 Estimation of Plane Equations

In order to compute the plane equation vector $\mathbf{n}_l$, we need to be able to map points in masked image M_{kl} onto the plane $\mathbf{n}_l^T \mathbf{x} = 0$. If $\mathbf{x}$ is a 3D world coordinate of a point and $\mathbf{u}_k$ is the image of $\mathbf{x}$ in camera $\mathbf{P}_k$, we have:

$$\mathbf{u}_k = \mathbf{P}_k \mathbf{x}$$

where equality is in the 2D projective space $\mathcal{P}^2$. Since $\mathbf{P}_k$ is of rank 3, we can write:

$$\mathbf{x} = \mathbf{P}_k^* \mathbf{u}_k + s\mathbf{p}_k \tag{4}$$

where $\mathbf{P}_k^* = \mathbf{P}_k^T (\mathbf{P}_k \mathbf{P}_k^T)^{-1}$ is the pseudoinverse of $\mathbf{P}_k$, s is an unknown scalar, and $\mathbf{p}_k$ is a vector in the null space of $\mathbf{P}_k$, i.e. $\mathbf{P}_k \mathbf{p}_k = 0$. If $\mathbf{x}$ lies on the plane $\mathbf{n}_l^T \mathbf{x} = 0$ we can solve for s, substitute into Equation (4), and obtain:

$$\mathbf{x} = \left((\mathbf{n}_l^T \mathbf{p}_k)\mathbf{I} - \mathbf{p}_k \mathbf{n}_l^T \right) \mathbf{P}_k^* \mathbf{u}_k. \tag{5}$$

Equation (5) allows us to map a point $\mathbf{u}_k$ in image M_{kl} onto the point on plane $\mathbf{n}_l^T \mathbf{x} = 0$, of which it is an image. Afterwards we can map this point onto its image in another camera $\mathbf{P}_{k'}$:

$$\mathbf{u}_{k'} = \mathbf{P}_{k'} \left((\mathbf{n}_l^T \mathbf{p}_k)\mathbf{I} - \mathbf{p}_k \mathbf{n}_l^T \right) \mathbf{P}_k^* \mathbf{u}_k \equiv \mathbf{H}_{kk'}^l \mathbf{u}_k \tag{6}$$

where $\mathbf{H}_{kk'}^l$ is a homography (collineation of $\mathcal{P}^2$). Equation (6) describes the image coordinate warp between the two images M_{kl} and $M_{k'l}$ which would hold if all the masked image pixels were images of world points on the plane $\mathbf{n}_l^T \mathbf{x} = 0$. Using this relation, we can warp all of the masked images onto the coordinate frame of one distinguished image, w.l.o.g. image M_{1l}, as follows:

$$\left(\mathbf{H}_{1k}^l \circ M_{kl} \right) (\mathbf{u}_1) \equiv M_{kl} \left(\mathbf{H}_{1k}^l \mathbf{u}_1 \right).$$

Here, $\mathbf{H}_{1k}^l \circ M_{kl}$ is the masked image M_{kl} warped into the coordinate frame of M_{1l}.

We can therefore solve for $\mathbf{n}_l$ by finding the value for which the homographies $\mathbf{H}_{1k}^l$ defined in Equation (6) best register the images onto each other. Typically, this value is found using some form of gradient decent, such as the Gauss-Newton method, and the optimization is performed in a hierarchical (i.e. pyramid based) fashion to avoid local extrema [5]. To apply this approach, we compute the Jacobian of the image warp $\mathbf{H}_{1k}^l$ with respect to the parameters of $\mathbf{n}_l$. Alternatively, we can first compute a set of unconstrained homographies using a standard mosaic construction algorithm, and then invoke a structure from motion algorithm to recover the plane equation (and also the camera matrices, if desired) [22, 37].

3.3 Estimation of Layer Sprites

Before we can compute the layer sprite images L_l, we need to choose 2D coordinate systems for the planes. Such coordinate systems can be specified by a collection of arbitrary (rank 3) camera matrices $\mathbf{Q}_l$.[6] Then, following the same argument used in Equations (5) and (6), we can show that the image coordinates $\mathbf{u}_k$ of the point in image M_{kl} which is projected onto the point $\mathbf{u}_l$ on the plane $\mathbf{n}_l^T \mathbf{x} = 0$ is given by:

$$\mathbf{u}_k = \mathbf{P}_k \left((\mathbf{n}_l^T \mathbf{q}_l) \mathbf{I} - \mathbf{q}_l \mathbf{n}_l^T \right) \mathbf{Q}_l^* \mathbf{u}_l \equiv \mathbf{H}_k^l \mathbf{u}_k \qquad (7)$$

where $\mathbf{Q}_l^*$ is the pseudo-inverse of $\mathbf{Q}_l$ and $\mathbf{q}_l$ is a vector in the null space of $\mathbf{Q}_l$. The homography $\mathbf{H}_k^l$ can be used to warp the image M_{kl} forward onto the plane, the result of which is denoted $\mathbf{H}_k^l \circ M_{kl}$. After we have warped the masked image onto the plane, we can estimate the layer sprite (with boolean opacities) by "blending" the warped images:

$$L_l = \bigoplus_{k=1}^{K} \mathbf{H}_k^l \circ M_{kl} \qquad (8)$$

where $\bigoplus$ is a blending operator.

There are a number of ways the blending can be performed. One simple method is to take the mean of the color or intensity values. A refinement is to use a "feathering" algorithm, where the averaging is weighted by the distance of each pixel from the nearest invisible pixel in M_{kl} [33]. Alternatively, robust techniques can be used to estimate L_l from the warped images.

3.4   Estimation of Residual Depth

In general, the scene will not be exactly piecewise planar. To model any non-planarity, we assume that the point $\mathbf{u}_l$ on the plane $\mathbf{n}_l^T \mathbf{x} = 0$ is displaced slightly in the direction of the ray through $\mathbf{u}_l$ defined by the camera matrix $\mathbf{Q}_l$, and that the distance it is displaced is $Z_l(\mathbf{u}_l)$, measured in the direction normal to the plane. In this case, the homographic warps used in the previous section are not applicable. However, using a similar argument to that in Sections 3.2 and 3.3, it is easy to show (see also [21, 11]) that:

$$\mathbf{u}_k = \mathbf{H}_k^l \mathbf{u}_l + Z_l(\mathbf{u}_l) \mathbf{t}_{kl} \qquad (9)$$

where $\mathbf{H}_k^l = \mathbf{P}_k \left((\mathbf{n}_l^T \mathbf{q}_l) \mathbf{I} - \mathbf{q}_l \mathbf{n}_l^T \right) \mathbf{Q}_l^*$ is the planar homography of Section 3.3, $\mathbf{t}_{kl} = \mathbf{P}_k \mathbf{q}_l$ is the epipole, and it is assumed that the plane equation vector $\mathbf{n}_l = (n_x, n_y, n_z, n_d)^T$ has been normalized so that $n_x^2 + n_y^2 + n_z^2 = 1$. Equation (9) can be used to map plane coordinates $\mathbf{u}_l$ backwards to image coordinates $\mathbf{u}_k$, or to map the image M_{kl} forwards onto the plane. We denote the result of this warp by $(\mathbf{H}_k^l, \mathbf{t}_{kl}, Z_l) \circ M_{kl}$, or $\mathbf{W}_k^l \circ M_{kl}$ for more concise notation.

To compute the residual depth map Z_l, we could optimize the same (or a similar) consistency metric as that used in Section 2.2 to estimate the plane equation. Doing so is essentially solving a simpler (or what [11] would call "model-based") stereo problem. In fact, almost any stereo algorithm could be used to compute Z_l. The algorithm should favor small disparities.

---

[6] A reasonable choice for $\mathbf{Q}_l$ is one of the camera matrices $\mathbf{P}_k$.

3.5   Pixel Assignment to Layers

In the previous three sections, we have assumed a known assignment of pixels to layer, i.e., known boolean masks B_{kl} which allow us to compute the masked image M_{kl} using $M_{kl} = B_{kl} \cdot I_k$. We now describe how to estimate the pixel assignments from n_l, L_l, and Z_l.

We could try to update the pixel assignments by comparing the warped images $\mathbf{W}_k^l \circ M_{kl}$ to the layer sprite images L_l. However, if we compared these images, we would not be able to deduce anything about the pixel assignments outside of the current estimates of the masked regions. To allow the boolean mask B_{kl} to "grow", we therefore compare $\mathbf{W}_k^l \circ I_k$ with:

$$\tilde{L}_l = \bigoplus_{k=1}^{K} \mathbf{W}_k^l \circ \tilde{M}_{kl},$$

where $\tilde{M}_{kl} = \tilde{B}_{kl} \cdot I_k$ and $\tilde{B}_{kl}$ is a dilated version of B_{kl} (if necessary, Z_l is also enlarged so that it declines to zero outside the masked region).

Given the enlarged layer sprites $\tilde{L}_l$, our approach to pixel assignment is as follows. We first compute a measure $P_{kl}(\mathbf{u}_l)$ of the likelihood that the pixel $\mathbf{W}_k^l \circ I_k(\mathbf{u}_l)$ is the warped image of the pixel $\mathbf{u}_l$ in the enlarged layer sprite $\tilde{L}_l$. Next, P_{kl} is warped back into the coordinate system of the input image I_k to yield:

$$\hat{P}_{kl} = (\mathbf{W}_k^l)^{-1} \circ P_{kl}.$$

This warping tends to blur P_{kl}, but this is acceptable since we will want to smooth the pixel assignment. The pixel assignment can then be computed by choosing the best possible layer for each pixel:

$$B_{lk}(\mathbf{u}_k) = \begin{cases} 1 \text{ if } \hat{P}_{kl}(\mathbf{u}_k) = \min_{l'} \hat{P}_{kl'}(\mathbf{u}_k) \\ 0 \text{ otherwise} \end{cases}.$$

The simplest ways of defining P_{kl} is the *residual intensity difference* [28]; another possibility is the residual normal flow magnitude [18]. A third possibility would be to compute the optical flow between $\mathbf{W}_k^l \circ I_k$ and $\tilde{L}_l$ and then use the magnitude of the flow for P_{kl}.

3.6   Layer Refinement by Re-synthesis

The layered stereo algorithm described above is limited to recovering binary masks B_{kl} for the assignment of input pixels to layers. If we wanted to, we could use an EM (expectation maximization) algorithm to obtain graded (continuous) assignments [10, 19]. However, EM models mixtures of probability distributions, rather than the kind of partial occlusion mixing that occurs at sprite boundaries [7]. Stereo techniques inspired by matte extraction [34] are needed to refine the color/opacity estimates for each layer [35]. Such an algorithm would work by re-synthesizing each input image from the current sprite estimates, and then adjusting pixel colors and opacities so at to minimize the difference between the original and re-synthesized images. We are planning to implement such an algorithm in future work.

4   Experiments

We have implemented our panorama 3D modeling system on a PC and tested it with single and multiple panoramas. The system consists of two parts: the interface (viewing the panorama with pan, tilt, and zoom control) and the modeler (recovering the camera pose and the 3D model). Figure 2 shows a spherical panoramic image on the left and a simple reconstructed 3D model on the right. The coordinate system on the left corner (red) is the world coordinate, and the coordinate system in the middle (green) is the camera coordinate. The panorama is composed of 60 images using the method of creating full-view panoramas [33]. The extracted texture maps (without top and bottom faces) are shown in Figure 3. Notice how the texture maps in Figure 3 have different sampling rates from the original images. The sampling is the best (e.g., Figure 3(b)) when the surface normal is parallel with the viewing direction from the camera center, and the worst (e.g., Figure 3(d)) when perpendicular. This explains why the sampling on the left is better than that on the right in Figure 3(a). Figure 4 shows two views of our interactive modeling system. Green lines and points are the 2D items that are manually drawn and assigned with properties, and blue lines and points are projections of the recovered 3D model. It took about 15 minutes for the authors to build the simple model in Figure 2. In 30 minutes, we can construct the more complicated model shown in Figure 5.

Figures 6 and 7 show an example of building 3D models from multiple panoramas. Figure 6 shows two spherical panoramas built from image sequences taken with a hand-held digital video camera. Figure 7 shows two views of reconstructed 3D wireframe model from the two panoramas in Figure 6. Notice that the occluded middle area in the first panorama (behind the tree) is recovered because it is visible in the second panorama.

We have applied our layered stereo modeling system to a number of multi-frame stereo data sets. A standard point tracking and structure from motion algorithm is used to recover a camera matrix for each image. To initialize our algorithm, we interactively specify how many layers and then perform a rough assignment of pixels to layers. Next, an automatic hierarchical parametric motion estimation algorithm similar to [5] is used to find the homographies between the layers, as defined in Equation (7). For the experiments presented in this paper, we set $Q_l = P_1$, i.e. we reconstruct the sprites in the coordinate system of the first camera. Using these homographies, we find the best plane estimate for each layer using a Euclidean structure from motion algorithm [40].

The results of applying these steps to the MPEG *flower garden* sequence are shown in Figure 8. Figures 8(a) and (b) show the first and last image in the subsequence we used (the first seven even images). Figure 8(c) shows the initial pixel labeling into seven layers. Figures 8(d) and (e) show the sprite images corresponding to each of the seven layers, re-arranged for more compact display. Note that because of the compositing and blending that takes place during sprite construction, each sprite is larger than its footprint in any one of the input images. This sprite representation makes it very easy to re-synthesize novel images without leaving gaps in the new image, unlike approaches based on a single

Fig. 2. 3D model from a single panorama.

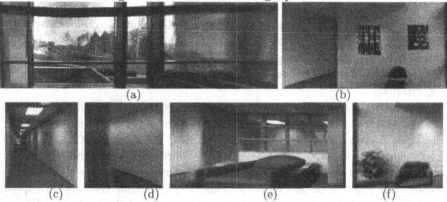

(a)   (b)

(c)   (d)   (e)   (f)

Fig. 3. Texture maps for the 3D model.

Fig. 4. Two views of the interactive system.

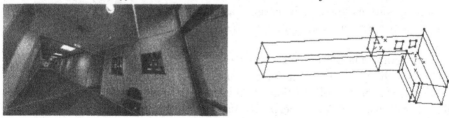

Fig. 5. A more complex 3D model from a single panorama.

Fig. 6. Two input panoramas of an indoor scene.

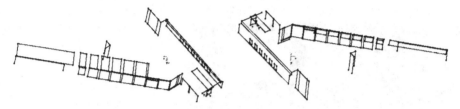

Fig. 7. Two views of a 3D model from multiple panoramas.

painted depth map [23]. Figure 8(f) shows the depth map computed by painting every pixel in every sprite with its corresponding color coded Z value, and then re-compositing the image. Notice how the depth discontinuities are much crisper and cleaner than those available with traditional stereo correspondence algorithms.

Our second set of experiments uses five images taken from a 40-image stereo dataset taken at a computer graphics symposium. Figure 9(a) shows the middle input image, Figure 9(b) shows the initial pixel assignment to layers, and Figure 9(c) shows the recovered depth map. Figures 9(d) and (e) show the recovered sprites, and Figure 9(f) shows the middle image re-synthesized from these sprites. The gaps visible in Figures 9(c) and 9(f) lie *outside* the area corresponding to the middle image, where the appropriate parts of the background sprites could not be seen.

5   Discussion and Conclusions

In this paper, we have prese nted two systems for interactively constructing complex (large-scale) 3D models from multiple images. Our modeling systems are able to construct accurate geometrical and photo-realistic 3D models because our approaches have much less ambiguity than traditional structure from motion or stereo approaches. Our results show that it is desirable and practical for the modeling systems to take advantage of as many regularities and priori knowledge about man-made environments (such as vertices, lines, and planes) as possible [41].

Our panorama 3D modeling system decomposes the modeling process into a zero baseline problem (panorama construction) and a wide baseline problem (stereo or structure from motion). Using the knowledge of the scene, e.g., known line directions, parallel or perpendicular planes, our system first recovers the camera pose for each panorama, and then constructs the 3D model using all possible constraints. In particular, we carefully partition the recovery problem into a series of linear estimation stages, and divide the constraints into "hard" and "soft" constraints so that each estimation stage becomes a linearly-constrained least-squares problem.

Our layered stereo modeling system makes use of a different kind of scene regularity, where input images are segmented into planar layers (with possible small depth offsets). By drastically reducing the number of unknowns (only 3

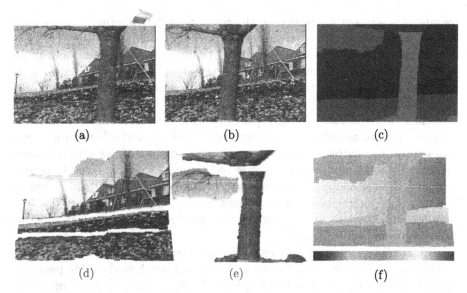

Fig. 8. Results on the *flower garden* sequence: (a) first and (b) last input images; (c) initial segmentation into six layers; (d) and (e) the six layer sprites; (f) depth map for planar sprites (bottom strip illustrates the coding of depths as colors)

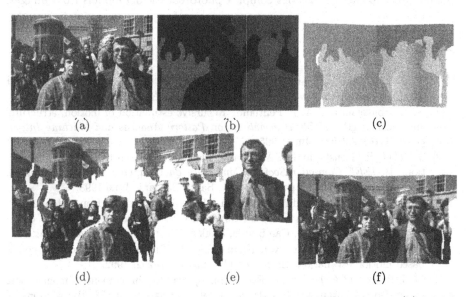

Fig. 9. Results on the *symposium* sequence: (a) third of five images; (b) initial segmentation into six layers; (c) recovered depth map; (d) and (e) the five layer sprites; (f) re-synthesized third image (note extended field of view).

parameters for each sprite plane), the recovery of 3D structure is much more robust than conventional stereo algorithms.

We are working on several extensions to improve the usability and generality of our system. Naturally, we want to automate even more parts of the interactive systems. For the panorama modeling system, we have implemented an automatic line snapping technique which snaps lines to their closest edges present in the panorama. We also plan to incorporate automatic line detection, corner detection as well as inter-image correspondence and other feature detections to further automate the system. If we use more features with automatic feature extraction and correspondence techniques, robust modeling techniques should also be developed [4]. For the layered stereo modeling system, we plan to automate the interactive masking process by only specifying layers in few (e.g., the first and the last) images and by incorporating motion segmentation and color segmentation techniques.

We are also planning to combine our layered stereo modeling system with the panorama modeling system. The idea is to build a rough model using panorama modeling system and refine it using layered stereo wherever it is appropriate (similar in spirit to the model-based stereo of [11]). We are also investigating representations beyond texture-mapped 3D models, i.e, image-based rendering approaches [17] such as view-dependent texture maps [11] and layered depth images [30]. Integrating all of these into one interactive modeling system will enable users to easily construct complex photorealistic 3D models from images.

References

[1] S. Ayer, P. Schroeter, and J. Bigün. Segmentation of moving objects by robust parameter estimation over multiple frames. In *3rd ECCV*, pages 316–327, 1994.

[2] A. Azarbayejani and A. P. Pentland. Recursive estimation of motion, structure, and focal length. *IEEE Transactions on Pattern Analysis and Machine Intelligence*, 17(6):562–575, June 1995.

[3] S. Baker, R. Szeliski, and P. Anandan. A layered approach to stereo reconstruction. In *IEEE Computer Society Conference on Computer Vision and Pattern Recognition (CVPR'98)*, pages 434–441, Santa Barbara, June 1998.

[4] P. Beardsley, P. Torr, and A. Zisserman. 3D model acquisition from extended image sequences. In *Fourth European Conference on Computer Vision (ECCV'96)*, volume 2, pages 683–695, Cambridge, England, April 1996. Springer-Verlag.

[5] J.R. Bergen, P. Anandan, K.J. Hanna, and R. Hingorani. Hierarchical model-based motion estimation. In *2nd ECCV*, pages 237–252, 1992.

[6] M. J. Black and A. D. Jepson. Estimating optical flow in segmented images using variable-order parametric models with local deformations. *IEEE Transactions on Pattern Analysis and Machine Intelligence*, 18(10):972–986, October 1996.

[7] J. F. Blinn. Jim Blinn's corner: Compositing, part 1: Theory. *IEEE Computer Graphics and Applications*, 14(5):83–87, September 1994.

[8] S. Bougnoux and L. Robert. Totalcalib: a fast and reliable system for off-line calibration of image sequences. In *IEEE Computer Society Conference on Computer Vision and Pattern Recognition (CVPR'97)*, June 1997. The Demo Session.

[9] R. T. Collins and R. S. Weiss. Vanishing point calculation as a statistical inference on the unit sphere. In *Third International Conference on Computer Vision (ICCV'90)*, pages 400–403, Osaka, Japan, December 1990. IEEE Computer Society Press.

[10] T. Darrell and A. Pentland. Robust estimation of a multi-layered motion representation. In *IEEE Workshop on Visual Motion*, pages 173–178, Princeton, New Jersey, October 1991. IEEE Computer Society Press.

[11] P. E. Debevec, C. J. Taylor, and J. Malik. Modeling and rendering architecture from photographs: A hybrid geometry- and image-based approach. *Computer Graphics (SIGGRAPH'96)*, pages 11–20, August 1996.

[12] O. Faugeras. *Three-dimensional computer vision: A geometric viewpoint.* MIT Press, Cambridge, Massachusetts, 1993.

[13] O. D. Faugeras. What can be seen in three dimensions with an uncalibrated stereo rig? In *Second European Conference on Computer Vision (ECCV'92)*, pages 563–578, Santa Margherita Liguere, Italy, May 1992. Springer-Verlag.

[14] O. D. Faugeras, Laveau S., Robert L., Csurka G., and Zeller C. 3-D reconstruction of urban scenes from sequences of images. *Computer Vision and Image Understanding*, 69(3):292–309, March 1998.

[15] G. Golub and C. F. Van Loan. *Matrix Computation, third edition.* The John Hopkins University Press, Baltimore and London, 1996.

[16] R. I. Hartley. Self-calibration from multiple views of a rotating camera. In *Third European Conference on Computer Vision (ECCV'94)*, volume 1, pages 471–478, Stockholm, Sweden, May 1994. Springer-Verlag.

[17] Workshop on image-based modeling and rendering. //graphics.stanford.edu/im98/, March 1998.

[18] M. Irani, P. Anandan, and S. Hsu. Mosiac based representations of video sequences and their applications. In *5th ICCV*, pages 605–611, 1995.

[19] A. Jepson and M. J. Black. Mixture models for optical flow computation. In *IEEE Computer Society Conference on Computer Vision and Pattern Recognition (CVPR'93)*, pages 760–761, New York, New York, June 1993.

[20] S. B. Kang and R. Szeliski. 3-D scene data recovery using omnidirectional multi-baseline stereo. In *IEEE Computer Society Conference on Computer Vision and Pattern Recognition (CVPR'96)*, pages 364–370, San Francisco, Cal, June 1996.

[21] R. Kumar, P. Anandan, and K. Hanna. Direct recovery of shape from multiple views: A parallax based approach. In *Twelfth International Conference on Pattern Recognition (ICPR'94)*, volume A, pages 685–688, Jerusalem, Israel, October 1994. IEEE Computer Society Press.

[22] Q.-T. Luong and O. Faugeras. Determining the fundamental matrix with planes: Instability and new algorithms. In *IEEE Computer Society Conference on Computer Vision and Pattern Recognition (CVPR'93)*, pages 489–494, New York, New York, June 1993.

[23] L. McMillan and G. Bishop. Plenoptic modeling: An image-based rendering system. *Computer Graphics (SIGGRAPH'95)*, pages 39–46, August 1995.

[24] R. Mohr, L. Veillon, and L. Quan. Relative 3D reconstruction using multiple uncalibrated images. In *IEEE Computer Society Conference on Computer Vision and Pattern Recognition (CVPR'93)*, pages 543–548, New York, N.Y., June 1993.

[25] Photomodeler. //www.photomodeler.com.

[26] M. Pollefeys, R. Koch, and L. Van Gool. Self-calibration and metric reconstruction in spite of varying and unknown internal camera parameters. In *Sixth International Conference on Computer Vision (ICCV'98)*, pages 90–95, Bombay, January 1998.

[27] H. S. Sawhney and A. R. Hanson. Identification and 3D description of 'shallow' environmental structure over a sequence of images. In *IEEE Computer Society Conference on Computer Vision and Pattern Recognition (CVPR'91)*, pages 179–185, Maui, Hawaii, June 1991. IEEE Computer Society Press.

[28] H.S. Sawhney and S. Ayer. Compact representations fo videos through dominant and multiple motion estimation. *PAMI*, 18(8):814–830, 1996.

[29] S. M. Seitz and C. M. Dyer. Photorealistic scene reconstrcution by space coloring. In *IEEE Computer Society Conference on Computer Vision and Pattern Recognition (CVPR'97)*, pages 1067–1073, San Juan, Puerto Rico, June 1997.

[30] J. Shade, S. Gortler, L.-W. He, and R. Szeliski. Layered depth images. In *Computer Graphics (SIGGRAPH'98) Proceedings*, Orlando, July 1998. ACM SIGGRAPH.

[31] A. Shashua. Projective structure from uncalibrated images: Structure from motion and recognition. *IEEE Transactions on Pattern Analysis and Machine Intelligence*, 16(8):778–790, August 1994.

[32] H.-Y. Shum, M. Han, and R. Szeliski. Interactive construction of 3d models from panoramic mosaics. In *IEEE Computer Society Conference on Computer Vision and Pattern Recognition (CVPR'98)*, pages 427–433, Santa Barbara, June 1998.

[33] H.-Y. Shum and R. Szeliski. Panoramic image mosaicing. Technical Report MSR-TR-97-23, Microsoft Research, September 1997.

[34] A. R. Smith and J. F. Blinn. Blue screen matting. In *Computer Graphics Proceedings, Annual Conference Series*, pages 259–268, Proc. SIGGRAPH'96 (New Orleans), August 1996. ACM SIGGRAPH.

[35] R. Szeliski and P. Golland. Stereo matching with transparency and matting. In *Sixth International Conference on Computer Vision (ICCV'98)*, pages 517–524, Bombay, January 1998.

[36] R. Szeliski and H.-Y. Shum. Creating full view panoramic image mosaics and texture-mapped models. *Computer Graphics (SIGGRAPH'97)*, pages 251–258, August 1997.

[37] R. Szeliski and P. Torr. Geometrically constrained structure from motion: Points on planes. In *European Workshop on 3D Structure from Multiple Images of Large-scale Environments (SMILE)*, Freiburg, Germany, June 1998.

[38] J. Torborg and J. T. Kajiya. Talisman: Commodity realtime 3D graphics for the PC. In *Computer Graphics Proceedings, Annual Conference Series*, pages 353–363, Proc. SIGGRAPH'96 (New Orleans), August 1996. ACM SIGGRAPH.

[39] P. Torr, A. W. Fitzgibbon, and A. Zisserman. Maintaining multiple motion model hypotheses over many views to recover matching structure. In *Sixth International Conference on Computer Vision (ICCV'98)*, pages 485–491, Bombay, January 1998.

[40] T. Viéville, C. Zeller, and L. Robert. Using collineations to compute motion and structure in an uncalibrated image sequence. *International Journal of Computer Vision*, 20(3):213–242, 1996.

[41] E. L. Walker and M. Herman. Geometric reasoning for constructing 3D scene descriptions from images. *Artificial Intelligence*, 37:275–290, 1988.

[42] J. Y. A. Wang and E. H. Adelson. Layered representation for motion analysis. In *IEEE Computer Society Conference on Computer Vision and Pattern Recognition (CVPR'93)*, pages 361–366, New York, New York, June 1993.

[43] Y. Weiss. Smoothness in layers: Motion segmentation using nonparametric mixture estimation. In *IEEE Computer Society Conference on Computer Vision and Pattern Recognition (CVPR'97)*, pages 520–526, San Juan, Puerto Rico, June 1997.

Integration of Multiple Range Maps through Consistency Processing

Philippe Robert, Damien Minaud

THOMSON multimedia R&D France
Av de Belle Fontaine, 35510 Cesson-Sévigné, France
Email:robertp@thmulti.com

Abstract. This paper presents a method for modeling the surfaces of some 3D scene from a set of registered range maps. The integration of range maps into a unique accurate representation is made tricky mainly because of the presence of noise in the viewpoints positions and in the range estimates. In the present case, the scene is captured by a CCD camera system and the depth maps are estimated by a stereovision technique. This approach makes the problem of integration particularly thorny. In fact, the range maps are generally redundant but corrupted by noise and not always coherent with each other. The integration method presented in this paper is based on a fundamental principle : whatever the scene is, the range maps must be consistent with each other. This principle is used as a constraint to discard noise and increase the 3D data accuracy and to identify and remove the redundancies leading to a minimal accurate representation. This phase is realized through the detection of inconsistencies between the range maps of the different viewpoints, the identification and the removal of the most inconsistent points, and the fusion of the remaining redundant points. The process is repeated until the depth maps are coherent with each other. Finally, the facet model is built by incrementally integrating the coherent depth maps. This system is independent of the depth estimation part and can process any set of depth maps of any scene.

1 Introduction

The construction of 3D models can be viewed as the problem of acquisition of 3D points, registration in a single reference system and integration of these points into a unique facet model. The resulting model must approximate the surfaces as precisely as possible. The data can be composed of unorganized sampled 3D points but are often captured through 2.5D range maps. This 2D image structure contains information about surface topology, and therefore usefully constrains the problem. The situation is that the range maps are noisy and generally overlap. Therefore, the construction of the model consists of a fusion process of the set of the maps as well as triangulation of the observed surfaces. Two approaches have been proposed for this process :

Reinhard Koch, Luc Van Gool (Eds.): SMILE '98, LNCS 1506, pp. 253-265, 1998.

- mesh integration
- volumetric fusion

In the mesh integration approach, the range images are first independently triangulated. The triangulation is generally constrained by discontinuities in depth/orientation.

Rustihauser *et al* [1] and Turk and Levoy [2] create a polygon mesh for each view; the individual meshes are then connected to form a single mesh covering the whole object. In both cases, the merging procedure is a rearrangement of the facets while preserving the 3D points. In fact, this re-arrangement may lead to unplausible surfaces.

Soucy and Laurendeau [3] divide the range maps into subsets of overlapping surface regions from the different views. In each subset, the redundancy of the views is used to improve the surface approximation. A virtual viewpoint is defined for each subset, the depth maps are projected on this virtual map, and the depth values are fused. However, the number of possible virtual viewpoints can be very high (2^n for n maps). Moreover, too little attention is paid to the projection of the depth maps, since points of different surfaces can be combined.

Pito [4] introduces a notion of consistency between triangles from different viewpoints. The test of similarity of two triangles is based on their relative distance and orientation. Then, the overlapping triangles are processed such that just one is kept : if two triangles are similar the one with the highest confidence is kept, if they are not, the occluding triangle is removed. Then several phases aim to integrate the meshes and to build a robust model.

In volumetric fusion of registered range maps, Pulli *et al.* [5] use a hierarchical octree representation and estimate a surface using a hierarchical space carving method that labels the cubes as outside the object, inside or on the boundary. This method does not tackle the problem of noise in the range maps.

Hilton *et al.* [6] propose an integration algorithm based on a continuous implicit surface representation that does not compensate for noise.

Wheeler *et al.*'s method [7] merges the set of range maps into a volumetric implicit-surface representation. The method called *the consensus-surface algorithm* deals with noise by requiring a quorum of observations before using them to build the model : the signed distance to the object surface is estimated by finding a consensus of locally coherent observations (in terms of 3D location and orientation) of the surface. A consensus surface is then derived by merging the selected observations and a surface mesh is obtained using a variant of the marching-cubes algorithm. As said in the paper, the algorithm assumes that it is possible to separate the noise from the relevant data by means of a threshold on the consensus value.

2 Presentation of the Context

Most of the techniques described above are applied to data issued from range scanners. In 3D reconstruction from passive vision, the presence of noise is particularly critical and a robust technique is required to integrate the range maps in a unique representation. Researchers have developed methods to build surface models in special cases (e.g. deformable models [8], elevation models [9]). The outliers detection and removal have been tackled by locally modeling the surfaces around the 3D points [10].

In the present case, a set of depth maps is estimated by means of a vision-based system [11]. This system exploits the luminance images provided by a single camera moving in front of an arbitrary static scene. The resulting depth maps are dense and redundant with each other. They are also noisy and not everywhere coherent with each other. In particular, due to the correspondence problem, erroneous areas may occur. Such noise is intra-frame and even inter-frame correlated, sometimes leading to a high consensus of 3D points for wrong surfaces.

The idea to use a volumetric approach is excluded : the scene can be complex, the density of the 3D observed data is generally irregular (the resolution depends on the shape of the scene as well as on the acquisition conditions). It makes noise removal through a simple density-based criterion difficult. Moreover it makes keeping the image resolution of the scene difficult.

Therefore we use the image grid as the support of the data and of the processing. The depth maps are supposed to be registered either by pre-calibration, on-line calibration or by robust registration such as in [12]. The integration method must be able to solve the inconsistencies between the range maps.

Two modeling approaches have been developed with a particular attention paid to solve the inconsistencies existing between the depth maps : the first one incrementally integrates the depth maps in the model and manages at each time instant the differences between the model and the current depth map [13]. In this method, the current model is projected on the new viewpoint and compared to the corresponding depth map. The new areas are approximated and triangulated, while the old ones are processed differently according to the similarity between the current depth map and the 3D model : if this similarity is high, they are simply adjusted; if there is a conflict, they are either maintained or corrected and retriangulated.

There is a conflict in presence of erroneous data. The problem is to identify what is erroneous on a given pixel : the 3D model or the current depth map? There is no robust local test to choose between the two candidates. In [13], a luminance-based criterion was defined to choose between the two values but some tests showed that this criterion is not reliable and does not solve the problem satisfactorily.

In the second approach [14], the range maps are all combined in order to detect and remove the outliers and to produce coherent maps; then, a 3D facet model is built by integrating these maps. This more robust approach has been recently improved and is presented in the following sections : what is an inconsistency is defined in section 3; the consistency processing is detailed in section 4 ; section 5 shows a set of results and gives the conclusion.

3 Definition of Inconsistency

The consistency processing is realized on the different viewpoints of the sequence, and relies on the properties of the 2D1/2 representation as provided by the depth maps. The objective is to make the depth maps consistent with each other and accurate before their integration in a unique 3D model. First, it is required to detect and solve the inconsistencies. What is an inconsistency ? Let us consider a given viewpoint. A depth map is assigned to this viewpoint. This depth map describes 3D points that are surface elements. The line joining the camera center to any 3D point of the depth map should not cross any other surface as this point is seen from this viewpoint. Therefore, there is an inconsistency when a surface seen from another viewpoint hides the surface seen on the current viewpoint when projected on it. This is the basic principle of inconsistency detection.

Figure 1a displays two examples in which two depth maps are consistent with each other :

in the first case, the two viewpoints see two different areas, and surface B is not incompatible with what viewpoint 1 sees (surface A).

in the second case, viewpoints 1 and 2 see the same surface, that is called A1 from viewpoint 1, and A2 from viewpoint 2. The surface measurements from viewpoints 1 and 2 are similar and therefore coherent with each other.

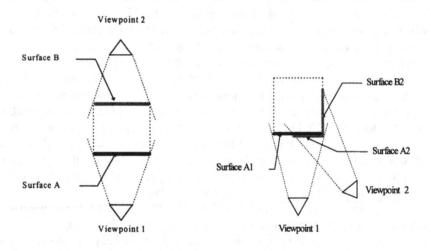

Fig. 1a. two examples of inter-image consistency

Figure 1b displays an example in which the two viewpoints see inconsistent data. Viewpoint 1 sees surface A1 while viewpoint 2 sees surfaces B2 and C2. The problem appears if what is seen from viewpoint 2 is observed from viewpoint 1. In this case, it appears that surface C2 hides surface A1 from viewpoint 1 : there is inconsistency. At least one of the two surfaces is false.

Let us notice that on the other hand if what is seen from viewpoint 1 is observed from viewpoint 2, there is no inconsistency : surface A1 is simply hidden by surface C2. Consequently, the detection of inconsistencies between two viewpoints requires to observe the two sets of data from the two views.

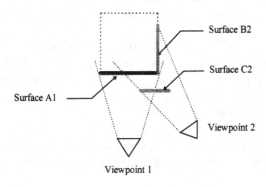

Fig. 1b. example of inter-image inconsistency

4   Consistency Processing

4.1 Overview of the Algorithm

The integration method is based on the principle that whatever the scene is, the range maps must be consistent with each other. This strong constraint is introduced to build a unique representation of the scene from the input noisy data. The objective is to estimate a new set of depth maps that are consistent with each other, as close to the input set as possible and locally smooth. The estimation problem can be formulated in terms of minimization of a set of three energy functions :

- E_c that measures the inconsistency between the depth maps
- E_f that measures the distance of the resulting depth maps to the observation maps
- E_s that introduces a weak smoothness constraint

Therefore, the objective is to estimate a set of filtered depth maps z() that minimize the global energy E :

$$\min_z E = \min_z (E_c + E_f + E_s)$$

Let us consider a set of N depth maps : each depth map is described by $z(p,i)$, in which z is the depth component, p is a given pixel of image i :

- the distance measure E_f is defined by the sum on all the pixels p of all images i of the distances between the observed depth values and the resulting ones :

$$E_f = \Sigma_i^N \Sigma_p^P c(p,i). ||\ z_f(p,i) - z_{obs}(p,i)||^2$$

  where $c(p,i)$ is the confidence value assigned to $z_{obs}(p,i)$.

- the consistency measure E_c is defined from the comparison of each depth map with the others :

$$E_c = \Sigma_i^N \Sigma_j^{N-1} \Sigma_p^P \mu(p,i). ||\ z_f(p,i) - z_f^{proj}(p,i,j)||^2$$

  where $z_f^{proj}(p,i,j)$ is issued from the projection of depth map j on i,
  and $\mu(p,i) = 1$ if $z_f(p,i)$ and $z_f^{proj}(p,i,j)$ correspond to the same surface,
  $= 0$ otherwise.

- the smoothness measure E_s is defined by :

$$E_s = \Sigma_i^N \Sigma_p^P ||\ z_f(p,i) - \Phi(z_f(p,i))||^2$$

  where $\Phi()$ is a local 2D operator on the depth map i. This intra-image constraint is mainly used to remove local artefacts.

The consistency processing is realized in two steps (figure 2) :

- inconsistency evaluation and outliers removal
- multiview fusion of the consistent data.

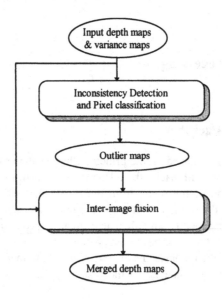

Fig. 2. consistency processing

4.2 Inconsistency Evaluation and Outlier Identification

In this section, we will answer the question how to detect and evaluate the inconsistencies in the set of depth maps and how to identify the outliers.

Inconsistency detection and evaluation. The inconsistencies between two viewpoints i and j are detected by comparing the depth map RMi of viewpoint i and the « projected » depth map PMji obtained by « projecting » the depth map RMj on viewpoint i. Inconsistencies are detected by comparing each pixel of RMi to the corresponding one in PMji. The depth difference ΔZ is compared to the threshold λ :
if $-\lambda < \Delta Z < \lambda$, the two points are supposed to belong to the same surface : there is consensus (consistency case)
if $\Delta Z < -\lambda$, the projected point is hidden by the current point (consistency case)
if $\lambda < \Delta Z$, the projected point hides the current point : there is inconsistency.
λ defines the separation threshold on the depth difference ΔZ between two surfaces. In case of inconsistency, the two points on the input depth maps RMi and RMj are potentially erroneous (at least one of them is wrong) and both are consequently penalized. In case of consensus, both points are « rewarded ». For each pixel, these confidence values are accumulated through the comparison to all the other maps and make up inconsistency maps. The procedure *InconsistencyDetection* describes the comparison between two views :

<u>**Procedure**</u> *InconsistencyDetection*
Input: range maps RMi and RMj of viewpoints i and j
Input: transformation matrix T(j,i) between viewpoints i and j
Input: outlier maps (l_i, l_j)
Output: inconsistency maps (c_i, c_j)

FOR $p_j \in 1...P$
    IF ($l_j(p_j) = 1$)   /* p_j is not an outlier */
        $(u_i, v_i, z_i) \leftarrow$ T(j,i) * $(p_j, RMj(p_j))$ /* (u_i, v_i) : 2D image components */
        p_i=closestpixel(u_i, v_i)
        PMji(p_i)=z_i
        IF ($l_i(p_i) = 1$)   /* p_i is not an outlier */
            IF ($\Delta Z = |$ RMi(p_i) - PMji(p_i)$|$ < λ)   /* consensus */
                $c_i(p_i) = c_i(p_i) + conf_+$
                $c_j(p_j) = c_j(p_j) + conf_+$
            ELSE   **IF** ($\Delta Z = ($ RMi(p_i) - PMji(p_i) $)$ > λ)   /* inconsistency */
                $c_i(p_i) = c_i(p_i) + conf_-$
                $c_j(p_j) = c_j(p_j) + conf_-$
End
The outlier maps discriminate the already identified outliers that have been discarded $(l_x=0)$ from the other points that are still processed $(l_x=1)$ (see below).

Outlier identification. Once all the comparisons have been done, the inconsistency maps are processed to classify each pixel as consistent/inconsistent. A first possible solution is to apply a threshold. However, as mentioned previously, in case of inconsistency between two points, both are penalized. Consequently, thresholding the inconsistency maps does not guarantee an ideal discrimination between the surface points and the outliers. In fact, we process the inconsistency detection and the outlier removal iteratively, starting with a high threshold μ that is progressively decreased : the suppression of the highest penalized points modifies the inconsistency maps that are re-evaluated (some inconsistent points can become consistent). As an example, the threshold can be chosen at each iteration so that it suppresses approximately the 10% of remaining points that are the most inconsistent. The process is applied until all depth maps are consistent with each other.

MainProcedure *InconsistencyEvaluation*
FOR $i \in 1...N$
FOR $p \in 1...P$
    $l_i(p)=1$ /* all points are initially valid*/
DO
    FOR $i \in 1...N$
    FOR $j \in 1...N,\ j \neq i$
    InconsistencyDetection
    Compute_μ
    FOR $i \in 1...N$
        OutlierMap
WHILE $a \neq 0$
End

Procedure *OutlierMap*
Input: inconsistency map c_i
Output: outlier map l_i and number of outliers a
$a=0$
FOR $p \in 1...P$
    IF $(\ c_i(p) > \mu\ )$
        $l_i(p)=0$ /* p is classified as outlier */
        $a = a+1$
End

4.3 Multiview Fusion

The consistent pixels in the depth maps are updated through a multiview fusion process. The points to be merged are identified by a projection step similar to the previous one. The depth components are then merged on each viewpoint taking into account the confidence maps attached to the observations. The surface orientation is also considered in the fusion process through the mesh of microfacets : a microfacet links three neighboring pixels of the image grid. The orientation of the projected microfacets is computed and their attached points are selected only if the orientation is right with regard to the viewpoint on which fusion is processed. A locally planar surface model is then applied to the resulting depth maps in order to smooth the surfaces and remove isolated noise. The resulting depth maps are more accurate than the input depth maps and more consistent with each other.

MainProcedure *MultiviewFusion*
FOR $i \in 1...N$
    FOR $j \in 1...N, j \neq i$
        MicroFacetProjection
    FOR $p_i \in 1...P$
        Fusion
End

Procedure *MicroFacetProjection*
Input: range map RMj, confidence map CMj and outlier map l_j of viewpoint j
Input: transformation matrix T(j,i) between viewpoints i and j
Output: projected range map PMji of range map j on viewpoint i
Output: orientation map OMji and confidence map CMji attached to PMji
FOR $p_j \in 1...P$
    $PMji(p_i) = \infty$
FOR $p_i \in 1...P$
    (u_i, v_i, z_i) $\leftarrow$ $T(j,i) * (p_j, RMj(p_j))$; /* (u_i, v_i) : 2D image components */
    p_i=closestpixel(u_i, v_i)
    IF ($z_i < PMji(p_i)$)
$PMji(p_i) = z_i$
$CMji(p_i) = CMj(p_j)$
IF at least one of the projected microfacets attached to p_j has the right orientation
        $OMji(p_i)=1$
ELSE $OMji(p_i)=0$
End

Procedure *Fusion*
Input: RMi, CMi, PMji, CMji and OMji
Output: fused range map FMi
FOR $p_i \in 1...P$
    IF ($RMi(p_i) \neq \infty$)
        conf=CMi(p_i)
        z_fus = RMi(p_i)*conf
        FOR $j \in 1...N, j \neq i$
            IF ($| RMi(p_i) - PMji(p_i) | < \lambda$ **AND** $OMji(p_i)=1$)
                z_fus = z_fus + PMji(p_i) * CMji(p_i)
                conf = conf + CMji(p_i)
        FMi(p_i) = z_fus / conf
Return Fmi

4.4 Geometry and Texture Representation

The multiview consistency processing described above provides coherent depth maps. It allows to keep the image resolution unlike the volumetric fusion techniques. From the resultant depth maps it is now possible to distinguish the various surfaces and to remove the redundancies. The next step is to build a compact representation of the scene. Two representations are possible and are presently under investigation for comparison :

- a geometry-based representation: it is an incremental construction of a 3D facet model that is made relatively simple once the depth maps are consistent with each other.
- an image-based representation (RGBZ) that is straightforward in our case.

The performance criteria are the compression ratio and rendered image quality.

5 Results and Conclusion

Synthetic scene. Figure 3a shows the top view of an original synthetic scene. A set of 284 depth maps 512rows*10lines have been created by moving a virtual camera in the scene; figure 3a displays a cross-section of the 3D scene. In a second step, noise has been added to the depth maps and figure 3b displays a cross-section of the 3D scene recovered from the set of the noisy depth maps.

The consistency processing has been applied on this set of images and the results of the various steps are shown in figures 4 : the 3D scene is shown once the outliers have been discarded (figure 4a) and at the end of the fusion (figure 4b). For comparison, figure 5 displays the results of a point rejection based on thresholding the 3D density of the points : some wrong surfaces remain while some right ones are removed that shows the unreliability of such discrimination. The inconsistency combined with an adaptive thresholding is a better discrimination parameter.

Real scene. Figures 6 show an example of images acquired by a moving camera. The sequence *Carton* is composed of 18 images, the camera motion is mainly vertical. Figures 6a, 6b and 6c correspond respectively to images n°1, 9 and 18. A joint recursive estimation of depth maps and camera motion is realised along the sequence. The depth maps corresponding to figures 6 are shown in figures 7. They are noisy and not everywhere coherent. The results of the consistency processing are displayed in figures 8. They clearly show the improvement brought by the processing. In particular, the inconsistencies on the top-right of the initial depth maps have been solved. Figures 9 display the interpolation of image n°10 from the images n°1 and n°18 : after consistency processing of the depth maps in figure 9a and from the original depth maps in figure 9b.

In conclusion, we have built a structure from motion system for arbitrary scenes and arbitrary small motions. A first step [11] provides a set of range maps with attached camera position. The second step presented in this paper is a robust method that provides coherent depth maps: the multiview consistency processing. In fact, this processing is independent from the other parts of the system : it can be introduced in any system with a set of input depth maps in order to make them consistent. Moreover, the consistency property is a strong constraint that can be added to the smoothness constraint in interpolation of sparse depth maps. Luminance is also planned to be taken into account to further constrain the processing.

6 References

1. M.Rutishauser, M.Stricker and M.Trobina.: Merging range images of arbitrarily shaped objects, Proceedings of IEEE Conference on Computer Vision and Pattern Recognition, 1994.

2. G.Turk and M.Levoy.: Zippered polygon meshes from range images, Proceedings of SIGGRAPH'94, July 1994.

3. M.Soucy and D.Laurendeau.: A general surface approach to the integration of a set of range views, IEEE PAMI, vol.17, n°4, April 1995.

4. R.Pito.: Mesh integration based on co-measurements, Proceedings IEEE ICIP, 96.

5. K.Pulli *et al.*: Robust meshes from multiple range maps, Proceedings of the international conference on recent advances in 3D Digital imaging and modeling, Ottawa, 12-15 May 1997.

6. A.Hilton, A.Stoddart, J.Illingworth and T.Windeatt : Reliable surface reconstruction from multiple range images, Proceedings of the 4th European Conference on Computer Vision, pages 117-126, Springer-Verlag, 1996.

7. M.Wheeler, Y.Sato and K.Ikeuchi : Consensus surfaces for modeling 3D objects from multiple range images, DARPA Image Understanding Workshop, New Orleans, Louisiana, 1997.

8. H.Delingette, M.Hebert, K.Ikeuchi.: Shape representation and image segmentation using deformable surfaces, Journal of Image and Vision Computing, 10(3):132-144, April 1992.

9. B.Hotz, Z.Zhang and P.Fua.: Incremental construction of local DEM for an autonomous planetary rover, Workshop on Computer Vision for Space Applications, Antibes, Sept.1993.

10. P.Fua and P.Sander.: Segmenting unstructured 3D points into surfaces, ECCV 92.

11. Ph.Robert, F.Ogor.: Joint estimation of depth maps and camera motion in the construction of 3D models from a mobile camera, in European workshop on combined real and synthetic image processing for broadcast and video production, 23-24 Nov. 1994. Proc. by Springer Verlag Ed.

12. P.J.Neugebauer.: Reconstruction of real-world objects via simultaneous registration and robust combination of multiple range images, International journal of shape modeling, pp 71-90, vol.3, No. 1&2, 1997.

13. D.Minaud and Ph.Robert.: Construction of 3D models from a mobile camera, IMAGE'COM96, Bordeaux, 20-22 May 1996.

14. D.Minaud and Ph.Robert.: Construction of 3D models from a mobile camera, Integration of a set of depth maps, International workshop on synthetic-natural hybrid coding and three-dimensional imaging (IWSNHC3DI'97), Rhodes (Greece), 5-9 September 1997.

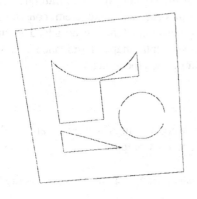

Fig. 3a

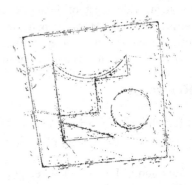

Fig. 3b

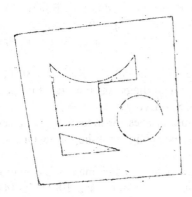

Fig. 4a

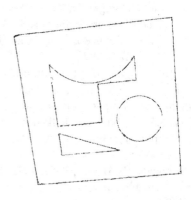

Fig. 4b

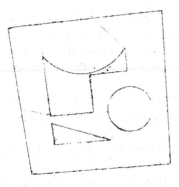

Fig. 5

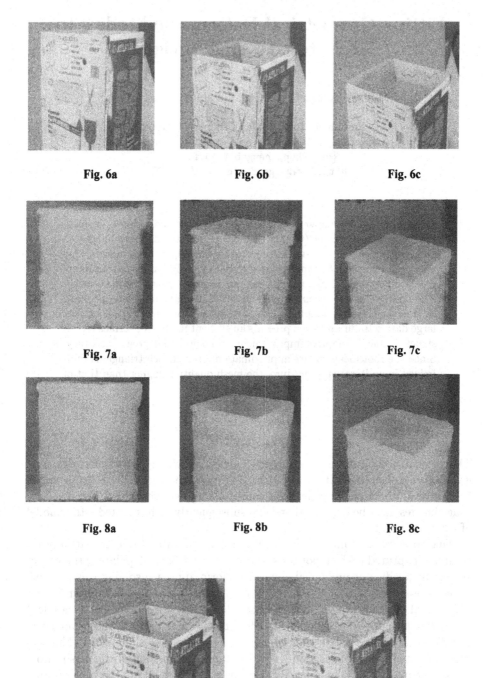

Fig. 6a   Fig. 6b   Fig. 6c

Fig. 7a   Fig. 7b   Fig. 7c

Fig. 8a   Fig. 8b   Fig. 8c

Fig. 9a   Fig. 9b

Fitting Geometrical Deformable Models to Registered Range Images

Stefan Großkopf and Peter Johannes Neugebauer

Fraunhofer Institute for Computer Graphics
Rundeturmstr. 6, D-64283 Darmstadt, Germany
{grosskop, neugeb}@igd.fhg.de
http://www.igd.fhg.de/www/igd-a7

Abstract. In this paper we present a method for adapting a geometrical deformable model (GDM) to a set of registered range images in order to reconstruct real-world objects from multiple range images. Our approach registers the range images simultaneously, carves out an intermediate volume and finally generates an accurate, sparse triangle mesh. The proposed GDM scheme refines an initial roughly approximated mesh by deformation and adaptive subtriangulation. Even in the case of very large data sets our approach presents an efficient method of surface reconstruction due to adaptive improvement to the desired degree of accuracy. Since the root mean square approximation error of each triangle is minimized in an iterative procedure, the mesh quality is higher than that of previous approaches.

1 Introduction

The reconstruction of complete object geometries with a 3D scanner device is generally not possible within one scan. Instead, the object has to be scanned from several directions in order to capture its complete geometry. The resulting range images must be registered and can subsequently be integrated into a model of the object surface.

Due to some amount of noise in the original data and due to partially incomplete captured surface portions, there is a need for interpolating the object surface at falsified or undefined gaps. A uniform approach solving this problem is the geometrical deformable model (GDM). The GDM was first described by Miller et al. [2,5] for the segmentation of volumetric data sets. Basically, a GDM is a triangle mesh that dynamically deforms by moving each mesh vertex in the direction of steepest descent along the surface of a cost function. The cost function integrates all constraints on the shape and position of the mesh into a consistent mathematical model. By minimizing the total costs the best solution considering all constraints is achieved.

However, a crucial drawback of this approach is the smoothing of fine details of the surface even in regions where it is defined properly, e.g., sharp edges. It is caused by improper weighting of internal cost terms which are intended to preserve the mesh smoothness and topology. We propose a deformation scheme

Reinhard Koch, Luc Van Gool (Eds.): SMILE '98, LNCS 1506, pp. 266–274, 1998.
© Springer-Verlag Berlin Heidelberg 1998

Fig. 1. (a) plaster bust of composer Richard Wagner (b) 3D model reconstructed from 27 scanned range images

that moves the vertices under constraint to minimize the external cost term exclusively. The presented optimization procedure achieves high quality of the mesh by moving the vertices along two types of forces, a spring force and an expansion force. The spring force maintains the mesh regularly whereas the expansion force drives the mesh towards the surface.

The remainder of this paper is organized as follows. Section 2 gives an overview of the processing steps. Section 3 discusses the definition of the implicit surface from multiple registered range images. Section 4 deals with the generation of the template mesh. Section 5 discusses topological improvements of the mesh applied during the deformation process. Section 6 presents two approaches to improve the vertex positions of a given mesh: a fast one [8] and the proposed GDM approach. In section 7 results are shown and discussed.

2   Overview

The processing steps and intermediate representations that yield an accurate, sparse triangulated surface starting from a set of range images is shown in Fig. 2. The first step is the registration of range images [7] and results in the model cluster. The cluster holds the information needed to define an implicit surface, i.e., the range images and their attached transformation matrices. For the calculation of Euclidean distances to the surface and for higher performance it also contains a distance transformed volume that assigns every voxel its distance to the nearest surface point. In a subsequent step, a binary volume is sculptured. By application of the marching cube algorithm a template triangle mesh is generated from the volume. By using an octree representation during sculpturing we are able to generate a volume of arbitrary resolution. Hence it is possible to construct meshes with the required number of triangles and surface topology. This template is then adapted to the surface by deformation and subtriangulation.

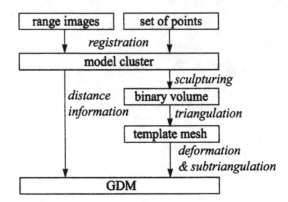

Fig. 2. Pipeline for adapting the GDM

3   Definition of the Implicit Surface

3.1   Distance Function

Initially, the surface of the object to be reconstructed is given by a number of range images that are already registered. The parameter grid of the range images is defined by the coordinate system of the scanner, e.g., a cylindrical or a perspective system. By interpolating between the grid points the surface can be continuously completed.

Now, we convert the range images to a signed distance function. For the definition of the distance we define for each range image a function $g_i(x)$ that measures the signed projection distance between a point in space and the interpolated surface in the range image. The corresponding point in the range image is found by projecting the point x onto the parameter grid of the range image. Thus, a positive distance indicates that the point lies between the scanner and the surface and consequently is visible whereas a negative distance indicates that the point lies below the surface and is invisible.

The synthesis of multiple range images is achieved by combining the functions $g_i(x)$ as shown in equation (1).

$$f(x) = \max_i \{ g_i(x) \} \tag{1}$$

The implicitly defined surface is given by the zero crossings of $f(x)$. It is now possible to calculate the intersection between an arbitrary ray and the surface of the object.

3.2 Distance Transformation

The distance function discussed in the previous subsection calculates the projection distance, which has the same zero crossings as the Euclidean distance. The function consequently is suitable for the definition of the implicit surface and for the definition of the visibility of a point. However, in order to approximate the Euclidean distance from a point to the nearest surface point, we propagate distances into space by calculating a distance transformed volume. This has the positive side effect that it also reduces the effort of calculating the distance, which otherwise depends linearly on the number of range images. In order to prevent loss of information the projection distance within the voxels that contain portions of the surface can be calculated additionally.

The distance transformed volume is generated by a floating point number based chamfering distance transformation. The distance is at first defined only for voxels that contain parts of the object surface. For initialization of these voxels the projection distance to the center of gravity of the voxel is calculated and stored to the voxel. By application of a two pass transformation algorithm [1] the distances are propagated successively into the neighborhood. After the distance transformation is completed, the invisible voxels are defined as to be negative.

4   Generating the Template Mesh

In order to achieve a first approximation of the object surface and to derive the topology of the object up to the desired level of detail, we use a sculpturing approach to build an intermediate volumetric model. For each voxel x of the volume the distance function $f(x)$ can be evaluated and we thus obtain the binary decision whether the point does belong to the object. In some cases, there remain some volumetric regions that do not belong to the object because the associated voxels e.g., lie on the back-face of the object, far below one of the range images defining the front side. However, after generating the intermediate volumetric model, the marching cube algorithm [4] with a look-up table that resolves ambiguous cases [6] can be applied to generate a polygonal representation. In order to delete wrong volumetric regions all connected meshes are detected and all but the largest mesh are deleted. The accuracy of this polygonal mesh is improved by moving the vertices of the mesh onto the surface implicitly defined by the registered range images [7].

5   Improving the Mesh Topology

To be able to approximate fine details of the surface our scheme refines the grid at surface portions with high curvature and removes triangles where the reconstructed surface is nearly flat. This benefits for a compact representation and accelerates operations performed on the mesh. We implemented the following operations.

5.1   Deletion of Short Edges

By merging those points connected by very short edges and deleting the corresponding triangles, the number of triangles can be reduced very easily.

5.2   Deletion of Redundant Points

For this operation mesh vertices are deleted if the normal of this vertex just differs slightly (i.e., within a predefined angle) from the normal of the neighboring vertices. Subsequently the surrounding polygon is retriangulated by a simple traversal algorithm.

5.3   Subdivision

Triangles are splitted into a number of faces if the distance of one of the centers of gravity of the three edges or of the center of gravity of the triangle is larger than a specified threshold value. The new vertices are found as the intersection of the mesh normal with the implicit surface. After determination of the point locations one of the subtriangulation schemes of Fig. 3 is chosen and the splitted triangle is replaced by the new triangles.

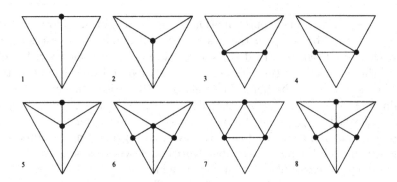

Fig. 3. Subdivision configurations without symmetric cases

5.4   Edge Swapping

The tessellation of a number of vertices is not unique. In order to generate the globally best triangulation local optimization can be applied. A triangulation is globally optimal iff it is locally optimal and a global criterion is improved in each local optimization step. A triangulation is called locally optimal iff a predefined criterion is true in each quadrilateral (2 triangles with one common edge).

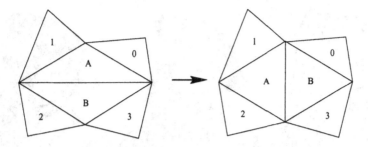

Fig. 4. Optimization by edge swapping

The criteria for performing the edge swapping (see Fig. 4) are as follows:

- The triangulation of a quadrilateral is optimal iff the smallest angle is greater than the smallest angle present in the alternative triangulation of the quadrilateral (*Max-Min-criterion*).
- The total area occupied by the triangles should not increase.
- The approximation error should not increase.

The edge swapping is activated for all quadrilaterals which do not fulfill the criteria mentioned above. This step is repeated for all quadrilaterals until no more improvements can be made.

6   Improving Vertex Positions

6.1   A Fast Approach: Smooth and Reproject

The initial triangulation can be improved by shifting the vertices of the mesh onto the center of gravity of the surrounding polygon (smoothing). We then define a ray that runs through the shifted vertex and parallel to the mean normal of the neighboring triangles. The vertex is now re-projected onto the surface by finding the nearest surface intersection. Hence we derive triangles of approximately equal size and inner angles. The visualization of the object appears to be greatly improved as small noise in the vertex coordinates only slightly influences the surface normal of the triangle. On the other hand, vertices may be delocalized apart from small step edges of the surface.

6.2   GDM

Force Definition The deformation of the GDM from the initial template is driven by the simulation of two forces. On one hand the edges act like springs. According to equation (2) the spring forces are normalized in order to yield equilateral triangles.

$$F_{\text{spring}}(x_i) = \sum_{(i,j) \in Vertices} \frac{x_j - x_i}{|x_j - x_i|} \tag{2}$$

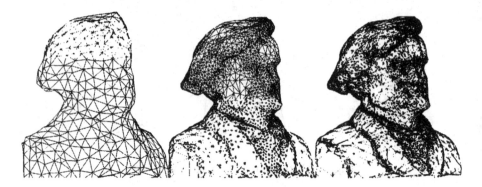

Fig. 5. Three stages of the adaption process with (a) 1300 (b) 7500 (c) 16000 triangles

On the other hand a pressure force defined along the surface normals causes a smooth deformation of the GDM as it is done for reprojection.

Optimization Procedure The deformation of the GDM is performed iteratively by moving each vertex along the direction of each force. The step size for this is chosen individually for both forces at each vertex. Two strategies are sensible.

1. As a first step, move the vertex along the spring force. The step size has to be smaller than the distance value of the starting point and shorter than the distance to the center of gravity of the surrounding polygon. If a defined distance value calculated for all adjacent triangles increases, this step is not performed. In a second step, move the vertex along the positive normal direction. The step size has to be smaller than or equal to the distance value of the starting point. If the distance value of the adjacent triangles increases, the negative normal direction is tested.
2. Since the second step of the above procedure assures for minimizing the distance of the adjacent triangles to the surface, the constraint for the movements along the spring force can be relaxed. This is done by a stochastic approach. We adapt an acceptance criteria from simulated annealing [3] which is shown in equation (3). If the probability P_{ij} is larger than an equally distributed random number in the interval of $[0 \ldots 1)$ the new state is accepted, otherwise rejected.

For the results shown in the next section the latter method has been used. In equation (3) T indicates the temperature of the system and $h(.)$ indicates the euclidean distance to the surface as mentioned in section 3.2.

$$P_{ij} = \begin{cases} 1 & \text{if } h(\boldsymbol{x}_i) \leq h(\boldsymbol{x}_j) \\ e^{-(h(\boldsymbol{x}_i) - h(\boldsymbol{x}_j)/T} & \text{if } h(\boldsymbol{x}_i) > h(\boldsymbol{x}_j) \end{cases} \tag{3}$$

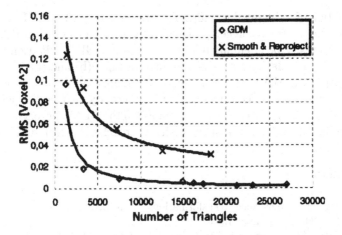

Fig. 6. Approximation error for both vertex optimization methods

In order to calculate the distance of an arbitrary point to the surface, the distance transformed volume is sampled at each vertex point and additionally at the center of gravity of each triangle. From these sample points the root mean square distance is calculated. As can be seen later the minimization of this average value results in high quality surface approximation. The optimization procedure terminates if the average vertex movement is below a given threshold value. The adaption algorithm is summarized as follows:

Adapt Mesh *(T)*
{
    loop {
        loop {
            remove short edges (T);
            remove redundant points (T);
            swap edges (T);
        } **until** *no more vertices are removed;*
        improve vertex positions (T);
        subdivision (T);
        swap edges (T);
        improve vertex positions (T);
    } **until** *the required accuracy is reached;*
}

7   Results

Results are presented for a bust of the composer Richard Wagner. The bust was reconstructed from 27 range images. The topology of the bust and a first approximation of its shape was sculptured in a volume of $23 \times 25 \times 16$ voxels. Fig. 5(a) shows the triangulation generated with the marching cube algorithm. Small edges have already been eliminated. Afterwards our GDM adaption procedure was applied to the data set as it is presented in Fig. 5(b) and (c).

Simultaneously the root mean square approximation error has been calculated as distance value of each triangle center of gravity resp. vertex point during each subdivision step. As can be seen from Fig. 6 the GDM approach leads to far lower approximation errors than the faster approach of smooth and reproject.

References

1. G. Borgefors.   Distance transformations in arbitrary dimensions.   *CVGIP*, 27(3):321–345, September 1984.
2. D.E. Breen, W.E. Lorensen, J.V. Miller, R.M. O'Bara, and M.J.Wozny. Geometrically deformed models: Method for extracting closed geometric models from volume data. *Computer Graphics*, 25(4):217–226, July 1991.
3. L. Ingber. Simulated annealing: Practice versus theory. *Mathl. Compu. Modelling*, 18(11):29–57, 1993.
4. W.E. Lorensen and H. E. Cline. Marching cubes: A high resolution 3d surface construction algorithm. *Computer & Graphics*, 21(4), 1987.
5. J.V. Miller. On GDM's: Geometrically deformed models for the extraction of closed shapes from volume data. Master's thesis, Rensselaer Polytechnic Institute, Troy, New York, December 1990.
6. C. Montani, R. Scateni, and R. Scopigno. A modified look-up table for implicit disambiguation of marching cubes. *Visual Computer*, 10(6), 1994.
7. P. J. Neugebauer. Reconstruction of Real-World Objects via Simultaneous Registration and Robust Combination of Multiple Range Images. *International Journal of Shape Modeling*, 3(1&2):71–90, 1997.
8. P. J. Neugebauer and K. Klein. Adaptive Triangulation of Objects Reconstructed from Multiple Range Images. In *IEEE Visualization '97, Late Breaking Hot Topics*, Phoenix, Arizona, Oktober, 20-24 1997.

The Use of Reality Models in Augmented Reality Applications

Gudrun Klinker, Didier Stricker, and Dirk Reiners

Fraunhofer Project Group for Augmented Reality at the ZGDV
Arabellastraße 17 (ECRC)
D-81925 Munich, Germany
{klinker, stricker, reiners}@igd.fhg.de
http://www.igd.fhg.de/www/igd-a4/

Abstract. Augmented reality (AR) is a technology by which a user's view of the real world is augmented with additional information from a computer model. AR applications require a very accurate model of the environment (a *reality model*) to augment the current view seamlessly with synthetic information (the *virtual model*). In this paper, we report on the problems we encountered with image data from real exterior construction sites. We discuss quality requirements for reality models in order to be useful in AR applications, and we outline potential further needs for reality models.

1 Introduction

With AR technology, users can work with and examine real 3D objects while receiving additional information about those objects or the task at hand [2, 3, 4, 21]. The virtual objects need to coexist in physically plausible manners with the real world: they occlude or are occluded by real objects, they are not able to move through real objects, and they cast shadows on such objects.

The automatic construction of reality models is a long-standing issue in computer vision research. In the context of the European CICC-project [7], we explore very applied, pragmatic approaches which are closely related to the requirements of rather realistic application pilots in the exterior construction. Other approaches towards semi-automatically generating architectural models from images have been reported by Debevec [9] and by Faugeras [10].

1.1 Reality Models for Exterior Construction Applications

Exterior construction applications impose very demanding challenges on the robustness and usability of evolving AR technologies. Real construction sites are huge. Information from many views, at close range and from long distances, has to be integrated. Furthermore, construction environments are not well structured. Natural objects such as rivers, hills, trees, and also heaps of earth or construction supplies are scattered around the site. Typically, no exact detailed 3D

Reinhard Koch, Luc Van Gool (Eds.): SMILE '98, LNCS 1506, pp. 275–289, 1998.

information of such objects exists making it difficult to generate a precise model of the site. Even worse, construction sites are in a permanent state of change. Buildings and landscapes are demolished, new ones are constructed. People and construction equipment move about, and the overall conditions depend on the weather and seasons. *Reality modelling* and *reality tracking* are thus very complex and demanding tasks. AR applications thus need to identify suitable simplified approaches for generating and dynamically maintaining appropriate models of the real environment.

1.2 AR Applications in Exterior Construction Projects

The first approach augments video sequences of large outdoor sceneries with detailed models of prestigious new architectures, such as TV towers and bridges that will be built to ring in the new milleneum (see Figure 1a). Since such video sequences are very complex, we currently pre-record the sequences and employ off-line, interactive calibration techniques to determine camera positions. Given all calibrations, the augmentation of the images with the virtual object is performed live, i.e., the virtual model can be altered and transformed while it is being seen in the video sequence.

The second approach operates on live video streams, calibrating and augmenting images as they come in. To achieve robust real-time performance, we need to use simplified, "engineered" scenes.

(a) Virtual bridge across   (b) Virtual wall and grid
a real river.   in a real room.

Fig. 1. Interactive vs. automatic video augmentation.

In particular, we place highly visible markers at precisely measured locations to aid the tracking process (Figure 1b). Such use of special markers is becoming a common practice [17, 20, 22, 24].

2   Reality Models

For optical camera calibration and to enforce physical interaction constraints between real and virtual objects, augmented reality systems need to have a precise description of the physical scene. Reality models don't need to be as complex as, for example, Virtual Reality (VR) models. VR models are expected to synthetically provide a realistic immersive impression of reality. Thus, the description of photometric reflection properties and material textures is crucial. AR, on the other hand, can rely on live optical input to provide a very high sense of realism. However, AR reality models have to be much more precise than VR models since users have an immediate quantitative appreciation of the quality of the integration between reality and augmentations.

2.1   Use of Existing Models

The most straightforward approach to acquiring 3D scene descriptions is to use existing geometric models, such as CAD data, output from GIS systems, and maps.

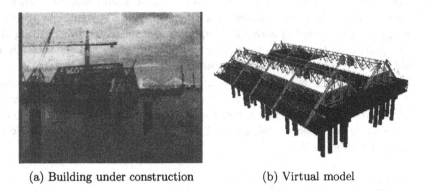

(a) Building under construction   (b) Virtual model

Fig. 2. Building under construction at the Expo 98 site in Lisbon.

Once a building has entered the construction phase, the virtual model of the building itself can begin serving as a reality model, as shown in Figure 2.

Yet, they cannot always be used for AR. The data in CAD models doesn't necessarily coincide with discernible features in images. Furthermore, the models often don't describe the evolving reality of a construction site in enough detail.

2.2   Manual Approach

The manual approach involves obtaining 3D measurements within the real world, using data bases and physical instruments. The 3D data points are entered into a small model. The approach works well when only very sparse reality models are needed but it cannot be used to generate elaborate descriptions of the real world. Figure 3a shows a thus generated reality model of our "tracking laboratory", a room with several carefully measured targets on its walls.

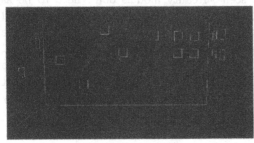
(a) Laboratory setup.

(b) At a real construction site.

Fig. 3. Example and use of manually created reality models.

Figure 3b shows use of a similar simplistic reality model of a small area at the Bluewater construction site in Kent, UK. The model data was collected with a 3D laser pointer that was attached to a differential GPS system. The location of the upper right corner of each black square was determined by orienting the 3D laser pointer at the square, thus yielding the orientation and distance (time-of-flight) between the square and the pointer.

Yet, the approach is prohibitively time-consuming, if thousands of points are to be measured this way to generate suitable surface approximations for occlucion handling. Furthermore, the approach depends upon the availability of professionals and special equipment. Thus, models cannot be expected to be obtainable on short notice.

2.3   Interactive Approach

In the European CICC project, we build a very sparse initial model of a landscape from external information such as maps and geodesic measurements. Our system helps us to interactively extend this model by superimposing it on a calibrated image. Models of new objects can then be entered into the model, using their two-dimensional position in a map and estimating their height from their alignment in several images.

From this model, we generate an initial camera calibration for a few site photos, interactively indicating how features in the image relate to the model (see Figure 4a).

Once an image has been successfully calibrated, the model is overlaid on the image, showing good alignment of the image features with the model features. Figure 4b illustrates the calibrated insertion of a new house into the model, using an initial much too large guess for the height of the building.

(a) Initial model.   (b) Interactively extended model.

Fig. 4. Interactively created and extended reality model of the city of London.

2.4 Towards Automatically Generated Models

Computer vision techniques are designed to automatically acquire three-dimensional scene descriptions from image data. Much research is currently under way, exploring various schemes to optically reconstruct a scene from multiple images, such as structure from motion [1, 10, 23, 25], (extended) stereo vision [9, 14, 16], and photogrammetric techniques [13].

In the context of the European project Cumuli [8], we explore to what extent automatically generated scene models can support AR and VR applications. In collaboration with INRIA and Lund University, we are developing and testing tools which exploit epipolar relationships between features in several images, geometric constraints on architectural structures, as well as city maps, to determine a set of progressively more precise projective, affine and finally euclidean properties of points in the three-dimensional scene.

Figure 5 shows a reconstructed model of the Arcades of Valbonne. Figure 5a shows the reconstructed geometric model. In Figure 5b, the model has been enhanced by mapping textures from the original image data onto the surfaces. Figure 5c illustrates how photo of the area can be augmented with synthetic objects, such as a Ferrari, once the images have been analyzed and calibrated.

2.5 Range Data Models

Alternatively to motion-based scene recognition, the RESOLV project uses three-dimensional range sensors to conduct a 3D survey of a building. The environment is scanned from a number of capture positions and reconstructed into a model, unifying measurements from all viewing positions (Figure 6). Surfaces are recognized by processing the range data and are textured from camera images.

2.6 Use of Reality Models for Camera Calibration

Precise camera calibration is a key issue in AR. Calibration algorithms are inherently sensitive to noise and to specific alignments of features in the reality

(a) Geometric model.   (b) Enhanced with texture maps.

(c) 2D picture of the plaza, augmented with a Ferrari.

Fig. 5. Automatically generated model of the arcades of Valbonne.

model. For example, houses in cityscapes tend to be aligned along a road or river. Many target features are thus approximately coplanar – considering a distance of several hundred meters between the camera and the houses – and cannot supply good 3-dimensional depth cues for camera calibration. In our work, we are emphasizing pragmatic concepts to cope with such real problems.

- Reality models should use targets in a nicely spread three-dimensional volume. For example, the inclusion of distant high rises and power poles in a model can greatly stabilize calibration results. The targets also need to be easily detectable and precisely locatable in image data.
- To help users correctly position image features, our system determines automatically which image feature currently has the largest influence on a calibration misalignment. By moving that feature by one pixel up, down, left, or right, a new calibration generates a much smaller mismatch between image features and projected scene features.
- We use as much externally available information as available, such as known internal camera parameters. Our algorithm can be further constrained when the approximate camera location and orientation is known from other tracking devices [15].

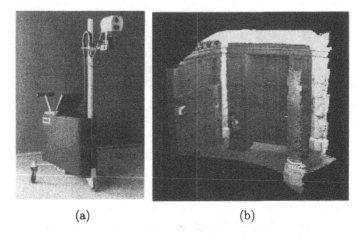

(a)   (b)

Fig. 6. a) RESOLV trolley b)Automatically generated model of part of the interior of the Royal Institute of Chartered Surveyors, London.

3 Augmenting Reality

With AR, such virtual geometric objects can be integrated into the real environment during all phases of the life cycle of a building. Before the construction project is started, AR can support marketing and design activities to help the customer visualize the new object in the environment (Figure 7). During construction, AR can help evaluate whether the building is constructed according to its design (Figure 8).

(a) Original scene.   (b) Augmented with planned footbridge.

Fig. 7. Side view of a new footbridge, planned to be built across the river Wear in Sunderland, UK.

Fig. 8. A virtual wall at a real construction site

(a) Original image.   (b) X-Ray view into the wall.

Fig. 9. Seeing the piping in the wall.

After the construction is completed, maintainance and repair tasks benefit from seeing hidden structures in or behind walls (Figure 9).

3.1   Occlusion Handling Using Geometric Reality Models or Depth Maps

Occlusions between real and virtual objects can be computed by geometric rendering hardware by first drawing the reality model transparently and then rendering the virtual objects. Other mixing approaches initialize the Z-Buffer from depth maps obtained with a laser scanner or stereo computer vision. As a result, the user sees a picture on the monitor that blends virtual objects with live video, while respecting 3D occlusion relationships between real and virtual objects (Figure 10).

Fig. 10. Virtual London bridge reflecting in the real water (partially occluded by the houses at the far side of the Thames).

3.2 Simulation of Illumination Effects and Physical Constraints

Objects in the real world not only determine their own shading, they also have an influence on the appearance of other, distant objects by means of shadows and reflections [11].

With the availability of reality models, the geometry of shadows cast by virtual objects onto real ones can be computed [22]. Reflections are a more difficult topic that can be solved for many useful special cases, such as reflections of virtual objects in planar real mirrors (Figure 10). Difficult to handle are reflective virtual objects, as in general they would have to reflect things from the surrounding environment that are not visible in the image. Rendering the reflections from the real environment onto virtual objects requires the availability of a high-quality reality model.

For an augmented world to be realistic the virtual objects not only have to interact optically with the real world, but also physically. This applies to virtual objects when animated or manipulated by the user. For example, a virtual chair shouldn't go through walls when it is moved, and it should exhibit gravitational forces [5]. Given a reality model, this behavior can be achieved using collision detection and avoidance systems that are known from Virtual Reality systems [26].

These two laws make up the most important physical constraints. A full physical simulation including more aspects of the interaction between real and virtual objects, such as elastic behavior and friction, would be desirable. For off-line applications this is possible if enough information about the virtual objects and a complete enough reality model is available. For real-time applications most simulation systems are not fast enough. Yet, even simple implementations of the above rules will make the system much more realistic.

4   Future Work

So far, we have used reality models for camera calibration, occlusion handling and a simple analysis of light reflections from virtual onto real objects. Yet, the concept of generating, using and updating reality models within AR applications goes far beyond this. We will now briefly allude to two other relevant aspects of AR that we expect to become important in the future.

4.1   Leaving Reality Behind

Augmented reality and virtual reality are not two discrete alternatives but rather part of a spectrum of mixed realities [21] with full virtual reality on one end and full physical reality on the other. Augmented Reality is in the middle, combining the best of both worlds. But sometimes it might be desirable to lean more in one direction or the other.

Since registered augmented reality by concept needs real images, its freedom of movement is limited to the places where an image recording device (possibly a human eye) can go. Virtual reality on the other hand allows complete freedom of movement, as computer generated images can be generated for every possible viewpoint. It may sometimes be desirable to leave the augmented reality behind and switch into the virtual reality to take a look from a point where it is physically impossible to go, e.g. from above.

When leaving reality behind, the view has to be constructed entirely from synthetic information, i.e., from the reality model plus new virtual objects. A very promising area of current computer graphics research in this direction is image based rendering [6, 12, 18, 19], which strives towards generating images from new viewpoints given some images from other viewpoints. A future system might employ a camera to record images while viewing the augmented scene and using them to incrementally refine the reality model. The ever-improving reality model allows the system to render increasingly realistic synthetic images from places that have not been visited by the user.

4.2   Diminishing Reality

Many construction projects require that existing structures be removed before new ones are built. Thus, just as important as augmenting reality is technology to diminish it.

Figure 11a shows one of several pictures of TV-towers on Monte Pedroso near Santiago de Compostela, Spain. Prior to augmenting the image with a model of a new TV tower, the existing towers need to be removed (Figure 11b). To this end, a part of the sky has to be extrapolated into the area showing the TV-towers and the barracks. Then the new tower can be put into place (Figure 11c).

We currently use interactive 2D tools to erase old structures from images (Figure14). This approach can only be used for static, individual photos, but not for video sequences from a live, dynamically moving camera.

(a) Original image.   (b) Diminished reality.   (c) Augmented reality.

Fig. 11. Monte Pedroso near Santiago de Compostela, Spain.

In principle, the problem of diminshing reality consists of two phases. First expiring buildings have to be identified in the image. When such structures are well represented in a reality model, they can be located by projecting the model into the image according to the current camera calibration.

The outdated image pixels then need to be replaced with new pixels. There is no general solution to this problem since we cannot know what a dynamically changing world looks like behind an object at any specific instant in time – unless another camera can see the occluded area. Yet, some heuristics can be used to solve the problem for various realistic scenarios. We can use morphological operators to extrapolate properties of surrounding "intact" areas (e.g: a cloudy sky) into outdated areas. Furthermore, when a building is to be removed from a densely populated area in a city, particular static snapshots of the buildings behind it could be taken and integrated into the reality model to be mapped as textures into the appropriate spaces of the current image. First results of such "X-ray vision" capabilities are shown in Figure 9b.

For video loops of a dynamically changing world, computer vision techniques can be used to suitably merge older image data with the new image. Faugeras et al. have shown that soccer players can be erased from video footage when they occlude advertisement banners: For a static camera, changes of individual pixels can be analyzed over time, determining their statistical dependence on camera noise. When significant changes (due to a mobile person occluding the static background) are detected, "historic" pixel data can replace the current values [27].

We use geometric constraints to compute pixelwise correspondences between regions in several images that outline a particular object (Figure 15). From such correspondances, we can trace specific points on the object across all images and we can decide in which images it is visible or occluded. Accordingly, occluded pixels can be replaced by visible ones, effectively removing the occluding object from the image. In more general schemes using mobile cameras, such techniques can lead towards incremental techniques to diminish reality. While moving about in the scene, users and cameras see parts of the background objects. When properly remembered and integrated into a three-dimensional model of the scene, such "old" image data can be reused to diminish newer images, thus increasingly effacing outdated objects from the scene as the user moves about.

Fig. 12. Automatic removal of a lego block.

5   Conclusions

Reality models are a crucial aspect of Augmented Reality work. Implicitly or explicitly, every AR application relies on knowledge about its surroundings in order to augment the reality appropriately. As reported in this paper, manual and semi-automatic techniques are commonly used to set up the models – a time consuming and complex task. Tools to automatically generate such models, e.g., via computer vision algorithms will greatly improve the quality and flexibility of AR applications. As a first step, the off-line generation of static scene descriptions will suffice. Yet, the long-term goal must be to automatically update and improve the models in real time while the application takes its course. At that point, AR applications will be able to deal with moving people and objects in the scene, such as objects that are being disassembled as part of the task. Users will also be able to temporarily leave reality behind to explore aspects otherwise unreached. Furthermore, they will not only be able to augment reality but also to diminish it, virtually removing objects by showing what is behind them – according to the current 3D information in the reality model.

Acknowledgments

The research is financially support by the CICC project (ACTS-017) in the framework of the European ACTS programme and by the Cumuli project (LTR-21914) in the ESPRIT programme. The laboratory space and the equipment is provided by the European Computer-industry Reseach Center (ECRC).

We are grateful to our current and former colleagues at Fraunhofer IGD, ZGDV and ECRC for many useful comments and insights which helped us develop and refine our work. Particular thanks go to Dieter Koller and Eric Rose who both participated in the research group in the past. Both the CICC and the Cumuli consortium have deeply influenced our approach.

Sources of Graphical Material

Sunderland Newcastle, UK (with Ove Arup and Partners): Figures 1a and 7a,b show a picture of the river Wear, Sunderland Newcastle, UK. The bridge model was provided by Sir Norman Foster and Partners.

Thames river, London, UK (with Ove Arup and Partners): Figures 4a,b, and 10 show pictures of the river Thames, London near St. Paul's Cathedral. The 3D model of a designed milleneum footbridge was provided Sir Norman Foster and Partners. The model was acquired for the CICC project by Ove Arup and Partners.

Bluewater Kent, UK (with Bovis and Trimble Navigation Limited): Figures 3b and 8b show a picture from a video sequence.

Santiago de Compostela, Spain (with Ove Arup and Partners): Figures 11a,b,c show a picture of Monte Pedroso near Santiago de Compostela, Spain. The model of the TV-tower was provided by Sir Norman Foster and Partners.

Gmunder Straße, Munich, Germany (with Philipp Holzmann AG, Germany): Figures 1b and 9a,b show indoor pictures of a bathroom under construction. Figure 8a shows an outdoor snapshot.

Valbonne, France (with INRIA Sophia-Antipolis): Figures 5a,b,c show a picture and a reconstructed model of the Arcades in Valbonne, France.

Royal Institute of Charted Surveyors, London, UK (work by U. Leeds, JRC and BICC): Figure 6 shows pictures of the RESOLV trolley and the reconstructed model of the Royal Institue of Charted Surveyors. Courtesy of the RESOLV project.

References

[1] A. Azarbayejani and A.P. Pentland. Recursive estimation of motion, structure, and focal length. *IEEE Trans. on Pattern Analysis and Machine Intelligence (PAMI)*, 17(6):562–575, June 1995.

[2] R.T. Azuma. A survey of augmented reality. *Presence, Special Issue on Augmented Reality*, 6(4):355–385, August 1997.

[3] W. Barfield and T. Caudell. *Augmented Reality and Wearable Computers*. Lawrence Erlbaum Press, 1998.

[4] J. Bowskill and J. Downie. Extending the capabilities of the human visual system: An introduction to enhanced reality. *Computer Graphics*, 29(2):61–65, 1995.

[5] D.E. Breen, E. Rose, and R.T. Whitaker. Interactive occlusion and collision of real and virtual objects in augmented reality. Technical Report ECRC-95-02, ECRC, Arabellastr. 17, D-81925 Munich, http://www.ecrc.de, 1995.

[6] S.E. Chen and L. Williams. View interpolation for image synthesis. In James T. Kajiya, editor, *Computer Graphics (SIGGRAPH '93 Proceedings)*, volume 27, pages 279–288, August 1993.

[7] CICC. Collaborative integrated communications for construction. ACTS AC-0017, 1995-1998, http://www.hhdc.bicc.com/cicc/, 1995.

[8] CUMULI. Computational Understanding of Multiple Images. Esprit LTR-21914, 1996-1999, http://www.inrialpes.fr/CUMULI/, 1996.

[9] P.E. Debevec, C.J. Taylor, and J. Malik. Modeling and rendering architecture from photographs: A hybrid geometry- and image-based approach. In *Proc. SIG-GRAPH*, pages 11-20, New Orleans, August 4-9 1996. ACM.

[10] O. Faugeras, S. Laveau, L. Robert, G. Csurka, and C. Zeller. 3D reconstruction of urban scenes from sequences of images. In A. Gruen, O. Kuebler, and P. Agouris, editors, *Automatic Extraction of Man-Made Objects from Aerial and Space Images*. Birkhauser, 1995.

[11] A. Fournier. Illumination problems in Computer Augmented Reality. *Journee Analyse/Synthese d'Images (JASI)*, pages 1-21, January 1994.

[12] S.J. Gortler, R. Grzeszczuk, R. Szeliski, and M.F. Cohen. The lumigraph. In Holly Rushmeier, editor, *SIGGRAPH 96 Conference Proceedings*, Annual Conference Series, pages 43-54. ACM SIGGRAPH, Addison Wesley, August 1996. held in New Orleans, Louisiana, 04-09 August 1996.

[13] B.K.P. Horn and M.J. Brooks. *Shape from Shading*. MIT Press, Cambridge, MA, 1989.

[14] T. Kanade, A. Yoshida, K. Oda, H. Kano, and M. Tanaka. A stereo machine for video-rate dense depth mapping and its new applications. In *Proc. 15th Computer Vision and Pattern Recognition Conference (CVPR)*, San Francisco, June 18-20 1996. IEEE.

[15] G. Klinker, D. Stricker, and D. Reiners. Augmented reality for exterior construction applications. In W. Barfield and T. Caudell, editors, *Augmented Reality and Wearable Computers*. Lawrence Erlbaum Press, 1998.

[16] G.J. Klinker, K.H. Ahlers, D.E. Breen, P.-Y. Chevalier, C. Crampton, D.S. Greer, D. Koller, A. Kramer, E. Rose, M. Tuceryan, and R.T. Whitaker. Confluence of computer vision and interactive graphics for augmented reality. *Presence: Teleoperators and Virtual Environments, special issue on Augmented Reality*, 6(4):433–451, August 1997.

[17] D. Koller, G. Klinker, E. Rose, D. Breen, R. Whitaker, and M. Tuceryan. Automated camera calibration and 3d egomotion estimation for augmented reality applications. In *7th Int'l Conf. on Computer Analysis of Images and Patterns (CAIP-97)*, Kiel, Germany, September 10-12, 1997, G. Sommer, K. Daniilidis, and J. Pauli (eds.), Lecture Notes in Computer Science **1296**, Springer-Verlag, Berlin, Heidelberg, New York, 1997.

[18] M. Levoy and P. Hanrahan. Light field rendering. In Holly Rushmeier, editor, *SIGGRAPH 96 Conference Proceedings*, Annual Conference Series, pages 31-42. ACM SIGGRAPH, Addison Wesley, August 1996. held in New Orleans, Louisiana, 04-09 August 1996.

[19] L. McMillan and G. Bishop. Plenoptic modeling: An image-based rendering system. In Robert Cook, editor, *SIGGRAPH 95 Conference Proceedings*, Annual Conference Series, pages 39-46. ACM SIGGRAPH, Addison Wesley, August 1995. held in Los Angeles, California, 06-11 August 1995.

[20] J.P. Mellor. Realtime camera calibration for enhanced reality visualization. In *Proc. of Computer Vision, Virtual Reality and Robotics in Medicine (CVRMed '95)*, pages 471-475, Nice, France, April 1995. IEEE.

[21] P. Milgram and F. Kishino. A taxonomy of mixed reality visual displays. *IEICE Transactions on Information Systems*, E77-D(12), December 1994.

[22] A. State, G. Hirota, D.T. Chen, W.F. Garrett, and M.A. Livingston. Superior augmented reality registration by integrating landmark tracking and magnetic tracking. In *Proc. SIGGRAPH*, pages 429–438, New Orleans, Aug 4-9 1996. ACM.

[23] R. Szeliski and S.B. Kang. Recovering 3d shape and motion from image streams using non-linear least squares. Technical Report CRL 93/3, Cambridge Research Lab, Digital Equipment Corporation, One Kendall Square, Bldg. 700, March 1993.

[24] M. Uenohara and T. Kanade. Vision-based object registration for real-time image overlay. In *Proc. of Computer Vision, Virtual Reality and Robotics in Medicine (CVRMed '95)*, pages 13–22, Nice, France, April 1995. IEEE.

[25] VANGUARD. Visualisation Across Networks using Graphics and Uncalibrated Acquisition of Real Data. ACTS AC-0074, 1995-1998, http://www.esat.kuleuven.ac.be/ konijn/vanguard.html, 1995.

[26] G. Zachmann. Real-time and exact collision detection for interactive virtual prototyping. In *Proc. of the 1997 ASME Design Engineering Technical Conferences*, Sacramento, CA, Sept 14–17 1997. ASME. CIE-4306.

[27] I. Zoghlami, O. Faugeras, and R. Deriche. Traitement des occlusions pour la modification d'objet plan dans une sequence d'image. Private communication; see also http://www.inria.fr/robotvis/ personnel/zimad/Orasis6/Orasis6/html, 1996.

Applying Augmented Reality Techniques in the Field of Interactive Collaborative Design

Hagen Schumann[1], Silviu Burtescu[1], and Frank Siering[2]

[1] Fraunhofer Institute for Computer Graphics,
Rundeturmstr. 6,
64283 Darmstadt, Germany
{schumann, burtescu}@igd.fhg.de
http://www.igd.fhg.de/www/igd-a7
[2] Computer Graphics Center,
Rundeturmstr. 6,
64283 Darmstadt, Germany

Abstract. In this paper we present a new interactive collaborative Augmented Reality system and demonstrate its functionalities in an collaborative design application. After a short investigation of the requirements of a collaborative AR-system we introduce the main components and key features of our implementation. An easy and intuitive method for augmenting video frames based on available 3D geometry is introduced. Our system is able to handle object interactions such as mutual occlusion of real and virtual objects or collision between objects of both types. 'Reality' is transmitted as a video stream to all partners in the collaboration. Compression technique is used to compress the PAL-size color video frames before transmission. Our system has been successfully tested in a test environment between Darmstadt and Rostock.

1 Introduction

Augmented Reality(AR) is similar to the widely known Virtual Reality (VR). In VR a user is completely immersed in a synthetic, computer-generated environment and cannot see the real world around him. In Augmented Reality a user is able to see his real environment and additional virtual objects are superimposed upon the users view. Therefore Augmented Reality enriches reality rather than completely replaces it. A user interacts with the real world in the usual, natural way and employs the computer simultaneously either to interact with virtual objects or to obtain additional information. As a result, compared with VR, AR requires less computer performance. Augmented Reality has been explored in several scenarios. In the field of medicine surgery can be trained, assisted and guided by superimposed, registered views of medical data (e.g. MRI, CT or ultrasound)[2][9][17]. Applications of Augmented Reality in the field of assembly, maintenance, and repair have been demonstrated[7][18][16]. Augmented Reality can also bee used for annotation [14][6], visualization [5] or planning purposes, e.g. urban planing[4]. Ahlers et al. demonstrated the use of Augmented

Reinhard Koch, Luc Van Gool (Eds.): SMILE '98, LNCS 1506, pp. 290–303, 1998.

Reality in the field of design[11]. In the field of design, Augmented Reality is a very promising technique. Visualization of products and new design ideas can be greatly improved by Augmented Reality. Nowadays the convincing presentation of new products is a lengthy and often very expensive task because realistic physical models or mock-ups have to be built. The use of computer-generated models in a VR scenario is an alternative to mock-ups or physical models. These models are then presented in virtual environments and users are allowed to explore them by flying over or walking through the models. In addition to that, Augmented Reality offers the advantage to present these computer models in the real environment, which can be given as a video, captured at the location where the real object will be placed later on. Users get a much clearer understanding and impression of the model within its intended real environment. In this paper we present an Augmented Reality system for design applications. Designing is often the task of a group and not only of a single person. Our system provides support for collaborative work of a group of users. A video stream of a real environment is distributed to all participants in the collaboration and functionalities are provided to collaboratively augment the video by adding and manipulating virtual objects. Interactions of real and virtual objects are taken into account by handling of occlusion and collision events.

2 System Requirements Analysis

2.1 Display Technology

Commonly used output devices in Augmented Reality systems are head-mounted displays (HMDs) (see-through[6] or non-see-through[17]) or computer monitors[11]. See-through HMDs in combination with electromagnetic trackers have the advantage that one does not have to deal with grabbing and displaying of video streams and only has to display virtual information. These systems are usually fast and can work in realtime. However, a significant disadvantage of see-through HMDs becomes apparent when mutual occlusion of virtual and real objects occurs. See-through HMDs cannot completely block off light from real objects at places were they are occluded by virtual ones and virtual objects always appear semi-transparent and are rather blended over instead into the real world. System latencies are critical, since synchronization of real world and virtual objects is a major problem. Virtual objects are delayed in movement when the user moves and appear rather to flow over the real world than to be part of it. Non-see-through HMDs display the real world as a video stream captured by one or usually two (for stereo) cameras attached to the HMD. The use of non-see-trough HMDs requires the additional afford to grab and display video streams. Compared to see-through-HMD, the use of non-see-through HMD requires a computer system with higher rendering performance. Synchronization is less problematic when using non-see-through HMDs since displaying of the augmented video frames can be delayed. "Floating" effects are only caused by registration errors. Mutual occlusion of real and virtual objects becomes possible since eg. depth information about the real world can be used when merging virtual objects and video. In collaborative AR-applications we must distinguish between two general scenarios. In scenario one all users are present at the same location, see virtual objects from different points and possibly interact with them. In the second scenario only one or a few users are present at the same location whereas other users are present at remote locations. In scenario one see-through HMDs can be used since the real world is directly available to all user. In the second scenario the real world is directly available only to a few users and has to be transmitted to other users. Non-see-through HMDs or computer monitors must therefore be used as output devices. In our collaborative design application where we assume that not all users are present at the same location computer monitors are used as output devices. A more comprehensive overview of displaying devices for Augmented Reality systems is given by Azuma[15] or Rolland et al.[13].

2.2 Tracking

Precise camera calibration and tracking is one of the most substantial problems in Augmented Reality. The demand of registration accuracy is much higher than in Virtual Reality. The reason for this demand lies in the nature of AR, in the combination of visual information with visual information. The human eye can easily detect offsets of a single pixel between e.g. a real object and its overlaid rendered model. To understand that we have to look at the anatomy of the human retina. Its central part, the so-called fovea, has a resolution of about 0.5 minute of arc[10]. Which means in that area the human eye can resolve alternating brightness bands that subtend one minute of arc. Most Augmented Reality systems use electromagnetic[14] or hybrid tracking technology[6][17] for tracking the movements of camera, user or objects. Vision-based tracking has been used by State et al. in an hybrid system[17] and by Koller et al.[12]. Electromagnetic tracking devices that are also commonly used in VR have an orientation accuracy of 0.15 (Polhemus Corporation 1996) and therefore are not able to track with the accuracy that is needed in AR[15]. Vision-based tracking is a very accurate but time consuming tracking methods. It fails when the used tracking marks are occluded or outside the field of view of the camera. Hybrid systems employing advantages of several tracking technologies may be most suitable for AR systems. Besides high accuracy and stability tracking techniques must offer feedback to measure and correct tracking errors. Standart electromagnetic tracking systems represent an "open-loop" controller system with no feed back of tracking errors to the system. There is no correleation between the tracking signal and the reference signal(video). With these kind of systems it is difficult to detect and correct tracking errors. In vision based tracking systems the tracking signal is identical with the reference signal and tracking errors can easily be detected, corrected and if desired fed back to the tracking system. The build up of a "closed-loop" controller system is therefore easier when using vision based tracking systems. In our collaborative AR applications we currently use vision-based tracking that employs tracking marks and kalman filter technique for fast and precise tracking.

2.3   Networking

Distribution of Augmented Reality is somewhat different from distributing e.g. VR. In AR not only virtuality and user interactions need to be distributed, but reality too in form of e.g. a video stream has to be transferred to all participants in the collaboration. Distribution of video streams means distribution of huge amounts of data. The normal approach to transfer only small images or images of low resolution cannot be accepted in AR since the "illusion" of reality is dominated by the view (video) of the real world. Therefore the network architecture that should be used in an distributed AR application must be able to handle a significant amount of data. There are several network architectures that are used in VR applications. Basically they can be reduced to three approaches: peer-to-peer, client-server and distributed. In the peer-to-peer model each user is connected to all other users by an one-to-one connection. Interactions have to transfer to each user separately. In an AR application such an approach is unacceptable, since the video stream would have to be transferred one time less than the number of users in the collaboration. Such an approach would decrease the performance of the application tremendously. However, this type of model is useful for creating private connections between certain users for e.g. distribution of restricted information or for audio channels. In the distributed approach, the state of the world is distributed amongst all users. This model is very complex and it is difficult to maintain data consistency and coherence. The third and most commonly used approach used is the client-server approach were data from a client are sent to the server and then become distributed to some or all other clients. This approach is ideal for filter operations which can lead to reduction of the network load. The server becomes a bottleneck when the number of users increases. Another problem in distributed applications is the location of data. This point needs consideration since it is very important for management mechanisms that have to be employed in order to maintain scene consistency. The most common data models are totally replicated database, shared central database and shared distributed database. In the last two models the database is stored just one time either at a central location or at several locations. In the case of a totally replicated database each user has its own database. Shared databases offer the advantage of an easy maintaining of scene consistency whereas a totally replicated database creates more problems concerning data consistency due to possible transfer losses or system latencies. In AR applications a total replicated database can be used when the users have computers with a high performance since in this case rendering is done locally and therefore all data have to be available locally. When using low-performance computers a central database may be more appropriate since rendering can be done by a central high-performance computer and only the rendered frames are sent to the user. Considering fast feedback for user interactions with virtual objects, a replicated database offers significant advantages. In our application we use a client-server architecture with a totally replicated database since we assume only a limited number of users in the collaboration using computers with a sufficiently high rendering performance.

3   Collaborative Design Application

3.1   Overview of the Augmented Reality System

In this chapter we present how Augmented Reality techniques can be used in a design application and give an overview of our collaborative Augmented Reality system.

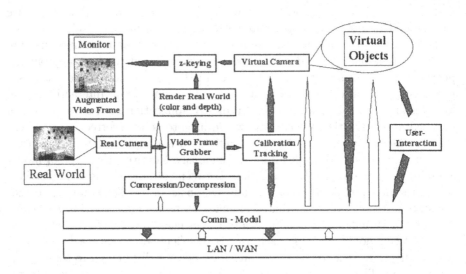

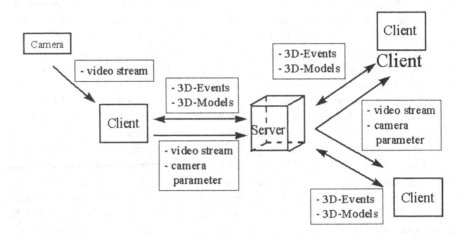

Fig. 1. Sketch of the principle components of our collaborative Augmented Reality system; top: local components(client); bottom: network structure

Figure 1 shows a sketch of the principal components of the implemented collaborative AR system. The input (video stream) is split and sent to the render system and to the tracking module. The video frame is rendered together with depth information of the real world. The calculated camera parameters are used to render the virtual objects. Video frame and virtual objects are combined by using z-keying. The combined video frame and virtual objects are then displayed. This approach leads to a delay in displaying the video frame but assures synchronization of video frame and rendered virtual objects. When a collaboration is established, video frame grabbing and tracking is done only by the client that controls the real camera. Video frames and calculated camera parameters are transmitted to all other users in the collaboration. The video frames are compressed prior to transmission. Virtual objects and interactions are sent to all users. In the following section we give a more detailed description of the implemented system.

3.2 User Interface

Figure 2 shows the user interface of our collaborative AR application. The collaborative scene is displayed in the main viewer. Additionally we provide two other viewer which allow the user to browse data bases and visualize objects without or before including them into the collaborative scene. In an collaborative session objects can be visualized locally (bottom viewer) or globally (top viewer). The model can be discussed about by all users and then be placed into the video. We do not share the camera position in this viewer to allow users an undisturbed investigation of the object. In a collaborative session users should be aware of their partners. We provide visual information about the partners in the collaboration by visualizing each partner as an icon on the interface below the viewer. In Figure 2 there are two icons representing two users. Note that there are three users in the collaboration since we do not visualize a user's own icon.

3.3 Calibration/Tracking

As already laid out, standard electromagnetic trackers work fast but not very accurate and are not suitable for AR applications. Optical tracking is much more time consuming and requires very fast computers but is very accurate. These algorithms work only in more or less tailored environments [12]. High accuracy is needed when dealing with occlusion problems which often occur in e.g. interior design applications. In our system we use an optical calibration and tracking algorithm that has been developed by Koller et al.[12] and is described in detail there. Here we give only a brief description. Figure 3 shows the setup that is used for camera calibration and tracking. The 8 black squares are used for calibration and tracking. The algorithm assumes that the exact 3D coordinates of the black squares are known. In a first calibration step the camera is calibrated fully automatically. The corners of the black squares are detected in the image with a sub pixel accuracy and matched with the known 3D-coordinates. Based on the sets of 2D-image and 3D-world coordinates the external and internal camera parameters are calculated. The black squares are also used for tracking. In each

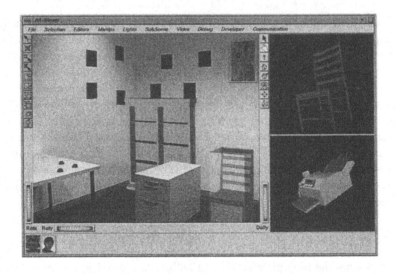

Fig. 2. User Interface of our AR-Application

frame the corners of the black squares are searched for locally. The starting point for the local search is predicted by applying extended kalman filter technique. Based on the new corner positions camera position and orientation are calculated and the kalman filter is updated.

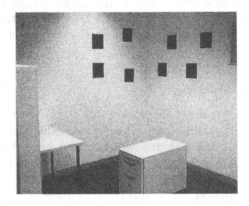

Fig. 3. Setup for calibration and tracking

3.4 Adding of Virtual Objects to the Real World

In Augmented Reality scenarios such as annotation, interactive placement or manipulation of objects is not necessary whereas in a design application users must be able to interact with the virtual objects. The used technique depends on the availability of geometrical information about the real world. In our collaborative design application we assume that a 3D-description of the real world is available. We use this to allow a very intuitive and easy way to incorporate virtual objects into the real world. Figure 4 shows an example. The interface allows a user to select and mark corresponding points in the video and on the visualized virtual object. These selected points are visualized as red spheres in order to give a visual feedback of the selection to the user. Based on these marked points position, orientation and, if desired, size of the virtual object is calculated and the object is then placed into the video frame. In the example a user wants to place the fax machine in the lower right window onto the table. He marks e.g. 3 points on the table and three points on the bottom of the fax machine. A copy of the fax machine is then placed at the marked 3D-position.

Fig. 4. Adding a virtual object to the video frame is done interactively by marking corresponding points in the scene; left(before including): red spheres on the table and on the bottom of the virtual object (fax machine in the lower right window); right(after including): The position, orientation and size of the virtual fax machine has been calculated and the object is placed into the video frame

3.5   Handling of Real - Virtual Object Interactions

An important issue in Augmented Reality is the handling of interactions between real and virtual objects. Basic interaction types are collision, occlusion and shadows. In some application fields such as annotation or guided surgery these kind of interactions are less important. In design applications one cannot neglect collision or occlusion handling. Proper collision and occlusion handling significantly increases the impression of virtual objects being part of the real world. Handling of collision and occlusion requires knowledge of the 3D geometry of the real world.

Mutual Occlusion of Real and Virtual Objects For occlusion handling two general cases must be dealt with. Real objects can occlude virtual ones and vice versa. Virtual objects can be combined with video frames by applying luminance keying. In this technique, virtual objects are rendered on a black background. Black areas are then replaced by the video signal. As a result of this technique, virtual objects always occlude real ones. Breen et al.[3] demonstrated occlusion handling in Augmented Reality by using a model-based and a depth-base method. Occlusion tests are performed on these depth-maps. Virtual objects are rendered in black and again luminance keying is used to achieve occlusion of virtual objects by real ones.

In our system z-keying is used to achieve occlusion effects. The known geometry of the real world, given as a polygonal model, is registered to the video frame and then rendered only into the z-buffer of the rendering system. The rendering process results in a registered depth map for each video frame of the real world. The virtual objects are then rendered using the initialized z-buffer for occlusion detection. Based on the result of the depth test, the color for each pixel of the output frame is chosen from the video or from the virtual object. Figure 5 shows an example for occlusion in AR. The virtual statue and chair occlude the real object wall and are partly occluded by the real office container.

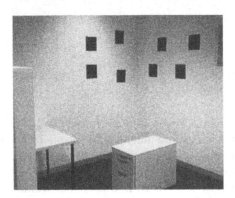 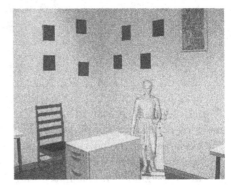

Fig. 5. left: Original video frame right: Virtual objects (chair, statue) occlude real objects (wall) and are partly occluded by a real object (office container)

Collision between Real and Virtual Objects Performing collision detection is more complicated than detection occlusion. Breen et al.[3] used registered depth-maps for collision detection. Collision is detected when the stored z-value is smaller than the z-value of a point of the bounding box of the virtual object. However this approach does not work in all cases. Consider a situation like the one depicted in Figure 5. The virtual chair can be moved behind the real office container since the office container stands sufficiently far away from the wall. The depth-map approach would not allow such a movement since the z-values of the chair are greater than the z-values of the container. Other approaches use axis aligned bounding box trees, sphere trees or oriented bounding box trees. In our application, where we assume that objects undergo only rigid motion, Oriented Bounding Box Trees (OBBTrees)[8] are used for accurate collsion detection at interactive rates. In this approach OBBTrees are calculated for each object and collision detection is carried out by performing hierarchical intersection tests between the OBBTrees of objects to be tested. This approach requires additional computing cost for calculating the OBBTree of each object. Fortunately this has to be done only once. In our implementation calculation of OBBTrees is done during initialization or when an object is added to the world. Figure 6 shows a sketch of the collision engine. When a user manipulates an object or a group of objects collision tests are performed between the manipulated objects (active objects) and all other objects (inactive objects) in the scene. No collision is performed between active objects. This can be done since in an active group objects do not change their position relative to other group members. A transformation that is applied to an active object is used to update the OBBTree and collision detection is performed at the new object position. When collision is detected the transformation is rejected and the OBBTree is reset. When no collision is detected the transformation is accepted and the OBBTree is not reset. The result of the collision detection is always returned to the AR application to allow further treatment. In case of collision we reject the last transformation and give an audible feedback to the user. As a result the object does not move any further when hitting another object. When no collision is detected, the transformation is accepted and the object is rendered at the new position. Moving objects in crowded worlds can be a lengthy and annoying task. To ease such tasks we allow the user to turn on and off collision detection interactively for selected objects. In the present implementation our collision detection engine is built upon RAPID[1].

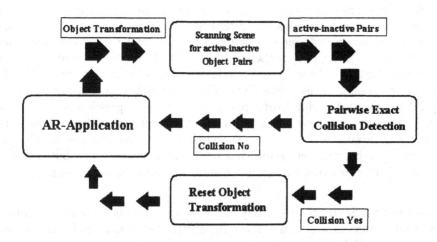

Fig. 6. Sketch of the collision engine

3.6 Distributing Augmented Reality

Network Architecture In our application we use a client-server architecture with a totally replicated database since we assume only a limited number of users in the collaboration using computers with a sufficiently high rendering performance. Figure 1 shows a sketch of the network architecture of our AR application and the principle data flow between the clients and the server. Transmission of video stream and camera parameter takes place only from one client to all other clients whereas transmission of 3D-models and 3D-events takes place from all clients to all clients.

Distributing 3D-Models and 3D-Events In a total replicated data base all models must be available locally at all clients sites and therefore needs to be distributed. Distributing large models over low bandwidth networks can take a considerable amount of time. Models should therefore be stored in an appropriate format such as VRML or OpenInventor. Both formats can be used to store 3D-information very effectively. VRML as an emerging standard for 3D description in the Internet is preferable but only an ASCII data format is specified. Our application is based on OpenInventor which offers the possibility to distribute objects in the binary OpenInventor format. Before distribution objects are written to a buffer in memory. After distribution the model data are read again from a buffer and included into the local data base. Distribution of 3D-events are less critical since only changes in transformation matrices need to be distributed.

Distributing of Video Stream and Camera Parameter A significant problem in collaborative AR applications is the distribution of the huge amount of data of the video stream. Several techniques can be used to reduce the amount of data. Size, resolution or number of channels of the frames can be reduced or compression techniques such as JPEG or MPEG can be used. In an AR application reduction of frame size or resolution cannot be used since the video frame is a significant part of the scene. MPEG offers a high compression rate but takes too long. The compression rate of JPEG is lower than that of MPEG but compression takes less time. Currently we use JPEG for frame compression and decompression. Using hardware compression/decompression instead of the currently used software solution will reduce the compression time significantly. Camera calibration and tracking is done only by the user who has the physical camera. Together with each frame the camera parameters are distributed so that synchronization between camera parameters and video frames is assured.

Maintaining Scene Consistency Since we use a totally replicated data base we need to take care of maintaining scene consistency and synchronizing user interactions. Global information about the data base(scene) are stored at a central position, the server. When a user interacts with the scene two general types of interactions are possible, global and local interactions. Local interactions and changes to the scene are not controlled by the server. Global interactions need to be authorized by the server before acceptance. Figure 7 shows an example for local and global interactions. User 1 marks points for including an object. The points are visualized as red spheres. This interaction is a local one and does not need to authorized and transmitted to other users. User 2 performs an global interaction by selecting an object(chair). The interaction needs to be authorized in order to maintain consistency of the scene. In the depicted example user 2 selects the chair. A locking request is sent to the server. The server compares the object with a list of locked objects. The chair is not locked by another user. The locking request is confirmed and a locking signal is sent to all other users. User 2 is allowed do manipulate the object whereas the object is locked for all other users. Locked objects are enclosed by an opaque bounding box to visualize the locking. When a locking request is rejected all manipulations done by the user who requested the lock are reset.

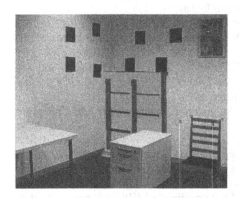 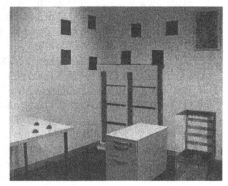

Fig. 7. left: local view of user 1; right: local view of user 2; user 1 performs local interaction (marking points for including an object); user 2 performs global interaction by selecting an object (chair)

4   Conclusion and Future Work

We have developed and tested an Augmented Reality system for interactive collaborative design tasks. Object interactions such as collision detection and occlusion are taken into account and handled byt the system. Fast and accurate collision detection is performed by using OBBTrees. Occlusion handling is based on geometric models of the real world. Video streams are compressed prior transmission to decrease network load. Scene consistency is maintained by applying locking mechanisms. The system has succesfully tested in trials between Rostock and Darmstadt. Besides the performed test trials we will test our collaborative design application in an transatlantic test environment between our institute in Darmstadt and our branch located in Providence (Rhode Island,

USA). Currently our system can only be used in pre-modeled static scenes. The used tracking algorithm relies on the black squares as tracking features. Future work will concentrate on the development of new tracking algorithms in order to be able to use our system in more general environments.

5 Acknowledgement

We are grateful for financial support from EU ACTS project VANGUARD (AC074).

References

[1] A Robust and Accurat Polygon Interference Detection library for large environments composed of unstructured models. http://www.cs.unc.edu/ geom/OBB/OBBT.html.

[2] Bajura, Mike, H.Fuchs, and R. Ohbuchi. Merging Virtual Reality with the Real World: Seeing Ultrasound Imagery Within the patient. In *Proceedings of SIG-GRAPH 92*, pages 26–31, 1992.

[3] D.Breen, E.Rose, R.Whitaker, and M. Tuceryan. Interactive Occlusion and Automatic Object Placement for Augmented Reality. In *EUROGRAPHICS 96 Proceedings*, pages 11–22. Blackwell Publisher, 1996.

[4] D. Drascic. Stereoscopic Vision and Augmented Reality. *Scientific Computing and Automation*, 9(7):31–34, 1993.

[5] D. Drascic, J. Grodski, P.Milgram, K. Ruffo, P. Wong, and S. Zhai. ARGOS: A Display System for Augmented Reality. In *Video Proceedings of INTERCHI 93: Human Factors in Computing Systems*, pages 24–29, April 1993.

[6] S. Feiner, B.MacIntyre, M. Haupt, and E. Solomon. Windows on the World: 2D Windows for 3D Augmented Reality. In *Proceedings of UIST 93*, pages 145–155, November 1993.

[7] S. Feiner, B. McIntyre, and D. Seligmann. Knowledge-based Augmented Reality. *Communications of the ACM*, 36(7):52–62, July 1993.

[8] S. Gottschalk, M. Lin, and D. Manocha. OBBTree: A Hierarical Structure for Rapid Interference Detection. In *Proceedings of ACM SIGGRAPH 96*, pages 171–180, 1996.

[9] W. Grimson, G. Ettinger, S. White, P. Gleason, T. Lozano-Prez, W. Wells, and R. Kikinis. Evaluating and Validating an Automated registration System for Enhanced Reality Visualization in Surgery. In *Proceedings of Computer Vision, Virtual Reality and Robotics in Medicine 95 (CVRMed 95)*, pages 3–12, April 1995.

[10] A. Jain. *Fundamentals of Digital Image Processing*. Prentice Hall, Englwood Cliffs, NJ, 1989.

[11] K.H.Ahlers, A.Kramer, D.E.Breen, P.Chevalier, C.Crampton, E.Rose, M.Tuceryan, R.T.Whitaker, and D.Greer. Distributed Augmented Reality for Collaborative Design Applications. In *Eurographics 95 Proceedings*, pages 3–14. Blackwell Publisher, Maastricht, NL, August 1995.

[12] D. Koller, G. Klinker, E. Rose, D. Breen, R. Whitaker, and M. Tuceryian. Real-time vision-based camera tracking for augmented reality applications. In *Proceedings of the Symposium on Virtual Reality Software and Technology*, September 1997.

[13] J.P. Rolland, R.L. Holloway, and H. Fuchs. A comparison of optical and video see-through head mounted displays. *SPIE Telemanipulator and Telepresence Technologies*, 2351:293–307, 1994.

[14] E. Rose, D. Breen, K. Ahlers, C. Crampton, M. Tuceryan, R. Whitaker, and D. Greer. Annotating Real-World Objects Using Augmented Reality. In *Proceedings of Computer Graphics International 95*, pages 357–370, June 1995.

[15] R.T.Azuma. A Survey of Augmented Reality. *Presence: Teleoperators and Virtual Environments*, 6(4):355–385, August 1997.

[16] D. Sims. New Realities in Aircraft Design and Manufacture. *IEEE Computer Graphics and Applications*, 14(2):91, March 1994.

[17] A. State, M. Livingston, G. Hirato, W. Garrett, H. Fuchs M. Whitton, and E. Pissano. Techniques for Augmented-Reality Systems: Realizing Ultrasound-Guided Needle Biopsies. In *Proceedings of SIGGRAPH 96*, pages 439–446, August 1996.

[18] M. Tuceryan, D. Greer, R. Whitaker, D. Breen, E. Rose C. Crampton, and K. Ahlers. Calibration Requirements and Procedures for Augmented Reality. *IEEE Transactions on Visualization and Computer Graphics*, 1(3):255–273, September 1995.

A Guided Tour Through Multiview Relations

Theo Moons

Katholieke Universiteit Leuven
ESAT / PSI, Kardinaal Mercierlaan 94
3001 Leuven, Belgium

Abstract. The aim of this paper is to give the non-specialist reader a comprehensible and intuitive introduction to multiview relations. It focusses on the geometric interpretation of the different image relationships, but also presents a concise mathematical formalism which allows to derive the algebraic expressions explicitly in an elementary and uniform manner. Special attention has been paid both to these multiview constraints as geometric incidence relations between image features (i.e. points and lines) in different views as well as to their use for image transfer. Moreover, an attempt has been made to provide sufficient pointers to the literature where the interested reader may find additional information on particular subjects as well as alternative viewpoints and mathematical formalisms.

1 Introduction

During the last years important progress has been made in the analysis and reconstruction of 3-dimensional (3D) scenes from multiple images and image sequences obtained by uncalibrated cameras. Many of these developments were made possible by the discovery and new insights gained in the interrelationships between corresponding geometric features observed in different images of the 3D scene. These *multiview relations* are derived and studied in an elaborate series of research papers by a multitude of methods and mathematical formalisms, each having there own advantages. For the interested, but non-specialist reader, however, it might not always be easy to select the reference that is best suited for his application. The aim of this paper therefore is to provide an intuitive and non-technical introduction to the key ideas and concepts of multiview relations. The focus of attention is on the geometrical interpretation of the interimage relationships and on how they relate to the 3-dimensional structure of the scene. As a stepping stone towards the different formal expressions encoutered in the literature, special care is taken to translate the geometrical relationships into algebraic formulas in a clear and concise manner which should help not only to memorize and recall the formulas, but also to provide the reader with a workable knowledge to derive the most favourable formulation for the problem at hand. Therefore, the mathematics is kept as simple as possible. Essentially, a working knowledge of linear algebra and analytical geometry suffice. Some familiarity with basic notions of projective geometry might be helpful, but is not a prerequisite for understanding the text.

Reinhard Koch, Luc Van Gool (Eds.): SMILE '98, LNCS 1506, pp. 304–346, 1998.
© Springer-Verlag Berlin Heidelberg 1998

It is clear that within the extend of this paper it is impossible to give a complete overview of all the results presented in the extensive literature on this subject, nor of the different approaches that have been used to derive them. Where possible, an attempt has been made to provide pointers to the literature where the interested reader may find additional information on particular topics or alternative viewpoints and mathematical formalisms. It should be realised, however, that also these references are not intended to provide a complete overview of the field.

The paper is organised as follows: Since our presentation is mainly geometric in nature, a good understanding of the image formation process is essential. Therefore, the paper opens in section 2 with an extensive treatment of the perspective camera model. Next, the binocular relations which hold between any two views of a static scene are discussed and the well-known epipolar constraint is derived in section 3. The trinocular relations between three views of the scene are elaborated in section 4. Apart from the underlying geometrical concept (sections 4.1 and 4.2), the interrelationship between the trifocal constraints for points and those for lines is explained in section 4.3. Special attention also goes to their use for point and line transfer between the images in section 4.4. The close connection between the epipolar and trifocal constraints is explored in section 4.5. The same "decoupling principle" then leads to the quadrinocular relations between four views and their interpretation in section 5. An interesting transfer principle between four views is derived as well. The general theory for n views is presented in section 6. It is first proven in section 6.1 that the relations between 5 or more views boil down to the epipolar, trifocal and quadrifocal constraints for the different image pairs, triples and quadruples that can be formed with the given views. Section 6.2 then completes the story by showing that the epipolar, trifocal and quadrifocal constraints presented in the previous sections cover all existing relations between two, three and four images.

Finally, it is emphasized that the results and insights formulated in this paper are influenced by many authors. Mentioning all publications to which this paper is indebted would amount to citing all the references listed at the end. However, the following articles have greatly influenced the presentation (in alphabetical order): [12,13,15,35,39,48,52].

2   The Perspective Camera Model

In this paper, the image formation process in a camera is modeled as a *perspective projection* of the scene onto an *image plane*. In mathematical terms, the *scene* is defined as a collection of points, lines and surfaces in Euclidean 3-space $I\!R^3$. The mathematical relation between the coordinates of a scene point and its projection in the image plane is easiest described in a *camera-centered reference frame*. This is a right-handed, orthonormal reference frame for the scene which is defined as in Figure 1 (left): The origin coincides with the center of projection (i.e. the center the lens of the camera), the Z-axis is the optical axis of the camera, and the XY-plane is the plane through the center of projection and perpendicular to the optical axis. The image plane is the plane with equation $Z = 1$. The camera-centered reference frame of the scene induces an orthonormal reference frame in the image, as depicted in the figure: The origin is the point of intersection of the image plane with the optical axis of the camera (i.e. the Z-axis); and the coordinate axes in the image are parallel to the X- and Y-axis of the camera-centered reference frame of the scene.

The image of a scene point $\mathbf{P}$ is the point of intersection $\mathbf{p}$ of the line through $\mathbf{P}$ and the origin of the camera-centered reference frame and the image plane with equation $Z = 1$. If $\mathbf{P}$ has coordinates $(X, Y, Z) \in \mathbb{R}^3$ with respect to the camera-centered reference frame, then the (u, v)-coordinates of its image $\mathbf{p}$ are $u = \frac{X}{Z}$ and $v = \frac{Y}{Z}$. It is important to note that the triple $(u, v, 1) \in \mathbb{R}^3$ can be interpreted both as the scene coordinates of the image point $\mathbf{p}$ with respect to the camera-centered reference frame, as well as *the direction vector of the ray of sight* of the camera which passes through the scene point $\mathbf{P}$.

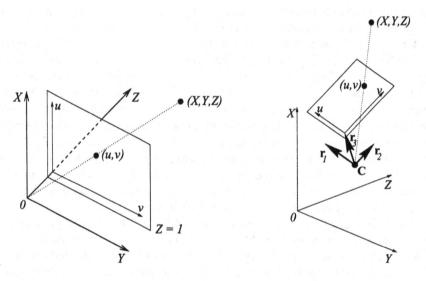

Fig. 1. Left: *In a camera-centered reference frame, the image of a scene point* (X, Y, Z) *is* $(u, v) = (\frac{X}{Z}, \frac{Y}{Z})$. Right: *The position and orientation of the camera in the scene are given by a position vector* $\mathbf{C}$ *and a* 3×3-rotation matrix $\mathbf{R}$. *The image* (u, v) *of a scene point* (X, Y, Z) *is then given by formula (1).*

When more than one camera is used, or when the objects in the scene are represented with respect to another, non-camera-centered reference frame (called the *world frame*), then the position and orientation of the camera in the scene is described by a point $\mathbf{C}$, indicating the origin, and a 3×3-rotation matrix R indicating the orientation of the camera-centered reference frame with respect to the world frame. More precisely, the column vectors $\mathbf{r}_i$ of the rotation matrix R are the unit direction vectors of the coordinate axes of the camera-centered reference frame, as depicted in Figure 1 (right). The coordinates of a scene point

P with respect to the camera-centered reference frame then are found by taking the dot products of the relative position vector **P** − **C** with the unit vectors $\mathbf{r}_i$; or equivalently, by pre-multiplying the column vector **P** − **C** with the transpose of the orientation matrix R : $R^t(\mathbf{P} - \mathbf{C})$. Hence, if **P** has coordinates (X, Y, Z) and **C** has coordinates (C_1, C_2, C_3) with respect to the world frame, then the projection of **P** into the image plane has (u, v)-coordinates:

$$
\begin{aligned}
u &= \frac{r_{11}(X - C_1) + r_{21}(Y - C_2) + r_{31}(Z - C_3)}{r_{13}(X - C_1) + r_{23}(Y - C_2) + r_{33}(Z - C_3)} \\
\text{and} \quad v &= \frac{r_{12}(X - C_1) + r_{22}(Y - C_2) + r_{32}(Z - C_3)}{r_{13}(X - C_1) + r_{23}(Y - C_2) + r_{33}(Z - C_3)} \;,
\end{aligned}
\tag{1}
$$

where r_{ij} is the (i, j)th entry of the rotation matrix R.

When working with digital images it is more natural to indicate the position of an image point in *pixel coordinates*. The transition from the geometrical (u, v)-coordinates to the pixel coordinates, which will be denoted as (x, y), is modeled by an (affine) transformation of the form:

$$
\begin{cases}
x = k_x\, u + s\, v + x_0 \\
y = k_y\, v + y_0
\end{cases}
\tag{2}
$$

Here, (x_0, y_0) are the pixel coordinates of the origin of the uv-reference frame, which is called the *optical center* of the image. k_x and k_y indicate the number of pixels per unit length in the horizontal and vertical direction respectively; and thus implicitly describe the length and width of a pixel. Their ratio k_x/k_y is called the *aspect ratio* of the camera. Furthermore, s measures how strong the shape of the pixels deviates from being rectangular. This parameter is usually referred to as the *skewness* of the pixels. $s = 0$ corresponds to rectangular pixels. Clearly, the numbers k_x, k_y and s depend on the focal length and the zooming distance of the lens. Together, k_x, k_y, s, x_0 and y_0 are referred to as the *intrinsic camera parameters*; whereas, the scene point **C** and the rotation matrix R representing the position and orientation of the camera, are called the *extrinsic camera parameters*.

More elegant formulas are obtained if one uses *extended coordinates* for the image points. In particular, if a point **p** in the image plane with pixel coordinates (x, y) is represented by the column vector $\mathbf{p} = (x, y, 1)^t$, and if its geometric coordinates (u, v) are represented by the column vector $(u, v, 1)$, then formula (2) becomes

$$
\mathbf{p} = \begin{pmatrix} x \\ y \\ 1 \end{pmatrix} = \begin{pmatrix} k_x & s & x_0 \\ 0 & k_y & y_0 \\ 0 & 0 & 1 \end{pmatrix} \begin{pmatrix} u \\ v \\ 1 \end{pmatrix} .
\tag{3}
$$

The 3×3-matrix

$$
K = \begin{pmatrix} k_x & s & x_0 \\ 0 & k_y & y_0 \\ 0 & 0 & 1 \end{pmatrix}
\tag{4}
$$

is called the *calibration matrix* of the camera. If $(u, v, 1)^t$ is interpreted as the direction vector of the ray of sight of the camera, which passes through the scene point $\mathbf{P}$, then the calibration matrix K can be viewed as *the transformation that relates an image point with its corresponding ray of sight in the camera-centered reference frame* of the camera. Furthermore, formula (1) can be rewritten as

$$\rho \begin{pmatrix} u \\ v \\ 1 \end{pmatrix} = \begin{pmatrix} r_{11} & r_{21} & r_{31} \\ r_{12} & r_{22} & r_{32} \\ r_{13} & r_{23} & r_{33} \end{pmatrix} \begin{pmatrix} X - C_1 \\ Y - C_2 \\ Z - C_3 \end{pmatrix} , \tag{5}$$

where $\rho = r_{13}(X - C_1) + r_{23}(Y - C_2) + r_{33}(Z - C_3)$ is a non-zero real number. Together, formulas (3) and (5) combine into the *projection equations*:

$$\rho \mathbf{p} = KR^t (\mathbf{P} - \mathbf{C}) \tag{6}$$

for some non-zero $\rho \in \mathbb{R}$. Many authors prefer to use extended coordinates for scene points as well. So, if $\tilde{\mathbf{P}} = (X, Y, Z, 1)^t$ are the extended coordinates of the scene point $\mathbf{P} = (X, Y, Z)^t$, then the projection equations (6) become

$$\rho \mathbf{p} = \left(KR^t \mid -KR^t\mathbf{C} \right) \tilde{\mathbf{P}} . \tag{7}$$

The 3×4-matrix $M = (KR^t \mid -KR^t\mathbf{C})$ is called the *projection matrix* of the camera. Readers who are familiar with projective geometry will observe that equation (7) defines a projective mapping from projective 3-space to projective 2-space. To this end, the extended coordinates $\mathbf{p}$ and $\tilde{\mathbf{P}}$ must be interpreted as (an instance of) the *homogeneous coordinates* of the corresponding image and scene point.

3 Relation Between Two Views: The Epipolar Constraint

When studying the relationships between different views of a static scene, it can be useful to ask oneself the following two questions:

(1) From which scene points can the geometric features (i.e. points and lines) that one observes in the image(s) be the projections?

(2) Where can these scene structures be observed in the other image(s)?

For example, a point $\mathbf{p}$ in one image is the projection of a scene point $\mathbf{P}$ that can be at any position along the ray of sight of the camera creating the image point $\mathbf{p}$. Therefore, the point $\mathbf{p}'$ corresponding to $\mathbf{p}$ in the second image (i.e. the projection $\mathbf{p}'$ of $\mathbf{P}$ in the second image) of the same scene must ly on the projection l' of this ray of sight in the second view, as depicted in Figure 2. To turn this into a mathematical formula, suppose for a moment that the camera parameters of both cameras are known. Then, according to formula (3), the direction of the ray of sight creating the image point $\mathbf{p}$ in the first camera is given by the 3-vector $K^{-1}\mathbf{p}$ in the camera-centered reference frame of the first camera, where K is the calibration matrix of the first camera. With respect to the world frame, this direction vector is $RK^{-1}\mathbf{p}$, where R is the rotation matrix expressing the orientation of the first camera in the world frame. As the position

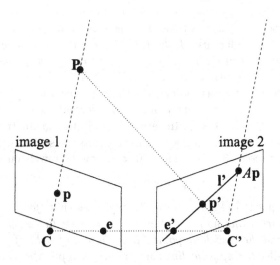

Fig. 2. *The point $\mathbf{p}'$ in the second image corresponding to a point $\mathbf{p}$ in the first image lies on the line $\mathbf{l}'$ which is the projection in the second image of the ray of sight creating the point $\mathbf{p}$ in the first camera.*

of the first camera in the world frame is given by $\mathbf{C}$, the parameter equations of the ray of sight in the world frame are:

$$\mathbf{P} = \mathbf{C} + \rho R K^{-1} \mathbf{p} \qquad \text{for some } \rho \in I\!\!R. \tag{8}$$

Note that this equation is just a rewriting of the projection equations (6). So, every scene point $\mathbf{P}$ satisfying equation (8) for some real number ρ projects onto $\mathbf{p}$ in the first image. If K', R' and $\mathbf{C}'$ are the camera parameters of the second camera, then, according to formula (6) again, the projection $\mathbf{p}'$ of $\mathbf{P}$ in the second image is given by

$$\rho' \mathbf{p}' = K' R'^t (\mathbf{P} - \mathbf{C}') \tag{9}$$

for some non-zero $\rho' \in I\!\!R$. Substituting expression (8) for $\mathbf{P}$ into this formula, yields

$$\rho' \mathbf{p}' = \rho K' R'^t R K^{-1} \mathbf{p} + K' R'^t (\mathbf{C} - \mathbf{C}') \ . \tag{10}$$

The last term in this equation corresponds to the projection $\mathbf{e}'$ of the position $\mathbf{C}$ of the first camera in the second image:

$$\rho'_e \mathbf{e}' = K' R'^t (\mathbf{C} - \mathbf{C}') \ . \tag{11}$$

$\mathbf{e}'$ is called the *epipole* of the first camera in the second image. The first term in the righthand side of the equality, on the other hand, indicates the direction of the ray of sight (8) in the second image. Indeed, recall that $R K^{-1} \mathbf{p}$ is the direction vector of the ray of sight in the world frame. In the camera-centered reference frame of the second camera, this vector is $R'^t R K^{-1} \mathbf{p}$. The corresponding position in the second image is then expressed (in homogeneous coordinates) by $K'R'^t R K^{-1} \mathbf{p}$. Put differently, $K'R'^t R K^{-1} \mathbf{p}$ *are the homogeneous coordinates of the vanishing point of the ray of sight (8) in the second image.*

To simplify the notation, put $A = K'R'^t RK^{-1}$. Then A is an invertible 3×3-matrix which, for every point $\mathbf{p}$ in the first view, gives the homogeneous coordinates $A\mathbf{p}$ of the vanishing point in the second view of the ray of sight observing $\mathbf{p}$ in the first camera. In terms of projective geometry, A is a matrix of the homography that maps the first image onto the second one via the plane at infinity of the scene [39]. Formula (10) can now be rewritten as

$$\rho' \mathbf{p}' = \rho A\mathbf{p} + \rho'_e \mathbf{e}' . \tag{12}$$

Observe that equation (12) algebraically expresses that, *for a given point $\mathbf{p}$ in one view, the corresponding point $\mathbf{p}'$ in the other view lies on the line $\mathbf{l}'$ through the epipole $\mathbf{e}'$ and the vanishing point $A\mathbf{p}$ of the ray of sight of $\mathbf{p}$* (see Figure 2). This line $\mathbf{l}'$ is called the *epipolar line* corresponding to $\mathbf{p}$ in the second image. This geometrical relationship is more efficiently expressed by formula (14) in the next proposition. But first, we fix some notation: for a 3-vector $\mathbf{a} = (a_1, a_2 a_3)^t \in \mathbb{R}^3$, let $[\mathbf{a}]_\times$ denote the skew-symmetric 3×3-matrix

$$[\mathbf{a}]_\times = \begin{pmatrix} 0 & -a_3 & a_2 \\ a_3 & 0 & -a_1 \\ -a_2 & a_1 & 0 \end{pmatrix} , \tag{13}$$

which represents the cross product with $\mathbf{a}$; i.e. $[\mathbf{a}]_\times \mathbf{v} = \mathbf{a} \times \mathbf{v}$ for all $\mathbf{v} \in \mathbb{R}^3$. Observe that $[\mathbf{a}]_\times$ has rank 2 if $\mathbf{a}$ is non-zero.

Theorem 1. (Epipolar constraint) [5,11] *For every two views I and I' of a static scene, there exists a 3×3-matrix F of rank 2, called the* fundamental matrix *of the image pair (I, I'), with the following property: If $\mathbf{p} \in I$ and $\mathbf{p}' \in I'$ are corresponding points in the images, then*

$$\mathbf{p}'^t F \mathbf{p} = 0 . \tag{14}$$

Moreover, the fundamental matrix F is given by $F = [\mathbf{e}']_\times A$, where $\mathbf{e}'$ is the epipole in I' and A is the 3×3-(homography-)matrix defined above.

Proof. According to equation (12), the point $\mathbf{p}' \in I'$ corresponding to $\mathbf{p} \in I$ lies on the epipolar line $\mathbf{l}'$ in I' which passes through $\mathbf{e}'$ and $A\mathbf{p}$. Since $\mathbf{p}'$, $\mathbf{e}'$ and $A\mathbf{p}$ actually are 3-vectors representing the homogeneous coordinates of the corresponding image points, this geometrical relationship is algebraically expressed as $|\mathbf{p}' \ \mathbf{e}' \ A\mathbf{p}| = 0$ where the vertical bars denote the determinant of the 3×3-matrix whose columns are the specified column vectors. Recall from linear algebra that this determinant equals

$$|\mathbf{p}' \ \mathbf{e}' \ A\mathbf{p}| = \mathbf{p}'^t (\mathbf{e}' \times A\mathbf{p}) ; \tag{15}$$

or, expressing the cross product as a matrix multiplication,

$$|\mathbf{p}' \ \mathbf{e}' \ A\mathbf{p}| = \mathbf{p}'^t [\mathbf{e}']_\times A \, \mathbf{p} . \tag{16}$$

This proves the theorem.   □

Remark 1. By definition of the fundamental matrix, $\mathbf{e}'^t F = 0$. So, the epipole $\mathbf{e}'$ in I' can be computed if F is known. Moreover, the epipolar constraint (14) brings, for each pair of corresponding image points $\mathbf{p}$ and $\mathbf{p}'$ in I and I' respectively, one homogeneous equation $\mathbf{p}'^t F \mathbf{p} = 0$ that is linear in the entries of the fundamental matrix F. Hence, F *can be computed linearly, up to a non-zero scalar factor, from (at least) 8 point correspondences between the two images.* Due to the presence of noise in the images, the matrix F computed from these point correspondences generally will not be of rank 2. Imposing the rank 2 constraint for the computation of F, however, results in a non-linear criterium. For an overview and comparison of different estimation procedures for F, the interested reader is referred to [26]. Robust methods for computing F can be found in [44].

4 Relations Between Three Views: The Trifocal Constraints

Next, suppose that three images of the same scene are given. If the fundamental matrices F_{13} and F_{23} between the first and the third, respectively the second and the third, view are known, then the position of the point $\mathbf{p}''$ in the third image, which corresponds to the points $\mathbf{p}$ in the first and $\mathbf{p}'$ in the second image, is easily found as the intersection of the epipolar lines $\mathbf{l}_1''$ of $\mathbf{p}$ and $\mathbf{l}_2''$ of $\mathbf{p}'$ in the third image, as is depicted in Figure 3. Unfortunately, this construction breaks

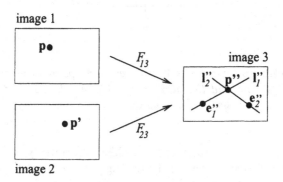

Fig. 3. *The point $\mathbf{p}''$ in the third image corresponding to the points $\mathbf{p}$ in the first and $\mathbf{p}'$ in the second view is the intersection of the epipolar lines $\mathbf{l}_1''$ and $\mathbf{l}_2''$ corresponding to $\mathbf{p}$ and $\mathbf{p}'$ respectively.*

down when the epipolar lines $\mathbf{l}_1''$ and $\mathbf{l}_2''$ coincide. This happens for scene points belonging to the plane defined by the three camera positions (i.e. the three centers of projection). Moreover, the construction is also poorly conditioned for scene points that are close to this plane. In [33] (see also [35]) trilinear relations between the homogeneous coordinates of corresponding points in three views were derived, which were proven to be are algebraically independent of the epipolar constraints in [23]. But, before writing down these formulas, let us examine the geometrical setting first.

4.1   The Fundamental Trifocal Constraint

The trifocal constraints essentially describe the geometric incidence relations between image points and lines in three views. The fundamental relationship is depicted in Figure 4 : Suppose **p**, **p′** and **p″** are corresponding points in three

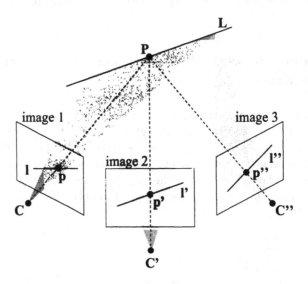

Fig. 4. *Two arbitrary lines* l′ *and* l″ *through corresponding points* **p′** *and* **p″** *in respectively the second and the third image define a line* **L** *in the scene whose projection* l *in the first image contains* **p**.

views I, I' and I'' of the same scene. Consider an arbitrary line l″ in the third image. The rays of sight in the world, creating the line l″ in I'', rule out a world plane π'' containing the center of projection **C″** of the third camera. Moreover, if the line l″ passes through **p″**, then this projecting plane π'' must also contain the scene point **P** of which **p**, **p′** and **p″** are the projections. Similarly, every line l′ through the point **p′** in the second view defines a projecting plane π' in the world which also contains **P**. Consequently, the projecting planes π' and π'' intersect in a line **L** through the point **P** in the scene. The projection l of **L** in the first image therefore must contain the image point **p** in I. Theorem 2 expresses this incidence relation algebraically. But first, we fix the following notation: An image line l with equation $a\,x + b\,y + c = 0$ is represented in the sequel by the column vector $(a, b, c)^t \in I\!\!R^3$. As the triple $(\lambda a, \lambda b, \lambda c)^t \in I\!\!R^3$ represents the same line for every non-zero $\lambda \in I\!\!R$, these column vectors have to be interpreted as the *homogeneous coordinates* of the given line. We will denote this by $l \simeq (a, b, c)^t$ where the symbol $\simeq$ means *"equality up to a scalar factor"*.

Theorem 2. (Fundamental trifocal constraint) [13] *For every three views* I, I' *and* I'' *of a static scene, there exists a* $3 \times 3 \times 3$-*tensor* $T = \left(T_k^{ij} \right)_{1 \leq i,j,k \leq 3}$, *called the* trifocal tensor *of the image triple* (I, I', I''), *with the following property: If* $\mathbf{p} \in I$, $\mathbf{p}' \in I'$ *and* $\mathbf{p}'' \in I''$ *are corresponding points in the images, then for every line* l' *through* $\mathbf{p}'$ *in* I' *and for every line* l'' *through* $\mathbf{p}''$ *in* I'',

$$l'^t [T\mathbf{p}] \, l'' = 0 , \tag{17}$$

where $[T\mathbf{p}]$ *is the* 3×3-*matrix whose* (i, j)th *entry is*

$$[T\mathbf{p}]_{ij} = T_1^{ij} x + T_2^{ij} y + T_3^{ij} \tag{18}$$

and with $\mathbf{p} = (x, y, 1)^t$. *Moreover, if, with the notations as before,* $A = \frac{1}{\rho'_e} K' R'^t R K^{-1}$ *and* $B = \frac{1}{\rho''_e} K'' R''^t R K^{-1}$, *then*

$$[T\mathbf{p}] = (A\mathbf{p}) \, e''^t - e' (B\mathbf{p})^t , \tag{19}$$

where e' *and* e'' *are the epipoles of the first camera in the second and the third view respectively. Furthermore, the entries* T_k^{ij} *of the trifocal tensor* T *are given by*

$$T_k^{ij} = a_{ik} (e'')_j - b_{jk} (e')_i \qquad \text{for } 1 \leq i, j, k \leq 3, \tag{20}$$

where $(e')_i$ *and* $(e'')_j$ *are the* ith *and* jth *entry of the epipoles* e' *and* e'', *and with* a_{ij} *and* b_{ij} *being the* (i, j)th *entry of the matrices* A *and* B *respectively.*

The theorem is proven by rephrasing the previous geometrical construction in algebraic terms. But first, we need to know how to find the projecting plane of a line in the image.

Lemma 1. [12] *The projecting plane* π *of a line* l *in the image obtained by a camera with projection matrix* $M = (KR^t \mid -KR^t C)$ *has equation*

$$l^t K R^t (\mathbf{P} - \mathbf{C}) = 0 \tag{21}$$

in the world frame. Homogeneous coordinates for π *are given by the 4-vector* $\pi \simeq M^t l \in \mathbb{R}^4$.

Proof. A world point $\mathbf{P}$ belongs to the projecting plane π generating the line l in the image *if and only if* the projection $\mathbf{p}$ of $\mathbf{P}$ in the image lies on the line l ; i.e. $l^t \mathbf{p} = 0$. According to the projection equations (6), $\mathbf{p}$ is given by $\rho \mathbf{p} = K R^t (\mathbf{P} - \mathbf{C})$ for some non-zero scalar $\rho \in \mathbb{R}$. Substituting this expression for $\mathbf{p}$ in the equality $l^t \mathbf{p} = 0$ yields formula (21) of the lemma. Using extended coordinates $\tilde{\mathbf{P}} = (X, Y, Z, 1)^t$ for the world points $\mathbf{P} = (X, Y, Z)^t$, equation (21) becomes $l^t (KR^t \mid -KR'^t C) \tilde{\mathbf{P}} = 0$. The middle matrix in the lefthand side of this equality is the projection matrix M of the camera. So, the equation can simply be rewritten as $l^t M \tilde{\mathbf{P}} = 0$, implying that the 4-vector $M^t l \in \mathbb{R}^4$ are homogeneous coordinates for π, as claimed by the lemma. □

Proof of Theorem 2. Let $\mathbf{P}$ be the scene point of which $\mathbf{p}$, $\mathbf{p}'$ and $\mathbf{p}''$ are the projections in the different images. According to Lemma 1, $\mathbf{P}$ belongs to the projecting plane π' generating the line $\mathbf{l}'$ in the second camera if and only if

$$\mathbf{l}'^t K' R'^t (\mathbf{P} - \mathbf{C}') = 0 \ . \tag{22}$$

Similarly, the scene point $\mathbf{P}$ belongs to the projecting plane π'' generating the line $\mathbf{l}''$ in the third camera if and only if

$$\mathbf{l}''^t K'' R''^t (\mathbf{P} - \mathbf{C}'') = 0 \ . \tag{23}$$

As $\mathbf{P}$ projects onto $\mathbf{p}$ in the first image, it must also ly on the ray of sight observing $\mathbf{p}$ in the first camera; i.e.

$$\mathbf{P} = \mathbf{C} + \rho \, R K^{-1} \mathbf{p} \qquad \text{for some } \rho \in I\!R, \tag{24}$$

by formula (8). Substituting this expression for $\mathbf{P}$ in equations (22) and (23) gives

$$\begin{cases} \mathbf{l}'^t K' R'^t (\mathbf{C} - \mathbf{C}') \ \ + \rho \, \mathbf{l}'^t K' R'^t R K^{-1} \mathbf{p} \ = 0 \\ \mathbf{l}''^t K'' R''^t (\mathbf{C} - \mathbf{C}'') + \rho \, \mathbf{l}''^t K'' R''^t R K^{-1} \mathbf{p} = 0 \end{cases} \tag{25}$$

Remember from formula (11) that $K' R'^t (\mathbf{C} - \mathbf{C}') = \rho'_e \, \mathbf{e}'$ gives the epipole $\mathbf{e}'$ of the first camera in the second view; and that $K'' R''^t (\mathbf{C} - \mathbf{C}'') = \rho''_e \, \mathbf{e}''$ gives the epipole $\mathbf{e}''$ of this camera in the third image. Take A and B as in the theorem. Then, after division by the non-zero scalars ρ'_e and ρ''_e respectively, system (25) becomes

$$\begin{cases} \mathbf{l}'^t \mathbf{e}' \ + \rho \, \mathbf{l}'^t A \mathbf{p} \ = 0 \\ \mathbf{l}''^t \mathbf{e}'' + \rho \, \mathbf{l}''^t B \mathbf{p} = 0 \end{cases} \tag{26}$$

Eliminating the unknown scalar $\rho \in I\!R$ in the previous two equations, gives

$$\left(\mathbf{l}'^t A \mathbf{p} \right) \left(\mathbf{l}''^t \mathbf{e}'' \right) - \left(\mathbf{l}'^t \mathbf{e}' \right) \left(\mathbf{l}''^t B \mathbf{p} \right) = 0 \ . \tag{27}$$

As $\mathbf{l}'^t \mathbf{e}' = \mathbf{e}'^t \mathbf{l}'$ and $\mathbf{l}''^t (B \mathbf{p}) = (B \mathbf{p})^t \mathbf{l}''$, equation (27) can be rewritten as

$$\mathbf{l}'^t \left[(A \mathbf{p}) \, \mathbf{e}''^t - \mathbf{e}' \, (B \mathbf{p})^t \right] \mathbf{l}'' = 0 \ . \tag{28}$$

Observe that the expression between square brackets is just the 3×3-matrix $[T\mathbf{p}]$ given in formula (19). The (i,j)th entry of this matrix is

$$[T\mathbf{p}]_{ij} = (A\mathbf{p})_i \, (\mathbf{e}'')_j - (\mathbf{e}')_i \, (B\mathbf{p})_j \ . \tag{29}$$

Using $\mathbf{p} = (x, y, 1)^t$, it follows from formula (18) that

$$T_k^{ij} = a_{ik} (\mathbf{e}'')_j - b_{jk} (\mathbf{e}')_i \qquad \text{for } 1 \le i, j, k \le 3, \tag{30}$$

as claimed by the theorem.   □

Remark 2. First of all, observe that the trifocal constraint (17) expresses a trilinear algebraic relation between (the homogeneous coordinates of) 1 image point and 2 image lines. In tensor terminology, this is expressed by stating that the trifocal tensor has one *covariant* and two *contravariant* indices, viz. k and ij respectively. Furthermore, it should also be emphasized that the lines l' and l'' in the theorem do *not* need to be *corresponding* lines in the images. Secondly, the attentive reader will have noticed the scalar factor $\frac{1}{\rho'_e}$ in the definition of the matrix A (and a similar factor in that of B), which was not present in the definition of A in section 3. Due to these factors, the scalars ρ'_e and ρ''_e could be factored out in the equations of system (26); thus resulting in nicer looking formulas. Since the epipolar constraint (14) in Theorem 1 is linear and homogeneous in the entries of the fundamental matrix F, defining A as $A = \frac{1}{\rho'_e} K' R'^t R K^{-1}$ in section 3 as well, will not affect the epipolar constraint (14) at all. Moreover, it is observed in Remark 1 that the fundamental matrix F can only be retrieved from the image data up to a non-zero scalar multiple. So, replacing A by $A = \frac{1}{\rho'_e} K' R'^t R K^{-1}$ will not even be noticed in practice.

4.2   The Trifocal Constraint for Corresponding Lines

The trifocal constraint (17) implies relations between corresponding points and between corresponding lines in three views, as we will show next. Recall that equation (17) actually expresses algebraically that the line l in the first image, which corresponds to the lines l' and l'' in respectively the second and the third image, passes through the image point $\mathbf{p} = (x, y, 1)^t$. Hence, the equation of l must follow directly from equation (17).

Proposition 1. (Trifocal constraint for lines) [12] *With the same notations as in Theorem 2: If l' and l'' are corresponding lines in the images I' and I'' respectively, then the homogeneous coordinates of the corresponding line l in the first view I are (up to a non-zero scalar factor) given by*

$$l \simeq \left(l'^t T_1 l'' , \, l'^t T_2 l'' , \, l'^t T_3 l'' \right)^t , \tag{31}$$

where T_k is the 3×3-matrix whose (i,j)-th entry is T_k^{ij}.

Proof. It follows directly from formula (18) that

$$[T\mathbf{p}] = T_1 x + T_2 y + T_3 . \tag{32}$$

Hence, equation (17) can be written as

$$l'^t \left(T_1 x + T_2 y + T_3 \right) l'' = 0 ; \tag{33}$$

or equivalently,

$$\left(l'^t T_1 l'' \right) x + \left(l'^t T_2 l'' \right) y + \left(l'^t T_3 l'' \right) = 0 . \tag{34}$$

As $\mathbf{p}$ can be any point on the line l, the latter formula actually is the equation of the line $l \simeq \left(l'^t T_1 l'' , \, l'^t T_2 l'' , \, l'^t T_3 l'' \right)^t$ in the first image.   □

Remark 3. Whereas the epipolar constraint (14) is the "simplest" — in the sense that it involves the smallest number of views — constraint that must hold between corresponding points in different images, so is equation (31) *the "simplest" constraint that must hold between corresponding lines in different images.* Indeed, if only two views of the scene are given, then any pair of lines in the two views might be corresponding lines, because they can always be interpreted as being the images of the intersection line **L** of their projecting planes, as observed before. To verify whether this is indeed the case, a third view — and Proposition 1 — is needed. In fact, formula (31) actually predicts where the corresponding line is to be found in the image. In other words, equation (31) allows to *transfer* lines from two images to a third one. In this respect, it is worth noting that the geometric construction underlying Theorem 2 and *Proposition 1 degenerates* if the projecting planes π' and π'' of the image lines l' and l'' coincide. This happens precisely *when* l *and* l'' *are corresponding epipolar lines* in the views I' and I'' respectively. Theorem 2, however, remains valid even in this case. Finally, it also interesting to note that the matrices T_k of the proposition can be written in matrix form as

$$T_k = \mathbf{a}_k\, \mathbf{e}''^t - \mathbf{e}'\, \mathbf{b}_k^t \qquad \text{for } 1 \leq k \leq 3, \tag{35}$$

with $\mathbf{e}'$ and $\mathbf{e}''$ the epipoles of the first camera in the second and the third views respectively, and where $\mathbf{a}_k$ and $\mathbf{b}_k$ denote the kth column of the matrices A and B of Theorem 2. Clearly, the range of T_k is contained in the linear subspace of $I\!R^3$ spanned by $\mathbf{a}_k$ and $\mathbf{e}'$. Hence, except for certain special camera configurations [31,29], T_k is of rank 2.

4.3   The Trifocal Constraints for Corresponding Points

On the other hand, the trifocal constraint (17) in Theorem 2 holds for *every* choice of lines l' and l'' through the corresponding points $\mathbf{p}'$ and $\mathbf{p}''$ in images I' and I'' respectively. All the lines l'' through a given point $\mathbf{p}''$ form a *pencil of lines* (i.e. a 1-parameter family of lines) in image I'', whose *top* is the point $\mathbf{p}''$. Recall from analytic geometry that the homogeneous coordinates of any line l'' in the pencil can be expressed as a linear combination of the homogeneous coordinates of two arbitrary, but fixed lines l_1'' and l_2'' in that pencil. When working with rectangular images, a natural choice for l_1'' and l_2'' are the horizontal $\mathbf{h}''$ and the vertical $\mathbf{v}''$ line passing through the image point $\mathbf{p}''$, as depicted in Figure 5. Hence, every line l'' through the point $\mathbf{p}''$ in I'' can be written as

$$l'' = \alpha\,\mathbf{h}'' + \beta\,\mathbf{v}'' \qquad \text{for some } \alpha, \beta \in I\!R. \tag{36}$$

The trifocal constraint (17) can thus be re-expressed as

$$\alpha\, l'^t\, [T\mathbf{p}]\, \mathbf{h}'' + \beta\, l'^t\, [T\mathbf{p}]\, \mathbf{v}'' = 0 \qquad \text{for all } \alpha, \beta \in I\!R; \tag{37}$$

or equivalently, by the system of equations

$$\begin{cases} l'^t\, [T\mathbf{p}]\, \mathbf{h}'' = 0 \\ l'^t\, [T\mathbf{p}]\, \mathbf{v}'' = 0 \end{cases} \tag{38}$$

Fig. 5. *Every line* l″ *through the image point* p″ *can be expressed as a linear combination of (the homogeneous coordinates of) the horizontal line* h″ *and the vertical line* v″ *through* p″.

because α and β are arbitrary real numbers. If the image coordinates of p″ are (x'', y'') — i.e. $\mathbf{p}'' = (x'', y'', 1)^t$ — then the horizontal line h″ through p″ has equation $y = y''$ and the vertical line v″ through p″ has equation $x = x''$. The homogeneous coordinates of h″ and v″ thus respectively are

$$\mathbf{h}'' \simeq (0, -1, y'')^t \quad \text{and} \quad \mathbf{v}'' \simeq (1, 0, -x'')^t \ . \tag{39}$$

System (38) yields *two algebraic equations involving the coordinates of corresponding image points* p *and* p″ *in respectively the first and the third view and an arbitrary line* l″ *passing through* p′ *in the second view*. This relationship will be discussed further in section 4.4 (Proposition 3) below.

Similarly, the line l′ passing through the point p′ in the second image can be written as a linear combination $\mathbf{l}' = \alpha' \mathbf{h}' + \beta' \mathbf{v}'$ of the horizontal line $\mathbf{h}' \simeq (0, -1, y')^t$ and the vertical line $\mathbf{v}'' \simeq (1, 0, -x')^t$ throught $\mathbf{p}' = (x', y', 1)^t$ in I'. Substituting this expression for l′ in system (38) yields

$$\begin{cases} \alpha' \, \mathbf{h}'^t \, [T\mathbf{p}] \, \mathbf{h}'' + \beta' \, \mathbf{v}'^t \, [T\mathbf{p}] \, \mathbf{h}'' = 0 \\ \alpha' \, \mathbf{h}'^t \, [T\mathbf{p}] \, \mathbf{v}'' + \beta' \, \mathbf{v}'^t \, [T\mathbf{p}] \, \mathbf{v}'' = 0 \end{cases} \tag{40}$$

Since these equations must hold for all $\alpha', \beta' \in \mathbb{R}$, it follows that

$$\begin{cases} \mathbf{h}'^t \, [T\mathbf{p}] \, \mathbf{h}'' = 0 \\ \mathbf{v}'^t \, [T\mathbf{p}] \, \mathbf{h}'' = 0 \\ \mathbf{h}'^t \, [T\mathbf{p}] \, \mathbf{v}'' = 0 \\ \mathbf{v}'^t \, [T\mathbf{p}] \, \mathbf{v}'' = 0 \end{cases} \tag{41}$$

These four, linearly independent, equations, which together are equivalent with the trifocal constraint (17) of Theorem 2, express the algebraic relations that must hold between the coordinates of corresponding image points in three views. Substituting the homogeneous coordinates of h′, v′, h″ and v″, and expanding the expressions, yields the well-known formulas calculated in [33] (see also [35]). An easier way to remember and use them is in the following form.

Proposition 2. (Trifocal constraints for points) [33] *If I, I' and I" are three views of a static scene, then each triple* **p**, **p'** *and* **p"** *of corresponding points in I, I' and I" respectively satisfies the matrix equation*

$$[\mathbf{p}]_\times [T\mathbf{p}]\,[\mathbf{p'}]_\times = 0_3 , \tag{42}$$

where $[T\mathbf{p}]$ *is the* 3×3*-matrix defined in Theorem 2 (formula (18)). Moreover, of the 9 relations collected in equation (42) only the 4 constraints that constitute the upper* 2×2*-submatrix are linearly independent relations.*

Proof. As **h'**, **v'**, **h"** and **v"** are column vectors and $[T\mathbf{p}]$ is a 3×3-matrix, system (41) can be written in matrix form as

$$\begin{pmatrix} \mathbf{h'}^t \\ \mathbf{v'}^t \end{pmatrix} [T\mathbf{p}]\,(\mathbf{h"}\ \mathbf{v"}) = 0_2 . \tag{43}$$

Substituting the homogeneous coordinates of **h'**, **v'**, **h"** and **v"**, gives

$$\begin{pmatrix} 0 & -1 & y' \\ 1 & 0 & -x' \end{pmatrix} [T\mathbf{p}] \begin{pmatrix} 0 & 1 \\ -1 & 0 \\ y" & -x" \end{pmatrix} = 0_2 . \tag{44}$$

Note that the leftmost matrix is formed by the first two rows of the skew-symmetric 3×3-matrix $[\mathbf{p'}]_\times$ that represents the cross product with the 3-vector $\mathbf{p'} = (x', y', 1)$, as defined in formula (13). Also recall that the rank of the matrix $[\mathbf{p'}]_\times$ is 2. As the first two rows of $[\mathbf{p'}]_\times$ clearly are linearly independent, the third row of $[\mathbf{p'}]_\times$ must be a linear combination of the first two. And indeed,

$$\text{row } 3 = -x'\,(\text{row } 1) - y'\,(\text{row } 2) . \tag{45}$$

Because the trifocal constraint (17) is linear in the 3-vector **l'**, adding this third row to the leftmost matrix of equation (44) will just add another 2 valid (but linearly dependent) relations to system (43). In fact, we just add the 2 equations in system (40) with $\alpha' = -x'$ and $\beta' = -y'$ to the matrix equation (44) (or equivalently, to system (41)). Hence, matrix equation (44) becomes

$$\begin{pmatrix} 0 & -1 & y' \\ 1 & 0 & -x' \\ -y' & x' & 0 \end{pmatrix} [T\mathbf{p}] \begin{pmatrix} 0 & 1 \\ -1 & 0 \\ y" & -x" \end{pmatrix} = 0_{3\times2} . \tag{46}$$

Similarly, the columns of the rightmost matrix in the lefthand side of equation (46) are, up to sign, the first two columns of the 3×3-matrix $[\mathbf{p"}]_\times$ that represents the cross product with the 3-vector $\mathbf{p"} = (x", y", 1)^t$. And again, the third column of $[\mathbf{p"}]_\times$ can be written as a linear combination of the first two:

$$\text{column } 3 = -x"\,(\text{column } 1) - y"\,(\text{column } 2) . \tag{47}$$

By the linearity of the trifocal constraint (17) in the 3-vector **l"**, adding this column to the rightmost matrix in the lefthand side of equation (46) will just add another 3 valid (but linearly dependent) relations to system (46). This brings us to

$$\begin{pmatrix} 0 & -1 & y' \\ 1 & 0 & -x' \\ -y' & x' & 0 \end{pmatrix} [T\mathbf{p}] \begin{pmatrix} 0 & 1 & -y'' \\ -1 & 0 & x'' \\ y'' & -x'' & 0 \end{pmatrix} = 0_3 \ , \qquad (48)$$

which, up to sign, is formula (42) of the proposition. □

4.4 The Trifocal Constraints as Incidence Relations and as Transfer Principle

Before going on, it is worth summarizing the different relations between three views, which have been derived yet. Table 1 gives an overview of the different trifocal relations ordered by the number and type of corresponding and incident geometric image features involved. The *"constraint"* number refers to the formula number where this constraint is expressed, and the *"number of equations"* refers to the number of *linearly independent* equations that exists for the homogeneous coordinates of the image features involved in that particular type of constraint. Except for constraint (31), which *predicts* the position of the line

image features	constraint	no. of equations
three points	(42)	4
two points, one line	(38)	2
one point, two lines	(17)	1
three lines	(31)	2

Table 1. *Overview of the different types of trifocal constraints.*

in the first view that corresponds to two given lines in the second and the third view respectively, all the (other) constraints express geometric *incidence* relations between the image features in the three views. In this form, the relations are well-suited for *verifying* whether particular image features — specified by their image coordinates — in the different views might be *corresponding* features of the image triplet. The trifocal constraint (31) for lines can also be expressed in this form by eliminating the common scalar factor.

Corollary 1. (Trifocal constraint for lines revisited) *Let I, I' and I'' be three views of a static scene. Three lines l, l' and l'' are corresponding lines in I, I' and I'' respectively — i.e. l, l' and l'' are the projections of one and the same 3D line in I, I' and I'' — if and only if*

$$\begin{cases} \ell_1 \left(l'^{t} T_3 \, l'' \right) - \ell_3 \left(l'^{t} T_1 \, l'' \right) = 0 \\ \ell_2 \left(l'^{t} T_3 \, l'' \right) - \ell_3 \left(l'^{t} T_2 \, l'' \right) = 0 \end{cases} \qquad (49)$$

where T_k are the 3×3-matrices defined in Proposition 1, and with $l = (\ell_1, \ell_2, \ell_3)^t$.

□

Remark 4. When corresponding image features are identified in the three views, then the relevant incidence relations summarized above all bring homogeneous linear equations in the entries T_k^{ij} of the trifocal tensor T. Hence, T can be computed linearly, up to a non-zero scalar factor, from these equations provided sufficient corresponding points and lines can be identified in the three views. More precisely, the trifocal constraint (42) for corresponding image points yields four linearly independent equations in the entries of T for each triple of corresponding points in I, I' and I'' ; and, the trifocal constraint (49) for corresponding image lines brings two linearly independent equations in the entries of T for each triple of corresponding lines in I, I' and I''. Because T has $3^3 = 27$ entries which have to be determined up to a non-zero scalar multiple only because all the relations in Table 1 are linear in the entries of T, *T can be computed linearly, up to a non-zero scalar factor, from n_p point and n_ℓ line correspondences between the three views if $4\,n_p + 2\,n_\ell \geq 26$* [13]. Consequently, T can be determined linearly, up to a non-zero scalar factor, from a minimum of 7 point correspondences or 13 line correspondences alone. But, as has been observed in section 4.2, each of the matrices T_k defined in Proposition 1 (see also formula (35)) has rank 2. Moreover, it has been proven in [38] that the rank of the trifocal tensor T is 4. In fact, the entries T_k^{ij} of T satisfy 8 non-linear algebraic relations such that T actually only has 18 degrees of freedom [7,22]. Due to the presence of noise in the images, the tensor T computed linearly from point and line correspondences between the images generally will not satify these non-linear relations. Imposing these relations in the computation of T, however, results in non-linear criteria [18,9,49]. A robust method for computing T can be found in [45] with improvements in [46].

Apart from having incidence relations which can be used to verify whether specific image points and lines in the different views are corresponding features, formulas such as the trifocal constraint (31) for lines, which predict where the corresponding feature in one view must be when their positions in the other two views are known, are also very useful. Therefore, we will now show how the trifocal constraints (42) for points can be used to *transfer* points from two views to a third one.

Corollary 2. (Trifocal constraint for points revisited) *Let I, I' and I'' be three views of a static scene. If $\mathbf{p}$ and $\mathbf{p}'$ are corresponding points in the images I and I' respectively, then the (extended) coordinates of the corresponding point $\mathbf{p}''$ in the third view I'' are (up to a non-zero scalar factor) given by*

$$\rho''\,\mathbf{p}'' = [T\mathbf{p}]_{1*}^t - x'\,[T\mathbf{p}]_{3*}^t \quad and \quad \tau''\,\mathbf{p}'' = [T\mathbf{p}]_{2*}^t - y'\,[T\mathbf{p}]_{3*}^t \ , \qquad (50)$$

where $[T\mathbf{p}]_{k*}$ denotes the kth row of the 3×3-matrix $[T\mathbf{p}]$ defined in Theorem 2, and with $\rho, \tau \in \mathbb{R}$ being non-zero scalar factors. In case of noise-free data, both equations are equivalent.

Proof. Recall from Proposition 2 that only the upper 2×2-submatrix in formula (42) yields linearly independent equations for $\mathbf{p}''$. This submatrix is given by formula (44) :

$$\begin{pmatrix} 0 & -1 & y' \\ 1 & 0 & -x' \end{pmatrix} [T\mathbf{p}] \begin{pmatrix} 0 & 1 \\ -1 & 0 \\ y'' & -x'' \end{pmatrix} = 0_2 \ . \tag{51}$$

Selecting the first row in the left matrix and the first column in the right matrix of the lefthand side of the equation, yields the relation

$$\begin{pmatrix} 0 & -1 & y' \end{pmatrix} [T\mathbf{p}] \begin{pmatrix} 0 \\ -1 \\ y'' \end{pmatrix} = 0 \ ; \tag{52}$$

or equivalently, when solving for y'',

$$\left\{ [T\mathbf{p}]_{23} - y' [T\mathbf{p}]_{33} \right\} y'' = [T\mathbf{p}]_{22} - y' [T\mathbf{p}]_{32} \ , \tag{53}$$

where $[T\mathbf{p}]_{ij}$ is the (i,j)th entry of the 3×3-matrix $[T\mathbf{p}]$. Similarly, the first row in the left matrix and the second column in the right matrix of the lefthand side of equation (51), yields the relation

$$\begin{pmatrix} 0 & -1 & y' \end{pmatrix} [T\mathbf{p}] \begin{pmatrix} 1 \\ 0 \\ -x'' \end{pmatrix} = 0 \ ; \tag{54}$$

or equivalently, when solving for x'',

$$\left\{ [T\mathbf{p}]_{23} - y' [T\mathbf{p}]_{33} \right\} x'' = [T\mathbf{p}]_{21} - y' [T\mathbf{p}]_{31} \ . \tag{55}$$

Equations (53) and (55) can be combined into the following matrix equation:

$$\left\{ [T\mathbf{p}]_{23} - y' [T\mathbf{p}]_{33} \right\} \begin{pmatrix} x'' \\ y'' \\ 1 \end{pmatrix} = \begin{pmatrix} [T\mathbf{p}]_{21} - y' [T\mathbf{p}]_{31} \\ [T\mathbf{p}]_{22} - y' [T\mathbf{p}]_{32} \\ [T\mathbf{p}]_{23} - y' [T\mathbf{p}]_{33} \end{pmatrix} \ . \tag{56}$$

Putting $\tau'' = [T\mathbf{p}]_{23} - y' [T\mathbf{p}]_{33}$ and using $\mathbf{p}'' = (x'', y'', 1)^t$ transforms this equation exactly into the right equation of formula (50) in the proposition. The left equation in formula (50) follows in exactly the same manner if one repeats this reasoning with the second row of the leftmost matrix in equation (51). □

Not only the trifocal constraints for points and for lines can be used to transfer corresponding image features from two views to a third one. The *2 points/ 1 line* relation (38) mentioned in Table 1 also provides an interesting transfer principle which goes as follows: Suppose a point $\mathbf{p}$ in the first view I and a line $\mathbf{l}'$ in the second view I' are given. Moreover, suppose that the line $\mathbf{l}'$ actually is the projection in I' of a line $\mathbf{L}$ in the scene that passes through the scene point $\mathbf{P}$ of which $\mathbf{p}$ is the projection in I ; but, that, for some reason or another, you are not able to identify the projection $\mathbf{p}'$ of $\mathbf{P}$ in I'. If the camera parameters of both cameras would be known, then the ray of sight creating the image point $\mathbf{p}$ in the first camera can be computed from formula (8); and, the projecting plane generating the line $\mathbf{l}'$ in the second camera is given by formula (21). The intersection of that ray of sight with this projecting plane gives the position of the underlying point $\mathbf{P}$ in the scene, as depicted in Figure 6. Generally, the camera

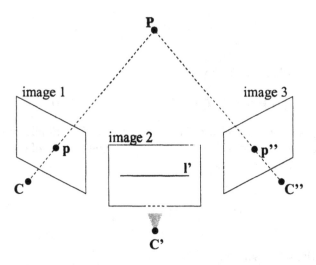

Fig. 6. *A line $\mathbf{l}'$ in the second image, containing the (possibly unknown) point $\mathbf{p}'$ corresponding to a point $\mathbf{p}$ in the first image suffices to compute the position of the point $\mathbf{p}''$, corresponding to $\mathbf{p}$ and $\mathbf{p}'$, in the third view.*

parameters are not known, but the projection $\mathbf{p}''$ of $\mathbf{P}$ in a third view can be determined from the *2 points / 1 line* relation (38) in Table 1, as is shown in the following proposition.

Proposition 3. (Point − line transfer) [52] *Let I, I' and I'' be three views of a static scene. If $\mathbf{p}$ is a point in image I and $\mathbf{l}'$ is a line in image I' which contains the (possibly unknown) point $\mathbf{p}'$ of I' corresponding to $\mathbf{p}$, then the (extended) coordinates of the point $\mathbf{p}''$ in the third view I'', corresponding to $\mathbf{p}$ (and $\mathbf{p}'$), are (up to a non-zero scalar factor) given by*

$$\tau'' \, \mathbf{p}'' = [T\mathbf{p}]^t \, \mathbf{l}' \, , \tag{57}$$

where $[T\mathbf{p}]$ is the 3×3-matrix defined in Theorem 2, and with $\tau'' \in \mathbb{R}$ being a non-zero scalar factor.

Proof. Recall that relation (38) consists of the following system of equations:

$$\begin{cases} \mathbf{l}'^t \, [T\mathbf{p}] \, \mathbf{h}'' = 0 \\ \mathbf{l}'^t \, [T\mathbf{p}] \, \mathbf{v}'' = 0 \end{cases} \tag{58}$$

where $\mathbf{h}''$ and $\mathbf{v}''$ are column vectors representing homogeneous coordinates of the horizontal and the vertical line through $\mathbf{p}''$ in I'' respectively (cf. formula (39)). Substituting the homogeneous coordinates $\mathbf{h}'' \simeq (0, -1, y'')^t$ and $\mathbf{v}'' \simeq (1, 0, -x'')^t$ for $\mathbf{h}''$ and $\mathbf{v}''$ in the system (58) yields two equations that can be solved for x'' and y'' explicitly, as we did in the proof of Corollary 2. But, the system can also be solved in a more analytical geometry-like manner. Indeed, system (58) can be interpreted as stating that the 3-vector

$$\left(\mathbf{l}'^t \, [T\mathbf{p}] \right)^t = [T\mathbf{p}]^t \, \mathbf{l}' \tag{59}$$

are homogeneous coordinates of an image point that lies both on the lines $\mathbf{h}''$ and $\mathbf{v}''$. Since, by construction, $\mathbf{p}''$ is the point of intersection of $\mathbf{h}''$ and $\mathbf{v}''$, the proposition follows. □

It is an easy exercise to verify that the geometrical construction of the point $\mathbf{p}''$ explained just before the statement of Proposition 3 really coincides with the point $\mathbf{p}''$ defined by formula (57) in the proposition. Indeed, given the image point $\mathbf{p}$ in the first image, the parameter equations of the ray of sight observing $\mathbf{p}$ in the first camera, according to formula (8), are

$$\mathbf{P} = \mathbf{C} + \rho \, RK^{-1} \mathbf{p} \qquad \text{with } \rho \in \mathbb{R} \; ; \tag{60}$$

and, by formula (21) in Lemma 1, the equation of the projecting plane π' generating the line $\mathbf{l}'$ in the second camera is

$$\mathbf{l}'^t K' R'^t \, (\mathbf{P} - \mathbf{C}') = 0 \; . \tag{61}$$

The point $\mathbf{P}$ of intersection of that ray of sight with the projecting plane π' is found by substituting expression (60) into formula (61) :

$$\mathbf{l}'^t \left\{ K' R'^t \, (\mathbf{C} - \mathbf{C}') + \rho \, K' R'^t RK^{-1} \mathbf{p} \right\} = 0 \; . \tag{62}$$

Recall from formula (11) that $K' R'^t (\mathbf{C} - \mathbf{C}') = \rho'_e \, \mathbf{e}'$ gives the epipole $\mathbf{e}'$ of the first camera in the second image, and from Theorem 2 that the matrix A in the definition of the trifocal tensor T is defined by $A = \frac{1}{\rho'_e} K' R'^t RK^{-1}$. Hence, equation (62) is equivalent to

$$\mathbf{l}'^t \mathbf{e}' + \rho \, \mathbf{l}'^t A\mathbf{p} = 0 \; . \tag{63}$$

This latter formula fixes the value of the parameter ρ of the scene point $\mathbf{P}$ in equation (60).

The projection $\mathbf{p}''$ of $\mathbf{P}$ in the third view, on the other hand, is given by the projection equations (cf. formula 6) :

$$\rho'' \mathbf{p}'' = K'' R''^t (\mathbf{P} - \mathbf{C}'') \ . \tag{64}$$

Substituting expression (60) for $\mathbf{P}$ in this equation, gives

$$\rho'' \mathbf{p}'' = K'' R''^t (\mathbf{C} - \mathbf{C}'') + \rho K'' R''^t R K^{-1} \mathbf{p} \ . \tag{65}$$

Using, as before, that $K'' R''^t (\mathbf{C} - \mathbf{C}'') = \rho''_e \mathbf{e}''$ gives the epipole $\mathbf{e}''$ of the first camera in the third image, and that the matrix B in the definition of the trifocal tensor T is defined by $B = \frac{1}{\rho''_e} K'' R''^t R K^{-1}$, one obtains

$$\rho'' \mathbf{p}'' = \rho''_e \mathbf{e}'' + \rho \rho''_e B \mathbf{p} \ . \tag{66}$$

Eliminating the non-zero scalar ρ from equations (63) and (66), and dividing by the non-zero scalar ρ''_e, one finds that

$$\tau'' \mathbf{p}'' = \mathbf{e}'' \left(\mathbf{l}'^t A \mathbf{p} \right) - \left(\mathbf{l}'^t \mathbf{e}' \right) B \mathbf{p} \ , \tag{67}$$

where $\tau'' = \frac{\rho''}{\rho''_e} (\mathbf{l}'^t A \mathbf{p})$. As $\mathbf{l}'^t A \mathbf{p} = (A \mathbf{p})^t \mathbf{l}'$ and $\mathbf{l}'^t \mathbf{e}' = \mathbf{e}'^t \mathbf{l}'$, equation (67) can be rewritten as

$$\tau'' \mathbf{p}'' = \left[\mathbf{e}'' (A \mathbf{p})^t - (B \mathbf{p}) \mathbf{e}'^t \right] \mathbf{l}' \ . \tag{68}$$

The expression between square brackets is the transpose of the 3×3-matrix $[T\mathbf{p}]$ in formula (19) of Theorem 2. This again proves Proposition 3.

Remark 5. In terms of projective geometry, the geometrical construction described here is *the homography that maps the first image plane onto the third one via the projecting plane of the line* $\mathbf{l}'$ *in the second image* [52]. It is also interesting to note that the projection $\mathbf{p}'$ of the scene point $\mathbf{P}$ on the line $\mathbf{l}'$ in the second view, which initially may be unknown, can now be calculated using the point transfer principle formulated in Corollary 2 (when switching the rôles of I' and I'', of course). Furthermore, it is worth mentioning that this geometrical construction underlying *Proposition 3 degenerates* if the ray of sight of $\mathbf{p}$ in the first camera lies into the projecting plane π' of the line $\mathbf{l}'$ for the second camera. This situation happens *when* $\mathbf{l}'$ *is the epipolar line corresponding to* $\mathbf{p}$ *in the second view.*

4.5   The Connection Between Epipolar and Trifocal Constraints

At first sight, there does not seem to be a direct connection between the epipolar and trifocal constraints discussed above. The epipolar constraint (14) gives a relation between (the coordinates of) corresponding image points in two views, whereas the fundamental trifocal constraint (17) expresses a relation between an image point in the first view and arbitrary lines through the corresponding point in the second and in the third view. The connection, however, lies in the word "arbitrary". Indeed, it was observed in section 4.3 that all the lines passing through a given point in the image form a pencil of lines (i.e. a 1-parameter family of lines) in that image, having the given point as top (see Figure 5). In other words, instead of considering 1 point in an image, it is completely equivalent to consider *all* the lines through that point in the image. At the scene level, an image point defines a ray of sight generating this point in the camera. A pencil of lines in the image, on the other hand, generates at the scene level a pencil (i.e. a 1-parameter family) of planes — viz. the projecting planes of the lines in the image — which all have the ray of sight of the top of line pencil in the image in common. So again, considering a ray of sight in the world space is completely equivalent to considering a pencil of projecting planes having this ray of sight in common. Remember that the epipolar constraint (14) expresses algebraically that, in order for a point $\mathbf{p}'$ in the second image I' to correspond to a point $\mathbf{p}$ in the first image I — i.e. in order for $\mathbf{p}$ and $\mathbf{p}'$ to be the projections of one and the same scene point $\mathbf{P}$ — $\mathbf{p}'$ must ly on the epipolar line corresponding to $\mathbf{p}$ in I': and that this epipolar line actually is the projection in I' of the ray of sight generating the image point $\mathbf{p}$ in the first camera. Put differently, the epipolar constraint essentially expresses that in order for two image points $\mathbf{p} \in I$ and $\mathbf{p}' \in I'$ to be corresponding, the two rays of sight generating $\mathbf{p}$ and $\mathbf{p}'$ in respectively the first and the second camera must intersect in the world space. Now, if one interprets the pencils of lines through the image points $\mathbf{p}'$ and $\mathbf{p}''$ in the trinocular case as projecting planes ruling out the rays of sight of $\mathbf{p}'$ and $\mathbf{p}''$ in the world space, then the trifocal constraint (17) basically expresses that the three rays of sight defined by the three corresponding image points must intersect in one and the same scene point. Indeed, all lines $\mathbf{l}'$ through $\mathbf{p}'$ in the second image rule out all possible world planes containing the projection center $\mathbf{C}'$ of the second camera and the scene point $\mathbf{P}$ of which $\mathbf{p}$, $\mathbf{p}'$ and $\mathbf{p}''$ are the projections in the respective images. Similarly, all lines $\mathbf{l}''$ through $\mathbf{p}''$ in the third image rule out all possible world planes containing the projection center $\mathbf{C}''$ of the third camera and the scene point $\mathbf{P}$. The intersections of the planes in the two pencils generate a family of 3D lines in the world space, all containing $\mathbf{P}$. The trifocal constraint (17), as proven in section 4.1, states that the projection of these lines in the first view all must contain the image point $\mathbf{p}$; or equivalently, that the ray of sight creating $\mathbf{p}$ in the first camera must intersect all the 3D lines generated by intersecting the projecting planes of the lines in the other views in the scene point $\mathbf{P}$. So, basically both constraints express the same geometrical condition, albeit involving a different number of views and in a slightly different manner. Consequently, it should be possible to express both constraints algebraically in the same way.

Consider again the binocular case, and let $\mathbf{p}$ and $\mathbf{p}'$ be corresponding image points in respectively the first and the second view. Then $\mathbf{p}$ and $\mathbf{p}'$ satisfy the epipolar constraint (14) : $\mathbf{p}'^t F \mathbf{p} = 0$. Following the reasoning above, the point $\mathbf{p}'$ is the top of a pencil of lines in the second image. So, two arbitrary, but distinct lines $\mathbf{l}'_1$ and $\mathbf{l}'_2$ of that pencil intersect in the image point $\mathbf{p}'$. Recall that $\mathbf{l}'_1$ and $\mathbf{l}'_2$ are represented as 3-vectors containing homogeneous coordinates for the image lines. Their cross product $l'_1 \times l'_2$ then yields homogeneous coordinates for the point of intersection of l'_1 and l'_2. Since l'_1 and l'_2 intersect in $\mathbf{p}'$, it follows that $l'_1 \times l'_2 = \rho \mathbf{p}'$ for some non-zero scalar $\rho \in \mathbb{R}$. Substituting this cross product for $\mathbf{p}'$ in the epipolar constraint (14) gives

$$(l'_1 \times l'_2)^t \, F \, \mathbf{p} = 0 \tag{69}$$

for all lines l'_1 and l'_2 through $\mathbf{p}'$ in the second image. On the other hand, recall from Theorem 1 that $F = [\mathbf{e}']_\times A$, where $\mathbf{e}'$ is the epipole in the second image and A is the 3×3-matrix $A = \frac{1}{\rho'_e} K' R'^t R K^{-1}$. Hence, $F \mathbf{p} = [\mathbf{e}']_\times A \mathbf{p} = \mathbf{e}' \times A \mathbf{p}$ and equation (69) can be written as

$$(l'_1 \times l'_2)^t \, (\mathbf{e}' \times A \mathbf{p}) = 0 \tag{70}$$

for all lines l'_1 and l'_2 through $\mathbf{p}'$ in the second image. Note that the lefthand side of equation (70), in fact, is the dot product of two cross products. From linear algebra we know that it is equal to

$$(l'_1 \times l'_2)^t \, (\mathbf{e}' \times A \mathbf{p}) = \left(l'^t_1 \mathbf{e}' \right) \left(l'^t_2 A \mathbf{p} \right) - \left(l'^t_1 A \mathbf{p} \right) \left(l'^t_2 \mathbf{e}' \right) . \tag{71}$$

As $l'^t_2 A \mathbf{p} = (A \mathbf{p})^t \, l'_2$ and $l'^t_2 \mathbf{e}' = \mathbf{e}'^t l'_2$, equation (70) can be rewritten as

$$l'^t_1 \left[\mathbf{e}' (A \mathbf{p})^t - (A \mathbf{p}) \mathbf{e}'^t \right] l'_2 = 0 \tag{72}$$

for all lines l'_1 and l'_2 through $\mathbf{p}'$ in the second image. Observe that the middle matrix in the lefthand side of equation (72) is, up to sign, exactly the 3×3-matrix $[T\mathbf{p}]$ of formula (19) in the fundamental trifocal constraint (17) of Theorem 2, provided the second and the third image are identical; i.e. $I' = I''$, $\mathbf{e}' = \mathbf{e}''$ and $A = B$.

Proposition 4. [2] *Let I and I' be two views of a static scene. If $\mathbf{p}$ and $\mathbf{p}'$ are corresponding points in the images I and I' respectively, then the following relation is equivalent to the epipolar constraint (14) for $\mathbf{p}$ and $\mathbf{p}'$: for every two lines l'_1 and l'_2 through $\mathbf{p}'$ in I',*

$$l'^t_1 [T\mathbf{p}] \, l'_2 = 0 , \tag{73}$$

where T is the trifocal tensor of the image triple (I, I', I'), as defined in Theorem 2.   □

In other words, *by replacing an image point by (the intersection of) two arbitrary lines through that point in the image, the epipolar constraint (14) can be written as a trifocal constraint (17) in which the second and the third view coincide; and, vice versa, by identifying the second and the third view in the trifocal constraint (17) the epipolar geometry of the image pair is recovered.* In [1] (see also [3]) explicit formulas are given on how the trifocal tensor of an image triple changes when the third camera is moved in the world. This allows to generate novel views of the scene from three given ones by using the trifocal constraints as a transfer principle. Moreover, these observations are used in [2] as a common framework, based on the trifocal tensor, for describing the multiview relations in image sequences.

5   Relations Between Four Views: The Quadrifocal Constraints

The methodology developed in the previous section to connect the epipolar constraint with the trifocal one can bring us on the track of the quadrifocal constraints that must hold between four views of a static scene. The fundamental trifocal constraint (17) expresses a relation between an image point in the first view and arbitrary lines through the corresponding point in the second and in the third view. Following the methodology of section 4.5, the image point $\mathbf{p}$ in the first view can be interpreted as the top of a pencil of lines through $\mathbf{p}$ in the first image. Algebraically, the point $\mathbf{p}$ in the fundamental trifocal constraint (17) can be replaced by the cross product $l_1 \times l_2$ of two arbitrary lines l_1 and l_2 passing through $\mathbf{p}$ in the first view. In this way, an algebraic relation is obtained between homogeneous coordinates of four arbitrary lines passing through corresponding points in the images. This relation is a degenerate case of the fundamental quadrifocal constraint (74), which occurs if one identifies the first and the second of the four views in Theorem 3. Hence, *the fundamental quadrifocal constraint is a relation between* (homogeneous coordinates of) *four lines in the respective images.* But what does this relation express geometrically? Well, recall from section 4.1 that the fundamental trifocal constraint (17) expresses algebraically that the projecting planes π' and π'' of the lines l' and l'' in respectively the second and the third view intersect in a 3D line $\mathbf{L}$ in the world space, which contains the scene point $\mathbf{P}$ of which the corresponding image points $\mathbf{p}$, $\mathbf{p}'$ and $\mathbf{p}''$ are the projections in the respective views; or equivalently, that the ray of sight observing the image point $\mathbf{p}$ in the first camera must intersect the 3D line $\mathbf{L}$ (consequently, in the scene point $\mathbf{P}$). Now, if the image point $\mathbf{p}$ is replaced by a pencil of lines through $\mathbf{p}$ in the first view, then each line of this pencil defines a projecting plane π in the world space, containing the ray of sight of $\mathbf{p}$ in the first camera. Since the ray of sight of $\mathbf{p}$ in the first camera is just the 3D line connecting the projection center $\mathbf{C}$ of the first camera with the scene point $\mathbf{P}$, each such projecting plane π must contain both $\mathbf{C}$ and $\mathbf{P}$. So, two arbitrary lines l_1 and l_2 passing through $\mathbf{p}$ in the first view, generate two world planes π_1 and π_2 both containing the projection center $\mathbf{C}$ of the first camera and the scene point $\mathbf{P}$ underlying $\mathbf{p}$ in the first image. Imagine that the projection center $\mathbf{C}$ would be split into two space point $\mathbf{C}_1$ and $\mathbf{C}_2$ and moved apart. In other words, assume that the first camera is "decoupled" into two separate cameras, which are then moved apart. Then the following situation occurs: There are four cameras — and thus four images — with projection centers $\mathbf{C}_1$, $\mathbf{C}_2$, $\mathbf{C}'$ and $\mathbf{C}''$ respectively. And, as before, the lines l' and l'' in the images obtained by the cameras at positions $\mathbf{C}'$ and $\mathbf{C}''$ still define, through their projecting planes, a 3D line $\mathbf{L}$ in the world space, which contains the scene point $\mathbf{P}$. The line l_2 in the image obtained from position $\mathbf{C}_2$ generates a projecting plane π_2 in the world space, which intersects the 3D line $\mathbf{L}$ in $\mathbf{P}$. This situation is generic for every triple of lines through corresponding image points in three views and does not yield a constaint. The fourth view, however, introduces a constraint, because the line l_1 in the image obtained from position $\mathbf{C}_1$ will contain the projection of the scene point $\mathbf{P}$ in this view *if and only if* the projecting plane π_1 of l_1 contains the 3D point $\mathbf{P}$ defined as the intersection of the (essentially arbitrary) projecting planes π_2, π' and π'' in the world. The fundamental quadrifocal constraint (74) expresses this constraint algebraically in terms of (homogeneous coordinates of) the lines in the images.

Theorem 3. (Fundamental quadrifocal constraint) [47,51,7] *For every four views I, I', I'' and I''' of a static scene, there exists a $3\times3\times3\times3$-tensor $Q = (Q^{ijk\ell})_{1\le i,j,k,\ell\le3}$, called the* quadrifocal tensor *of the image quadruple (I, I', I'', I'''), with the following property: If $\mathbf{p} \in I$, $\mathbf{p}' \in I'$, $\mathbf{p}'' \in I''$ and $\mathbf{p}''' \in I'''$ are corresponding points in the images, then for every line 1 through $\mathbf{p}$ in I, for every line l' through $\mathbf{p}'$ in I', for every line l'' through $\mathbf{p}''$ in I'' and for every line l''' through $\mathbf{p}'''$ in I''',*

$$\sum_{i=1}^{3}\sum_{j=1}^{3}\sum_{k=1}^{3}\sum_{\ell=1}^{3} Q^{ijk\ell} u_i u_j' u_k'' u_\ell''' = 0 , \tag{74}$$

where $l^{(i)} \simeq (u_1^{(i)}, u_2^{(i)}, u_3^{(i)})^t$ are homogeneous coordinates for the lines $l^{(i)}$ ($0 \le i \le 3$) in the images — the superscript $^{(i)}$ indicating the number of primes. Moreover, if, with the notations as before, $A = \frac{1}{\rho_e'} K'R'^t RK^{-1}$, $B = \frac{1}{\rho_e''} K''R''^t RK^{-1}$ and $C = \frac{1}{\rho_e'''} K'''R'''^t RK^{-1}$, then

$$Q^{ijk\ell} = \det \begin{pmatrix} \delta_{i1} & \delta_{i2} & \delta_{i3} & 0 \\ a_{j1} & a_{j2} & a_{j3} & (\mathbf{e}')_j \\ b_{k1} & b_{k2} & b_{k3} & (\mathbf{e}'')_k \\ c_{\ell1} & c_{\ell2} & c_{\ell3} & (\mathbf{e}''')_\ell \end{pmatrix} \qquad for\ 1 \le i,j,k,\ell \le 3, \tag{75}$$

where δ_{ij} denotes the Kronecker delta; a_{ij}, b_{ij} and c_{ij} denote the (i,j)th entry of the matrices A, B and C respectively; and with $(\mathbf{e}')_j$, $(\mathbf{e}'')_j$ and $(\mathbf{e}''')_j$ being the jth coordinate of the epipoles $\mathbf{e}'$, $\mathbf{e}''$ and $\mathbf{e}'''$ of the first camera in respectively the second, third and fourth view.

Proof. We just have to express that the four projecting planes of the image lines 1, l', l'' and l''' have the scene point $\mathbf{P}$, projecting onto the corresponding image points $\mathbf{p}$, $\mathbf{p}'$, $\mathbf{p}''$ and $\mathbf{p}'''$, in common. By Lemma 1, this means that $\mathbf{P}$ satisfies the following system of equations:

$$\begin{cases} 1^t KR^t (\mathbf{P} - \mathbf{C}) & = 0 \\ l'^t K'R'^t (\mathbf{P} - \mathbf{C}') & = 0 \\ l''^t K''R''^t (\mathbf{P} - \mathbf{C}'') & = 0 \\ l'''^t K'''R'''^t (\mathbf{P} - \mathbf{C}''') & = 0 \end{cases} \tag{76}$$

Or, expressed in matrix form,

$$
\begin{pmatrix}
\mathbf{l}^t K R^t & -\mathbf{l}^t K R^t \mathbf{C} \\
\mathbf{l}'^t K' R'^t & -\mathbf{l}'^t K' R'^t \mathbf{C}' \\
\mathbf{l}''^t K'' R''^t & -\mathbf{l}''^t K'' R''^t \mathbf{C}'' \\
\mathbf{l}'''^t K''' R'''^t & -\mathbf{l}'''^t K''' R'''^t \mathbf{C}'''
\end{pmatrix}
\begin{pmatrix} \mathbf{P} \\ 1 \end{pmatrix}
=
\begin{pmatrix} 0 \\ 0 \\ 0 \\ 0 \end{pmatrix}
\tag{77}
$$

As this homogeneous system of linear equations clearly has a non-zero solution, the leftmost 4×4-matrix must be singular. Because the rank of a matrix does not change if the matrix is multiplied with a regular matrix, the matrix

$$
\begin{pmatrix}
\mathbf{l}^t K R^t & -\mathbf{l}^t K R^t \mathbf{C} \\
\mathbf{l}'^t K' R'^t & -\mathbf{l}'^t K' R'^t \mathbf{C}' \\
\mathbf{l}''^t K'' R''^t & -\mathbf{l}''^t K'' R''^t \mathbf{C}'' \\
\mathbf{l}'''^t K''' R'''^t & -\mathbf{l}'''^t K''' R'''^t \mathbf{C}'''
\end{pmatrix}
\begin{pmatrix} R K^{-1} & \mathbf{C} \\ \mathbf{0}^t & 1 \end{pmatrix}
=
\begin{pmatrix}
\mathbf{l}^t & 0 \\
\rho'_e \mathbf{l}'^t A & \rho'_e \mathbf{l}'^t \mathbf{e}' \\
\rho''_e \mathbf{l}''^t B & \rho''_e \mathbf{l}''^t \mathbf{e}'' \\
\rho'''_e \mathbf{l}'''^t C & \rho'''_e \mathbf{l}'''^t \mathbf{e}'''
\end{pmatrix}
\tag{78}
$$

must be singular as well. In particular, the determinant of matrix (78) must be zero. After expansion and division by the non-zero factor $\rho'_e \rho''_e \rho'''_e$, this determinant is the quadrifocal constraint (74) of the theorem. As the determinant yields a quadrilinear expression in the entries of $\mathbf{l}$, $\mathbf{l}'$, $\mathbf{l}''$ and $\mathbf{l}'''$, the entries $Q^{ijk\ell}$ of the quadrifocal tensor Q can be found by substituting the appropriate standard unit 3-vector $\mathbf{u}_1 = (1,0,0)^t$, $\mathbf{u}_2 = (0,1,0)^t$ or $\mathbf{u}_3 = (0,0,1)^1$ for $\mathbf{l}$, $\mathbf{l}'$, $\mathbf{l}''$ and $\mathbf{l}'''$ in the determinant. More precisely, $Q^{ijk\ell}$ is found by taking $\mathbf{l} = \mathbf{u}_i$, $\mathbf{l}' = \mathbf{u}_j$, $\mathbf{l}'' = \mathbf{u}_k$, $\mathbf{l}''' = \mathbf{u}_\ell$. For every 3-row-ed matrix M, $\mathbf{u}_i^t M$ is equal to the ith row of M. Hence, $Q^{ijk\ell}$ equals the determinant of the 4×4-matrix whose rows respectively are the ith row of the 3×4-matrix $(I_3 \mid \mathbf{0})$, the jth row of the matrix $(A \mid \mathbf{e}')$, the kth row of $(B \mid \mathbf{e}'')$ and the ℓth row of $(C \mid \mathbf{e}''')$, as in formula (75). □

As in section 4.3, the fundamental quadrifocal constraint (74) can be transformed into incidence relations involving the coordinates of one or more of the image points $\mathbf{p}$, $\mathbf{p}'$, $\mathbf{p}''$ or $\mathbf{p}'''$ by taking for $\mathbf{l}$, $\mathbf{l}'$, $\mathbf{l}''$ and / or $\mathbf{l}'''$ the horizontal and vertical lines through the given image point(s). Table 2 gives an overview of

image features	no. of equations
four points	16
three points, one line	8
two points, two lines	4
one point, three lines	2
four lines	1

Table 2. *Overview of the different types of quadrifocal constraints.*

the different quadrifocal relations ordered by the number and type of geometric image features involved. Again, the *"number of equations"* refers to the number

of *linearly independent* equations that exists for the homogeneous coordinates
of the image features involved in that particular type of constraint. It is important to note that, in the cases involving both points and lines, different types
of relations are possible, depending on which particular view(s) the point(s) are
taken from. As before, this variability is *not* taken into account in the *"number
of equations"*.

Remark 6. As with the epipolar and the trifocal constraints, if corresponding
image features are identified in the four views, then the relevant incidence relations mentioned in Table 2 all bring homogeneous linear equations in the entries
$Q^{ijk\ell}$ of the quadrifocal tensor Q. Hence, Q can be computed linearly, up to
a non-zero scalar factor, from these equations provided sufficient corresponding
points and lines can be identified in the four views. More precisely, the quadrifocal constraints for corresponding image points yields 16 linearly independent
equations in the entries of Q for each quadruple of corresponding points in I,
I', I'' and I'''. Because Q has $3^4 = 81$ entries which can be determined up to
a non-zero scalar multiple only, one would expect that 5 point correspondences
that could be identified in the four views would suffice to compute Q linearly,
up to a non-zero scalar factor, because 5 point correspondences yield 80 homogeneous linear equations in the entries of Q. Unfortunately, it is proven in [15]
that for $n \leq 5$ point correspondences between the four views the homogeneous
system of 80 linear equations in the entries of Q has rank $16\,n - \binom{n}{2}$, where $\binom{n}{2}$ is
the binomial coefficient $\binom{n}{2} = \frac{n(n-1)}{2}$. Thus, 5 point correspondences yield only
70 linearly independent equations, which is not enough to solve for the entries of
Q. For $n \geq 6$, on the other hand, 80 linearly independent equations are found.
Consequently, *Q can be computed linearly, up to a non-zero scalar factor, from
(at least) 6 point correspondences between the four images* [15]. Furthermore, it
is proven in [22] that the quadrifocal tensor Q has rank 9. In fact, the entries
$Q^{ijk\ell}$ of Q satisfy 51 non-linear algebraic relations, in addition to the scale ambiguity, such that Q actually only has 29 degrees of freedom [19]. Due to the
presence of noise in the images, the tensor Q computed linearly from point correspondences between the images most certainly will not satify these non-linear
relations. Moreover, it is clear that one cannot ignore the 51 non-linear relations
in the 81 entries of Q and hope to get reasonable results. Imposing these relations
in the computation of Q results in non-linear criteria. A practical and accurate
algorithm for the compution of Q is given in [19].

The quadrifocal constraints mentioned in Table 2 express geometric *incidence*
relations between between the image features in the four views. As in the trifocal
case, these quadrifocal constraints can also be converted to *transfer* equations,
predicting the position of an image feature in one view from the positions of
related features in the other views. One case is worth mentioning here: Recall
from the beginning of this section that three arbitrary lines in three views generate three projecting planes in the world space, which generally intersect in a
singe world point **P**, as depicted in Figure 7. The fundamental quadrifocal constraint (74) gives a necessary and sufficient condition for the projecting plane of

a line in the fourth view to contain that particular world point **P** as well. Obviously, the projections of **P** in the different views are the corresponding image points mentioned in Theorem 3. Replacing the line l''' in the fourth image by the horizontal and the vertical line through the point **p**''' in the fourth view, not only yields the *1 point / 3 lines* constraints in Table 2, but also gives a means to compute the position of **p**''' in the fourth view.

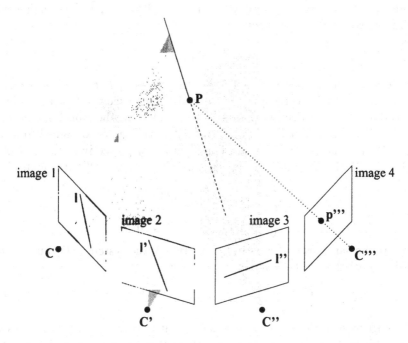

Fig. 7. *Three lines* l, l' *and* l'' *in three images, all containing the (possibly unknown) projections of a scene point* **P**, *suffice to compute the projection* **p**''' *of* **P** *in the fourth image.*

Proposition 5. (3 lines transfer) *Let* I, I', I'' *and* I''' *be four views of a static scene. If* l, l' *and* l'' *are arbitrary lines in the images* I, I' *and* I'' *respectively, containing the (possibly unknown) projections* **p**, **p**' *and* **p**'' *of a scene point* **P**, *then the (extended) coordinates of the projection* **p**''' *of* **P** *in the fourth view* I''' *are (up to a non-zero scalar factor) given by*

$$\tau''' \mathbf{p}''' = \left[\mathbf{l}^t [Q^{(k\ell)}] \mathbf{l}' \right]^t \mathbf{l}'' , \qquad (79)$$

where $[Q^{(k\ell)}]$ *is the* 3×3*-matrix whose* (i,j)*th entry is* $Q^{ijk\ell}$, $\left[\mathbf{l}^t [Q^{(k\ell)}] \mathbf{l}' \right]$ *is a* 3×3*-matrix whose* (k, ℓ)*th entry is* $\mathbf{l}^t [Q^{(k\ell)}] \mathbf{l}'$, *and with* $\tau''' \in \mathbb{R}$ *being a non-zero scalar factor.*

Proof. Before proving the proposition, let us first rewrite the fundamental quadrifocal constraint (74) in a more compact form. Let, for a moment, the indices k and ℓ be arbitrary, but fixed. Then all entries $Q^{ijk\ell}$ of the quadrifocal tensor Q obtained by varying the indices $1 \leq i, j \leq 3$, but keeping k and ℓ fixed, define a 3×3-matrix which we will denote by $[Q^{(k\ell)}]$. If 1 and $1'$ are two lines in respectively the images I and I', then $1^t[Q^{(k\ell)}]1'$ is a real number, depending on the choice of the indices k and ℓ. When varying the indices $1 \leq k, \ell \leq 3$, one again obtaines a 3×3-matrix, which we will denote by $\left[1^t[Q^{(k\ell)}]1'\right]$. The fundamental quadrifocal constraint now is equal to

$$1''^t \left[1^t[Q^{(k\ell)}]1' \right] 1''' = 0 \ . \tag{80}$$

Now, consider three lines 1, $1'$ and $1''$ in the images I, I' and I'' respectively. Furthermore, let $\mathbf{p}'''$ be the projection in the fourth view I''' of the point of intersection of the projecting planes of 1, $1'$ and $1''$ in the world space. Then the (extended) coordinates $\mathbf{p}''' = (x''', y''', 1)^t$ of $\mathbf{p}'''$ can be obtained from formula (80) by replacing the arbitrary line $1'''$ in I''' by respectively the horizontal line $\mathbf{h}''' \simeq (0, -1, y''')^t$ and the vertical line $\mathbf{v}''' \simeq (1, 0, -x''')^t$ through $\mathbf{p}'''$ in I''' :

$$\begin{cases} 1''^t \left[1^t[Q^{(k\ell)}]1' \right] \mathbf{h}''' = 0 \\ 1''^t \left[1^t[Q^{(k\ell)}]1' \right] \mathbf{v}''' = 0 \end{cases} \tag{81}$$

Following the same argument as in Proposition 3, the system (81) can be interpreted as stating that the 3-vector

$$\left(1''^t \left[1^t[Q^{(k\ell)}]1' \right] \right)^t = \left[1^t[Q^{(k\ell)}]1' \right]^t 1'' \tag{82}$$

are homogeneous coordinates of an image point that lies both on the lines $\mathbf{h}'''$ and $\mathbf{v}'''$. Since, by construction, $\mathbf{p}'''$ is the point of intersection of $\mathbf{h}'''$ and $\mathbf{v}'''$, the proposition follows. $\square$

Remark 7. Observe that the geometrical construction underlying *Proposition 5 degenerates* if (at least) two of the three projecting planes coincide. This situation happens *when (at least) two of the three lines 1, $1'$ and $1''$ are corresponding epipolar lines in their images*. Also note that, when $\mathbf{p}'''$ is known, the corresponding points $\mathbf{p}$, $\mathbf{p}'$ and $\mathbf{p}''$ in the other images can be found by the point–line transfer principle described in Proposition 3. Finally, the attentive reader will remark that the projection $\mathbf{p}$ of the scene point $\mathbf{P}$ in the first image can also be obtained as the point of intersection of the image line 1 with the projection in I of the 3D line defined by the intersection of the projecting plane of $\mathbf{p}'$ and that of $\mathbf{p}'''$ in the world space, as given by formula 31 in Proposition 1. The corresponding point $\mathbf{p}'''$ in the fourth view can then be found by the point–line transfer principle described in Proposition 3. Observe, however, that this latter construction needs the estimation of two trifocal tensors between different image triples. Proposition 5 has the advantage of providing an explicit formula (79) and an independent construction of $\mathbf{p}'''$.

6   Relations Between n Views: The General Picture

What about the relations between five views? Clearly, the "decoupling trick" of section 5 does not work anymore, because the fundamental quadrifocal constraint (74) is a relation between image lines and does not (explicitly) involve image points anymore. It will be shown in this section (Theorem 4) that for five or more views of a static scene there essentially are no other relations than the ones discussed before (i.e. the epipolar, trifocal and quadrifocal constraints between every combination of two, three or four views out of the given ones).

6.1   Relations Between $n \geq 5$ Views

Let us first consider the n-view constraints for (the extended coordinates of) corresponding image points. Hence, let $I^{(0)}$, $I^{(1)}$, $\ldots$, $I^{(n-1)}$ be n views of a static scene. You may think of the superscript $^{(i)}$ as indicating the number of primes used in the previous sections. Furthermore, suppose that $\mathbf{p}^{(0)} \in I^{(0)}$, $\mathbf{p}^{(1)} \in I^{(1)}$, $\ldots$, $\mathbf{p}^{(n-1)} \in I^{(n-1)}$ are corresponding points in the respective images, meaning that they are all the projection of a single scene point $\mathbf{P}$ in the different views. In particular,

$$\rho^{(i)} \mathbf{p}^{(i)} = K_i R_i^t \left(\mathbf{P} - \mathbf{C}_i \right) \qquad \text{for all } 0 \leq i \leq n - 1, \tag{83}$$

where the world point $\mathbf{C}_i$ and the 3×3-rotation matrix R_i indicate the position and orientation of the $(i+1)$th camera in the scene, K_i is its calibration matrix, and the $\rho^{(i)} \in \mathbb{R}$ are non-zero scalar factors. Or, equivalently,

$$K_i R_i^t \mathbf{P} - K_i R_i^t \mathbf{C}_i - \rho^{(i)} \mathbf{p}^{(i)} = 0 \qquad \text{for all } 0 \leq i \leq n - 1. \tag{84}$$

All these projection equations can be expressed in matrix form as

$$\begin{pmatrix} K_0 R_0^t & -K_0 R_0^t \mathbf{C}_0 & \mathbf{p}^{(0)} & 0 & \cdots & 0 \\ K_1 R_1^t & -K_1 R_1^t \mathbf{C}_1 & 0 & \mathbf{p}^{(1)} & \cdots & 0 \\ \vdots & \vdots & \vdots & \vdots & \ddots & \vdots \\ K_{n-1} R_{n-1}^t & -K_{n-1} R_{n-1}^t \mathbf{C}_{n-1} & 0 & 0 & \cdots & \mathbf{p}^{(n-1)} \end{pmatrix} \begin{pmatrix} \mathbf{P} \\ 1 \\ -\rho^{(0)} \\ -\rho^{(1)} \\ \vdots \\ -\rho^{(n-1)} \end{pmatrix} = \begin{pmatrix} 0 \\ 0 \\ \vdots \\ 0 \end{pmatrix} \tag{85}$$

Observe that the column vector at the lefthand side of the matrix equation (85) contains the variable parameters whereas the leftmost matrix contains all the camera and image information. So, one may consider this matrix equation as representing a homogeneous system of linear equations from which the world coordinates of the scene point $\mathbf{P}$ and the unknown scalars $\rho^{(0)}, \rho^{(1)}, \ldots, \rho^{(n-1)}$ can be determined if the camera parameters and the projections $\mathbf{p}^{(0)}, \mathbf{p}^{(1)}, \ldots,$ $\mathbf{p}^{(n-1)}$ of $\mathbf{P}$ in the respective images are given. The entry equal to 1 in the column vector proves that this homogeneous system of linear equations has a non-zero solution; or equivalently, that the rank of the (leftmost) matrix

$$\begin{pmatrix} K_0 R_0^t & -K_0 R_0^t \mathbf{C}_0 & \mathbf{p}^{(0)} & \mathbf{0} & \dots & \mathbf{0} \\ K_1 R_1^t & -K_1 R_1^t \mathbf{C}_1 & \mathbf{0} & \mathbf{p}^{(1)} & \dots & \mathbf{0} \\ \vdots & \vdots & \vdots & \vdots & \ddots & \vdots \\ K_{n-1} R_{n-1}^t & -K_{n-1} R_{n-1}^t \mathbf{C}_{n-1} & \mathbf{0} & \mathbf{0} & \dots & \mathbf{p}^{(n-1)} \end{pmatrix} \qquad (86)$$

is strictly less than the number of columns of that matrix. As K_i and R_i are 3×3-matrices, and $\mathbf{C}_i$, $\mathbf{p}^{(i)}$ and $\mathbf{0}$ are 3-vectors, the matrix (86) has $3n$ rows and $n + 4$ columns. Thus, this rank condition on matrix (86) only yields a constraint if the number of rows is greater than the number of columns; i.e. $3n \geq n+4$, or equivalently, if $n \geq 2$. In other words, *there only is a constraint on the position of corresponding image points if there are at least 2 views of the scene*; an observation that was already made in section 3.

Suppose that $n \geq 2$. Then the rank condition on matrix (86) implies that all $(n+4) \times (n+4)$-submatrices of this matrix must be singular; or equivalently, that all $(n+4) \times (n+4)$-submatrices of matrix (86) must have zero determinant. Obviously, each $(n+4) \times (n+4)$-submatrix is obtained by choosing $n+4$ rows among the $3n$ rows of matrix (86); or equivalently, by deleting $3n - (n+4) = 2n - 4$ rows from matrix (86). In this matrix each view $I^{(i)}$ is represented by 3 rows, namely

$$\begin{pmatrix} K_i R_i^t & -K_i R_i^t \mathbf{C}_i & \mathbf{0} & \dots & \mathbf{0} & \mathbf{p}^{(i)} & \mathbf{0} & \dots & \mathbf{0} \end{pmatrix} . \qquad (87)$$

So, if none of the three rows corresponding to the $(i+1)$th view $I^{(i)}$ is contained in the $(n+4) \times (n+4)$-submatrix, then the $(4+i+1)$th column of the $(n+4) \times (n+4)$-submatrix is zero; and, its determinant trivially becomes zero. Hence, *only $(n+4) \times (n+4)$-submatrices containing at least 1 row from each view yield a non-trivial constraint* between the coordinates of corresponding image points. On the other hand, if a $(n+4) \times (n+4)$-submatrix of matrix (86) contains exactly one row corresponding to image $I^{(i)}$, then the $(4+i+1)$th column of this submatrix contains only one non-zero entry. Developing the determinant of this submatrix along this $(4+i+1)$th column results in a relation between corresponding image points in the views $I^{(0)}, \dots, I^{(i-1)}, I^{(i+1)}, \dots, I^{(n-1)}$; and, one ends up with a constraint between only $n-1$ of the n views. So, view $I^{(i)}$ will participate in a multiview constaint *if and only if at least two rows of the submatrix (87) are contained in the $(n+4) \times (n+4)$-submatrix of matrix (86)*. Put differently, *in order for the view $I^{(i)}$ to participate in a multiview constraint, at most 1 row of the submatrix (87) may be deleted from matrix (86) to form a $(n+4) \times (n+4)$-submatrix*. Since $3n$ increases more rapidly with n than $n+4$, the number of rows in matrix (86) increases more rapidly with the number of views that the number of columns. Consequently, there must be a minimal number of views n^* for which the previous condition — i.e. deleting at most 1 row for each view $I^{(i)}$ — cannot be maintained for all of the n^* views. This situation occurs if the number of rows to be deleted from matrix (86) (i.e. $2n^* - 4$) is greater than the number of views involved; i.e. $2n^* - 4 > n^*$, or equivalently, $n^* > 4$. In other words, a non-trivial constraint involving image points from all the n views $I^{(0)}, I^{(1)}, \dots, I^{(n-1)}$ only exists if $n \leq 4$. Put differently, *all the multiview* *relations that exist between the image coordinates of corresponding image points in 5 or more views of a static scene are expressed by the epipolar constraints between any pair, the trifocal constraints between any triplet, and the quadrifocal constraints between any quadruple of views among the given images.*

Next, let us investigate what happens when also image lines are involved. A line $l^{(i)}$ in image $I^{(i)}$ passes through the image point $\mathbf{p}^{(i)}$ in $I^{(i)}$ if and only if the projecting plane generating the line $l^{(i)}$ in the $(i+1)$th camera contains the scene point $\mathbf{P}$ of which $\mathbf{p}^{(i)}$ is the projection in $I^{(i)}$. According to Lemma 1, $\mathbf{P}$ must therefore satisfy the equation

$$l^{(i)^t} K_i R_i^t (\mathbf{P} - \mathbf{C}_i) = 0 \; ; \tag{88}$$

or equivalently,

$$l^{(i)^t} K_i R_i^t \mathbf{P} - l^{(i)^t} K_i R_i^t \mathbf{C}_i = 0 \; . \tag{89}$$

Writing this in matrix form in confirmity with matrix equation 85 gives

$$\left(\begin{array}{cccccc} l^{(i)^t} K_i R_i^t & -l^{(i)^t} K_i R_i^t \mathbf{C}_i & 0 & 0 & \ldots & 0 \end{array} \right) \begin{pmatrix} \mathbf{P} \\ 1 \\ -\rho^{(0)} \\ -\rho^{(1)} \\ \vdots \\ -\rho^{(n-1)} \end{pmatrix} = 0 \; . \tag{90}$$

Thus, when using a line $l^{(i)}$ through the point $\mathbf{p}^{(i)}$ in image $I^{(i)}$ instead of $\mathbf{p}^{(i)}$ itself, the 3 rows (87) in matrix (86) are replaced by only 1 row, viz.

$$\left(\begin{array}{cccccc} l^{(i)^t} K_i R_i^t & -l^{(i)^t} K_i R_i^t \mathbf{C}_i & 0 & 0 & \ldots & 0 \end{array} \right) \; . \tag{91}$$

Let us express this more precisely. Suppose that in m of the n views $I^{(0)}$, $I^{(1)}$, $\ldots$, $I^{(n-1)}$ corresponding image points $\mathbf{p}^{(i)} \in I^{(i)}$ will be used, whereas in the other $k = n - m$ views image lines $l^{(j)} \in I^{(j)}$ through the corresponding point $\mathbf{p}^{(j)}$ are being considered. Without loss of generality, we may assume that the points $\mathbf{p}^{(i)}$ are taken from the first m views $I^{(0)}$, $I^{(1)}$, $\ldots$, $I^{(m-1)}$; and, that the lines $l^{(j)}$ are taken from the last k images $I^{(m)}$, $I^{(m+1)}$, $\ldots$, $I^{(n-1)}$. Then the projection equations yield a homogeneous system of linear equations (as in formula (85)) whose matrix now is

$$\begin{pmatrix} K_0 R_0^t & -K_0 R_0^t \mathbf{C}_0 & \mathbf{p}^{(0)} & \ldots & 0 \\ \vdots & \vdots & \vdots & \ddots & \vdots \\ K_{m-1} R_{m-1}^t & -K_{m-1} R_{m-1}^t \mathbf{C}_{m-1} & 0 & \ldots & \mathbf{p}^{(m-1)} \\ l^{(m)^t} K_m R_m^t & -l^{(m)^t} K_m R_m^t \mathbf{C}_m & 0 & \ldots & 0 \\ \vdots & \vdots & \vdots & & \vdots \\ l^{(n-1)^t} K_{n-1} R_{n-1}^t & -l^{(n-1)^t} K_{n-1} R_{n-1}^t \mathbf{C}_{n-1} & 0 & \ldots & 0 \end{pmatrix} \; . \tag{92}$$

As before, this homogeneous system of linear equations must have a non-zero solution; or equivalently, the rank of this matrix is strictly less than the number of columns. Matrix (92) has $3\,m + k$ rows and $m + 4$ columns. The rank condition therefore only yields a constraint if the number of rows is greater than the number of columns; i.e. $3\,m + k \geq m + 4$, or equivalently, if $2\,m + k \geq 4$. In other words, *there only is a multiview constraint involving image points and lines if either there are at least 2 points in 2 views, or 1 point and 2 lines in 3 views, or 4 lines in 4 views.* Remark that this is in agreement with respectively the epipolar constraint (14) for 2 views, the fundamental trifocal constraint (17) for 3 views, and the fundamental quadrifocal constraint (74) for 4 views.

Suppose that indeed $2\,m + k \geq 4$. Then the rank condition on matrix (92) implies that all $(m+4) \times (m+4)$-submatrices of (92) must have zero determinant. Each $(m+4) \times (m+4)$-submatrix is obtained by choosing $m+4$ rows among the $3\,m + k$ rows of matrix (92); or equivalently, by deleting $(3\,m + k) - (m + 4) = 2\,m + k - 4$ rows from matrix (92). We already know that, in case of an image point $\mathbf{p}^{(i)}$, at most 1 row may be deleted for the submatrix (87) corresponding to image $I^{(i)}$ in matrix (92) in order for the view $I^{(i)}$ to participate in the constraint. On the other hand, we also know that, in case of an image line $\mathbf{l}^{(j)}$, the image $I^{(j)}$ is only represented in matrix (92) by the single row (91). Therefore, this row may not be deleted in order for image $I^{(j)}$ to participate in the constraint. Put differently, *for all views to participate in the constraint, only rows corresponding to image points may be deleted from matrix (92), and, moreover, at most 1 of the 3 rows corresponding to an image point may be removed.* The minimal number of views n^* for which this condition cannot be maintained, is reached when the number of rows to be deleted from matrix (92) (i.e. $2\,m + k - 4$) is greater than the number of image points involved; i.e. $2\,m + k - 4 > m$, or equivalently, $m + k > 4$. As $m + k = n$, the number of views, a non-trivial constraint involving image points and lines from all of the n views $I^{(0)}, I^{(1)}, \ldots, I^{(n-1)}$ only exists if $n \leq 4$. This proves the following theorem.

Theorem 4. (Relations between $n \geq 5$ views) [47,48] *All multiview relations that exist between (homogeneous coordinates of) image points and lines in five or more views of a static scene are expressed by the epipolar constraints between any pair, the trifocal constraints between any triple, and the quadrifocal constraints between any quadruple of views among the given images.* □

6.2 Have All Relations Between $n \leq 4$ Views Been Found?

Critical readers may remark that the analysis performed in section 6.1 proves the statement in Theorem 4, but that it is not at all clear that the determinants of the $(m+4) \times (m+4)$-submatrices of matrix (92) are equivalent with the epipolar, trifocal and quadrifocal constraints derived in the previous sections. Therefore, we will now investigate these determinants more closely and show that each determinant corresponds to one of the relations derived earlier. But first, an observation is made, which simplifies the calculations significantly. Recall from linear algebra that the rank of a matrix does not change when it is multiplied with an invertible matrix. So, the rank condition underlying the results of this section will not change if matrix (92) is multiplied on the right by the invertible $(m+4) \times (m+4)$-matrix

$$
\left(
\begin{array}{cc|cccccc}
R_0 K_0^{-1} & C_0 & 0 & 0 & \ldots & 0 \\
0^t & 1 & 0 & 0 & \ldots & 0 \\
\hline
0 & 0 & 1 & 0 & \ldots & 0 \\
0 & 0 & 0 & \rho_e^{(1)} & \ldots & 0 \\
\vdots & \vdots & \vdots & \vdots & \ddots & \vdots \\
0 & 0 & 0 & 0 & \ldots & \rho_e^{(m-1)}
\end{array}
\right) .
\tag{93}
$$

The resulting matrix can be simplified by using the notation A_i for $A_i = (1/\rho_e^{(i)}) K_i R_i^t R_0 K_0^{-1}$ in the first column; and, by observing that the expression $K_i R_i^t (\mathbf{C}_0 - \mathbf{C}_i) = \rho_e^{(i)} \mathbf{e}^{(i)}$ in the second column gives the epipole $\mathbf{e}^{(i)}$ of the first camera in the $(i+1)$th image $I^{(i)}$. The non-zero scalar factors $\rho_e^{(i)}$ in the rows of the resulting matrix can then be removed by pre-multiplying it with the *inverse* of the following $(3m+k) \times (3m+k)$-diagonal matrix

$$
\left(
\begin{array}{cccc|ccc}
I_3 & 0 & \ldots & 0 & 0 & \ldots & 0 \\
0^t & \rho^{(1)} I_3 & \ldots & 0 & 0 & \ldots & 0 \\
\vdots & \vdots & \ddots & \vdots & \vdots & & \vdots \\
0^t & 0^t & \ldots & \rho^{(m-1)} I_3 & 0 & \ldots & 0 \\
\hline
0^t & 0^t & \ldots & 0^t & \rho^{(m)} & \ldots & 0 \\
\vdots & \vdots & & \vdots & \vdots & \ddots & \vdots \\
0^t & 0^t & \ldots & 0^t & 0 & \ldots & \rho^{(n-1)}
\end{array}
\right) .
\tag{94}
$$

The resulting $(3m+k) \times (m+4)$-matrix, which satisfies the same rank condition as matrix (92), is

$$
\left(
\begin{array}{cccccccc}
I_3 & 0 & \mathbf{p}^{(0)} & 0 & \ldots & 0 \\
A_1 & \mathbf{e}^{(1)} & 0 & \mathbf{p}^{(1)} & \ldots & 0 \\
\vdots & \vdots & \vdots & \vdots & \ddots & \vdots \\
A_{m-1} & \mathbf{e}^{(m-1)} & 0 & 0 & \ldots & \mathbf{p}^{(m-1)} \\
1^{(m)t} A_m & 1^{(m)t} \mathbf{e}^{(m)} & 0 & 0 & \ldots & 0 \\
\vdots & \vdots & \vdots & \vdots & & \vdots \\
1^{(n-1)t} A_{n-1} & 1^{(n-1)t} \mathbf{e}^{(n-1)} & 0 & 0 & \ldots & 0
\end{array}
\right) .
\tag{95}
$$

Moreover, the diagonal form of the matrix (94) guarantees that the determinants of the $(m+4) \times (m+4)$-submatrices formed from this matrix (95) only differ up to a non-zero scalar factor from the determinants of the corresponding $(m+$

4) × $(m + 4)$-submatrix of the original matrix (92). Put differently, exactly the same constraints are found when performing the same operation either on the original matrix (92) or on the transformed matrix (95).

Before going on, it might be useful to indicate how this algebraic transformation of the problem relates to the geometry it describes. To this end, observe that the first 4 columns of the original matrix (92) actually contain the camera matrices $M_i = (K_i R_i^t \mid -K_i R_i^t C_i)$ for $0 \le i \le n - 1$ — eventually premultiplied with the transpose $\mathbf{1}^{(i)\,t}$ of the line coordinates $\mathbf{1}^{(i)}$ — of the camera set-up in the world space. In the transformed matrix (95), on the other hand, the first 4 columns are $(I_3 \mid \mathbf{0})$ for the first 3 rows, and $(A_i \mid \mathbf{e}^{(i)})$ for the others $(1 \le i \le n-1)$ — again eventually pre-multiplied with the transpose $\mathbf{1}^{(i)\,t}$ of the line coordinates $\mathbf{1}^{(i)}$. Recalling that $A_i = (1 / \rho_e^{(i)}) K_i R_i^t R_0 K_0^{-1}$ and that $K_i R_i^t (C_0 - C_i) = \rho_e^{(i)} \mathbf{e}^{(i)}$, it is easy to see that

$$M_0 = (K_0 R_0^t \mid -K_0 R_0^t C_0) = (I_3 \mid \mathbf{0}) \begin{pmatrix} K_0 R_0^t & -K_0 R_0^t C_0 \\ \mathbf{0}^t & 1 \end{pmatrix}$$

and $\quad M_i = (K_i R_i^t \mid -K_i R_i^t C_i) = \rho_e^{(i)} (A_i \mid \mathbf{e}^{(i)}) \begin{pmatrix} K_0 R_0^t & -K_0 R_0^t C_0 \\ \mathbf{0}^t & 1 \end{pmatrix}$.

$$(96)$$

Thus, when multiplying the original matrix (92) on the right with the matrix (93), the original projection equations

$$\rho^{(i)} \mathbf{p}^{(i)} = (K_i R_i^t \mid -K_i R_i^t C_i) \begin{pmatrix} \mathbf{P} \\ 1 \end{pmatrix} \tag{97}$$

(in extended coordinates) were replaced by the equations

$$\rho^{(0)} \mathbf{p}^{(0)} = (I_3 \mid \mathbf{0}) \begin{pmatrix} \hat{\mathbf{P}} \\ 1 \end{pmatrix} \quad \text{and} \quad \rho^{(i)} \mathbf{p}^{(i)} = \rho_e^{(i)} (A_i \mid \mathbf{e}^{(i)}) \begin{pmatrix} \hat{\mathbf{P}} \\ 1 \end{pmatrix} , \tag{98}$$

where the 3-vector $\hat{\mathbf{P}}$ is defined by

$$\begin{pmatrix} \hat{\mathbf{P}} \\ 1 \end{pmatrix} = \begin{pmatrix} K_0 R_0^t & -K_0 R_0^t C_0 \\ \mathbf{0}^t & 1 \end{pmatrix} \begin{pmatrix} \mathbf{P} \\ 1 \end{pmatrix} , \tag{99}$$

or equivalently, by

$$\hat{\mathbf{P}} = K_0 R_0^t (\mathbf{P} - C_0) . \tag{100}$$

In other words, by multiplying the original matrix (92) on the right with the matrix (93), a change of coordinates is performed in the world space, making the world frame camera-centered for the first camera. As geometrically is clear, the images only depend on the set-up of the cameras relative to the scene, but not on the particular choice of the world frame. Consequently, the inter-image relations should not depend on the choice of the world frame either. Making the world frame camera-centered to the first camera will therefore not alter the multiview relations, but it certainly makes the algebra easier, as will become clear in a moment. Coming back to equation (98), after division by the non-zero scalar factor $\rho_e^{(i)} \in \mathbb{R}$, the projection equations of the other cameras become

$$\tau^{(i)} \, \mathbf{p}^{(i)} = \left(A_i \mid \mathbf{e}^{(i)} \right) \begin{pmatrix} \hat{\mathbf{P}} \\ 1 \end{pmatrix} \tag{101}$$

with $\tau^{(i)} = \rho^{(i)} / \rho_e^{(i)}$ for all $1 \leq i \leq n-1$. This division was performed algebraically by pre-multiplication with the inverse of the diagonal matrix (94).

Now let us verify that the vanishing of the determinants of the $(m+4) \times (m+4)$-submatrices of matrix (95) indeed yield the multiview constraints derived in the previous sections. Let us starts with the 2 view case. Taking features from all images, the number m of points and the number k of lines must sum up to the number n of views: i.e. $m + k = 2$; and, moreover, an n-view relation only occurs if $2m + k \geq 4$. So, for two views, only a relation between (the image coordinates) of 2 corresponding points exists. Using the notations from section 3 again, the appropriate matrix (95) is

$$\begin{pmatrix} I_3 & 0 & \mathbf{p} & 0 \\ A & \mathbf{e}' & 0 & \mathbf{p}' \end{pmatrix} . \tag{102}$$

This matrix being square, the rank condition is equivalent to the vanishing of its determinant:

$$\det \begin{pmatrix} I_3 & 0 & \mathbf{p} & 0 \\ A & \mathbf{e}' & 0 & \mathbf{p}' \end{pmatrix} = 0 . \tag{103}$$

Denote this determinant by Δ_2. Then Δ_2 is easiest calculated by using Laplace's rule, which is a generalisation of developing a determinant along a row or column. In particular, developing Δ_2 with respect to the first three rows gives the following non-zero terms:

$$\begin{aligned}
\Delta_2 = (-1)^{1+2+3} \big\{ \, & (-1)^{1+2+5} \, |\mathbf{u}_1 \ \mathbf{u}_2 \ \mathbf{p}| \, |\mathbf{a}_3 \ \mathbf{e}' \ \mathbf{p}'| \\
& + (-1)^{1+3+5} \, |\mathbf{u}_1 \ \mathbf{u}_3 \ \mathbf{p}| \, |\mathbf{a}_2 \ \mathbf{e}' \ \mathbf{p}'| \\
& + (-1)^{2+3+5} \, |\mathbf{u}_2 \ \mathbf{u}_3 \ \mathbf{p}| \, |\mathbf{a}_1 \ \mathbf{e}' \ \mathbf{p}'| \big\} \, ,
\end{aligned} \tag{104}$$

where $\mathbf{a}_i$ is the ith column of the matrix A, $\mathbf{u}_1 = (1,0,0)^t$, $\mathbf{u}_2 = (0,1,0)^t$ and $\mathbf{u}_3 = (0,0,1)^t$ are the standard unit vectors in $\mathbb{R}^3$, and with vertical bars denoting the determinant of the 3×3-matrix whose columns are the specified column vectors. As $\mathbf{p} = (x, y, 1)^t$ and $|\mathbf{a}_i \ \mathbf{e}' \ \mathbf{p}'| = -|\mathbf{p}' \ \mathbf{e}' \ \mathbf{a}_i| = -\mathbf{p}'^t(\mathbf{e}' \times \mathbf{a}_i)$, Δ_2 is equal to

$$\begin{aligned}
\Delta_2 &= -1 \, \mathbf{p}'^t(\mathbf{e}' \times \mathbf{a}_3) - y \, \mathbf{p}'^t(\mathbf{e}' \times \mathbf{a}_2) - x \, \mathbf{p}'^t(\mathbf{e}' \times \mathbf{a}_1) \\
&= -\mathbf{p}'^t [\mathbf{e}' \times (x \, \mathbf{a}_1 + y \, \mathbf{a}_2 + 1 \, \mathbf{a}_3)] \\
&= -\mathbf{p}'^t (\mathbf{e}' \times A\mathbf{p}) = -\mathbf{p}'^t [\mathbf{e}']_\times A \, \mathbf{p} .
\end{aligned} \tag{105}$$

Putting $F = [\mathbf{e}']_\times A$ again, condition (103), i.e. $\Delta_2 = 0$, equals the epipolar constraint (14) expressed in Theorem 1.

Next, consider the case of 3 views. Taking m points and k lines in 3 views means that $m + k = 3$; and, to have a 3-view relation, $2m + k \geq 4$. So, for three views, only the following type of relations exist: *3 points, 2 points / 1 line* and *1 point / 2 lines* (cf. Table 1). Notice that the option "*3 lines*" is not found here, because the combination $m = 0$ and $k = 3$ does not satisfy the condition $2m + k \geq 4$. At first sight this may seem contradictory to Proposition 1 and Corollary 1, but it is not. Indeed, Proposition 1 and Corollary 1 only are valid for *corresponding* lines in the images (i.e. image lines that are the projection of one and the same 3D line in the scene). The image lines considered in this section do *not* have to be corresponding to each other. They only need to contain the image point that corresponds to the point(s) selected in the other images; but, apart from that, they are completely arbitrary. This latter situation does also apply for the *3 points, 2 points / 1 line* and *1 point / 2 lines* constraints referred to in Table 1.

Let us first look at the "*3 points*" case. Using the notations from section 4 again, the appropriate matrix (95) is

$$
\begin{pmatrix}
I_3 & 0 & \mathbf{p} & 0 & 0 \\
A & \mathbf{e'} & 0 & \mathbf{p'} & 0 \\
B & \mathbf{e''} & 0 & 0 & \mathbf{p''}
\end{pmatrix} . \tag{106}
$$

This matrix has 9 rows and 7 columns. The rank condition therefore is equivalent to the vanishing of the determinants of all its 7×7-submatrices. In other words, 2 rows have to be deleted from this matrix to obtain a constraint; and, moreover, to get a relation involving all 3 views, these 2 rows should be taken from different camera matrices. As only 2 rows may be deleted, it is clear that one camera matrix will be untouched. This explains the special rôle of one image when compared to the other two views in the trifocal constraints. In section 4, the first image I served that rôle. Deleting one row in the A- and one in the B-line of matrix (106) and computing the determinant of the resulting 7×7-submatrix yields one of the 9 constraints in equation (42) of Proposition 2, as can be verified by explicit calculation. Here, however, we follow an alternative strategy, namely to study the effect on the computation of the determinant of deleting one row in the $3 \times (m + 4)$-submatrix corresponding to one camera in matrix (95).

Lemma 2. *With the notations of this section: The constraint involving the image point* $\mathbf{p}^{(i)}$ *in image* $I^{(i)}$, *obtained by deleting the first (respectively, the second) row of the* $3 \times (m + 4)$-submatrix

$$
(\ A_i \quad \mathbf{e}^{(i)} \quad 0 \ \ldots \ 0 \quad \mathbf{p}^{(i)} \quad 0 \ \ldots \ 0 \ ) \tag{107}
$$

of matrix (95) in order to form a $(m + 4) \times (m + 4)$-*determinant, is equivalent to the constraint obtained by chosing the horizontal line* $\mathbf{h}^{(i)}$ *(respectively, the vertical line* $\mathbf{v}^{(i)}$*) through that point* $\mathbf{p}^{(i)}$, *instead of* $\mathbf{p}^{(i)}$ *itself, in image* $I^{(i)}$. *The constraint obtained by deleting the third row of submatrix (107) is equivalent to the constraint obtained by chosing the line through* $\mathbf{p}^{(i)}$ *and the image origin. Homogeneous coordinates of this line are given by the third row of the skew-symmetric* 3×3-matrix $\left[\mathbf{p}^{(i)} \right]_{\times}$.

Proof. First of all, notice that the column vector $\mathbf{p}^{(i)}$ in camera submatrix (107) is part of the $(i+5)$th column of matrix (95); and, moreover, that these are the only non-zero entries in that column. If the first row of camera submatrix (107) is deleted to form a $(m+4) \times (m+4)$-submatrix of matrix (95), then the remaining rows of (107) are

$$
\begin{pmatrix}
(A_i)_{2*} & y_e^{(i)} & 0 & \dots & 0 & y^{(i)} & 0 & \dots & 0 \\
(A_i)_{3*} & 1 & 0 & \dots & 0 & 1 & 0 & \dots & 0
\end{pmatrix} ,
\tag{108}
$$

where $(A_i)_{k*}$ denotes the kth row of matrix A_i and we also used that $\mathbf{p}^{(i)} = (x^{(i)}, y^{(i)}, 1)^t$ and $\mathbf{e}^{(i)} = (x_e^{(i)}, y_e^{(i)}, 1)^t$. Remember from linear algebra that the value of a determinant does not change when a scalar multiple of one row of the matrix is added to another row. Hence, the determinant of the $(m+4) \times (m+4)$-submatrix will not change if one subtracts $y^{(i)}$ times the second row from the first one in camera submatrix (108). The resulting submatrix is

$$
\begin{pmatrix}
(A_i)_{2*} - y^{(i)} (A_i)_{3*} & y_e^{(i)} - y^{(i)} & 0 & \dots & 0 & 0 & 0 & \dots & 0 \\
(A_i)_{3*} & 1 & 0 & \dots & 0 & 1 & 0 & \dots & 0
\end{pmatrix} ,
\tag{109}
$$

Due to this operation, the 1 in the $(i+5)$th column of submatrix (109) becomes the only non-zero entry in that column of the $(m+4) \times (m+4)$-submatrix of matrix (95). Developing the determinant of that $(m+4) \times (m+4)$-submatrix along this $(i+5)$th column thus results in a $(m+3) \times (m+3)$-determinant obtained by deleting the $(i+5)$th column corresponding to the image point $\mathbf{p}^{(i)}$ as well as the last row of submatrix (109). Put differently, the point $\mathbf{p}^{(i)}$ has disappeared completely from the determinant, and the submatrix (109) corresponding to the $(i+1)$th camera has been replaced by only one row, viz.

$$
\begin{pmatrix}
(A_i)_{2*} - y^{(i)} (A_i)_{3*} & y_e^{(i)} - y^{(i)} & 0 & \dots & 0 & 0 & \dots & 0
\end{pmatrix} .
\tag{110}
$$

Recall from formula (39) that the horizontal line $\mathbf{h}^{(i)}$ through $\mathbf{p}^{(i)}$ in the $(i+1)$th image $I^{(i)}$ has homogeneous coordinates $\mathbf{h}^{(i)} \simeq (0, -1, y^{(i)})^t$. Pre-multiplying the matrix A_i with the transpose of $\mathbf{h}^{(i)}$ gives

$$
\mathbf{h}^{(i)t} A_i = -(A_i)_{2*} + y^{(i)} (A_i)_{3*} ,
\tag{111}
$$

which, up to sign, is the first part of row (110). Furthermore, pre-multiplying the epipole $\mathbf{e}^{(i)} = (x_e^{(i)}, y_e^{(i)}, 1)^t$ with the transpose of $\mathbf{h}^{(i)}$ gives

$$
\mathbf{h}^{(i)t} \mathbf{e}^{(i)} = -y_e^{(i)} + y^{(i)} ,
\tag{112}
$$

which, up to sign, is the 4th entry of row (110). So, row (110), up to sign, equals

$$
\begin{pmatrix}
\mathbf{h}^{(i)t} A_i & \mathbf{h}^{(i)t} \mathbf{e}^{(i)} & 0 & \dots & 0 & 0 & \dots & 0
\end{pmatrix} ,
\tag{113}
$$

which is nothing else but the single row corresponding to the $(i+1)$th camera, which would have been included in the original matrix (95) if the (horizontal) line $\mathbf{h}^{(i)}$ was chosen in image $I^{(i)}$ instead of the image point $\mathbf{p}^{(i)}$. This proves the claim for deleting the first row in camera submatrix (107).

The claim for deleting the second row in camera submatrix (107) follows in exactly the same manner, but using the vertical line $\mathbf{v}^{(i)}$ through $\mathbf{p}^{(i)}$ in image $I^{(i)}$, which has homogeneous coordinates $\mathbf{v}^{(i)} \simeq (1, 0, -x^{(i)})^t$. Finally, removing the third row in camera submatrix (107) and repeating this type of reasoning leads to replacing the point $\mathbf{p}^{(i)}$ in image $I^{(i)}$ by the line with homogeneous coordinates $(-y^{(i)}, x^{(i)}, 0)^t$. This line is the line through the point $\mathbf{p}^{(i)}$ and the origin in image $I^{(i)}$. $\square$

Since the last row of the skew-symmetric 3×3-matrix

$$
\left[\mathbf{p}^{(i)} \right]_\times = \begin{pmatrix} 0 & -1 & y^{(i)} \\ 1 & 0 & -x^{(i)} \\ -y^{(i)} & x^{(i)} & 0 \end{pmatrix} \tag{114}
$$

is a linear combination of the first two rows, as shown in formula (45); and, because the first two rows of this matrix contain homogeneous coordinates of respectively the horizontal line $\mathbf{h}^{(i)}$ and the vertical line $\mathbf{v}^{(i)}$ through the point $\mathbf{p}^{(i)}$, it follows from Lemma 2 that the constraint obtained by deleting the last row in a camera submatrix (107) is a linear combination of the constraints obtained by respectively removing the first and the second row of that camera submatrix. This proves the following proposition.

Proposition 6. *The linearly independent determinant constraints involving image points $\mathbf{p}^{(i)}$ can be obtained from the determinant constraints on image lines by replacing the line $\mathbf{l}^{(i)}$ in view $I^{(i)}$ by respectively the horizontal line $\mathbf{h}^{(i)}$ and the vertical line $\mathbf{v}^{(i)}$ through $\mathbf{p}^{(i)}$ in $I^{(i)}$, as was done in the previous sections. In particular, all linearly independent n-view relations can be derived by this procedure from the n-view relation involving the maximal number of image lines.* $\square$

In practice, since for a n-view relation involving m points and k lines one needs $m + k = n$ and $2m + k \geq 4$, it follows from Proposition 6 that for 3 views the relation involving the maximal number of lines is the one with 1 point and 2 lines; whereas that "fundamental" relation for 4 views is the one involving 4 lines only. To prove the claim made at the beginning of this section — viz. that all the constraints given by the $(m + 4) \times (m + 4)$-determinants described in section 6.1 are equivalent to the multiview relations derived in the previous sections — it suffices to show that the "*1 point / 2 lines*" relation in the 3-view case corresponds to the fundamental trifocal constraint (17) of Theorem 2 and that the "*4 lines*" relation in the case of 4 views is just the fundamental quadrifocal constraint (74) of Theorem 3.

First consider the "*1 point / 2 lines*" situation for 3 views. The appropriate matrix (95) for this case is

$$
\begin{pmatrix}
I_3 & 0 & \mathbf{p} \\
\mathbf{l}'^t A & \mathbf{l}'^t \mathbf{e}' & 0 \\
\mathbf{l}''^t B & \mathbf{l}''^t \mathbf{e}'' & 0
\end{pmatrix} ,
\tag{115}
$$

where the notations of section 4 are used again. This matrix being square, the rank condition on this matrix is equivalent to the vanishing of its determinant:

$$
\det
\begin{pmatrix}
I_3 & 0 & \mathbf{p} \\
\mathbf{l}'^t A & \mathbf{l}'^t \mathbf{e}' & 0 \\
\mathbf{l}''^t B & \mathbf{l}''^t \mathbf{e}'' & 0
\end{pmatrix} = 0 .
\tag{116}
$$

Denote this determinant by Δ_3. Then Δ_3 is easiest calculated by using Laplace's rule again. In particular, developing Δ_3 with respect to the first three rows gives the following non-zero terms:

$$
\Delta_3 = (-1)^{1+2+3} \left\{ (-1)^{1+2+5} \, | \, \mathbf{u}_1 \ \mathbf{u}_2 \ \mathbf{p} \, | \begin{vmatrix} \mathbf{l}'^t \mathbf{a}_3 & \mathbf{l}'^t \mathbf{e}' \\ \mathbf{l}''^t \mathbf{b}_3 & \mathbf{l}''^t \mathbf{e}'' \end{vmatrix} \right.
$$

$$
+ (-1)^{1+3+5} \, | \, \mathbf{u}_1 \ \mathbf{u}_3 \ \mathbf{p} \, | \begin{vmatrix} \mathbf{l}'^t \mathbf{a}_2 & \mathbf{l}'^t \mathbf{e}' \\ \mathbf{l}''^t \mathbf{b}_2 & \mathbf{l}''^t \mathbf{e}'' \end{vmatrix}
\tag{117}
$$

$$
\left. + (-1)^{2+3+5} \, | \, \mathbf{u}_2 \ \mathbf{u}_3 \ \mathbf{p} \, | \begin{vmatrix} \mathbf{l}'^t \mathbf{a}_1 & \mathbf{l}'^t \mathbf{e}' \\ \mathbf{l}''^t \mathbf{b}_1 & \mathbf{l}''^t \mathbf{e}'' \end{vmatrix} \right\} ,
$$

where $\mathbf{a}_i$ and $\mathbf{b}_i$ are the ith column of respectively the matrix A and B, and with $\mathbf{u}_1$, $\mathbf{u}_2$ and $\mathbf{u}_3$ the standard unit 3-vectors, as before. Using that $\mathbf{l}''^t \mathbf{e}'' = \mathbf{e}''^t \mathbf{l}''$ and $\mathbf{l}''^t \mathbf{b}_i = \mathbf{b}_i^t \mathbf{l}''$ for all i, the 2×2-determinants in the previous equality can be written as

$$
\begin{vmatrix} \mathbf{l}'^t \mathbf{a}_i & \mathbf{l}'^t \mathbf{e}' \\ \mathbf{l}''^t \mathbf{b}_i & \mathbf{l}''^t \mathbf{e}'' \end{vmatrix} = (\mathbf{l}'^t \mathbf{a}_i)(\mathbf{e}''^t \mathbf{l}'') - (\mathbf{l}'^t \mathbf{e}')(\mathbf{b}_i^t \mathbf{l}'') = \mathbf{l}'^t \left[\mathbf{a}_i \, \mathbf{e}''^t - \mathbf{e}' \, \mathbf{b}_i^t \right] \mathbf{l}'' .
\tag{118}
$$

As $\mathbf{p} = (x, y, 1)^t$, determinant (117) is equal to

$$
\Delta_3 = 1 \, \mathbf{l}'^t [\, \mathbf{a}_3 \, \mathbf{e}''^t - \mathbf{e}' \, \mathbf{b}_3^t \,] \mathbf{l}'' + y \, \mathbf{l}'^t [\, \mathbf{a}_2 \, \mathbf{e}''^t - \mathbf{e}' \, \mathbf{b}_2^t \,] \mathbf{l}'' + x \, \mathbf{l}'^t [\, \mathbf{a}_1 \, \mathbf{e}''^t - \mathbf{e}' \, \mathbf{b}_1^t \,] \mathbf{l}''
$$

$$
= \mathbf{l}'^t \left[(\, x \, \mathbf{a}_1 + y \, \mathbf{a}_2 + 1 \, \mathbf{a}_3 \,) \, \mathbf{e}''^t - \mathbf{e}' \, (\, x \, \mathbf{b}_1 + y \, \mathbf{b}_2 + 1 \, \mathbf{b}_3 \,)^t \right] \mathbf{l}''
$$

$$
= \mathbf{l}'^t \left[(\, A \mathbf{p} \,) \, \mathbf{e}''^t - \mathbf{e}' \, (\, B \mathbf{p} \,)^t \right] \mathbf{l}'' .
\tag{119}
$$

Putting $[T\mathbf{p}] = (A\mathbf{p}) \, \mathbf{e}''^t - \mathbf{e}' (B\mathbf{p})^t$ as in formula (19), the condition $\Delta_3 = 0$ equals the fundamental trifocal constraint (17) expressed in Theorem 2. This proves the claim for the 3-view case.

In case of 4 views, on the other hand, the fundamental quadrifocal constraint (74) in Theorem 3 was proven precisely as explained in this section. So, nothing more has to be said about this case. Having shown that all the relations between multiple views of a static scene are covered by the constraints derived in the previous sections also concludes our guided tour through multiview relations.

References

1. S. Avidan and A. Shashua, Novel view synthesis in tensor space, *Proceedings of the IEEE Conference on Computer Vision and Pattern Recognition (CVPR'97)*, Puerto Rico, IEEE Computer Society Press, Los Alamitos, 1997, pp. 1034–1040.
2. S. Avidan and A. Shashua, Unifying two-view and three-view geometry, *Proceedings of the ARPA Image Understanding Workshop (IUW'97)*, Morgan Kaufmann Publishers, Orlando, FL, 1997.
3. S. Avidan and A. Shashua, Novel view synthesis by cascading trilinear tensors, submitted to *IEEE Transactions on Visualisation and Computer Graphics (TVCG)*.
4. P.A. Beardsley, P.H.S. Torr, and A. Zisserman, 3D Model acquisition from extended image sequence, pp. II.683–II.695, in : B. Buxton and R. Cipolla (eds.), *Computer Vision — ECCV'96*, LNCS, Vol. **1065**, Springer-Verlag, Berlin, 1996.
5. O.D. Faugeras, What can be seen in three dimensions with an uncalibrated stereo rig, pp. 563–578, in : G. Sandini (ed.), *Computer Vision — (ECCV'92)*, Lecture Notes in Computer Science, Vol. **588**, Springer-Verlag, Berlin, 1992.
6. O. Faugeras, *Three-Dimensional Computer Vision : A Geometric Viewpoint*, MIT Press, Cambridge, MA / London, UK, 1993.
7. O. Faugeras and B. Mourrain, On the geometry and algebra of the point and line correspondences between N images, *Proc. 5th International Conference on Computer Vision (ICCV'95)*, Cambridge, MA, IEEE Computer Society Press, Los Alamitos, CA, 1995, pp. 951–956.
8. O. Faugeras and B. Mourrain, About the correspondences of points between N images, *Proceedings of the IEEE workshop on the Representation of Visual Scenes*, Boston, MA, IEEE Computer Society Press, Los Alamitos, CA, 1995.
9. O. Faugeras and T. Papadopoulo, A nonlinear method for estimating the projective geometry of three views, *Proc. 6th International Conference on Computer Vision (ICCV'98)*, Bombay, India, Narosa Publishing House, New Delhi / London, 1998, pp. 477–484.
10. A.W. Fitzgibbon and A. Zisserman, Automatic camera recovery for closed or open image sequences, pp. I.311–I.326, in : H. Burkhardt and B. Neumann (eds.), *Computer Vision — ECCV'98*, LNCS, Vol. **1406**, Springer-Verlag, Berlin, 1998.
11. R.I. Hartley, Estimation of relative camera positions for uncalibrated cameras, pp. 579–587, in : G. Sandini (ed.), *Computer Vision — (ECCV'92)*, Lecture Notes in Computer Science, Vol. **588**, Springer-Verlag, Berlin, 1992.
12. R.I. Hartley, Projective reconstruction from line correspondences, *Proceedings of the IEEE Conference on Computer Vision and Pattern Recognition (CVPR'94)*, Seattle, WA, IEEE Computer Society Press, Los Alamitos 1994, pp. 903–907.
13. R.I. Hartley, Lines and points in three views — a unified approach, *Proceedings of the ARPA Image Understanding Workshop (IUW'94)*, Monterey, CA, Morgan Kaufmann Publishers, Orlando, FL, 1994, pp. 1009–1016.
14. R.I. Hartley, A linear method for reconstruction from lines and points, *Proceedings of the 5th International Conference on Computer Vision (ICCV'95)*, Cambridge, MA, IEEE Computer Society Press, Los Alamitos, CA, 1995, pp. 882–887.

15. R.I. Hartley, Multilinear Relationships between coordinates of corresponding image points and lines, *Computer Vision Applied Geometry*, Nordfjordeid, Norway, 1995.

16. R.I. Hartley, In defence of the 8-point algorithm, *Proceedings of the 5th International Conference on Computer Vision (ICCV'95)*, Cambridge, MA, IEEE Computer Society Press, Los Alamitos, CA, 1995, pp. 1064–1070.

17. R.I. Hartley, Lines and points in three views and the trifocal tensor, *International Journal of Computer Vision*, Vol. **22** (1997), no. 2, pp. 125–140.

18. R.I. Hartley, Minimizing algebraic error in geometric estimation problems, *Proceedings of the 6th International Conference on Computer Vision (ICCV'98)*, Bombay, India, Narosa Publishing House, New Delhi / London, 1998, pp. 469–476.

19. R.I. Hartley, Computation of the quadrifocal tensor, pp. I.20–I.35, in : H. Burkhardt and B. Neumann (eds.), *Computer Vision — ECCV'98*, Lecture Notes in Computer Science, Vol. **1406**, Springer-Verlag, Berlin, 1998.

20. R.I. Hartley and A. Zisserman, *Multiple View Geometry in Computer Vision*, Cambridge University Press, Cambridge, UK, to appear.

21. R. Hartley, R. Gupta, and T. Chang, Stereo from uncalibrated cameras, *Proceedings of the IEEE Conference on Computer Vision and Pattern Recognition (CVPR'92)*, IEEE Computer Society Press, Los Alamitos, CA, 1992, pp. 761–764.

22. A. Heyden, A common framework for multiple view tensors, pp. I.3–I.19, in : H. Burkhardt and B. Neumann (eds.), *Computer Vision — ECCV'98*, Lecture Notes in Computer Science, Vol. **1406**, Springer-Verlag, Berlin, 1998.

23. A. Heyden and K. Åström, Algebraic varieties in multiple view geometry, pp. II.671–II.682, in : B. Buxton and R. Cipolla (eds.), *Computer Vision — ECCV'96*, LNCS, Vol. **1065**, Springer-Verlag, Berlin, 1996.

24. A. Heyden and K. Åström, Algebraic properties of multilinear constraints, *Mathematical Methods in the Applied Sciences*, Vol. **20** (1997), pp. 1135–1162.

25. H.C. Longuet-Higgins, A computer algorithm for reconstructing a scene from two projections, *Nature*, Vol. **293** (1981), no. 10, pp. 133–135.

26. Q.-T. Luong and O.D. Faugeras, The fundamental matrix: Theory, algorithms, and stability analysis, *Intern. Journal Computer Vision*, Vol. **17** (1996), pp. 43–75.

27. Q.-T. Luong and T. Viéville, Canonic representations for the geometries of multiple projective views, pp. I.589–I.599, in : J.-O. Ecklund, *Computer Vision — ECCV'94*, LNCS, Vol. **800**, Springer-Verlag, Berlin, 1994.

28. Q.-T. Luong and T. Viéville, Canonic representations for the geometries of multiple projective views, *Comp. Vision Image Understanding*, Vol. **64** (1996), pp. 589–599.

29. S.J. Maybank, The critical line concruence for reconstruction from three images, *Applic. Algebra in Engineering, Comm. & Computing*, Vol. **6** (1995), pp. 89–113.

30. S.J. Maybank and A. Shashua, Ambiguity in reconstruction from images of six points, *Proc. 6th International Conference on Computer Vision (ICCV'98)*, Bombay, India, Narosa Publishing House, New Delhi / London, 1998, pp. 703–708.

31. N. Navab, O.D. Faugeras, and T. Viéville, The critical sets of lines for camera displacement estimation : A mixed Euclidean–projective and constructive approach, *Proc. of the 4th International Conference on Computer Vision (ICCV'93)*, Berlin, Germany, IEEE Computer Society Press, Los Alamitos, CA, 1993, pp. 713–723.

32. T. Papadopoulo and O.D. Faugeras, A new characterization of the trifocal tensor, pp. I.109–I.123, in : H. Burkhardt and B. Neumann (eds.), *Computer Vision — ECCV'98*, LNCS, Vol. **1406**, Springer-Verlag, Berlin, 1998.

33. A. Shashua, Trilinearity in visual recognition by alignment, pp. I.479–I.484, in : J.-O. Ecklund, *Computer Vision — ECCV'94*, Lecture Notes in Computer Science, Vol. **800**, Springer-Verlag, Berlin / Heidelberg / New York / Tokyo, 1994.

34. A. Shashua, Projective structure from uncalibrated images, *IEEE Trans. Pattern Analysis and Artificial Intellingence (T-PAMI)*, Vol. **16** (1994), no. 8, pp. 778–790.
35. A. Shashua, Algebraic functions for recognition, *IEEE Trans. Pattern Analysis and Artificial Intellingence (T-PAMI)*, Vol. **17** (1995), no. 8, pp. 779–789.
36. A. Shashua, Multiple-view geometry and photometry and the trilinear tensor, *Computer Vision and Applied Geometry*, Nordfjordeid, Norway, 1995.
37. A. Shashua, Trilinear tensor: The fundamental construct of multiple-view geometry and its applications, *Proceedings of the International Workshop on Algebraic Frames for the Perception Action Cycle (AFPAC97)*, Kiel, Germany, 1997.
38. A. Shashua and S. Avidan, The rank 4 constraint in multiple ($\geq$ 3) view geometry, pp. II.196 – II.206, in : B. Buxton and R. Cipolla (eds.), *Computer Vision — ECCV'96*, LNCS, Vol. **1065**, Springer-Verlag, Berlin, 1996.
39. A. Shashua and N. Navab, Relative affine structure: Theory and application to 3D reconstruction from perspective views, *Proc. IEEE Conference on Computer Vision and Pattern Recognition (CVPR'94)*, Seattle, WA, IEEE Computer Society Press, Los Alamitos, CA, 1994, pp. 483–489.
40. A. Shashua and M. Werman, Trilinearity of three perspective views and its associated tensor, *Proc. 5th International Conference on Computer Vision (ICCV'95)*, Cambridge, MA, IEEE Computer Society Press, Los Alamitos, 1995, pp. 920–925.
41. M.E. Spetsakis, A linear method for point and line-based structure from motion, *CVGIP: Image Understanding*, Vol. **56** (1992), no. 2, pp. 230 – 241.
42. M.E. Spetsakis and J. Aloimonos, A unified theory of structure from motion, *Proceedings of the DARPA Image Understanding Workshop (IUW'90)*, Morgan Kaufmann Publishers, Orlando, FL, 1990, pp. 271 – 283.
43. G.P. Stein and A. Shashua, On degeneracy of linear reconstruction from three views : linear line complex and applications, pp. II.862 – II.878, in : H. Burkhardt and B. Neumann (eds.), *Computer Vision — ECCV'98*, Lecture Notes in Computer Science, Vol. **1407**, Springer-Verlag, Berlin / Heidelberg / New York / Tokyo, 1998.
44. P.H.S. Torr and D.W. Murray, The development and comparison of robust methods for estimating the fundamental matrix, *International Journal of Computer Vision*, Vol. **24** (1997), no. 3, pp. 271 – 300.
45. P.H.S. Torr and A. Zisserman, Robust parameterization and computation of the trifocal tensor, *Image and Vision Computing*, Vol. **15** (1997), pp. 591 – 605.
46. P.H.S. Torr and A. Zisserman, Robust computation and parameterization of multiview relations, *Proc. 6th International Conference on Computer Vision (ICCV'98)*, Bombay, India, Narosa Publishing House, New Delhi / London, 1998, pp. 727 – 732.
47. B. Triggs, Matching constraints and the joint image, *Proc. 5th International Conference on Computer Vision (ICCV'95)*, Cambridge, MA, IEEE Computer Society Press, Los Alamitos, CA, 1995, pp. 338–343.
48. B. Triggs, The geometry of projective reconstruction I : matching constraints and the joint image, submitted to *International Journal of Computer Vision*, (1995).
49. B. Triggs, *A new approach to geometric fitting*, unpublished paper, 1998. (Can be obtained from: http://www.inrialpes.fr/movi/people/Triggs/publications.html).
50. J. Weng, T.S. Huang, and N. Ahuja, Motion and structure from line correspondences: Closed-form solution, uniqueness, and optimization, *IEEE Trans. Pattern Analysis and Artificial Intellingence (T-PAMI)*, Vol. **14** (1992), no. 3, pp. 318–336.
51. M. Werman and A. Shashua, The study of 3D-from-2D using elimination, *Proceedings of the 5th International Conference on Computer Vision (ICCV '95)*, Cambridge, MA, IEEE Computer Society Press, Los Alamitos, CA, 1995, pp. 473 – 479.
52. A. Zisserman, *A Users Guide to the Trifocal Tensor*, Department of Engineering Science, University of Oxford, 1996. Also a chapter in [20].

Author Index

Lecture Notes in Computer Science

For information about Vols. 1–1447

please contact your bookseller or Springer-Verlag

Vol. 1483: T. Plagemann, V. Goebel (Eds.), Interactive Distributed Multimedia Systems and Telecommunication Services. Proceedings, 1998. XV, 326 pages. 1998.

Vol. 1484: H. Coelho (Ed.), Progress in Artificial Intelligence – IBERAMIA 98. Proceedings, 1998. XIII, 421 pages. 1998. (Subseries LNAI).

Vol. 1485: J.-J. Quisquater, Y. Deswarte, C. Meadows, D. Gollmann (Eds.), Computer Security – ESORICS 98. Proceedings, 1998. X, 377 pages. 1998.

Vol. 1486: A.P. Ravn, H. Rischel (Eds.), Formal Techniques in Real-Time and Fault-Tolerant Systems. Proceedings, 1998. VIII, 339 pages. 1998.

Vol. 1487: V. Gruhn (Ed.), Software Process Technology. Proceedings, 1998. VIII, 157 pages. 1998.

Vol. 1488: B. Smyth, P. Cunningham (Eds.), Advances in Case-Based Reasoning. Proceedings, 1998. XI, 482 pages. 1998. (Subseries LNAI).

Vol. 1489: J. Dix, L. Fariñas del Cerro, U. Furbach (Eds.), Logics in Artificial Intelligence. Proceedings, 1998. X, 391 pages. 1998. (Subseries LNAI).

Vol. 1490: C. Palamidessi, H. Glaser, K. Meinke (Eds.), Principles of Declarative Programming. Proceedings, 1998. XI, 497 pages. 1998.

Vol. 1491: W. Reisig, G. Rozenberg (Eds.), Lectures on Petri Nets I: Basic Models. XII, 683 pages. 1998.

Vol. 1492: W. Reisig, G. Rozenberg (Eds.), Lectures on Petri Nets II: Applications. XII, 479 pages. 1998.

Vol. 1493: J.P. Bowen, A. Fett, M.G. Hinchey (Eds.), ZUM '98: The Z Formal Specification Notation. Proceedings, 1998. XV, 417 pages. 1998.

Vol. 1494: G. Rozenberg, F. Vaandrager (Eds.), Lectures on Embedded Systems. Proceedings, 1996. VIII, 423 pages. 1998.

Vol. 1495: T. Andreasen, H. Christiansen, H.L. Larsen (Eds.), Flexible Query Answering Systems. IX, 393 pages. 1998. (Subseries LNAI).

Vol. 1496: W.M. Wells, A. Colchester, S. Delp (Eds.), Medical Image Computing and Computer-Assisted Intervention – MICCAI'98. Proceedings, 1998. XXII, 1256 pages. 1998.

Vol. 1497: V. Alexandrov, J. Dongarra (Eds.), Recent Advances in Parallel Virtual Machine and Message Passing Interface. Proceedings, 1998. XII, 412 pages. 1998.

Vol. 1498: A.E. Eiben, T. Bäck, M. Schoenauer, H.-P. Schwefel (Eds.), Parallel Problem Solving from Nature – PPSN V. Proceedings, 1998. XXIII, 1041 pages. 1998.

Vol. 1499: S. Kutten (Ed.), Distributed Computing. Proceedings, 1998. XII, 419 pages. 1998.

Vol. 1501: M.M. Richter, C.H. Smith, R. Wiehagen, T. Zeugmann (Eds.), Algorithmic Learning Theory. Proceedings, 1998. XI, 439 pages. 1998. (Subseries LNAI).

Vol. 1502: G. Antoniou, J. Slaney (Eds.), Advanced Topics in Artificial Intelligence. Proceedings, 1998. XI, 333 pages. 1998. (Subseries LNAI).

Vol. 1503: G. Levi (Ed.), Static Analysis. Proceedings, 1998. IX, 383 pages. 1998.

Vol. 1504: O. Herzog, A. Günter (Eds.), KI-98: Advances in Artificial Intelligence. Proceedings, 1998. XI, 355 pages. 1998. (Subseries LNAI).

Vol. 1506: R. Koch, L. Van Gool (Eds.), 3D Structure from Multiple Images of Large-Scale Environments. Proceedings, 1998. VIII, 347 pages. 1998.

Vol. 1507: T.W. Ling, S. Ram, M.L. Lee (Eds.), Conceptual Modeling – ER '98. Proceedings, 1998. XVI, 482 pages. 1998.

Vol. 1508: S. Jajodia, M.T. Özsu, A. Dogac (Eds.), Advances in Multimedia Information Systems. Proceedings, 1998. VIII, 207 pages. 1998.

Vol. 1510: J.M. Zytkow, M. Quafafou (Eds.), Principles of Data Mining and Knowledge Discovery. Proceedings, 1998. XI, 482 pages. 1998. (Subseries LNAI).

Vol. 1511: D. O'Hallaron (Ed.), Languages, Compilers, and Run-Time Systems for Scalable Computers. Proceedings, 1998. IX, 412 pages. 1998.

Vol. 1512: E. Giménez, C. Paulin-Mohring (Eds.), Types for Proofs and Programs. Proceedings, 1996. VIII, 373 pages. 1998.

Vol. 1513: C. Nikolaou, C. Stephanidis (Eds.), Research and Advanced Technology for Digital Libraries. Proceedings, 1998. XV, 912 pages. 1998.

Vol. 1514: K. Ohta,, D. Pei (Eds.), Advances in Cryptology – ASIACRYPT'98. Proceedings, 1998. XII, 436 pages. 1998.

Vol. 1515: F. Moreira de Oliveira (Ed.), Advances in Artificial Intelligence. Proceedings, 1998. X, 259 pages. 1998. (Subseries LNAI).

Vol. 1516: W. Ehrenberger (Ed.), Computer Safety, Reliability and Security. Proceedings, 1998. XVI, 392 pages. 1998.

Vol. 1517: J. Hromkovič, O. Sýkora (Eds.), Graph-Theoretic Concepts in Computer Science. Proceedings, 1998. X, 385 pages. 1998.

Vol. 1518: M. Luby, J. Rolim, M. Serna (Eds.), Randomization and Approximation Techniques in Computer Science. Proceedings, 1998. IX, 385 pages. 1998.

Vol. 1520: M. Maher, J.-F. Puget (Eds.), Principles and Practice of Constraint Programming - CP98. Proceedings, 1998. XI, 482 pages. 1998.

Vol. 1521: B. Rovan (Ed.), SOFSEM'98: Theory and Practice of Informatics. Proceedings, 1998. XI, 453 pages. 1998.

Vol. 1522: G. Gopalakrishnan, P. Windley (Eds.), Formal Methods in Computer-Aided Design. Proceedings, 1998. IX, 529 pages. 1998.

Vol. 1524: G.B. Orr, K.-R. Müller (Eds.), Neural Networks: Tricks of the Trade. VI, 432 pages. 1998.

Vol. 1526: M. Broy, B. Rumpe (Eds.), Requirements Targeting Software and Systems Engineering. Proceedings, 1997. VIII, 357 pages. 1998.

Vol. 1529: D. Farwell, L. Gerber, E. Hovy (Eds.), Machine Translation and the Information Soup. Proceedings, 1998. XIX, 532 pages. 1998. (Subseries LNAI).

Vol. 1531: H.-Y. Lee, H. Motoda (Eds.), PRICAI'98: Topics in Artificial Intelligence. XIX, 646 pages. 1998. (Subseries LNAI).

Vol. 1096: T. Schael, Workflow Management Systems for Process Organisations. Second Edition. XII, 229 pages. 1998.